Untouchable Castes in India

Untouchable Castes in India

The Raigar Movement (1940–2004)

SHYAMLAL

RAWAT PUBLICATIONS

Jaipur • New Delhi • Bangalore • Hyderabad • Guwahati

ISBN 81-316-0029-7

Reprinted, 2010

Published by
Prem Rawat for **Rawat Publications**
Satyam Apts., Sector 3, Jawahar Nagar, Jaipur 302 004 (India)
Phone: 0141 265 1748 / 7006 Fax: 0141 265 1748
E-mail: info@rawatbooks.com
Website: www.rawatbooks.com

New Delhi Office
4858/24, Ansari Road, Daryaganj, New Delhi 110 002
Phone: 011-23263290

Also at *Bangalore, Hyderabad* and *Guwahati*

Typeset by Rawat Computers, Jaipur
Printed at Chaman Enterprises, New Delhi

in loving memory

of my mother

Bhani Bai

Contents

Preface

The present study presents a systematic and comprehensive picture of traditional, transitional and emerging pattern of a dominant scheduled caste – the Raigar in northern India. It also reports and analyses a mass activity which provides a vivid picture of various dimensions on untouchable caste in the pre- and post-independent India.

Based on a single dominant scheduled caste, spread over eight different states (Rajasthan, Gujarat, Maharashtra, Madhya Pradesh, Delhi, Uttar Pradesh, Haryana, and Punjab), I have presented a rich treasure of data on scheduled caste socio-political changes both at a diachronic and synchronic levels. On a diachronic level the study covers:

- the genesis and development of Raigar socio-religious and educational consciousness in various regions of the country, and
- the role of the various Raigar saints played at different points of time in different regions and the socio-cultural movement moulding the contemporary Raigar leaderships and their involvement in national movement and lastly the emergence of recent political parties including the contemporary movements in the Raigar community.

On a synchronic level four important changes were recognised which had occurred or which ought to have occurred in the life and world of Raigars. First, due to policies of protective discrimination, an upward social mobility had been experienced among Raigars in terms of social, educational, economic and political settings. Second, there had been an unprecedented rise in socio-political consciousness among Raigars. Third, caste consciousness and caste based solidarity in the untouchable communities in general and Raigars in particular had increased, rather weakening caste system. Finally, Raigars are asserting an independent identity or to mobilise people for collective action.

This volume is an off-spring of national fellowship on "Social Justice and Untouchable Movement in Northern India during the span of 1940-2004", which this author carried out at the Department of Sociology, University of Rajasthan, between 2003-2005. Dr B.R. Ambedkar National Fellowship was awarded and financially supported by the Indian Council of Social Science Research, New Delhi. I thank V.R. Panchamukhi, Chairman of ICSSR for awarding National Fellowship and providing financial support to undertake this work.

Many organisations and individuals had lent their support and cooperation in various ways at different stages in this work. I have had a very fruitful discussion on various parts of the work with Indu Mathur, Department of Sociology, University of Rajasthan, Shyam Lal Verma, Department of Political Science, University of Rajasthan, and Gopal Bhardwaj, Jai Narain Vyas University, Jodhpur. I am grateful to them for their valuable comments and encouragement.

I owe a special debt to the leaders and masses of ABRM and authorities of various organisations for supplying valuable material for historical study of the various aspects of ABRM and also extending all cooperation in completing this study, but for which it would not have been possible for me to complete the work.

Activists connected with Raigar movement, programmes and activities, provided important research material. Through the years discussions and interaction with activists, office bearers of ABRM and intellectuals of Raigar movement and the other social movements have been essential in helping me sharpen and formulate my perspective. I owe thanks to K.L. Kamal, Chandanmal Naval, Roop Chand Jalutharia, P.M. Jalutharia, P.N. Rachhoya, M.L. Bhatt, Shyam B. Sevalia, Dau Lal Mathur, Kishan Lal Kurdia, Shiv Narain Sarsunia, Kusum Meghwal, S.S. Saxena, P.M. Bairwa, and many others.

I would like to thank those whose support, stimulation and research aid was crucial in completing this work. K.S. Saxena, former Director, Academic Staff College, Jai Narain Vyas University, Jodhpur not only for taking interest but also facilitating this work and my friends Jagdish Roy and Ishwar Modi for helpful suggestions and pertinent comments on earlier versions of this study. My family has supported me through this long period of research and writing and to them my affectionate thanks.

Finally, I would like to thank Sushila Jain, former Head of the Department and present Head of the Department of Sociology, Leena Parmar, University of Rajasthan, for providing facilities for completion of this manuscript.

I am also indebted to Shri Kailash Rawat of Rawat Publications for accepting the proposal and publishing it in such a short time.

Shyamlal

List of Abbreviations

AIHSS	All India Harijan Sewak Sangh
AG	Accountant General
ABKRM	Akhil Bharatiya Koli Rajput Mahasabha
ABRM	Akhil Bharatiya Raigar Mahasabha
AKP	Arya Kanya Pathshalla
ASS	Asmarth Sahayata Samiti
ARRYM	Akhil Rajasthan Raigar Yua Mahasabha
ABBM	Akhil Bharatiya Bairwa Mahasabha
AMO	Assistant Medical Officer
AMASNNS	Ambedkar Mission Avam Samaj Nav Nirvan Sansthan
ANS	Ambedkar Navyuvak Sangh
ABSCSTWU	Akhil Bharatiya Scheduled Castes and Scheduled Tribes Welfare Union
AMES	Ambedkar Memorial Education Society
DPRP	Delhi Prantiya Raigar Panchayat
DPRSCP	Delhi Prantiya Raigar Subha Chintak Parisad
DPRMPC	Delhi Prantiya Raigar Mandir Prabandhan Committee
DPRSSM	Delhi Prantiya Raigar Swayam Sewak Mandal
DPRYS	Delhi Prantiya Raigar Yuvak Sangh

HSS	Harijan Sewak Sangh
HSS	Harijan Sudhar Samiti
JPPS	Jagrati Patra Prakashan Samiti
LSS	Labhunath Satsangh Sabha
MMSS	Marwar Mehtar Sudhar Sabha
MM	Meghwal Mahasabha
MJSM	Meghbansh Jati Sudharak Mandal
PM	Praja Mandal
PBSMH	Prince Bijay Singh Memorial Hospital
RHSS	Rajasthan Harijan Sewak Sangh
RAS	Rajasthan Administrative Services
RPF	Railway Protection Force
RMSS	Rajputana Mehtar Sudhar Sabha
RVP	Raigar Vidhyarti Parisad
RJSSM	Raigar Jati Swayam Sewak Mandal
RSS	Raigar Shikshit Samaj
RSAS	Raigar Sanyukta Agragami Sangh
RPSCP	Raigar Prantiya Subha Chintak Parisad
RNYS	Raigar Nav Yuvak Sangh
RSCSS	Raigar Subha Chintak Sabha, Sindh
RSRHS	Raigar Society Ravivans Hitkarni Sabha
RSS	Raigar Sewak Sangh
RRPS	Rajasthan Raigar Pragatisheel Sabha
RVSR	Raigar Vikas Sansthan Rajasthan
RSSVASJ	Raigar Samaj Samuhik Vivah Aayojan Samiti, Jaipur
RMMP	Rajasthan Meghwal Mahasabha, Pushkar
RSSS	Raigar Samaj Shiksha Samiti
RS	Raigar Sabha
SMRSS	Sri Moji Ram Sat Sangh
SDSS	Sanatan Dharm Satsangh Sabha
SDUS	Satsangh Dharmo Updesh Sabha
SPRPA	Shat Patti Raigar Panchayat, Ajmer

SHMDCT	Sri Hazarimal Manohar Devi Charitable Trust
SRSKS	Sri Raigar Sudharak Karyakarini Sangh
SMU	Safai Mazdoor Union
SCUU	Scheduled Castes Uplift Union
SCSTEUB	Scheduled Castes and Scheduled Tribes Employees Union, Banswara
UOA	Untouchability Offence Act
VSKM	Valmiki Sangit Kalla Mandir

1

The Problem

Throughout the country the lower untouchable castes/communities are organising themselves to fight against socio-religious disabilities, atrocities, caste based discrimination and the economic exploitations. They agitate for their legitimate rights in economic opportunities, educational privileges and political power. Widespread collective mobilisation, centred around such interests has led to organised social movements with the defined ideology and leadership, which have brought about significant socio-economic and political changes in the communities from where they originate. In the present study, an attempt has been made to analyse the genesis, growth dynamics and socio-economic consequences of movement among the scheduled castes in northern India.

Legally Constituted Terms: SCs and STs

Scheduled castes and scheduled tribes are specified terms applied to two different categories of the people who have been singled out by the Government of India (originally used by imperial state) for specific treatment which together formed about one-fourth of the total population of India in 1991. While the scheduled castes comprised one-sixth of the total population of India, the scheduled tribes constituted the twelfth of it. Certain castes and tribes are scheduled in the Constitution of India by the President, hence the terms scheduled castes and scheduled tribes. The castes and communities included under scheduled castes and scheduled tribes categories are entitled to three kinds of privileges – educational facilities, government employment and representation at different levels on the political bodies. Students belonging to scheduled castes and scheduled tribes generally get free education in educational institutions, a stipend for books, admission in hostels, lowering of normal eligibility conditions for admission to schools, colleges, technical and professional courses and scholarship to pursue higher studies. A certain quota of government jobs are also reserved for them at all levels and conditions of promotion are also liberal. Similarly, they have reserved seats of representation in the village panchayats, panchayat samities, district councils, state assemblies and parliament.

The special privileges that the scheduled castes and scheduled tribes enjoy today did not however materialise overnight. This has been a cumulative result of several organised protest movements that emerged over a period of a century in British India. In order to understand the development of social reform movement among the lower untouchable castes/communities, it is necessary to consider the nature of the caste system in traditional India.

Caste System and Social Discrimination in Traditional India

The 'varna' system that was established in ancient India functioned at the larger framework within which the caste society was formed. According to Rigveda, the oldest of the four Vedas, distinction between the four varnas dates back to the origin of the human race. That is to say at the time of the creation, the Brahmins were born from the mouth of Purusa, the Kshatriya from his arms, the Vaishya from his thigh and Shudra from his feet.

The Brahmin who made up the highest ranked varna, monopolised the position of priest and preacher of the Vedas, the Kshatriyas took charge of politics and military, the Vaishyas formed the commoner ranks of cultivators, traders and merchants and Shudras were relegated to the position of servants. The top three varnas were the regular members of Aryan society. They were called the Dvijati or 'twice born' and were allowed to participate in the religious worship presided over by the Brahmins. Their second birth was the initiation ceremony into the Vedic studies (Upanayana) which they performed while they were young. In contrast, the Shudras were segregated from 'Dvijati' as 'Ekajati' who were born only once from their mother's wombs. Under Shudras, a class of inferior people existed, in which the 'Chandals' or the untouchables were placed. In other words social discrimination appeared in a stratified form.

The upper caste category included such castes as the Brahmins, Rajputs, Baniyas or Vaish. All castes belonging to upper caste category exercised control over different sources of power. The Brahmins enjoyed ritual supremacy and as priests controlled access to sacred Sanskrit texts and they were also a source for reinforcing the caste system.

At the bottom of the caste hierarchy was the category of untouchable castes who came to be designated as the depressed/ exterior/out caste during the British rule. It included such castes as Chamars, Bhambhis, Meghwals, Balais, Raigars, Jatavs, Dholis, Damamis, Bunkars, Khateeks, Valmikis, Bhangis, Mehtars, etc., in Rajasthan – northern India. These castes are mainly bonded agricultural labourers. They also worked as sweepers, folk musicians, basket makers, cloth weavers, meat sellers and performed various manual jobs for their higher caste patrons. They were considered to be unapproachable and untouchables and therefore, suffered from many civic and religious disabilities. They were neither allowed to enter in the temples of the high caste Hindus nor were they admitted to the educational institutions. Financially, they were dependent and in some cases even slaves. In the villages and towns, they were segregated from the upper castes. They did not have any access to the streets used by the upper castes. Nor were they allowed to use the public tanks, and wells. Socially, there were many forms of discrimination with regard to the terms of address, difference in speech and other modes of behaviour. They were prevented from dressing in caste Hindu style and from wearing of gold and silver ornaments.

Untouchable Movements during British India

Since independence, numerous studies have been published in connection with social movements in India[1] which have greatly contributed in throwing new light on the socio-economic life of the untouchables as well as other social groups.

In the pre-independence period anti-caste movement comprised strong non-Brahmin movements in Maharashtra and Tamilnadu as well as untouchable movements in Maharashtra, Punjab (the Adi-dharam movement), western Uttar Pradesh (the

Adi-Hindu movement), Bengal (Nama Shudras), Kerala (Narain Swami Guru's movement), Tamilnadu (Adi-Dravidas), Coastal Andhra (Adi-Andhras) and Hyderabad (Adi-Hindus).[2] In addition there were non-Brahmin ideological trends elsewhere and weaker or unorganised untouchables assertions in such areas as Rajasthan and Bihar. These movements can be termed in the language of functionalist sociological theory, as 'value-oriented movements' as opposed to 'norm-oriented movements'. That is, they challenged and sought to transform the basic structure of the Indian social system, replacing caste and the accompanying social oppression, economic exploitation and political domination by an equalitarian society. There were, of course, reformist trends in the movements as in the other social movements of Indian society. These were represented within the untouchable movement by leaders such as Jagjivan Ram of Congress, G.A. Gavai and his organisations, within the non-Brahmin movements the justice party. Reformist trends were also embodied in Gandhi's Harijan movements which stood in the tradition of broad upper castes social reform tradition which sought to cleanse Hinduism of its impurities. The lower or untouchable castes movements were widespread both in south and north India.

The main figures of this larger anti-caste movement, Jotiba Phule,[3] Babasaheb Ambedkar,[4] and E.V. Ramasami 'Periyar' with many others throughout India – Narain Swami Guru[5] in Kerala, Achutanand in Uttar Pradesh,[6] Mangoo Ram in Punjab, all attacked the system of exploitation at all levels, culturally, economically and politically.

Untouchable Movements in Rajputana and Neighbouring States during Pre-Independence Period

The decade of 1920 saw the emergence of the Bhangis leadership vis-a-vis social reform movement as a conscious and organised force in the socio-religious life of the Bhangis of Rajasthan. Here, the reform movement of Arya Samaj emerged more distinctly in the Bhangi basties of Jodhpur city. Being influenced by Arya Samaj movement in the region, the Bhangi reform movement concentrated on socio-religious evils. The aims of the movement were as follows:

1. To wean the Bhangis away from eating beef, dead animals, left-overs and consumption of alcoholic drinks.

2. To inculcate the idea of cleanliness in them and give them a sense of improved standards of living.
3. To create the feeling of Hinduism, and
4. To eradicate Muslim influence from their socio-religious spheres.[7]

More precisely, there emerged the Arya Samaj movement in 1923 in Jodhpur which challenged the influence of Muslim culture on the Bhangi community. With the result, the Bhangis relinquished the Muslim influence in almost every walk of life and laid the basis for influencing Bhangi's socio-religious life and movement including the process of sanskritisation. The important leaders of Arya Samaj were Shankar Lal Gaur, Bhajan Singh Bhati, Bhom Singh Bhati and others. Through organising of meeting throughout the various Bhangi bastis, the Bhangi social workers had enhanced the urban area base. During 1940, in the princely state of Jodhpur a political agitation among the Bhangis started. It was chiefly aimed against the economic exploitation of sweepers by municipal authorities.

In 1942, the leaders and workers of Marwar Lok Parishad, a political organisation in princely states which struggled for the rights of people against the rulers, discussed with the Bhangis the possibility of organising a Bhangi union. Getting favourable response from the latter, Safai Mazdoor Union of the Bhangis was formed. Prabhudanji, the then eminent Bhangi of Jodhpur, was made honorary President and Bhabji Maharaj General Secretary, Jai Narain Vyas and his colleagues felt that if they had Bhangis with them, their political agitation could be more successful and widespread. It would be easier to get the support through union. In order to guide and help the Bhangis in their social and political activities two Congress workers namely – Amar Kishan Vyas and Saint Lada Ram were attached in organisation. From 1942 onwards, the Bhangis were drawn more into the orbit of social reform movement and politics. Their contact with higher caste political and social workers increased. The social and political workers also realised the necessity of expanding their field of activities.

In 1945, a handful of illiterate old caste Panchas and old and young workers who had been meeting in Jodhpur, began serious discussions about developing a reform movement and political struggle. The key leaders were – Prabhudan Gharu, Bhagwan Das Gund, Sri Ram Sarvate, N.D. Gujarati, Achlu Ram Barashah, Roop

Chand Chanwaria and so on. These leaders were guided by Marwar Lok Parishad's leaders and workers. As a result, Marwar Mehtar Sudhar Sabha (MMSS) emerged as an organised movement of the Bhangis in 1946 in Jodhpur with Prabhudan Gharu as its President. This was the beginning of articulate protest among the Bhangis.

In 1946, the political climate changed in the princely states substantially. His Highness of Jodhpur State set up a six-men committee for removing grievances of the Bhangi employees of the Jodhpur Municipality, with Rai Bahadur, Dr L.D. Joshi, the Legal Rememberance, Government of Jodhpur as Chairman. Five persons were nominated as members. The main object of the committee was to look into the grievances of the Bhangi employees of Jodhpur. The first person selected for representation on the Committee was N.D. Gujarati – a Bhangi from Sindhio-ka-Bass, who had been in touch with Jai Narain Vyas and Mathura Das Mathur. His revised status enabled him to speak in political terms and won him respect and admiration of his community.

Soon after this His Highness issued an order advising the State Government to hand over the government building situated in Udai Mandir Bhangi basti to Bhangis to run a school for their children. In solving the water problem of the Bhangis, a separate water tank was constructed in Moka Bhangi basti. Orders were issued by the ruler pertaining to education. He also permitted the admission of the Bhangi children in the state owned educational institutions. Thus, one boy Hari Bhajan was admitted in the Muslim School and Dau Lal Jawa in Darbar High School.

It was soon discovered by the Bhangi leaders of the MMSS that it was not enough to unite at district level or local level but they also realised the need for a wider organisation. Consequently, in order to expand the geographical boundary of the Sabha, Sarvate and Gujarati negotiated with Bhangi leaders of the other regions and tried to create a social consciousness among the fragmented and disorganised masses of the Bhangis. Therefore, in order to meet this need and to expand the geographical boundary of the Sabha, an attempt to forge a united front of the Bhangis for unity and upliftment reached its peak in 1948 when a large joint meeting of Rajputana Bhangi Sammelan was held at Udai Mandir Bhangi basti. It was, according to its participants and organisers, the most inspired spectacle ever witnessed in Jodhpur attended by about 500-600 persons having representation from Bikaner, Jaipur, Nagaur, Pali, Churu, Ladnu, Barmer, Ajmer, Sojat, Beawar, etc.

Gopalanand Maharaj of Baroda – well known Bhangi Monk and social reformer presided over the function and Jai Narain Vyas, an eminent Congress leader, inaugurated the Sammelan. Thus, Rajputana Mehtar Sudhar Sabha was established. Straight away two changes in the caste organisations should be noted. First, the word 'Marwar' was replaced by the word 'Rajputana' which facilitated the inclusion of the Bhangis of various regions in the Sabha fold. Second, the socio-religious reform activities of the caste were transformed into the general caste association convening all-round reform and development of the Bhangis. Nagar Mal from Churu was elected President and Ghasi Ram from Jaipur was made Secretary of the newly constituted union.

In fact, Sarvate and Gujarati were the first Bhangis to hold Sammelan of the Bhangis in Rajasthan. Besides, they formed Safai Mazdoor Union in 1942 and Gujarati also published Hindi Paper Samajik Azadi. They also fought against Jajmani system. Gujarati published a few books on Bhangis. One such important book is *Samarpeet Sewa* (1994). They also opened a few library centres in different Bhangi bastis. They were also leaders of temples and hotel entry campaign in Jodhpur.

In early 1935, the members of the Praja Mandal, particularly Heera Lal Shastri, circulated secretly a pamphlet titled Aka (unity) among the public of Jaipur city. In this published pamphlet Shastri aimed to bring different castes (including lower and untouchable castes), sects and religions closer to one another. It should be remembered that because of the courage shown by reformers, reform and integration of the lower castes gradually came to be accepted by the general public. The first meeting was held at Kalu Ram Pradhan's house at Chand Pole Bhangi basti, which was attended by some members such as Chiranji Lal Aggarwal, Radha Vallabh Aggrawal and others including Bhangis such as Ram Narain, Jamna Prasad Chanwaria, etc. It was decided to form a group called Satsang Mandali. The basic objects of the Mandali were:

1. to get together once a week;
2. to sing the religious songs;
3. to promote socio-religious reform programmes among the caste fellows;
4. through these programmes unite the Samaj; and
5. to pay one anna as contribution.

It is fairly clear that at that time, as even today, Bhangis were living in a miserable and deplorable condition.

Thus, the whole atmosphere stirred these reformers and motivated them. In 1935, for the first time in the community's history, they started in Jamna Prasad Chanwaria's house at Ghatgate, a residential school for the exclusive benefit of the Bhangi's children. Bhangi parents sent their children to school, namely Kanhaiya Lal Daboria, Lalita Prasad Chanwaria, Banshi Lal, Ram Narain, Ram Swaroop, etc. (all boys) and Kalu Bai, Sharda, Gulabi, Chhota (all girls). Along with educational activities they were working for community reforms too. The Bhangi children were given books, slates, pencils, writing materials, etc., free of cost.

Bhajan Lal, Raghu Nandan, Om Prakash and Ram Ratan were the first Brahmin teachers from Uttar Pradesh and Jaipur city respectively to work in the Bhangi Schools, as teachers. The Praja Mandal decided to bear their expenses and these teachers joined the school. They were paid Rs 15 per month. Besides teaching, these Brahmin teachers used to visit bastis to preach social reform. Knowing the advantages of education, numerous Bhangis sent their children to school. The boys and girls were generally examined. After the examination, prizes were given to the children.

Another organised attempt of Praja Mandal towards education began with the opening of another school with 30 Bhangi children in Chand Pole Bhangi basti in the year 1936. Thereafter, education began to spread through the efforts of the social reformers. Mohan Lal and Bhajan Lal both Brahmins by caste from Uttar Pradesh and Prem Shankar Solanki from Madhya Pradesh were the first to teach Bhangi children. The children were given books, slates, pencils, writing materials, etc., free of cost.

In the middle of twentieth century, particularly in the fourth decade, the Chamars had asserted a distinct identity and had even refused to be referred to as Chamars. It was felt that the word referred to them as Chamars, Meghwals, Bhambhis, Balais, etc., was derogatory, insulting and humiliating. It was in 1940 that Sohan Lal Chamar of Delhi held a series of meetings with caste-men namely Swami Vivekanand (Chamar) and felt the necessity of introducing a self-internal reform movement. It is said that from 1940-42, Sohan Lal toured all over Rajputana[8] and towns such as Baroda, Bombay, Agra, Mathura and Bulandshahar. During his visit to these places he held several meetings with caste-men. In 1943, in order to discuss the issue further, he met with Munishwaranand of Jaipur, Sarvjeet Lal of Ajmer and Jhuta Lal of Indore separately and discussed the issue in details. The main concern of such discussions was to moderate the caste's name and customs and promote internal reforms of the Jati (caste). But these efforts were local in approach and specific in nature. The Chamars of Delhi and Rajputana held many meetings with caste-men and conceived the idea of a new name for caste as a whole. Later during late 1943, Sohal Lal again discussed the issue with Swami Vivekanand, an influential saint of Delhi. Vivekanand also supported Sohan Lal's view and advised him to organise a caste sabha as through caste council or sabha, social reform measures would prove effective.

A meeting on the caste's geneological history took place at Jaipur. In the meeting, Munishwaranand in the course of his deliberations on the history of the caste, mentioned that Chamars, Bhambhis Balais, Jatias, Meghwals, etc., were descendants of a common stock. Apparently, according to him, differences amongst them had arisen with occupational variation in social setting in which the units of the community were placed. Munishwaranand believes that there are references to a word 'Bairwa' in Mahabharat and that it was therefore, we would trace our origin from Bairwa. Later, during late 1944, Sohan Lal also went to Indore to consult Jhuta Lal for introducing reforms amongst the Chamars.

In Indore, Jhuta Lal, popularly known as the 'Master', the supporter of caste reforms, had been devoting his life to the upliftment of the Chamar community since 1930. First of all he agreed with the views of Munishwaranand to relinquish all the traditional callings and accept the new name Bairwa. At the same time, Jhuta Lal also advised Sohan Lal to persuade caste fellows for organising a community meeting. Sohan Lal's success, in this respect, was remarkable.

Now, Sohan Lal along with others worked day and night for holding a community meeting for introducing reforms amongst the Chamars. As a result of such efforts, consciousness for betterment of their community was generated amongst the Chamars. Consequently, in 1944 the Chamars of Delhi organised a meeting at Padampur, Delhi, and it was attended by a few thousand caste fellows. Most of them were from different localities of Delhi and a few were from the neighbouring states such as Rajputana, Uttar

Pradesh, etc. This was the first social meeting of the Chamars. The leaders appealed to their fellow brethren to take some constructive decision for caste reform. They said that taking of decision would mean that we were supporting the social reforms, which they should implement in word and deed. Their appeal was heeded by the caste fellows and following decisions were taken.

First, they took the decision to be called as 'Bairwa' as a caste distinct from Chamars, Bhambhis, Meghwals, etc. Second, at all-India level, a new organisation be formed immediately. Third and last, an appeal was made to the gathering that assembled at Padampur, Delhi to initiate an agitation in order to express their resentment and protest against the atrocities perpetrated on the caste fellows particularly in Rajasthan.

The above decisions having been taken in the gathering, the leaders appealed to the community to follow decisions adopted for forming a new organisation. Thus, a new organisation under the banner of 'Akhil Bharatiya Bairwa Rajput Sabha' (ABBRS) came into existence in 1944.

Swami Vivekanand was nominated as President with Mangalsen as Vice-President, Sohan Lal as the General Secretary and Bhora Lal as Treasurer. Ishwar Lal and Kalyan Singh were nominated as Prachar Mantri of the Sabha. At last, Sohan Lal's dream of 1940s became a reality.

In early 1946, a few leaders such as Hari Shanker Sidharth Shastri (Jaipur), Master Jhuta Lal (Indore), Babu Surjeet Lal (Ajmer), Babu Hardayal (Bandikui) and few others, assembled at Delhi. They were worried about the word 'Rajput'. On the same line, Swami Vivekanand, Sohan Lal Chaudhary, Manak Chand, Ghosi Ram and others were also worried about the use of the word Rajput. Consequently, in April 1946, an urgent meeting of the Sabha was called at the residence of contractor Ghasi Ram Patalwasha at Delhi. They considered that the country would soon become free. According to them, it was nothing but to harm the caste and therefore, they should drop it immediately. Thus, the proposal placed by Hari Shanker Sidharth Shastri in a meeting was passed unanimously and straight away three changes in the caste sabha were made. First, the socio-educational activities were transformed into general caste sabha covering all round development of Bairwas. Second, the word Rajput was dropped. Third, and last, the word 'Sabha' was replaced by the word 'Mahasabha' which facilitated the inclusion of various other sub-groups, who claimed Chamars status in the Mahasabha fold. However, no specification was made regarding the word Bairwa.

The members felt the need for a written constitution for carrying out the programmes and activities for all round development of the Bairwa caste. The leaders also knew that all the members were illiterate except other two members. Under such circumstances, Bheem Sen, a high caste Hindu and a legal expert, was approached and requested to draft a model constitution. When the draft constitution was ready, it was placed before the members, who approved it in the year 1946.

The aims of ABBM was to bring together the scattered Bairwas by merging them into a single organisation at all-India level and carrying out the functions for an all-round development of the caste. In order to attain the goals, the constitution laid down the following activities:

1. To develop a feeling of unity in diversity amongst all untouchables including Bairwas, ABBM should take initiative.
2. To eradicate social evils and vices such as early marriage, death feasts, dowry, consuming liquor, etc., and to impose a ban on these through ABBM.
3. To encourage the process of sanskritisation.
4. To eradicate untouchability and make Bairwas free from inferiority complex.
5. To expand education amongst the children of Bairwas in general and girls in particular.
6. To improve the low and poor economic conditions of the caste, Bairwas should be encouraged to discard their traditional occupation and accept the non-traditional occupations.

Rajputana (now Rajasthan) has been stronghold of the Meghwals. Rajasthan has eight dominant untouchable castes and Meghwal is one of them. The Rajasthan Meghwals Mahasabha Pushkar (RMMP)[9] was established in the year 1920 at a meeting held at Ajmer under the leadership of Swami Gokul Das Maharaj, who was the moving spirit behind this campaign. The RMMP was actively engaged in the programmes of prohibition of liquor and in the anti-social evils movement. The name of RMMP was later changed to 'Meghwal Mahasangh'. Its activities extended to Punjab, Delhi, Madhya Pradesh, Gujarat and Maharashtra.

Besides the Bhangis, the Chamars and the Meghwals in the year 1944, the Raigars in different regions of the country – Rajasthan, Haryana, Punjab, Delhi, Uttar Pradesh, Hyderabad (now in Pakistan), Madhya Pradesh, Gujarat, and Maharashtra formed an 'Akhil Bharatiya Raigar Mahasabha' (ABRM), which initiated self-reform movement.

The present work is an attempt to analyse the genesis, growth, dynamics and social and the cultural consequences of the movement amongst one scheduled caste or untouchable community of India. This community, the Raigars of north India in general and Rajasthan and Delhi in particular, represents a unique case of socio-religious and political activities amongst the depressed and disadvantaged minorities of Indian society, i.e., untouchables. The Raigars are in many ways a unique community in the social history of modern India, for two reasons: First, by virtue of their functional role in the village community, they had occupied a somewhat special position in the hierarchy of the lower untouchable castes. Second, under the leadership of Swami Atma Ram Lakshya the Raigars were the first untouchable community to organise a conference at all-India level and agitated against their social deprivation and disability.

The socio-political movement of the Raigars which dates back from the fourth decade of the twentieth century, is very distinguished both by its longevity and continuity as well as due to its organisational works. The Raigars are also notable in the sense that their religious guru, Swami Atma Ram Lakshya was one of the chief architects of ABRM and stipulated that the Raigars self-reform themselves. The Raigar caste, therefore, affords a significant instance for the study of the socio-political activities in its broadest sense of the untouchables and similarly placed groups in Indian society.

No scholar, except a few both in Rajasthan and in India have tended to focus on the Raigars or had dealt with extensively with socio-political development in the post-independence era. Therefore, this study intends to:

1. Bring out the historical development of the Raigar caste and the socio-political movement that it enshrined.
2. Develop the movement through phased agitations and a search for social reforms, formation of ABRM and rift in the ABRM, fight against the untouchability, mobilisation and awakening of

a new consciousness through literature and cultural activities be studied.

3. Study other aspects of ABRM's role in political parties and elections and its bargaining power with the government.
4. Examine the role of the Raigars and their diverse activities in the freedom movement.

Methods

The sources on which this work is based is predominantly primary in nature. The intent in relying heavily on primary sources has been to see the Raigar movement from within, from the perspective of the participants as they understand their past to transform the conditions under which they live.

Examination of Documentary Material

The study began with documentation work. First of all, the small booklets, souvenirs, pamphlets and hand-bills published by the Raigar leaders or by various units of the organisations, were studied in detail to formulate the history of the organisation and to note the views and beliefs of the leaders on certain socio-political decisions. The most important books etc. are:

Raigad Jati ka Mahatava, (1941).

Jati Beejak Mool Prakash: Raigar Samaj, (Year not mentioned).

Raigar Kshstriyo Pradesh-Gayan, (1942).

Unnati Path Pradershan Athva Dhan ka Duropayog, (1947).

Bharatiya Janganana Vibhag Rajasthan Ajmer Rajyakey Bulletin No. 12 – Parishist No. 2 ke prashano key Pariganit Raigar Samaj ka Uttar (1950).

Raigar Kaun aur Kya? (1964).

Akhil Bharatiya Raigar Mahasabha: Vidhan, (1965).

Smarika – Kalyan Sangh, (1971).

Rajasthan Prantiya Raigar Mahasabha, Jaipur – Smarika, (1972).

Prachin Raigar Itihas, (1973).

Raigar Itihas ki Khoj tatha Jatpath Sambandhi Vichar, (1980).

Akhil Bharatiya Raigar Panchayat, Pushkar Mandir Vyabyastha Committee, Pushkar, Rajasthan, Aaya-Vyaya Vivran, (Year not mentioned).

Raigar Dharmshala, Birla Road, Haridwar Aaya-Vyaya Vivran (1982-83), (Year not mentioned).

Dilli Prantiya Raigar Panchayat, (Year not mentioned).

Dilli Prantiya Raigar Mandir Prabandhak Committee ka Aaya-Vyaya Prativedan, (Year not mentioned).

Akhil Bharatiya Raigar Mahasabha Karyakarini Samiti avam Karyakarta Sammelan, 8 avam 9 November, 1981.

Raigar Samaj – Atma Ram Lakshya, (1986).

Raigar Jati ka Itihas, (1986).

Pancham Akhil Bharatiya Raigar Mahasabha, Raigar Gaurav Smarika, (1986).

Dilli Prantiya Raigar Swayam Sewak Mandal, Dev Nagar, New Delhi, Swaran Jayanti, 1938-1987, (1987).

Smarika: Dashak Samaroh, 30-31 May, 1993, (1993).

Smarika Dharamguru Swami Gian Swaroop Janam Satabdi Avam Akhil Bharatiya Raigar Mahasabha Swaran Jayanti Samaroh, (1995).

Gian Bhajan Prabhakar, (1998).

Prachin Raigar Itihas, (1998).

Akhil Rajasthan Raigar Yuva Mahasabha, Pratham Maha Sammelan Smarika, (1998).

Raigar Samaj Samuhik Vivaha Ayojan Samiti, Jaipur, Madhur Smiriti – Smarika, (1998).

Raigar Samaj Samuhik Vivaha Ayojan Samiti, Jaipur: Dwitiya Samuhik Vivaha Samaroh Madhur Smiriti – Smarika, (1999).

Raigar Vikas Sanstha Rajasthan, Jaipur, Tritiya Samuhik Vivaha Samaroh Madhur Smiriti Smarika, (2000).

Surya-Sagar Ganga Smarika, Tritiya Raigar Samaj Samuhik Vivaha Sammelan, Pushkar, (2001).

Parivarik Jyoti, (2001).

Raigar Jati ka Itihas, (2001).

Kavya Piyush, (2001).

Raigar, (2002).

The leading regional daily papers – Rajasthan Patrika, Dainik Navjyoti and Dainik Bhaskar (all Jaipur editions) were read for caste's activities. Likewise caste periodical Raigar Pragatisheel Patrika, Jaipur (1982), Phalak, Jaipur (1992), Raigar Uthan, Indore (1993), Raigar Sudhar, Fatehabad (1999), Raigar Jyoti, Barmer (2000), Vikas Kiran, Tonk (2001), Raigar Rakshak, Jaipur (2001), Lakshya Rakshak, Delhi (2001) and Parivarik Jyoti, Bhilwara, (2001) were consulted for socio-economic and political issues. Efforts were also made to acquire the pamphlets and handbills published by Raigar leaders or by various units of the organisation and were used wherever available.

Rapport Building and Observation

Prior to this fieldwork, the author was already in contact with some of the leaders of the Sabha and therefore, it had an added advantage of starting work without spending much time for rapport building. During the fieldwork we participated in some of Sabha's activities and functions, where the leading figures of the organisation assembled. This helped us in listening to gossips, establishing rapport with the members of the Sabha and talking at length with different Raigars who came there for various purposes. During our work we developed personal relationship with some of the leaders who often discussed their personal, organisational and political problems with us. Some meetings and Sammelan of Sabha were attended by us. All this provided us an excellent opportunity to look deep into the social problems of the community and to make a first-hand observation which helped us in developing a clear insight into the subject under investigation.

Conversation and Talk

In order to have an overall view of the process of the Raigars' involvement in the Mahasabha's activities, a few important Raigars, who were in close touch with Mahasabha either as supporters or critics, were interviewed. Besides MLAs, ministers and office bearers of the Mahasabha were also interviewed. Interviews were carried out with open-ended questions in the conversational form. The major talking points were about socio-cultural and political activities and their attitude towards the Mahasabha, the 'savarnas', government, political parties and elections. We also asked their views on certain socio-political decisions of the Mahasabha.

The material for the work was gathered first in 2003 and then in 2004.

Plan of the Work

Chapter 1 discusses the formulation of the problem with reference to the empirical context. It also discusses genesis, growth and consequences of social movements which occurred in other regions of the country.

Chapter 2 gives a background analysis of caste system in Rajasthan alongwith a discussion of sub-division among the Raigar caste category and analysis of disabilities.

Chapter 3 deals with the major socio-religious reforms introduced by various saints for the eradication of social evils. It also discusses early efforts made towards ideological changes.

Chapter 4 and 9 focus on the year 1810-1993 and 1940-2004 respectively, the period said to be the turning point, describes the emergence of Raigar movement as organisational forces in Delhi and Sindh – Hyderabad as also in Rajasthan, Uttar Pradesh, Gujarat, Madhya Pradesh, Haryana and Punjab respectively. It also deals with the construction of temples, schools, dharmshallas, etc.

Chapter 5 deals with the period (1940) of emergence of Akhil Bharatiya Raigar Mahasabha (ABRM) as an organisational force in many regions of India, taking different situations in eight regions (Rajasthan, Delhi, Madhya Pradesh, Uttar Pradesh, Gujarat, Maharashtra, Haryana and Punjab) focussing on the period 1940 onwards as agenda of Raigar movement. It describes further the discarding of traditional occupation and confrontation of Raigars and issues of caste raised by Raigar movement with upper caste Hindus on the one hand and the quest for respectable place in the Hindu society on the other. The Chapter also deals with the years of radicalism in Rajasthan when ABRM was actively involved in leading the struggles. The success of this period to develop into a broad movement unifying social and anti-caste Hindu struggle was perhaps decisive for Raigars.

Chapter 6 focuses on the participation of Raigars in the freedom movement from 1940-1947, while Chapter 7 describes the decline in the activities of ABRM and the issue of rift in ABRM and Chapter 8 focuses on the origin and the development of various social and educational organisations in Rajasthan during 1950-2004. It also deals with major caste issue – fight against socio-religious disabilities and untouchability.

Chapter 10 concentrates on Raigar's migration to Maharashtra in pre-independence period.

Chapter 11 concentrates on Raigar periodicals during 1948-2002.

Chapter 12 focuses on 1952-2004 period as emergence of politicians, discusses the caste representation in the state assembly, in parliament and in ministry on the one hand and shifting of caste sentiment from Congress to other political parties on the other.

Chapter 13 deals with social and cultural transformation among the caste fellows in the pre- and post-independence period.

Notes

1. For a discussion on Dalit movements that stress the role of both political and social organisation in the pre- and post-independence period and their socio-political consequences, see F.G. Bailey, *Caste and Economic Frontier: A Village Highland in Orissa,* Manchester. The Manchester University Press, 1957; Bernard S. Cohn, 'The Changing Status of a Depressed Caste' in Mackim Marriott (ed.), *Village India,* Chicago. University of Chicago Press, 1960; G.S. Bhatt, 'Trends and Measures of the Status Mobility Among the Chamars of Dehradun' in E.A., Vol. 14; No. 3, 1961; S. Patwardhan, *Change Among India's Harijan,* New Delhi, Orient Longman, 1973; Omen M. Lynch, *The Politics of Untouchability, Social Mobility and Social Change in a City of India,* Delhi, National Publishing House, 1974; L.P. Vidhyarthi and N. Misra, *Harijan Today,* New Delhi, Prentice Hall of India, 1977; Sachhidanand, *The Harijan Elite: A Study of their Status, Network Mobility and Role in Social Transformation,* Faridabad, Thomson Press, 1977; V.D. Divekar (ed.), *Social Reform Movement in India: A Historical Perspective,* Mumbai, Popular Prakashan, 1991; Jaya Shree Gokhale, *From Concession to Confrontation: The Politics of an Indian Untouchable Community,* Mumbai, Popular Prakashan, 1993.
2. Gail Omvedt, *Dalits and the Democratic Revolution: Dr Ambedkar and the Dalit Movement in Colonial India,* New Delhi, Sage Publications, 1994, p. 10.
3. Dhananjay Keer, *Mahatma Joti Rao Phule: The Father of Indian Social Revolution,* Bombay, Popular Prakashan, 1974.
4. Dhananjay Keer, *Dr Ambedkar; Life and Mission,* Mumbai, Popular Prakashan, 1995.
5. G. Gopinathan, "The process of Rehumanisation initiated by Sri Narayan Guru and Its impact on Kinship and other social relationship in Kerala" in Asok Parpola and Sirpa Tenhunen (ed.), *Changing Pattern of Family and Kinship in South Asia,* Helsinki, 1998. pp. 87-109; M.S.A. Rao, *Social Movements and Social Transformation: A Study of Two Backward Classes Movement in India,* Madras, Macmillan Company of India, 1979.
6. W.N. Kuber, "Dalit Movements in India", in V.D. Divekar (ed.), *Social Reform Movements in India: A Historical Perspective.* Mumbai, Popular Prakashan, 1991, p. 102.
7. Shyamlal, *The Changing Bhangis of India: A Study of Caste Association,* Jaipur, Sublime Publication, 1999, pp. 59-64. Also, see, Shyam Lal,

Caste and Political Mobilisation: The Bhangis, Jaipur, Panchsheel Prakasan, 1981.

8. Shyam Lal, *Untouchable Movements in India*, Jaipur, Sublime Publications, 2002, pp. 48-53.
9. Swami Gokul Das, *Meghwal's Itihas*, Ajmer, Arya Brothers Book Seller, 1993. Also see, *Meghwal Kirti Smarika*, 1998.

2

Raigars in Traditional Rajputana Society

The Raigar movement which was set in Rajasthan, today (census 1991) has a population of 4,40,05,990[1] (males 2,30,42,780 and females 2,09,63,210). Out of these figures Chamars and scheduled castes account for roughly 76,07,820[2] which is 17.28 per cent of the total population. Out of 76,07,820 scheduled castes in Rajasthan, Chamars represent nearly 28.6 per cent of the population or roughly 21,81,935.[3] Hence, Chamars are the most populous scheduled castes in Rajasthan, followed by Meghwal, Bairwa, Balai and Nayak respectively. (Counting all the communities related with leather occupation, i.e., at serial nos. 16, 17 and 46, the Chamars number roughly 35,67,719 or 46.89 per cent of the total population).[4] Among other scheduled castes Meghwal had the largest number 13,83,583 or 18.18 per cent, Bairwa 6,21,111 or 8.16 per cent, Balai 5,14,908 or 6.76 per cent and Nayak 4,71,411 or 6.19 per cent. The overwhelming majority of the scheduled castes are rural dwelling (82.83% rural, 17.16% urban for Chamars, 90.27% rural, 9.27% urban for Meghwal and 84.57% rural, 15.42% urban for the Bairwa). Moreover, out of the total scheduled castes workers, roughly 72.47 per cent are represented in agriculture and agricultural labourers accounting for over 23.13 per cent and cultivators 49.3 per cent.

The population of Rajasthan in 1961 had been 2,01,55,602.[5] By 1971, the population of Rajasthan was enumerated to be 2,57,65,806,[6] and by 1981, it had become 3,42,61,862.[7] Similarly, in 1991, the population of Rajasthan was estimated to be 4,40,05,990[8] and by 2001 it had become 5,64,73,122.[9]

It would be noted that Raigars have not been listed separately in the Census of India, but along with Chamars. In 1961, Raigars along with six other sub-castes known as Bhambhi, Jatia, Jatava, Mochi, Raidas and Ramdasia were listed under the category of 'Chamar'. If we compare the proportion of the Raigars including sub-division among the Chamar category of caste to the total population of Rajasthan, then in 1961, they had numbered around 14,54,502,[10] in 1971, 15,80,888,[11] in 1981, 18,72,133,[12] in 1991, 21,81,935,[13] and in 2001, 5,64,73,122.[14] This was an overwhelming rural population. The Raigars derived their livelihood from their traditional occupation, such as tanning of hides. They performed as agricultural labourers as well, to augment their earnings.

If the present population distribution trends are any indication, the Raigars must have been represented in fairly equal numbers in all areas of Rajasthan. Thus, in traditional society, Raigars were a population of untouchable community and village servants, scattered fairly throughout Rajasthan. They were integrated into the village community, albeit in the permanently inferior untouchable position as they occupied the lowest reaches of social as well as ritual hierarchy. Table 2.1 gives a broad picture of their strength.

A good attempt was made by Chandan Mal Naval during 1986 to write a brief history on Raigar community. Though Raigars, according to Naval, are spread over whole of Rajasthan, they are mostly found in abundance in the north rather than in the south. The Raigars are then numerically the largest social group in Delhi. Similarly, in a good number, the Raigars also reside in Gujarat, but a few in Maharashtra. Table 2.2 gives a broad picture of their residential distribution in the different regions.

The social structure of traditional Rajasthan contained three major elements:

1. Savarnas or caste Hindus from Brahmin to Vaishya.
2. Artisans: blacksmith, Suthar, Nai, tailor, etc.
3. Untouchables: Meghwal, Chamar, Bhambhi, Mochi, Khateek, Raigar, Bhangi.

Table 2.1

Castewise Break-up: 1981 and 1991 (Census)
(Population Size Arranged in Descending Order)

S. No.	Name of Scheduled Castes	Scheduled Castes Population		Decadal Variation	% of Variation
		1991	1981		
Large size communities 1,00,000 or more					
1	Chamar, Bhambhi, Bambhi, Bhambhi, Jatia, Jatav, Jatava, Mochi, Raidas, Rohidas, Regar, Raigar, Ramdasia	2,18,19,35	18,72,133	3,09,802	16.55
2	Megh, Meghval, Meghwal, Menghvar	13,83,583	8,89,300	4,94,283	55.58
3	Bairwa, Berwa	6,21,111	4,29625	1,91,486	44.57
4	Balai	5,14,908	4,62,925	51,983	11.23
5	Thori, Nayak	4,71,411	3,47,613	1,23,798	35.61
6	Koli, Kori	3,38,504	2,65,767	72,737	27.37
7	Bhangi, Chura, Mehter, Olgana, Rukhi, Malkana	3,17,125	2,63,565	53,560	20.32
8	Khatik	2,71,380	2,15,089	56,291	26.17
9	Baori	2,42,607	1,80,054	62,553	34.74
10	Dhobi	1,28,789	1,04,252	24,537	23.54
11	Majhabi	1,03,441	80,344	23,097	28.75
Medium size communities 10,000 or more					
12	Sargara	89,192	77,169	12,023	15.58
13	Dholi	85,880	72,282	13,598	18.81
14	Dhanak, Dhanuk	84,504	82,234	2,270	2.76
15	Mehar	47,416	31,450	15,966	50.77
16	Kalbelia, Sapera	47,126	30,874	16,252	52.64
17	Gavaria	46,078	30,268	15,810	52.23
18	Sansi	45,032	31,997	13,035	40.74
19	Bawaria	41,903	31,903	10,000	31.35
20	Salvi	32,876	19,409	13,467	69.39
21	Garo, Garura, Gurda, Garoda	32,398	28,888	3,510	12.15
22	Nat, Nut	31,585	23,223	8,362	36.01
23	Bagri, Bagdi	30,646	25,326	5,320	21.01
24	Kanjar, Kunjar	29,264	21,001	8,263	39.35
25	Madari, Bazigar	22,162	11,191	10,971	98.03
26	Jingar	21,958	12,327	9,631	78.13

Contd...

Contd...

27	Rawal	20,459	12,649	7,810	61.74
28	Bhand	18,023	12,058	5,965	49.47
Small size communities less than 10,000					
29	Dhankia	9,355	6,477	2,878	44.43
30	Kamad, Kamadia	8,181	6,270	1,911	30.48
31	Badi	7,205	5,698	1,507	26.45
32	Bedia, Beria	6,926	2,361	4,565	193.35
33	Dantia, Satia	6,925	5,372	1,553	28.91
34	Khangar	6,170	4,320	1,850	42.82
35	Garancha, Gancha	6,152	5,168	984	19.04
36	Bansphor, Bansphod	5,671	3,929	1,742	44.34
37	Mahar, Taral, Dhegumegu	4,185	7,635	3,450	45.19
38	Dome, Dom	4,141	3,692	449	12.16
39	Bargi, Vargi, Birgi	3,751	3,725	26	0.70
40	Singiwala	3,457	1,786	1,671	93.56
41	Turi	3,328	2,041	1,287	63.06
42	Tirgar, Tirbanda	2,866	2,170	696	32.07
43	Aheri	2,830	2,736	94	3.44
44	Kapadia Sansi	2,518	1,768	750	42.42
45	Dabgar	2,270	1,166	1,104	94.68
46	Bola	2,201	5,945	-3,744	-62.98
47	Pasi	1,739	943	796	84.41
48	Bajgar	1,442	3,085	-1,643	-53.26
49	Mahyavanshi, Dhed, Dheda, Vankar, Maru, Vankar	1,394	1,868	-474	-25.37
50	Kooch Band, Kuchband	1,222	1,509	-287	-19.02
51	Chandal	1,174	1,105	69	6.24
52	Mang, Matang, Minimadig	1,087	241	846	351.04
53	Godhi	1,053	263	790	300.38
54	Adi Dharmi	1,000	780	220	28.21
55	Koria	991	2,794	1,803	-64.53
56	Gandia	869	159	710	446.54
57	Bidakia	718	245	473	193.06
58	Sarbhangi	654	613	41	6.69
59	Mang Garodi, Mang Garudi	610	177	433	244.63
All Scheduled Castes		76,07,820	58,38,879	17,68,941	30.30

Source: Directorate of Census, Rajasthan.

Table 2.2

The Bastis and Domicile of Raigars

S. No.	State/District	Name of Mohalla/Basti/Residential Place
1.	*Rajasthan*	
	Jaipur	Ghatgate, Chandpole, Hasanpura, Jhotwara, Sanganer, Amer, Keshupura, Bas Badanpura, Kho-nagoran, Ghati-Karolan, Jansi-Sanganeri-gate, Rakadi, Gajsinghpura, Mangiavas, Ravji-ka-bagh, Badanpura, Khor, Shastri Nagar, Murlipura, Nidar-Hadmara, Khora-bisal, Khatipura, Sirsi, Bindayaka, Dhawas, Khokhabas, Jagatpura, Kundanpura, Malviya Nagar, Jhalana Kacchi Basti, Baiji ki Kothi, Mansinghpura, Luniawas, Ambedkar Basti Adarsh Nagar, Ambedkar Nagar, Chitragupta Nagar, Tagore Nagar, Bhagwati Nagar, 2nd; Saini Colony 1, 2, and 3, Bal Nagar, Kalyan Nagar, Mahesh Nagar, Gujar ki Thadi, Govind Nagar, DCM, Dudu
	Ajmer	Digi Mohalla Ganj, Pattan Bazar, Pahar Ganj, Malusar, Kalyanpura, Parvatpura, Khanpura, Makhupura, Doraitaboji, Salampur, Boraj, Lohagarh, Raidaspura, Narwinpura, Topdha, Pratap Mohalla, Pratap Mohalla, Ganj-Mohalla, Shanti Nagar, Sukhadia Nagar, Phaisagar, SubashNagar, Malusar Road, Raigaro ka Chota Bas and Raigaro ka Bada Bas (both in Pushkar), Chandravardhai Nagar, Shiv Nagar
	Beawar	Badabas, Chhotabas, Jamalpura, Raidaspura, Marsinghpura, Nehru Nagar, Jatia Para, Om Nagar – Outside Nehru Gate, Indira Colony, Bakolia Colony, Saket Nagar, Housing Boad, Tanwar Colony
	Jodhpur	Bhadwashia, Nagori Gate, Maderna Colony, Parihar Nagar, Kirti Nagar, Ravidas Nagar, Ashok Nagar, Pipad City, Mathania,Tibri, Bhopalgarh, Balkha, Angwa, Satlana, Dhudhada
	Pali	Suraj Pole, Sarvodaya Nagar, Sojat City, Khod
	Barmer	Barmer City, Chauhatan, Dhorimana, Balotra, Samdadi
	Tonk	Tonk city, Niwai, Devli, Malpura,Toda Rai Singh city, Pachver
	Jaisalmer	Pokaran
	Sirohi	Abu Road, Pindwada, Sirohi City, Revdar
	Kota	Kota City
	Udaipur	Udaipur City
	Nagaur	Badli, Chenar, Railway Station Nagaur, Housing Board Nagaur, Merta City, Didwana, Kuchaman City, Nava City, Minda, Ladnun, Makrana, Degana, Gachipura, Parbatsar, Colony behind Agricultural Mandi
	Bikaner	Shiv Badi, Bhinasar,Udai Ramsar, Vyas Colony, Nokha

Contd...

Contd...

2.	*Delhi*	Raigarpura, Sat Nagar, Bapa Nagar, Rameshwari Nehru Nagar, Dev Nagar, Indra Puri, Rajori Garden, Tilak Nagar, Pankha Road, Lajpat Nagar, Madipura, Nangloi, Mangol Puri, Sultan Puri, Bidan Pura, Khichadi Pur, Pandav Nagar, Vikas Puri, Panchim Puri, Raghuveer Nagar, Uttam Nagar, PaschimVihar, M Block, Giragadhi, Rohini
3.	*Gujarat*	
	Ahmedabad	Kuber Nagar, Thakkarbapa Nagar, Ganganar, Vadaj, Girdhar Nagar, Jamalpur Darwaja, Pathro-ki-Chali, Gandhi Nagar, Narayan Pura,Chanakyapuri, Solagram, Sewage Farm
4.	*Maharashtra*	
	Bombay (now Mumbai)	Thakkarbapa Colony, Chembur, Dadar, Navi Mumbai
5.	*Madhya Pradesh*	Mandsor, Neemuch, Indore, Ujjain, Ratlam and Bhopal
6.	*Haryana*	Hansi, Dabwali Mandi, Siwani, Fatehbad, Hisar, Anandpura
7.	*Punjab*	Rama Mani, Abohar, Firozpur, Amritsar, Vareta
8.	*Uttar Pradesh*	
	Mathura	Raigar Mohalla Mathura, Vrandavan, Govardhan, Chhata, Chandanvan, Moti Kunj, Refinary Nagar, Naya Nagla, Shergarh
	Agra	Prakash Nagar, Jivni Mandi, Ghadhapada, Sultanpur, Agra Chhavni, Avas-Vikas Colony Bedla, Kamla Nagar, Janta Quarters, Balkeshwar Colony, Shahid Nagar
	Meerut	Meerut Chhavni
	Lucknow	Lucknow
	Ghaziabad	Ghaziabad, Noida
	Mah Mayanagar	Mah Mayanagar
	Aligarh	Aligarh
	Rae Bareli	Rae Bareli
	Kanpur	Kanpur

Sources: 1. Chandanmal Naval, *Raigar Jati-ka-Itihas*, Jodhpur, Shyam Printing Press, 1986, pp. 45-46.
2. Also gleaned from eminent Raigar Social Activists and Workers.

Besides these groups, there are Christians, Muslims, Sikhs and others who did not fit into any of the caste divisions of Hindus in Rajasthan.

According to social hierarchy, Brahmins were regarded as the highest caste and the Bhangis the lowest of the low. Under the princely states of Rajputana Rajasthan, the Brahmins were in ascendancy, as they controlled the society. Brahmins as a caste consolidated their position as religious preceptors under the Rajput laws. Moreover, individual Brahmins in their capacity as priests, administrators of the temples and religious preceptors also received grants of land from the state. Finally, Brahmins were also astrologers.

The Rajputs (Kshatriyas) were in ascendancy as they ruled the state. The Rajputs as a ruling caste consolidated their position as Jagirdars, Jamindars, landlords, etc., in the Rajput regions.

The trading communities were represented primarily by the Oswal, Aggarwal, Maheshwari, etc., largely castes belonging to the category of trading communities. They were socially and economically dominant and major moneylender caste in Rajputana and in that capacity wielded significant power at the state level. By and large these trading communities were independent business communities in the state and held significant economic power.

Ranking below twice-born castes were the tenant cultivators, artisans and other service castes. This category consisted of such specific castes as Jat, Ahir, Gujjar and Artisan castes – Luhar, Khati, Nai, Darjee and various other castes. All these castes were above the pollution line and were considered clean but low-caste Hindus. Low-caste Hindus neither owned any significant area of land nor had any political status. They were under the economic political status. They were under the economic and political control of landowning castes.

The untouchables were the third major social category in the traditional social structure while there were numerous untouchable castes, the Chamars were the most populous, followed by Bhambhis, Meghwals and Raigars. The untouchables were, by no means, a homogenous or unified group but were placed by divisions which displayed a hierarchy of their own.

The socio-economic distinction between the three tiers of the traditional social hierarchy, while by all means clear, were as rigid as they were in other parts of north India. Moreover, there were certain norms and rituals which served to separate them and to endow it with a distinct identity. Socio-cultural distinction had permeated the region.

Describing the miserable conditions of the untouchable communities/castes in the traditional Rajasthan, G.M. Sharma writes:

> Under this system, the position of lower castes and specially that of untouchables who had to do all necessary services for

> society and in return they were despised was most deplorable. They had to remain content with life which was not better than death.[15]

> He further says:

> This shows that they were looked down as quite outside of the pale of the society and one who touched them accidentally had to clean and wash himself.[16]

Such unjustifiable social tyranny was prevalent all over Rajputana and in all major regions during the 19th century. The caste rules observed from generation to generation were the supreme law of the land. The fact was that the highest and lowest were equally slaves of social order of hereditary customs which had been sanctioned by antiquity. Some of the most inviolated caste rules and relationship will be illustrated as we look into the socio-religious conditions of the Raigars. Until recently, they were one of the most backward communities in terms of the educational, religious, social and economic status.

The Raigars had produced their own 'Dharm-gurus' (religious preachers) and thus, no doubt, had an effect on the formation of the social and cultural consciousness among the community. Moreover, their place in the village community was as village servants and recognition of their role was vital to the functioning of the village which also provided a medium through which, community became conscious of itself and hence could organise itself for the socio-political rights.

Who are the Raigars?

The term 'Raigar' has been interpreted in a number of ways. Local traditions regarding the origin of the Raigars are recorded in the book of Naval published in 1986. As per the story prevalent, Maharaja Rewat founded a new town called Kush-Isthal. After Maharaj's death, there was a warrior king named 'Rewar'. His children and descendants came to be known as Rewar. Over a period of time, the term Rewar emerged as 'Raigar'. It shows that Raigars were originally Kshatriyas of Rajputana.[17]

An altogether different version of the term was given by Ramesh Chandra Gunarthi. According to him, it has been derived from the word Rang + gar. Because the powder prepared from Babool (Acacia), Aavala-ki-chhal (bark of emblica) along with Dhamas, Namak (salt) and Tejab (acid) is good chemical for dyeing the things, it is called Rang and also used in dyeing the skins of cattle. Thus, persons engaged in dyeing work, were called Rangar and over a period of time, came to be known as Raigar.[18] They are ranked as untouchable and ranked at the bottom of the system. In Rajputana, Raigar refuse to touch the hide of a deer and dye its skin and according to local customs if persons were to dye the skin of deer, he would lose his caste.[19]

Others like Munshi Hardayal Singh, Bajrang Lal Lohia and K.S. Singh have tried to trace the origin of the term 'Raigar' from their traditional business of dyeing the skins of cattles. Hardayal Singh says that Raigar means: those associated with filthy work, namely, dyeing the skins of cattles.[20] According to Lohia, dyeing of skins of cattle, had traditionally been the task of untouchables and those who performed this kind of work are known as Raigar".[21] K.S. Singh says, literally, the word 'Raigar' means dyeing. In fact, they dye leather.[22] N.L. Pingolia says that Raigars are also known as Rehgar, Reghad and Rayagar.[23]

Another title for Raigar is Jatia. Some say that the Jatias were originally camel drivers as their name Jat indicates. Others connect them with the Jat caste and claim that they are the offspring of mixed union of Jat and Chamar.[24]

The castes coming under this category are to be found in different parts of India and are known as Bagri in Punjab, Raigar in Delhi, Mumbai and Ahmedabad, the Jatia and Raigar in Rajasthan. There are also several sub-regional names, such as Bola (in Mewar and Harauti regions), the Jatia and Raigar (in Marwar and western regions), Rangia in Bikaner region, Sindhi Raigar (those settled down in Sind province, Pakistan) Sindhi Jatia (who migrated from Sindh, Pakistan) in Jodhpur, Ajmer and Beawar and Laskaria Raigars in Bharatpur and Deeg in Rajasthan; Laskaria Raigar in Gwalior (Madhya Pradesh) and in Agra and Mathura (Uttar Pradesh). Throughout this book, we shall use only name 'Raigar' to represent an ethnic category including the cognate castes of Rajasthan and since they are most commonly known in Rajasthan and elsewhere as 'Raigar'.

The origin of Raigars is shrouded in mystery and is controversial.[25]

Local traditions regarding the origin of Raigars are recorded in the 1891 Census of Marwar. Accordingly, Raigars are a branch of the Chamar. Raidas was a venerable saint of Chamar caste. He had two wives and had children. Children from her first wife came to be known as Chamars. It is said that Raidas was a devotee of Mata Ganga. In the course of Bhakti, he acquired spiritual power and was considered to be an accomplished person (siddha), capable of performing miracles and fulfilling the wishes of his followers. Thus, Raidas emerged as a charismatic saint. It is believed that Raigars are the offsprings of Siddha Raidas.[26] Bajrang Lal Lohia also took a similar view, i.e., that Raigars are descendants of Saint Raidas.[27]

But against this point of view that the Raigars are descendants of Saint Raidas, it is believed that they were descendants of Kshatriyas. In 1941, after careful examination of the religious scripture and historical evidences, the State Hindu Mahasabha, Ajmer, issued a statement called 'Appeal' to caste Hindus which was published in weekly paper 'Aawaj' on July 28, 1941. Hindu Mahasabha believes that the Raigars were the original Kshatriyas. The appeal is as follows:

> *Yeh pramanit kiya jata hai ki sastro, itihas aur prachin granthoo key anusheelan sey yah sidh hota hai ki yeh raigar jati 'gar' kshastriyo sey utpanna hui hai. Aatah sab hindu arya nar nariyoo sey nivedan kiya jata hai ki vey inkey sath kshastriyo key saman puran vyavhar karey.*[28]

Hindu Mahasabha believes that there are references which show that Raigar's origin is from Kshatriyas and therefore, they were not the descendants of Saint Raidas. Similarly, Gunarthi produces historical evidence to show that Raigars were the original Rangar Rajputs of Bhatinda. According to him Firoz Shah Tuglak attacked Bhatinda in Samvat 1408 and fought a victorious battle against the Rangar Rajputs. He captured thousands of them to accept Islam. During this period Rangar Rajputs were also pressurised to dye the cow's skins. This indicates that Rangar Rajputs and other Hindus who did the work of dyeing the cow's skin were called Raigar and this marked the beginning of Raigar caste.[29] It is also believed that term 'Raigar' comes from Rangna which means dyeing[30] and therefore, the Raigars belonged to Rangar Rajputs (also Raghad Rajput). The same version of the name is given in Jiwan Ram Gunshaiwal's, *Prachin Raigar Itihas*.[31]

An altogether different connotation of the term has been put forward in Jaspat Rao Girdhar's *Rayagar Itihas-ki-Khoj Tatha Jatpat Sambandhi Vichar*. According to him, in the history, we do not find the term Raigar. Different scholars have interpreted it in different ways which has created a lot of confusion. There is not a single scholar who has proved the origin of caste on historical evidences. Some scholars, as stated earlier, are of the opinion that they are descendants of Saint Raidas while some say that they are descendants of Maharaja Sagar Shogar. All these interpretations are baseless. According to him, if the term 'Re' is replaced by Raiya, meaning advise, and that those who advise someone means Raiyagar[32] (adviser). Thus, the term Raiya (advise) according to Jaspat Rao Girdhar, was used for the highly placed persons in the society, such as 'Raiya Bahadur', 'Raiya Saheb', etc., therefore Raigars are 'Raiyagar'.[33]

The Raigars generally followed traditional occupation and were responsible for disposal of the dead animals. Mathur mentioned that their traditional occupation was skinning the dead animals and tanning and curing of the hides and skins.[34] Besides this, they were agricultural labourers and manufacturers of shoes and sandles. They also repaired old shoes. They had a few titles granted to them, such as 'Kanwar'.[35]

Raigars ranked parallel to Chamars in caste hierarchy.[36] Since the Chamars are recognised as 'untouchable' the Raigar accordingly belonged to the low untouchable castes, i.e., outside the 'verna' system. There are however, other much lower castes such as Bhangis and Churas compared with whom, the Raigars boast of having a higher social status. In fact, they are included in the scheduled castes.

It was the rule of purity and pollution that chiefly governed caste hierarchy. There was not only touch pollution but also distance pollution. A certain number of low castes were regarded as being permanently impure and therefore permanently capable of causing pollution by touch. Any caste Hindu who came in direct contact with such an untouchable himself became impure and demanded ceremonial purity, i.e., he must bathe himself and wash his clothes. Thus we know that eleven castes will not touch a Bhangi; seventeen will not touch a Chamar; ten will not touch a Dhakar; sixteen will not touch a Dhobi or a Dom.[37] Pollution was a peculiar and notorious custom prevailing in Rajputana. Distance pollution to which it is usually referred means not only by touch but by approaching within a specific distance.

Traditionally, all the castes included in the category of Raigars enjoy equal status and do not have a hierarchy of sub-castes. The Raigars in Rajasthan, Delhi and Madhya Pradesh occupied an equal rank and have conventional and matrimonial relations. The Raigars followed patriarchal system of inheritance.

The clans of Raigars were divided into several parts/groups. Thus, according to Lohia, the Raigars of Rajputana were divided into 68 clans. They are:[38]

1	Kansotia	2	Singaria	3	Mandavaria
4	Motaria	5	Jetaliya	6	Umbaria
7	Bachwadia	8	Kankharia	9	Chukriya
10	Muriya	11	Gidia	12	Aduliya
13	Bora	14	Uojiniya	15	Khutvaria
16	Gadegavalia	17	Kuroliya	18	Makriwal
19	Gusaiwal	20	Jajiriya	21	Bhopriya
22	Kurriya	23	Bukariya	24	Sundariwal
25	Movanpuriya	26	Mudooliya	27	Umrikha
28	Koovariya	29	Masiwal	30	Palavriya
31	Gagrodia	32	Janwaley	33	Khoolwal
34	Dewatwal	35	Sunwasa	36	Mandriya
37	Nogiya	38	Chomiya	39	Sakriya
40	Jaroliya	41	Garoliya	42	Jatta
43	Hingunia	44	Kharetia	45	Rigolia
46	Mosiwal	47	Mishalpuria	48	Savlaniya
49	Alooriya	50	Mishalpuria	51	Kariwal
52	Dooniya	53	Jabardia	54	Khuliya
55	Paliya	56	Balootiya	57	Jagarwal
58	Khemkariya	59	Dileep	60	Widhabhadia
61	Mooriya	62	Varia	63	Khadwalia
64	Baleytia	65	Tagiya	66	Basiwal
67	Bakuliya	68	Bajirpuria		

The Raigars of western Rajasthan were divided into 75 clan groups.[39] In Rajasthan there were several clan groups among Raigars. The total number of clans, according to Naval, are more than 400. Altogether different number of clan groups were given by Ramesh Chandra Gunarthi. According to him, the Raigars of Rajasthan were divided into 198 clan groups.[40] Members of each group having similar patronymics are believed to have a common ancestry. They belong to the same family. Therefore, intra-clan marriages are forbidden.

The Raigars of Rajasthan asserted their claims of being a Kshatriya's origin. The change in their social and ritual hierarchy of Hindus first began when they were conquered by the invaders. Having been defeated and overcome by the invaders, they were incorporated permanently with a low social position and in the course of time, they came to be known as an untouchable castes. As such, the Raigars case, is by no means, unique but is a typical process of degradation or to use Shyam Lal's concept. 'Asprashyeekaran'[41] by which the defeated castes were absorbed into untouchable castes.

Raigars had no military traditions but occasionally a few Raigars were selected as soldiers and they showed fighting prowess during the internal and external aggressions. According to Naval, no scholars or historians had focused on it. However, through the efforts of Bhat (gencologist of Raigar community) Naval succeed in digging out the mythological and historical brave Raigar soldiers. As this is a very significant aspect, it is worth describing in some details. He (1986) spoke of the Raigars as excellent soldiers as brave, industrious and orderly as Sikhs and Rajputs were.

According to Naval, in Samvat 603, Raigar soldier Raju Malpuria (Malpura) fought bravely in the war which took place between Nawabs of Tonk and Maharaja of Jaisalmer.[42] He was killed in Samvat 732. Beejmer Mania (Peeplod) was killed during the Maratha aggression.[43] During various fights and invasions Raigar soldiers exhibited their bravery. In Samvat 1153, Gujal Sanwasia (Delhi) fought bravely in the war fought between King Prithvi Raj Chauhan and Mughals and was killed.[44] In his memory a monument was erected in the old fort of Delhi.

Vena Kurdia (Nagaur) under the leadership of Amar Singh Rathore fought in the war.[45] In Samvat 1561, Kheta Kurdia (Peepard) also under the leadership of Darbar Summer Singh fought bravely.[46] Likewise, during the fight between Rathore Rajputs and Dodi Rajputs Manak Badaria (Kheda Kisangarh) fought.[47] All the three were killed. During the Mughal invasion in Samvat 1303, and in Samvat 1613, Kalu Bansiwal (Bassi) and Hema Bansiwal (Bassi Sarward) were killed respectively. Shiv Shankar Mandarial (Chittorgarh) was killed in the war fought between the Rajputs and Mughals.[48]

As has already been mentioned earlier that untouchables including the Raigars were not recruited in the armed forces. However, it was noticed that during the Mughal and British period, they were recruited in the Mughals and British Indian Army. According to Kanwar Surya Mal Maurya of Beawar, in 1489, the Emperor Aadil Shal appointed Chandra Rao Maurya as the Senapati (commander) of his forces at Jawali place.[49]

During the British Raj, after 1900, the Ajmer Meharwara Infantry Company headed by General Diksan began recruiting the soldiers to British Indian Army. Then the untouchable Raigars were consistently being forced to work at the construction site of Beawar fort. To avoid himself from doing the forced labour as free, i.e., *Begar*, Panna Maurya son of Nagji Maurya of Beawar left the house and went to Ajmer in search of employment.[50] Here, he came to know about the recruitment in army. The army officers found Panna Maurya suitable for the profession of arms and soon thereafter, was promoted to the rank of Hawaldar.[51] During the Kabul War in 1920, the Indian soldiers including Panna exhibited exemplary bravery – published as news item in Raigar Sudhar published from Phatehabad, Haryana (Year 1, Issue 1, February 2000). One Hawaldar Panna Maurya (Raigar) fought bravely in the Kabul War and on May 7, 1921, the then Viceroy recommended Panna, 1373 of 44 Ajmer-Marwar Infantry Campaign No. 1 for award of Jangi (warrior) Medal and also sanctioned pension to him for three generations.[52]

The martial element has added a new dimension to the Raigar ideology in the sense that Raigar provide a fighting force, which is the characteristic of Kshatriyas.

As has been stated above, the Raigars had no military tradition. Similarly Raigars too had no Sati tradition contrary to the prevalent system in the then ruling caste, the Rajputs whose impact on Raigar women followed Sati tradition throughout the State of Rajputana. It was because a few Raigar soldiers exhibited their bravery during the various wars and invasions. They also fought bravely during the period of Rana Kumbha, Rana Sangha, Rana Ratan Singh and Gogdev Chauhan against the Mughals. Naval spoke of Raigar women as esteemed Sati as Rajput Sati. As per available inscriptions and other evidences, according to Naval there still exist evidences of Sati tradition at places like Soyal, Run, Phulia, Ren, Bilada, Kaluda and Khord.[53] A monument called 'Seven Sati Memorial' in the memory of upper caste Sati women, had been erected in Bilara and out of these seven, one Sati was from Raigar caste.[54] In Samvat 1760 Shrimati Dharmi wife of Udai Jatolia (grandson of Manak Jatolia) became Sati. Naval narrated in detail the events from Samvat 513 to 1760 to illustrate how brave and sacrificing were the Raigar women and added that the Raigar Satis had earned a name for themselves also. He pointed out all names along with other particulars of the Raigar Satis. As regards total number of Satis, he showed as many as 39 in all.[55] He said Raigar society is proud of the Satis. The Raigars occasionally arrange fairs (Mela) where men, women and children meet at Satis Samadhi or place and where they pray to fulfil their wishes.

In order to understand the contribution made by a few wealthy Raigars during the droughts and famines to the humanity, it is necessary to describe their achievement in brief. In Samvat 1925 Vena Kanwaria a resident of Narwar, Kishangarh distributed food-grains, cloths and money during the drought period to poor and needy persons irrespective of caste, creed and religion. Due to his dedication he was able to save the lives of downtrodden to some extent.[56] Similarly in Samvat 1956 another wealthy man, Hema Ugirpuria of Govindgarh also took the initiative and distributed food-grains and cloths during the famous drought called 'Famine of Fifty-six' to poor and needy persons.[57]

Apart from Vena Kanwaria and Hema Ugirpuria, there were Shanwata and Gangaram Kurdia – the great brave men of Jalia village and Peepad City respectively. Coming from poor Raigar families, they showed their mighty power in killing the lions.[58] These are the sporadic examples of Raigar community.

By improving their social-economic conditions the Raigars, like other untouchable castes or communities had followed the path of sanskritisation by various methods. Sanskritisation is a process of adopting customs and rituals of upper castes particularly to Brahminical ceremonies. The Raigars now don the sacred thread. Moreover, Raigars patronymics are adopted and Bhatt, Chauhan, Sukhadia, Rathi, the clan name endings of Brahmins, Rajputs, Aggarwals and Maheshwaries have been added to their names. For example Balotia has changed into Bhatt and gradually called Bhatt.[59] Another clan such as Swansia, Khatnawaliya and Randia have changed into Chauhan, Sukhadia, Khanda (also Khanna, Khandekar, Naval) and Rathi.[60] The first clan name appears to be that of a Rajput, the second looks like Aggarwal – a trading community while the last symbolises the clan name of Maheshwari – again a business community.

Nature of Disabilities

As has been noted earlier, the Raigars were untouchables and as such they were obliged to perform those tasks which were considered polluting the Hinduism.

The integration of the Raigars into the traditional Rajputana society meant, therefore, that they were obliged to perform those tasks which were deemed polluting and unclean by the Hindus. As an untouchable, Raigar existed in the realm of the impure and this required their performing the most unpleasant tasks of the village. Their position also demanded that contact between them and the caste Hindus were strictly controlled and regulated by the norms of caste Hindu society. The position of the untouchables contained within it a curious circularity. They were impure by birth and therefore, were constrained to perform the most impure social duties. Yet the very act of performing these duties confirmed their untouchability and sealed the distance between them and the upper caste Hindus. One of the important issues of Raigar Reform Movement, consequently had been to reject the traditional tasks of Raigars especially pertaining to the handling and disposal of dead animals. This rejection had also figured prominently as a symbol and a theme in the reform movement. Therefore, the refusal by Raigars to perform their ancient duties in the villages of Rajputana had significant socio-political repercussion. It had even occasioned violent conflicts between Raigars and high caste Hindus, particularly the Brahmins, Jagirdars, Jamindars who predominated in the village community.

Yet as long as the Raigars performed their traditional duties without reservation or complaint and as long as they accepted the stigma of their birth and behaved accordingly, the social order of traditional Rajputana guaranteed their continued existence, if not their prosperity. During the princely states an individual Raigar was not permitted to follow other occupations, through which he could improve his position. Indeed the relationship between caste and occupation was rigid.

The state power maintained the socio-economic position of the untouchables and ensured that they did not deviate from their prescribed duties. Naval cites several cases from different areas which reveal the extent to which the upper castes supported the prevailing division of labour. Thus, in several cases, the Raigars who had started non-traditional work were given punishment. The social and ritual order of caste, therefore, had socio-religious content and the caste system acquired under the Rajput regime was directly related to the kind of decisions made by the socio-religious authorities.

Contact between Raigars and the caste Hindus took place within well specified and circumscribed limits. Like other untouchables Raigars could not live within the village proper or even too close to village. They had to maintain discreet distance from the caste Hindus. Therefore, they had to reside either in some blocks (mohallas) on outer skirts of the village or in their own hamlets away from village. Thus it can be said that 'residential pattern in a village' have been an indication of caste discrimination.[61] This discrimination may also have been true in the case of other untouchable castes in Rajputana.

This will be evident from the two following statements on the condition of untouchables which appeared in the *Hindustan Times*. The first appeared in the issue of March 8, 1945, written by one Kesari Lal Bordia, Headmaster of a School called 'Vidya Bhawan' in Udaipur. It reads as follows:[62]

> Many are the disabilities under which the Harijans in Mewar live. They cannot enter in temples, nor can they draw water from the public wells. They cannot join the caste Hindus in festivals and processions. They have to take out their Rath Yatra or Doll procession through a different route and on a different day. And they cannot ride through the village.
>
> Even silver ornaments, let alone gold ones on their person are resented by the Caste Hindus. The result is, they have to content themselves with tin and brass articles. Age-old usage prevents them from using butter or gur in wedding feasts.
>
> In schools and other public places, Harijan boys cannot sit with the children of caste Hindus. They are asked to absent themselves on the inspection day in order to save the inspector from embarrassment.
>
> A memorandum has been submitted to the State Government. If the Government chooses to declare in unequivocal terms and the disapproval of these disabilities, the hands of non-official bodies which are fighting untouchability will be strengthened.

The second was in the form of a statement issued by the President of the Harijan Sevak Sangh and refers to the condition of the untouchables in the State of Mewar. It reads as under:

The Mewar Harijan Sevak Sangh has sent a Memorandum to the Mewar government drawing their attention to the various disabilities of the Harijans in the State and their consequent hardship. The memorandum brings out how civil liberties of Harijans are curtailed in several ways by the orthodoxy and prejudices of caste Hindus.

I enumerate below some of the unjust practices which still persist in the State and for the rectification of which the State has taken no effective measures. They are as follows:

1. Harijans have no liberty in the selection of clothes to wear. The form of dress must follow the age-long pattern; personal tastes and desires have no place in the choice of the dress.
2. At wedding feasts they have no choice in the selection of food materials. Even on payment they cannot use costly articles.
3. They cannot ride on a horse in the village.
4. They are not allowed accommodation in public vehicles.
5. On religious festivals they cannot take out procession of their idols except through the specified routes.
6. They have no access to wells and temples.

The writer adds:

Three years ago in company with Thakur Bapa, I travelled all over the State and placed before the Government and public my impression of the conditions prevailing there and pleaded for reform. On perusal of the above mentioned memorandum and other reports sent to me, I find that the past few years have hardly brought any change and conditions are more or less static.

It is heart breaking to find that passage of time cuts no ice with us. The result is that there is hardly any change in our age-long practices and prejudices. This perversity which blinds us to the tyranny and injustices of our ways also makes us impervious to the incalculable harm we have already suffered as a result of it. Even if the ignorant prejudice of the common-man is unshaken the enlightened governments of the Twentieth Century ought to be more alive to their responsibilities.

The dates of these communications are important. They are of the year 1945. None can say that this Hindu established order is a thing of the ancient past. The fact that these latest accounts refer to the Indian states should not be understood to mean that the established order has vanished from free India.

They could not use the village well nor could their children be educated in the village schools. Education in those days was in the hands of the upper castes, particularly Brahmins, who taught to higher caste children and the untouchables were forbidden to study there. In pre-independence period, therefore, the Raigar community like other untouchable communities were overwhelmingly illiterate. To acquire an education, in order to inhance ability to think critically about themselves and about society in which they lived, was restricted.

The untouchables could not take water from the Hindu well at all. They could not build a *pucca* brick well for themselves even though they might have the money to do so. For having a *pucca* well for themselves means an attempt to raise themselves to the status of the Hindus which was contrary to the established social order. Not only this, according to social rules, the untouchables must not remain seated on a cot in the presence of a upper caste Hindu. Untouchables standing in front of them was beneath the dignity of caste Hindus. It must be observed by the untouchables. If untouchables defied these rules, they were seriously tortured by caste Hindus.

In the traditional Rajputana society other forms of social contacts were also denied to the untouchables. In some cases free use of village streets was forbidden. If lower caste people saw someone from upper castes coming along the same street or road from the opposite direction they were supposed to step aside for them. Penalties for transgressing caste norms were severe and were used with devastating effect against transgressors. As a corollary to the pollution customs, the lower castes were not allowed to enter the temples frequented by the caste Hindus. They were also forbidden to wear good clothes, their women were not allowed to wear any gold or silver ornaments, they were not allowed to construct pucca houses like Hindu castes. They were allowed to build only *kacha* houses and required to call the houses in which they lived as 'huts' whereas Brahmins called their houses, as 'house' and Rajputs as 'rawla'.

The untouchables must not wear decent and clean clothes and they must not wear gold or silver ornaments. If the untouchables defied these rules, the Hindus would not hesitate to bring them to book. The untouchables have been trying to defy these rules. What consequences will be seen from the following incidents which have been reported in the newspapers:[63]

> Until 1922, the untouchable caste of Dalai in Berar district of Bundi, were forbidden to eat wheat. In February 1922, a Chamar woman was put on the Rock in Sakatgarh, Jaipur, simply because she was wearing silver ornaments on her feet. The reason given was that only men of the high castes were allowed to wear silver or to eat wheat. The low caste people should not dare to aspire to these things.

The Times of India, in its issue of January 4, 1928, reports the tyranny and oppression practised upon the Balais who form an untouchable community in Central India for their daring to wear clean clothes and golden ornaments. Observes The Times of India:

> In May (1927) high caste Hindus viz. Kalotas Rajputs and Brahmins including the Patils and Patwaris of villages Kanaria, Bicholee Hafsi, Bicholi Mardana and of about 15 other villages in the Indore district informed the Balais of their respective villages that if they wished to live among them, they must conform to the following rules:
>
> 1. Balais must not wear gold lace bordered pugrees;
> 2. They must not wear dhotis with coloured or fancy borders;
> 3. They must convey intimation of the death of any Hindu to relatives of the deceased – no matter how far away these relatives may be living;
> 4. In all Hindu marriages, the Balais must play music before the processions and during the marriages;
> 5. The Balai women must not wear fancy gowns or jackets;
> 6. Balai women must attend all cases of confinement of Hindu women;
> 7. The Balais must render services without demanding remuneration and must accept whatever a Hindu is pleased to give; and

8. If the Balais do not agree to abide by these terms, they must get out of the villages.

> The Balais refused to comply; and the Hindus proceeded against them. Balais were not allowed to get water from the village wells; they were not allowed to let their cattle graze. Balais were prohibited from passing through land owned by a Hindu; so that if the field of a Balai was surrounded by fields owned by the Hindus, the Balai could have no access to his own field. The Hindus also let their cattle graze down the fields of the Balais.
>
> The Balais submitted petitions to the Darbar of Indore against these persecutions, but as they could get no timely relief and the oppression continued, hundreds of Balais with their wives and children, were obliged to abandon their homes in which their ancestors lived for generations, and to migrate to adjoining states, viz. to villages in Dhar, Dewas, Bagli, Bhopal, Gwalior and other states.

The untouchables must not eat rich food even if they can afford it. It is an offence for the untouchables to live above their status in life.

The Pratap, in its issue of February 26, 1928, relates the following occurrence:

> In the State of Jodhpur at a place Chandayal, you will still see men who do not think that the Harijans have even the right to eat Halwa. One of the untouchable castes is that of Sargaroes. Sometime back on the occasion of the marriage ceremony of two or three girls, Halwa was prepared for the members of the marriage party. For this purpose, Maida (white flour) was also brought from the Thakur Sahib. At meal time, the marriage party came for meals but just at that time the Kanwar Sahib of Chandawal sent orders to the Sargaroes that they could not eat Halwa. Some cringing sycophants negotiated a compromise in this way that the Kanwar Sahib be presented with Rs 200.00 and then permission will be given to eat Halwa. At this the Sargaroes got infuriated and refused to pay the money.

To lead a marriage procession through the main streets of the village is the right of every caste Hindu. It is also in evidence that the community which enjoys this right is accepted as a respectable community. The untouchables have no such right.

One of the major benefits received by the landlords, jamindars, jagirdars and upper caste Hindus from the untouchables including Raigars was the access to forced labour (begar) and services. They could be summoned for sowing or harvesting the lands of these castes, and could also be required to tend public land for which they were not paid.

The Hindus treated the untouchables as having been born to serve the Hindu castes. It being his duty to serve, the untouchables could not refuse to serve the Hindus whenever the latter called upon to do so. The Hindus of village held the belief that they could command the labour of untouchables. The system was known as 'begar' or forced labour. The untouchables of rural areas were seriously tortured by the upper caste Hindus for refusing Begar.

Within the existing socio-religious framework, therefore, the untouchables had very few means through which they could alter their position. As we have seen challenges to the existing social order by the untouchables were not tolerated. Defiance of caste norms resulted in massive punishment in the form of the Bahiskar. Mobility within caste system, in Srinivas' phrase 'sanskritisation' was also not available to the untouchables, they were too low and impure for that to be feasible. Moreover, the material prerequisites for sanskritisation, the generation of an economic and political base was also beyond their reach. The untouchables did not possess the economic resources which could be translated into power and thus could not make a convincing case for raising the social status.

The only resource open to Raigars on the socio-religious plank was to become followers of Kabir sect, which had as a central tenet the abolition of caste. With the establishment of the Arya Samaj in Rajasthan in twentieth century some sections of the Raigars community had also become the followers of Arya Samaj.

With the advent of the British Raj the traditional order was disrupted fundamentally, with the establishment of Arya Samaj in India in 1875 and the initiative of political movement offered new modes of socio-political activities and finally to provoke an intellectual ferment within Indian society which questioned the very principles of Hinduism and the social structure which embodied them.

Notes and References

1. Puranmal, *Ashprashyata Avam Dalit Chetna,* Jaipur, Pointer Publishers, 1999, p. 40.
2. Ibid., p. 40.
3. Census Directorate of Rajasthan, Jaipur, Distribution of Scheduled Caste Population by Sex Population 1991, Sheet 1, Serial No. 17, p. 3.
4. Ibid., p. 2, 3 and 6. Also see, p. 6,1, 1, 7.
5. Puranmal, op. cit., p. 40.
6. Ibid.
7. Ibid.
8. Ibid.
9. Census Directorate of Rajasthan, Jaipur (tentative figures).
10. U.B. Mathur, *Ethnographic Atlas of Rajasthan* (with reference to Scheduled Castes and Scheduled Tribes), 1969, p. 4.
11. R.B. Chari, Census of India, 1971, Serial 1. Paper 1 of 1975, Scheduled Castes and Scheduled Tribes, 1975. Castes at serial nos. 23 and 24 at page 78 respectively have been clubbed.
12. Census of India, 1991. Castewise Break-up: 1981 and 1991 (population size arranged in descending order). Census Directorate of Rajasthan, Jaipur.
13. Distribution of Scheduled Castes Population by Sex Population, 1991. Sheet 1, Ibid., Caste at Serial No. 17.
14. Census Directorate of Rajasthan, Jaipur (tentative figures).
15. G.M. Sharma, *Social Life in Medieval Rajasthan (1500-1800 AD),* Agra, Lakshmi Narayan Agarwal, 1968, p. 107.
16. Ibid., p. 99.
17. Chandanmal Naval, *Raigar Jati-ka-Itihas,* Jodhpur, Shyam Printing Press, 1986, p. 20.
18. Ibid., p.20.
19. Munshi Hardayal Singh, Marwar Census Report, 1891, Jodhpur, Government Press 1896 (Reprinted in 1997), p. 541.
20. Ibid.
21. Bajrang Lal Lohia, *Rajasthan-ki-Jatia,* Calcutta, Vishal Bharat Book Depot, 1954, p. 214.
22. K.S. Singh (ed.), *People of India, Rajasthan*, Part Two, Mumbai, Popular Prakashan, 1998, p. 19.

23. Raigar writers have given many analysis of origin of Raigar caste, see particularly, Jiwan Ram Gunshaiwal, *Pracheen Raigar Itihas,* Delhi, *Gunsai Sahitya Ismarak Nidhi,* 1973, pp. 14-17; Jaspal Rai Girdhar, Raigar *Itihas-ki-Khoj Tatha Jat-pat Samandhi Vichar,* New Delhi, Karol Bagh, 1980, pp. 1-5; Bhagat Bhagirath, *Jati Bijak Mool Prakash: Raigar Samaj,* Nasirabad (Ajmer), Jain Printers, year not mentioned, p. 8; Chandanmal Naval, *Raigar Jati-ka-Itihas,* Jodhpur, Shyam Printing Press, 1986; Roop Chand Jalutharia, *Raigar Jati-ka-Itihas,* Jaipur, Capital Printers, 2001, pp. 7-16.
24. Fuchs, Stephen, *At the Bottom of Indian Society: The Harijan and other Low Castes,* New Delhi. Munshiram Manoharlal Publishers, 1981, p. 203. See also Bajrang Lal Lohia, op. cit., p. 214. Munshi Hardayal Singh, Marwar Census Report 1891, Reprinted in 1997, pp. 541-42.
25. It is also suggested that they are the occupational offshoot of the Yadu tribe from which Krishna came. Although the Jatiyas of the Punjab work in camel and horse hides, Gaur Brahmins condescend to officiate in their religious ceremonies. For this reason alone they may be considered as the highest sub-caste of the Chamars. For more details, see particularly Stephen Fuchs, Ibid., p. 203.
26. Munshi Hardayal Singh, Marwar Census Report 1891, Jodhpur, Government Press (reprinted in 1997), p. 541.
27. Bajrang Lal Lohia, *Rajasthan ki Jatia.* Ibid., p.214.
28. Chandanmal Naval, op. cit., p. 24. See also Jiwan Ram Gunsaiwal, *Pracheen Raigar Jati-ka-Itihas,* op. cit., p. 20.
29. Ramesh Chandra Gunarthi, *Rajasthani Jatio-ki-Khoj,* Ajmer, Vedic Yantralaya, 1950, pp. 269-271.
30. Jiwan Ram Gunshaiwal, *Pracheen Raigar Jati-ka-Itihas,* op. cit., pp. 14-17.
31. Chandanmal Naval, op. cit., p. 20.
32. Jaspat Rai Girdhar, *Raigar Itihas-ki-Khoj Tatha Jatpat Sambandhi Vichar,* New Delhi, 1980, pp. 4-5.
33. Ibid., p. 5.
34. U.B. Mathur, *Ethnographic Atlas of Rajasthan* (with reference to SCs and STs), 1969, op. cit., p. 12.
35. Chandanmal Naval, op. cit., p. 105.
36. Bajrang Lal Lohia, op. cit., p. 214.
37. E.A.H. Blunt, *The Caste System of Northern India,* New Delhi, S. Chand & Co., First Indian Reprint, 1969, p. 102.
38. Bajrang Lal Lohia, op. cit., pp.214-215.

39. Munsi Hardayal Singh. Marwar Census Report 1891 (Reprinted 1997), pp. 542-43.
40. Ramesh Chandra Gunarthi, *Rajasthani Jatio-ki-Khoj*, Ajmer, Vedic Yantralaya, 1950, pp. 271-272; *See also* Chandanmal Naval. Ibid., p. 35.
41. Shyam Lal, *From Higher Caste to Lower Caste: The Process of Asprashyeekaran and Myth of Sanskritisation*, Jaipur, Rawat Publications, 1997.
42. Chandanmal Naval, op. cit., p. 65.
43. Ibid.
44. Ibid., p. 64.
45. Ibid.
46. Ibid.
47. Ibid.
48. Ibid., p. 65.
49. For more details, see in particular, pamphlet *Raigad Jati ka Mahatava*, written by Kanwar Surya Mal Maurya (Beawar), in 1941 and was published and circulated amongst Raigars by Budha Ram Mantri, Sindh Hyderabad (now in Pakistan), Prabhat Printing Press.
50. *Hame garv hai Raigad Sudhar*, Fatehabad, Haryana, February 15-19, 2002, p. 2.
51. Ibid.
52. Ibid.
53. Chandanmal Naval, *Raigar-Jati-ka-Itihas*, 1986, op. cit., 61.
54. Ibid., p. 61
55. Ibid., pp.62-63.
56. Ibid., p. 69
57. Ibid.
58. Ibid., p. 70.
59. Ibid., p. 43.
60. Ibid., pp. 43-44.
61. Masanori Sato, "The Chamars of South-eastern Rajasthan AD 1650-1800" in H. Kotani (ed.), *Caste System, Untouchability and Depressed*, New Delhi, Manohar Publishers, 1999, p. 32.
62. For most important sources for atrocities on the untouchables and the situation of low castes in Rajputana and neighbouring states is "Untouchability and Lawlessness" in *Dr Baba Saheb Ambedkar: Writings and Speeches*, Volume 5, Mumbai, Government of Maharashtra, 1989, pp. 48-59. Other useful studies on tyrannies and

oppressions practised by the caste Hindus against untouchables especially in Rajasthan are those of Girdhar Behari Sharma, "Law as an Instrument for Abolition of Untouchability: Case of Rajasthan" in *EPW*, Vol. X, No. 15, April 12, 1975, p. 635 and Sapna Bhatia, "Untouchability and Atrocities: A Case Study of Rural Rajasthan", M.Phil dissertation, submitted in the Department of Sociology, University of Rajasthan, 1999-2000 (unpublished).

63. *Dr Baba Saheb Ambedkar: Writings and Speeches*, Volume 5, 1989, p. 48, 49 and also 52.

3

Emergence of Raigar Movement (1878-1955)

Rajputana

The decade of 1940s saw the emergence of untouchable movement as a conscious organised force in the social and political life of untouchable castes/communities in general and the Bairwas, Raigars and Chamars, in particular. Though much ground for the advancement of the untouchables has been laid earlier in terms of education and social activities, the 1940s saw a qualitative leap forward.

At the national level the campaign against untouchability was marked by the promise made by Mahatama Gandhi to the untouchables as set out in Gandhi-Ambedkar Poona Pact in the year 1932. It was the period of advancing mass struggle and ideological upheavals in India when the untouchables began their major era of the organisation under the leadership of Dr Ambedkar. The untouchables' struggle arose against the upper caste Hindus due to oppression and atrocities perpetuated by them and local organisations or campaign against the untouchability were founded in many areas, though it was not until the late 1940s that an all India untouchable organisation was established. The Congress' new mass base was associated with the dominance of Gandhi and his call for social reform all linked with assertion of untouchable identity.

Harijan Sewak Sangh struggle, reformist trend embodied in Gandhi's Harijan movement, rise of Praja Mandal, Arya Samaj efforts and growing radical mass nationalism, all provided the ideological and organisational environment within which early untouchable movement took place. At the same time, untouchables' initiative, put pressures on these sections making the issue of untouchability a socio-political one. This process to some degree occurred everywhere. In the case of untouchables this was marked by the formation of All India Raigar Mahasabha in 1944 in North India and by Bairwa, another major untouchable community in 1940. Thus, we can get a better idea of the patterns analysing organising capacity of Raigars in Rajputana.

Dharmgurus' Contribution Towards Reform Movement of Raigars

The period from the year 1878 to 1955 represents the formative period in the history of the Raigar movement. It was, during this period that the individual efforts, dedicated to the upliftment of the Raigars as an untouchable community, were initiated and spearheaded by Dharmgurus under the leadership of Swami Laxman Ram Maharaj, Swami Jiva Ram Maharaj, Swami Gian Swaroop Maharaj, Swami Atma Ram Maharaj and others, which began to acquire a socio-religious and educational consciousness. This period of development of Raigar movement has two distinct stages, which were characterised by a different set of issues, leadership and style.

The first stage, dating roughly from the year 1873 to 1955 may be termed an era of self-reform. During this period, the organisations that were formed for reform in orientation and their major concern seems to have been the social upliftment and advancement of Raigar community. This advancement was to be effected through the medium of education, with the elimination of those practices and customs, which branded the Raigars as the untouchable community. Moreover, these individuals accepted the Hindu orders as social as well as ideological system and did not fundamentally question that order. Change and progress among the Raigars were to occur within the Hindu framework and that progress demanded self-reform of the Raigars as well as the transformation of the attitude of the caste Hindus; the destiny of the untouchables was seen as inseparable from that of the larger Hindu society. In the self-directed modernisation of the community lay the solution to untouchability. Untouchability was defined largely with reference to cultural ideological criteria, the attitudinal and behavioural aspects of social life. Varna and jati were accepted as principles of social organisation, hence the progress of the untouchables was to occur within the social and ideological order of Hinduism rather than in opposition to it. It is important to note that these characteristics of Raigar movement at its inception were not unique but indeed were common to many untouchable castes movements emerging at this time. Self-reform within the Hindu framework was the shared perspective of movements among lower castes and untouchables that arose in Andhra Pradesh, Karnataka, Tamil Nadu, as well as Kerala. And in their reformist stance, these movements were within the tradition of caste Hindu reformers or modernisers, who formed organisations such as Arya Samaj and Prarthana Samaj. In this respect, this phase of mobilisation represented one possible response to the challenge posed by the West to all strata of Indian society.

By the year 1944, the Raigar movement, however, moved towards a new direction with the displacement of the old leadership, the appearance of different issues and a new style in the conduct of the movement. The second phase of the movement saw the emergence and then the predominance of political and social workers of Raigars as the leader of the movement. With the ascendancy of educated Raigars, the previous goals of the socio-cultural regeneration of the Raigar community played a significant role. The Hindu framework was no longer acceptable as it was, and its parameters were no longer considered as binding on the untouchable communities. Rather the social and ideological order of Hindu society was to be confronted. Untouchability was no longer seen merely as a ritually defined, attitudinally conditioned and behaviourally manifested disability, but rather as a form of secular slavery whose imprint was felt in all aspects of social life – particularly the socio-economic. Finally, it was decided that it must be emphasised on the community that the development of Raigar movement did not occur in a vacuum, but was closely affected by social and political changes occurring in the broader environment.

Indian society as a whole was undergoing the process of social mobilisation by way of its attendant dislocations with the elaboration of new modes of thought and action. Developments in the Raigar community were both influenced by, as well as reflected the process of social mobilisation. The origin of Raigar movement may be seen as an instance of that process. The larger political contact was characterised by the growth of Indian Nationalist Movement, the political awaking of other community and the prospects for the devolution of power by the British, all of which affected the contours and direction of the Raigar movement.

Self-Reform as the Solution of Untouchability

The origin of the Raigar movement and its early development may be seen as exemplifying the process of social mobilisation. In Karl Deutsch's formulation, "social mobilisation encompasses a variety of changes – psychological, behavioural, sociological and political, ... that characterize a society in transition from traditional to modern ways of life. These changes have a far-reaching effect on political behaviour and patterns of political action in these transitional societies. The scope of the 'politically relevant strata' is widened and new non-traditional elites emerge. New modes of political interaction develop. The range of human needs that are considered politically significant expand".[1]

An examination of the early Raigar movement reveals that it did undergo the kinds of changes contained in the concept of social mobilisation. The emergence of a new elite, which was influenced by modern ideas and was prepared to exhort its community to reject traditional values and roles was particularly crucial development in the Raigar community and in the growth of the Raigar movement. The new Raigar elite, which was both a product as well as a beneficiary of modernisation brought by the British, was the single indispensable feature in the inception of Raigar movement.

The beginning of the movement[2] dates back from the year 1878 when Raigar Dharmgurus emerged in different parts of northern India and began to work to reform their community. They travelled extensively throughout the regions and held religious gatherings in which they tried to spread the message in order to effect the social and educational awakening of Raigar community. They also attempted to organise Raigars in the various regions of northern India.

When a teacher evolves into a guru,[3] he commands natural respect not just respect but love and devotion too. The discipline becomes so devoted to the guru that he can sacrifice his life for him, though a true guru never expects any sacrifice.[4] The guru shares his being, his love and light with his disciples, unconditionally.[5]

Describing the role of the guru, Osho says: "the role of the guru is to give you a glimpse of the real – not teaching, but an awakening. The guru is not a teacher: The guru is an awakener".[6]

'Gu' means darkness[7] and 'ru' means dispeller.[8] One who dispels your darkness is your Guru.[9] The unique role played by Raigar Dharmguru must be considered against this socio-religious background. It was the influence and reputation of the Dharmguru's as a 'Raigar Saint' that reached illiterate Raigars.

Dharmgurus of Raigars

Gunshai Baba Saint Pitambar Maharaj (1638-1718)

Gunshai Baba Saint Pitambar Maharaj was born on Jeth Sudhi Teej in the year 1638 at Phagi, a village situated 50 kilometres away from Jaipur.[10] His father, Mahant Chuha Ram Gunshaiwal, a poor Raigar, was enjoying his family life in traditional style. His mother was Holi Bai. Saint Pitambar Maharaj's childhood name was 'Peeta'. Throughout his childhood and youth, he remained with Sadhus and Sanyasis eating in their groups. In the course of his wandering, he realised the pitiable socio-economic conditions of the untouchables. The poor untouchables were engulfed by the social evils and vices. The Maharaj realised their deplorable condition and in order to improve their condition, thought of doing something to ameliorate it. He vowed to remain Brahmachari (unmarried) for whole life and devote himself to work for eradication of social evils, customs, etc. After becoming Sanyasi, he was popularly known as Saint Pitambar alias "Gunshai Baba."[11]

Maharaj was active as a socio-religious reformer in his youth and he took Samadhi on Bhadwa Sudi Punam in the year 1698 at Gunshai Ghahat Phagi.[12] During a period of about sixty years, he introduced different kinds of socio-religious changes, which were remarkable. He formulated his system of thought which was oriented towards social reforms and maintained that the reformation of Raigar community was a necessary adjunct for the upliftment of the Raigars. He made a direct attack on social evils especially on gambling, child marriage, use of liquor and eating of meat, death feast and unmatching marriages. Thus, he campaigned against social evils and created a stir amongst his caste fellows. One of the programmes of action, directed towards the achievement of this goal, was to promote communal relations with the members of the lower untouchable castes. Maharaj was certain that till the Raigars follow the social vices and other evil customs, they would not be able to improve their social and economic backwardness. Hence, he toured from village to village and from house to house, which gave them a sense of self-consciousness. He asked his caste-men to leave social evils and bad customs. He gave them the slogan 'Satnam'[13] and encouraged them, for self-reform. He believed that progress in the social and economic spheres was the basis for upward social-mobility and keeping this in mind encouraged social reforms.

It is believed that Maharaj acquired spiritual powers to fulfil the wishes of his followers. Thus, Maharaj emerged as a charismatic Sadhu in the year 1668. For instance, Jiwan Ram Gunshaiwan, a resident of Delhi, has given a detailed account of miracles of Maharaj in his small book *Prachin Raigar Itihas* published in January 1973. According to him, once during the year 1668,[14] Maharaj, along with his younger brother, Bhudhar were going to village Niwai. When they reached on the boundary of Niwai, they observed that the villagers were going to the cremation ground with a dead body. On enquiry, it was told that the only son of the local Thakur had died. Younger brother Bhudhar made a request to Maharaj to give life to the dead boy. Upon this, Maharaj asked his brother to convey his message to Thakur Sahib to allow him to see the dead body of the boy, if he so desired. When the message was communicated, Thakur Sahib agreed and allowed the Maharaj to see the dead body of his son.[15] Maharaj wrapped himself in coarse cloth and sat in meditation. To the great surprise of the Thakur and the villagers, the boy regained his life. This miracle had been described in the following song (Bhajan).[16]

Daya kari gurudev ney, jab niwai gram mein aaya
Raigar ram peerdhan key, chit charno meain lagya.
Meri aaur niharo hey, satguru deen dayal,
Ladka mar gaya rao ka, raigar bhaya udas.
Karam dekhoon kya gaon ki, nahi kisi ki pichan,
Sheelgai sauda gaya, gaon ram ki aan,
Daya drishti guru kari, jab balak jeewat jaan,
Adbhut parcho paiya, turant hatheli maaye,
Aur dev dishe nahi, satnam tat saar.
Balak jeewat ker diya, satguru key aadhar.
Daya bhaye gurudev ki, lagi nishaney choot,
Pita Gunshai, phagi ke, rahey naam ki oot.

This incident attracted the attention of Maharaja of Jaipur State. Later, Maharaj allotted a piece of land measuring two and half bigha to Raigars at village Phagi.[17] At the tail end of his life on Bhadhwa

Sudi Purnima in the year 1698, he took Samadhi at Phagi. Here Raigars built a Raigar Dharmshala and dug a well. Phagi where Maharaj took Samadhi has become a centre of pilgrimage for Raigars. The caste men established Gusai Sahitya Smarak Nidhi at Delhi. The Sansthan is dedicated in spreading the Maharaj's message. The pilgrims make wishes and offer prayer to Maharaj which are usually fulfilled. Thus, even after his death the spiritual regeneration among the Raigars continues.

Jivan Ram Gunshai led the Raigar movement with his poetic talent. He spearheaded the movement in local language and exposed the cruelties of the upper castes through his poems. His long narrative poem Santvani Vilas (in four parts) shows, how the Raigars could ameliorate their socio-religious conditions in order to escape the humilities inflicted upon them by the upper castes. His major work is *Ayurved Chikitsa Padhati* in which he described the importance of Ayurvedic medicines. He was well versed in Ayurvedic medicines and to cure the diseases, he used to administer Ayurvedic medicine. Jiwan Ram Ganshai also made an attempt to write on the part played by the saints in bringing social awakening amongst the down-trodden masses and he published a small booklet, *Bharatiya Sant Itihas*. He realised that the influence of religion was essential for making progress in the socially low untouchable and educationally backward community. The publication of another book *PrachinVansh Pradeep* provides the origin of the caste.

Laxmandas Maharaj[18] *(1878-1933)*

Sadhu Laxmandas, son of Balu Ram Sunkaria, was born in the year 1878 in a village in district Pali. His mother's name was Smt Siya Devi. Laxmandas received his early education in Sindh (now in Pakistan) and passed his class 10th examinations from Sindhi High School, Phooleli. After passing his High School Examination, Laxmandas returned to his native place, Pali. From the very beginning he exhibited his rare spiritual temperament. He evinced keen interest to get rid of social evils and practices in the world. At that time Achaldas Maharaj, native of Jodhpur was gaining high command in Raigar community. Laxmandas found a positive philosophy in Maharaj Achaldas's socio-religious teachings. He was greatly influenced by his teachings and became his disciple. With the help of guru, Laxmandas learnt about philosophy, vedant, yoga, etc. Laxmandas, although educated at Sindhi School at Sindh, spoke Hindi at home. He was a good orator and writer in Hindi. He started his work to reform his community. He formed a group of few devotees, with the help of which he attempted to organise the scattered Raigars in the various regions of Rajputana. He travelled throughout the region, holding kirtans (religious gathering) in which he tried to spread the message that untouchability was not a divine creation but was instead a social artefact. The major issues addressed included, the necessity of education, the abandonment of evil practices (such as child marriage and unmatching marriage), discarding the death feast, and access to non-traditional jobs. The call for the reform was put within the bounds of an enlightened Hinduism (according to the teachings of the Brahmin reformers of the 19th century); there was rarely the suggestion that Raigars challenge or defy the Hindu order. Rather, Raigar gurus exhorted their community to rid itself of those practices which Hindu principles considered evil.

The extent of support Laxmandas Maharaj was able to command can be gauged and according to guru's account in his *Raigar Jati-ka Itihas.*[19] The author of the book said that there are indications, however, that he was quite far ahead of his time and therefore succeeded in securing many followers. The author further mentioned that Laxmandas's image among the masses was not far from the one commonly found amongst them about 'Saints' with great power. What is significant about Laxmandas's movement is that it represented the first attempt by Raigars to organise themselves.

In this way Laxmandas Maharaj tried to persuade his caste fellows to abandon the social evils and practices. In addition to the religious preaching and the work of his society, he wrote two granths.[20] They are Gian Divakar and Avgunoshadhi. Today, in fact Gian Divakar is not available.

We should also note that Laxmandas Maharaj was an intellectual of Hindi language. As a poet he used various kinds of stanzas (Chanda) in this work, especially poetry,[21] Idav Chanda, Tribhangi Chanda, Kundalia Chanda, Mukti Bhadam Chanda, Manhar Chanda, Trotak Chand, Aril Chanda, Chhapya Chand, Bujang Prayat Chand, Chaupai Chand, Drumila Chand, Harijeet Chand and Narach Chand in all 13 in number are few exemplary cases.

Further, from language, Chand, Alankar, sermon and spiritualism view point 'Gian Divakar' is really a unique granth. In 'Gian Divakar', Idav Chanda was used effectively and typically:[22]

Kal karal sada shir gajat, tu nahi cheytat mootha ajani
Aayu ghatey chhan hi chhan bhitar, javat jyo? Sarita kar pani.
Tel ghatey jab butey ut tyo tan chhijat sow nahi jani.
Laksh kahey harinam bhajey bin, jayey padya nar key abhimani.

Gian Swaroopanand Maharaj[23] *(1895-1984)*

Gian Swaroopanand was born in the year 1895 in village Gohana in Beawar tehsil, district Ajmer.[24] His parents named him Gena Ram. His father's name was Uda Ram Gosaniwal and his mother was Medibai. He received his primary education in his village Gohana. When he passed the Primary School examination from Gohana the very school was shifted to Rajiabash and thus he could not continue his studies further.[25] It is said that from the very beginning, he took keen interest in religious affairs. He used to keep with him a few small religious books such as *Geeta, Ramayan, Yog Vashit, Bharatri Satak*, etc.[26] In addition to his active participation in spiritual affairs, he also disassociated himself from worldly affairs. He wanted to make his life fruitful. Gena Ram was a handsome boy. His personality attracted the attention of Raigars of nearby villages and they wanted to marry him. When he was at the marriageable age, he disappeared and reached Mirpur Khas, Sindh. In the course of his wandering, he came in contact with Swami Moji Ram Maharaj in Sindh (now in Pakistan) who 'was well versed in philosophy and Yoga and was considered to be an accomplished person ('siddha'), capable of performing miracles. Since then he remained closely associated with Moji Ram Maharaj. After thoroughly examining Gena Ram from all points of view and after satisfying himself, Moji Ram Maharaj accepted Gena Ram as his disciple and thereafter he (Gena Ram) was rechristianised as 'Swami Gian Swaroopanand'.[27] Swami was active as socio-religious reformer in the year 1917 and he died in the year 1984.[28] During a period of about seventy years, the kind of radical changes he ushered in were remarkable. Tandu Ashram of Sindh, where Swami Moji Ram Maharaj had built his Ashram and Swami Gian Swaroopanand Maharaj lived until 1947, had become a centre of pilgrimage for Raigars. After the partition Swami Gian Swaroopanand Maharaj shifted the Ashram from Sindh to Beawar (Ajmer).[29]

When Swami Gian Swaroopanand saw the miserable socio-economic conditions of his caste, he evinced interest to uplift his caste. Later, he toured throughout India. During his all-India tour he organised several meetings of the local Raigars. His greatest contribution to the Raigar movement was his learned attack on the social evils and vices. Like Swami Laxmandas, he was also an orator and writer in Hindi. His connections with the social reforms date back to 1939, because from 1940 onwards he worked as a moving force of social reforms in various ways and capacities. He unfurled the Raigar flag at Dausa's conference, held in the year 1944 and remained its major force till his death in the year 1984.[30] The Swami was certain that though Raigars had adopted the ways of Brahmins, they would not be allowed to participate in their religious institutions. Hence, he advocated separate institution which gave them a sense of achievement.

In an attempt to establish temples, Dharamshalas, educational institutions, Swami toured all over Rajasthan and neighbouring states. He brought the high degree of identity amongst the Raigars who shared his view and ideology. There are today a large number of temples, shrines and Ashrams.

Naval (1986) who has given an account of the events in the Swami's life shows that Swami was associated with diverse kind of activities with regard to religious activities. He took an active interest in writing and producing religious books and granths for a good and happy life. Swami wrote three important granths namely[31]:

1. Atam Bodh Gian Bhaskar,
2. Gian Kundlia, and
3. Gian Bhajan Prabhakar.

In this regard, Naval further records that in the first part of Gian Bhajan Prabhakar there are nearly 400 religious songs (bhajans) regarding *Pram Bhakti Yoga, Upasana avan Atma*. Similarly, in the second part of the same granth, there are 375 stanzas (*chhanda*) regarding Ishwar Esthuthi, 'Guru Esthuthi', 'Updesh' and 'Patibrat Dharam'.[32]

On February 25, 1985 Swami died at Pipad.[33] His disciple Swami Ramanand Maharaj took an active interest in collecting funds for construction of an Ashram in the memory of late Swami Gian Swaroopanand Maharaj. Swami Ramanand Maharaj constructed a famous Ashram at Pipad. The expenditure incurred on the construction of his Ashram was roughly Rs 6 lacs.[34] An idol of Swami Gian Swaroopanand Maharaj was installed on August 6, 1993 and the total expenditure incurred on this installation was nearly Rs 35,000.[35] Several services are offered to Swami's idol (pratima) – pilgrims make wishes and offer prayers to Swami and they are usually fulfilled. The pilgrims are provided free meals. The food prepared is first offered to Swami, by placing it before his idol. This is known as Guru Prasad. Thus even after his death, the spiritual regeneration among Raigars continues.

Jiva Ram Maharaj (1901)

Jiva Ram Maharaj is also a notable guru for his socio-religious zeal in his missionary work amongst the untouchables and touchables. He was born in the year 1901 in village Bhavpura in district Jaipur.[36] His father, Ladu Ram Bakolia, was a poor untouchable Raigar. He renounced the world early in his youth and was greatly influenced by Kabir Panthi Saint Bhadu Ram's ideas, because his disciples had begun to work amongst the Raigars of Rajputana and Delhi to reform the community. His teachings were religious and social reformative in character.

On the Krishna Janamashtami festival in the year 1940, he founded a new sect called 'Ramjan Pánth'[37] in Delhi, through which he attempted to organise the Raigars in various regions of Rajputana, Delhi and neighbouring areas. He travelled throughout the various regions, holding Kirtan (religious gathering) in which he tried to spread the message that the lowest amongst the low is the best for God[38] was the creed of the sect. Later on Ramjan Path was rechristianised Ramjan Mandal.[39] The influence of his teachings expanded mostly amongst the rural untouchables.

The most significant feature of Jiva Ram's movement was that like Swami Atma Ram Lakshya, Jiva Ram Maharaj also clearly admitted the spiritual debt to Kabir and therefore, can be considered as another person who could implement Kabir's ideas amongst the Raigar untouchables.

In a decade or so the Raigar movement operated through several forms primarily in Rajputana and Delhi. During this period no united leadership or organisation emerged.

In this way Jiva Ram Maharaj tried to initiate the process of social transformation. In addition to Kirtan and work of his community, he also wrote several granths. According to Naval, numbers of such written granths are 22 in all.[40] Some of the most important are:

1. Sriram Bhajan Bodh Sagar,
2. Bhakti Prakash Prabhakar
3. Manushya Bodh Bhajan Mala,
4. Anubhav Prakash,
5. Vani Sangrah,
6. Santvani Vilas,
7. Brahmgyan,
8. Vaniprakash,
9. Aadi Jiwan Ram,
10. Jivaram,
11. Jivanand, and
12. Jiva Das.

Jiva Ram Maharaj was an active socio-religious reformer and he died on July 6, 1983.[41] During a period of 60 years, the kind of changes he brought out, were remarkable. On July 8, 1983, Jiva Ram Maharaj was buried at Sri Ram Nagar Colony, Sanganer, Jaipur.[42] According to Naval, nearly 30 thousand people gathered on this occasion.[43] His disciples took an active interest in collecting donations for construction of a temple in the memory of late Jiva Ram Maharaj. Disciples constructed the temple at Sri Ram Nagar Colony, Sanganer, Jaipur. On another occasion, on his 84th birthday, an idol was installed on August 18, 1985 at Sri Ramjan Mandir, Bapu Nagar, New Delhi, under the aegis of Sri Ramjan Mandal.[44] Thus, even after his death the spiritual regeneration among the Raigars continues.

Swami Atma Ram Maharaj 'Lakshya' (1907)

Atma Ram was born in Jaipur (Rajasthan) in the year 1907 in the family of Ganesh Ram Khorwal of Shivdaspura village.[45] Ganesh Ram was a poor and illiterate man. His wife Panchi Devi was a simple woman. They were the members of the Raigar Jati. Parents called him 'Kanhaiya Lal'.[46] When Kanhaiya Lal was three years old his parents died. Thereafter, he was brought up by his Bhuva (father's sister) at Delhi.[47] He was married at a very early age but he was not happy with his wife. As a child he is said to have had spiritual vent. He had great faith in God. In his early life, he came in contact with Kabir Panthis. He was impressed by the Kabir philosophy and left the family. He went to Tandu Adam (now in

Pakistan). In the course of his wandering, he reached Swami Gian Swaroopanand Maharaj's Ashram at Tandu Adam, a place of high spiritual achievement in Sindh.[48] At that time Swamiji was a famous religious guru of Raigar community. Here he was greatly influenced by the teachings of Swami Gian Swaroopanand Maharaj and took 'updesh' (sermon) from him. He accepted Swami Gian Swaroopanand Maharaj as his guru.[49] He became an inmate of the Ashram. Swami Gian Swaroopanand Maharaj rechristianised his name from Atma Ram to Swami Atma Ram. Here both Moji Ram Maharaj and Gian Swaroopanand Maharaj of Ashram provided financial support. Swami not only provided financial assistance to Atma Ram Maharaj for elementary education but also engaged a tutor at the Ashram. The tutor was Pandit Lachhi Ram, a learned teacher. In addition to all these activities, Atma Ram Maharaj studied the famous granth Vichar Sagar (in Hindi) under the guidance of his tutor.

Shree Tarachand Jai Ram Dass Sanskrit Pathshala (STJDSP) was a popular school in Hyderabad (now in Pakistan). Swamiji was a progressive guru, who realised the importance of Sanskrit to study the religious scripts. So he encouraged Atma Ram Maharaj to learn Sanskrit.[50] He was admitted in the school. While he was studying Sanskrit in school, he came in contact with Fateh Chand who was then supposed to be a good teacher. Later, he went to Kashi and passed the examination of Vyakran Bhooshnacharya[51] from Kashi Vidhyapeeth, Kashi. Looking to the pitiable socio-economic as well as the educational conditions of the Raigars, Swami Gian Swaroopanand Maharaj was shocked. He concentrated his attention to carrying out actively a programme of social reform. Swami envisaged the need for socio-religious reform to improve the pitiable socio-economic and educational conditions of the Raigars. In Swami Atma Ram Maharaj he found the ability of an organiser. Swami Gian Swaroopanand Maharaj therefore, assigned this important responsibility to his disciple Atma Ram Maharaj and encouraged him to do so. To materialise the dream of his guru and in order to devote his time and energy to strengthen and to spread socio-religious and spiritual reforms amongst the Raigars, Atma Ram Maharaj took vow to make social reform as an object of his life.

Since then he had been publically known as Atma Ram 'Lakshya'.[52] With these views and visions in his mind, Swami Atma Ram 'Lakshya' dedicated himself in spreading the message of

Swami Gian Swaroopanand Maharaj. He used to wear Khadi clothes and cap. From 1940 onwards Swami Atma Ram 'Lakshya' toured a large number of villages and towns. He concentrated his attention on two issues: (i) formation of all India organisation, and (ii) making it a symbol of national identity by submerging the regional names and to carry out a programme of social reform. Early and unmatching marriage posed a serious problem in some cases. Another problem which attracted the attention of Swami was illiteracy and alcohol, because only a few Raigars were teetotallers and vegetarians. Most of them drank liquor uninhibitedly and Swami strongly advocated for vegetarianism and teetotalism.

A significant feature of Swami Atma Ram 'Lakshya's' movement was that it clearly admitted intellectual and spiritual debt to Kabir and therefore can be considered as the first 'untouchable' man to implement Kabir's ideas. The untouchable's poverty and disabilities, as well as high caste's atrocities on them, help to explain their importance in the development of Raigar movement. In fact the impact of the movement was at different places and regions.

Swami also introduced certain positive programmes of reform. He encouraged sanskritisation. Swami was against the practice of untouchability. Attempts were made to protest against the caste atrocities on the untouchables by Jamindars, Jagirdars, Brahmins and others. He insisted that Raigars themselves should leave the traditional occupations and this was enthusiastically followed by the Raigars from all over northern India in general, and Rajasthan in particular. Such programmes were published and praised. Swami was active as socio-religious reformer since the very beginning and he died on November 20, 1946.[53] During a period of about 30 years the kind of radical changes he ushered in, were remarkable. He reformed his system of thought, oriented towards social transformation. From an account of the events in Swami's life given by Naval (1986) Swami was associated with diverse kinds of activities with regard to reform programmes. He took an active lead in opposing the atrocities perpetrated by the upper castes on the untouchable communities in different rural areas of Rajputana.

Due to the emergence of a powerful leader like Swami Atma Ram 'Lakshya' from 1940 onwards some events took place in and outside Rajasthan. His ideas were vehemently opposed by Jagirdars, Jamindars, Brahmins and upper caste Hindus, who were seen as exploiters of the untouchables. A bitter social rivalry between

Raigars and Savarnas developed which resulted into beating of Swami Atma Ram 'Lakshya' and others mercilessly.[54] When the Jagirdars and upper caste people of Holkar state, for instance, came to know about his entry in Kangatti for propagating and preaching the ideas of social reforms, they were beaten with lathis.[55] Similarly, when Swami went to village Khavda, Jaipur, he was also beaten by the Samant of the village. He was virtually not only beaten this time but also arrested.[56]

With such a background and bitter experience, Swami went to Delhi for discussions in the year 1944.[57] Here he discussed social reforms and other issues with some eminent Raigars such as Ram Swaroop Jajoria, Kanwar Sen Maurya, Khushal Chand Mohanpuria, Shambhu Dayal Dadegaonlia and others.[58] These persons were also interested in the programme of social reforms. They appreciated the contribution made so far by Swami Atma Ram 'Lakshya' to the reform movement. However, Swami himself was dissatisfied with the progress and wanted to form an organisation. He thought this would strengthen the society from purely a reformist organisation to an organisation bringing about socio-political renaissance among the Raigars of northern India. The main decision of the meeting was to organise a huge caste sammelan with a view to politicise and gaining the support of Raigars for its organisation and Swami was authorised to do so.

Swami Ramanand Maharaj 'Jigyasu' (1915)

Swami Ramanand 'Jigyasu' was born in the year 1915 in Sindh, Hyderabad (now in Pakistan).[59] His original name was Tek Chand alias Bhag Chand, but his father called him 'Ram' out of love.[60] His father was Kesha Ram Mosalpuria and mother Jhaniku. He received his early education at Banaras and later at Jaipur.[61] He passed 'Prabhakar' in Hindi and 'Prathma' in Sanskrit.[62] He passed his middle class examination in Sindhi also.[63]

From his early age Bhag Chand took keen interest in Bhajan and Kirtan. During this period he came in contact with a few saints. When he came in contact with saints he evinced keen interest in the affairs of religion, in addition to his active participation in the affairs of Bhajan and Kirtan. He kept himself aloof and away from the worldly activities. Looking at his tilt towards spiritual affairs, Mahatma Tulsi Das, a famous saint of Sindh, declared that one day, he would be a great saint and this worried his parents.[64] As in the case of Swami Atma Ram 'Lakshya', the members of Bhag Chand's parents wanted to get him married as early as possible. Soon his marriage was fixed with a girl named Tulsi, daughter of Ganesh Ram Phalwadia,[65] resident of Sindh, Hyderabad. His parents made all the preparations for the marriage according to the social customs and norms. Bhag Chand's relatives from different places arrived for participation in the marriage. While the marriage preparations were in full swing, Bhag Chand on the other hand felt acute eye pain and later on lost his eye sight and became blind.[66] Naval mentioned that this untoward incident happened in the year 1935 when he was only 20 years old.[67] As a result of this, the marriage could not take place. This incident changed the direction of his life.

Like Swami Atma Ram 'Lakshya', Tek Chand alias Bhag Chand too became a disciple of Swami Gian Swaroopanand Maharaj. When Swami observed Bhag Chand's 'zeal' or 'curiosity' in knowing the truth, Swami rechristianised (Bhag Chand) his name as Swami Ramanand 'Jigyasu'. Like all other Maharaj's, Swami Ramanand 'Jigyasu' also toured throughout the country and agitated against the social evils and vices.

In order to initiate reform programmes he made his life's aim to devote his time and energy to strengthening and spreading socio-religious spiritual reforms amongst the Raigars.

In the early years, he concentrated his attention on some social issues like child marriage, unmatching marriages and dowries which posed serious problems in the community. He expressed his unhappiness against such practices and also condemned the meaningless funerary feast (after death) which was expensive too.

Another problem which attracted the attention of 'Jigyasu' was alcohol. Only some Raigars were teetotallers and vegetarians. Most of them drank liquor uninhibitedly and 'Jigyasu' strongly advocated for both vegetarian food and non-alcohol teetotalism. He also strongly advocated for sending their children to schools.

With such rich experience and background, 'Jigyasu' came for the first time to the city in district Jodhpur in the year 1942[68] and in 1948 he settled down there permanently. He also established here his own Ashram with an estimated cost of Rs 6 lacs.[69]

'Jigyasu' also introduced certain positive programmes of reform. He encouraged construction of hostels and Dharmshalas. Since admission of the untouchables in the schools and hostels were prohibited, Jigyasu pleaded for opening of community schools, hostels and dharmashalas. In Jodhpur, he established a hostel called Gian Ganga Chhatrawas as early as 1963 and in Haridwar, Uttar Pradesh, he constructed Raigar Dharmshala in 1983.

In addition to being an eminent social reformer, he was a famous saint, a well known Vaid, a good orator and one of the founder members of Akhil Bharatiya Raigar Mahasabha (ABRM).

Swami Gopal Ram Maharaj (1922)

Co-terminous with earlier period of Swami Laxman Das Maharaj, Swami Gian Swaroopanand Maharaj, Swami Jiva Ram Maharaj, Swami Atma Ram 'Lakshya' and Swami Ramanand 'Jigyasu's activity, another important figure in the Raigar movement is Swami Gopal Ram Maharaj, a Raigar from Nagaur.[70] Gopal Ram was born in the year 1922 in Village Badli in district Nagaur.[71] His father was Ridha Ram Kurdia and mother Gogi Devi.[72] The economic condition of his family was good. He received his early education in Nagaur, Jodhpur, and Delhi.[73] He also learned Gujarati and Urdu. He was an intelligent student and in 1940 passed 9th class examination. He wanted to continue his studies further, but his parents did not allow him and entrusted him with the responsibility of looking after their small business.[74] Like other untouchable communities, Raigar community was very backward and depressed and looking to the desire to achieve self-directed change to the extent that may fulfil their aspirations, it needed support by some one. Interestingly, this was the reason which compelled Gopal Ram to initiate the process of radical reforms to educate the Raigars. In 1941, he started imparting free education to the poor Raigars[75] and other untouchable communities at his residence, which gave a momentum to their educational and social progress.

Naval stated that religious atmosphere at Ridha Rama Kurdia's family had influenced Gopal Ram. Thus, it was this atmosphere which had inspired him for Bhajan Kirtan and encouraged his interest in spiritual affairs.[76] In course of his wanderings in the year 1948 he came in contact with Mahatma Kishna Ram Maharaj alias Alfu Ram Maharaj.[77] Gopal Ram was greatly influenced by the teachings of Alfu Ram Maharaj and he instantly became his disciple.

Gopal Ram Maharaj was especially more active as a religious guru and organiser after 1948. In the following years, he made extensive tour of Luni, Sojat Road, Didwana, Merta, Gatmanglong and other neighbouring rural areas.[78] During these sammelans (big meetings) he urged his fellow Raigars to abandon their evils and vices and to give up customs and ritual practices which impeded their social progress.

In order to publicise the need for the reforms, socio-religious activities in different regions were not enough by holding the sammelans. We have noted that a decade ago Swami Gopal Ram Maharaj had initiated the process of education. A hostel called Mahatma Gandhi Hostel[79] for Raigar boys was started in Nagaur. Naval accounts that before he started the hostel, Swami Gopal Ram Maharaj consulted the Raigar masses in order to enlist their help. In addition, Gopal Ram Maharaj like Swami Atma Ram 'Lakshya' and other Raigar gurus, took initiative to solve the drinking water problem at Gatmanglong. He urged Raigars to contribute for construction of water tank at Gatmanglong where thousands of Raigars assembled every year to participate in Mata's religious fair. Mahatma Gopal Ram's organisational efforts culminated in the construction of a big water tank and Dharmshala at Gotmanglong.[80] The expenditure incurred was roughly over Rs 50,000.[81]

In order to make the religious changes effective Mahatma realised the importance of having temples, ashrams and categories of monks, priests and missionaries and he therefore constructed an ashram at Nagaur. Thus, he created a set of religious institutions which were parallel to the Brahminical ones and this gave the Raigars an opportunity to participate in Brahminical Hinduism which had been denied to them for centuries. In 1976 it was renovated, at the cost of Rs 5 lacs.[82] In the ashram a canotaph ('chhatri') was constructed in Swami's memory, where his Charan Paduka (shoes) were placed.[83] The expenditure incurred over it was Rs 20,000.[84]

In this way, an examination of the Raigar Dharmgurus movement would reveal that it did undergo the kinds of changes contained in the concept of social mobilisation.

Whatever were each Dharmguru's programmes, what was common was that they all used their great influence well enough for mobilising the Raigar masses and justifying their particular reform programmes. Raigar followers who participated from the beginning and contributed in socio-religious movements appealed in the name of Dharmgurus, saying that joining the socio-religious movement was exactly what Dharmgurus desired. Dharmguru's name was thus a valuable instrument for promoting Raigar unity. Their birth-days were celebrated throughout Rajasthan. Although their names were beyond their particular castes, yet they remained nothing more than the Raigar's gurus (caste gurus).

These issues of reforming the customs, education and economic improvement are to be considered together since these were inseparable but related to each other through education as budding centres. Apart from the critique of the caste discrimination, the necessity of spreading education amongst the community, occupied a primal place in the discourse and activities amongst the Raigar Dharmgurus of the time. When the Dharmgurus discussed the issue with Raigar notables and masses, the best way to ensure the community progress, they invariably emphasised education as the most appropriate measure.

For Dharmgurus, becoming educated was the fastest possible route to social mobility. At the same time producing as many educated Raigar persons as possible, was considered as the best route to the community reforms, the result of which was a resolution of caste disabilities, their attempts to reform age-old customs were connected with their goal to spread education amongst them. The women's dress and accessories were also scrutinised by the Dharmgurus. Their ceremonies and customs were regarded not only as disgraceful and meaningless but also waste of money and time, which could have been utilised in spreading education.

The ultimate goal, viz., education, forced the Dharmgurus to reflect on the economic problem facing the Raigar commoners. Without their economic betterment, they had neither any chance to get education nor was there any possibility of bringing forth self-respect, essential to protest against caste related injustice.

Their concern for social evils are especially important in the history of socio-religious movement in Raigars. The fact that the entire Raigar community was encircled by all these social evils, pressed the Raigar gurus to advocate how they could get rid of these social evils. For instance, the socio-religious reformers launched a campaign against these evils like more children and early marriages unmatching marriages, death feasts, etc., which could be banished immediately.

The phenomenon of sanskritisation has been pointed out in a number of movements amongst all the untouchables and lower castes. And self-temperance was one of the criteria of that phenomenon. Seeing that many Raigars were accustomed to alcohol and eating meat, we may ask how Raigar gurus and leaders came to deal with this problem. This became all the more complex when gurus preached "do not eat meat and drink alcohol". It cannot be denied that, during the course of Raigar's caste movement, self-temperance was encouraged. Yet it is doubtful whether Raigar leaders thought it advisable or possible for the Raigar en masse to leave their age-old habits of alcohol drinking and eating meat. Their efforts were rather prominent in drawing the society's attention to bad habits. They did condemn it and their concern was so much about social bad habits and evils that it was asserted that their low social status did necessarily drove them from traditional evils.

In the following years, a variety of educational programmes, on the pattern of local initiative and leadership, were initiated throughout Rajputana – the then princely state. The main objective of most of these activities was the promotion of education amongst the Raigar untouchables. In Rajasthan, Raigars established hostels called Atma Ram 'Lakshya' Hostel at Ringus[85] and Shri Gian Ganga Chhatravas at Jodhpur.[86]

Thus, around the turn of independence period, the Raigars in several regions were aware of the benefits of modern education and organised themselves into regional associations. The activities of the early reform movement concentrated on the promotion of education and founded hostels and also ran a few schools. Their efforts to seek modern education were complementary to their attempts to raise their low social status through socio-religious reformation. The leadership in different regions came from the affluent sections of Dharmgurus of the caste – they influenced caste fellows and the disciples and a few educated Raigars.

In the socio-religious matters, a variety of works like construction of temples, Dharmshalas and shrines etc., on the pattern of local heritage, were started throughout the regions. The main objective of most of these activities was promotion of socio-religious programme among the Raigar community. As early as 1550,[87] Bheroji Sawariya a wealthy Raigar from village Siyala spent his own money in the construction of 5 historical temples at different places, which still exist. They are located at Khord, Towali, Basi and Darjio-ki-Mandali. Another Raigar, Nanakji Jatolia[88] also dedicated a constructed temple 'Gusai Temple' to the Raigar community in Siyala in 1650. At Phagi in district Jaipur, a few years later, in 1700, he constructed a Samadhi of Raigar Saint Gusai Baba Saint Pitamber Maharaj[89] and a well for the Raigar community.

There is another point to be reckoned within its formative period Naval writes in his book (1986) which provided much information about the Raigar movement in the Samvat 989,[90] one noted reformer Badri Bakolia, a Raigar from village Gundi, district Jaipur, constructed a ghat, known as 'Gau Ghat' at Pushkar, district Ajmer and dedicated it to the community at Pushkar.

A noteworthy issue in the 20th century, which attracted wide-spread attention among the Raigars in which court allowed the ownership of Gau Ghat to Raigars is an important event in the restoration of the ownership of Gau Ghat. In the year 1916[91] Mrs Teja Bakolia and Mrs Govind Rithadia, from nearby Ragar basti at Pushkar, went to Gau Ghat to bring water. The local Brahmins not only stopped them from taking water from Gau Ghat and not only terrorised them but also beat Raigar women mercilessly.[92] As a result, Mrs Teja Bakolia died on the spot.[93] This led to a conflict between the Raigars and Brahmins. It was a local custom which forbade Raigars and other untouchable castes (Chamars, Meghwals, Bhangis, etc.) to use this Ghat. However, this incident forced Raigars to protest against this incident and they filed a case against the Brahmins in the court at Ajmer.[94] The Raigars, with the help of caste genealogist not only provided evidences but also staked their claim over the Gau Ghat. The court allowed the Raigars to use the Gau Ghat and this made the Raigars owners of the Ghat.[95]

It is necessary to point out that over a period of time particularly after Gandhi's murder in 1948, Gau Ghat was renamed as Gandhi Ghat[96] because ashes of Gandhi were submerged here. Later a statue of Gandhi was also installed.

Thus, the untouchable Raigars achieved success in respect of their right over the Gau Ghat. But the most significant consequence of the ownership controversy was the widespread social awakening of the community with regard to their right, which came as a result of the efforts of religious gurus.

Similarly, in 1947, the Raigar community collected donations from the caste fellows for construction of famous shrine called 'Ganga Mata Temple' and Dharmshala at Pushkar, Ajmer which was dedicated to the cause of advancement of Raigars and which would provide a organisational forum for their socio-religious activities.[97] Statues were installed in the temples in the year 1951. The expenditure incurred on the maintenance of these temples depended on the contributions made by the members of the community. The collections made by way of donation every year were good enough to run the charitable institutions. In his book, written by Naval, which provides the information about the annual income and expenditure of the temples in the financial year 1981-1982, brings out that the total income for the temples was Rs 29,914.55 and the expenditure incurred was Rs 15,197.64.[98]

From 1928 onwards the wealthy Raigars from different areas assumed active role in the social and religious affairs of their people. Long ago, Pandit Ghisu Lal Sawanlia, a prominent activist and supporter of social reforms from the village Aalnias in district Pali, came to Beawar and later settled down there permanently.[99] Especially in the field of socio-religious affairs, Ghisu Lal made a significant contribution. In the year 1930, he constructed Ganga Mata's temple at Raigar Badabas Colony, Beawar. What is particularly noteworthy about this temple is that a 'seth' (businessman) from upper caste opposed the construction of this temple.[100] Naval writes that the seth lodged a complaint against Ghisu Lal and Raigar community. As a result, Ghisu Lal was summoned by the then Commissioner, Ajmer. After hearing him, the Commissioner allowed to resume the construction of the temple with the condition that the whole construction work will be completed within a day and night,[101] failing which he would not be allowed to complete it. This order put Ghisu Lal in a poignant situation. Interestingly, Naval writes, that in spite of the condition Ghisu Lal constructed a big temple within the prescribed time limit for Raigar community, which was named after Ganga Mata.[102] He did a lot to reform his community.

In the year 1246, a large number of Raigar families migrated from Khandar to Merta and other places in Nagaur. A few families settled in Maji also. There were 150 families of Khatnavaliya gotra of Raigars.[103] According to Naval, there was a Raigar family of Jassa Khatnavaliya, whose sons were – Gangaji, Rupaji and Ashuji. We should also note here that Ganga's wife gave birth to a male child named Jiva.[104] It should be mentioned here that Jiva acquired spiritual power or gift of curing diseases of men and fulfilling the wishes of his followers. Thus, the local Raja was highly impressed by the charismatic personality of Jiva and honoured him with the title 'Kunvar'.[105] Since then he was known as Jiva Ji Kunvar what is particularly noteworthy about this saint is that Jivaji was the first and the last Raigar to be honoured by the local Raja. After his death, a temple was constructed in his memory in the year 1778.[106]

At Dhaneshwar Mahadev Triveni in Phoolia Kalla – a small village in Bhilwara district, the Raigar community constructed a temple called the Temple of Ganga Mata. Rs 8 lacs had been collected from caste fellows and this amount was spent on the construction work.[107] At Matra Kundia – another small place in Chittorgarh district, the Raigar community constructed another famous shrine called Ganga Mata's temple. Rs 3 lacs were collected and were spent over it.[108] The facts show that caste notable's were not entirely confined to journalism but also demonstrated in action. It will be seen that the principal deity in all the community temple shrines is 'Ganga Mata'.

Dharmgurus realised the need for constructing Dharmshala at Haridwar and appealed to the Raigar community to discharge its responsibility to contribute towards the construction of the Dharmshala for the community. With the blessings of Swami Gian Swaroopanand Maharaj and Swami Kevalanand Maharaj, Swami Gopal Ram Maharaj and Swami Ramanand Maharaj took the lead to discuss the question of constructing Raigar Dharmshala. In the following years both Swami Gopal Ram and Swami Ramanand Maharaj appealed to wealthy Raigar government officials, political workers and elites, common men and others to contribute towards this goal. Since the cost of construction of the Dharmshala was very high, the Dharmgurus frequently appealed to its caste fellows for financial help, as they depended on caste fellows.

The Dharmshala's importance for Raigar movement lies in three areas: First, it would provide, the boarding and lodging to the sadhus, sanyasis and members of the Raigar community who would be coming to Haridwar from all over India. Second, these Dharmshalas will provide spacious place for meetings and 'sammelans' gatherings by the caste fellows and third, it had its importance for the development of Raigar movement in Uttar Pradesh.

Swamis directly contributed in the organisational work of Raigar movement. Thus, Swamis played an important role in bringing its caste fellows together. Their main request was for the contribution to Dharmshala.

From 1980 onwards the caste fellows and Raigars residing in Maharashtra took cognizance of its problems and offered financial help for amelioration of Raigars. A few years later, in 1980-81, a trust was formed in order to effect the construction of Dharmshala of Raigar community. This organisation drew a few eminent persons of Raigar community – notably Lala Ram Kurdia (Bombay), Chiranji Lal Bakolia, Kalyandas Peepliwal and Kishan Lal Kurdia (all Delhi).[109] The trust received financial help from Raigars of Thakkarbapa Colony, Bombay and also collected donations from other communities. In such a short span of time nearly Rs 2 lacs were collected.[110] In that year seth Ram Rakh Dholkhedia, a wealthy Raigar from Bikaner, Rajasthan contributed a heavy amount for construction of Dharmshala at Haridwar. The trust took initiative in holding meetings for the purchase of a plot for Raigar Dharmshala. They also took concrete measures for purchasing a constructed building for the purpose of Dharmshala. In 1982, the members ultimately purchased a building for utilising it as Dharmshala. On June 19, 1983, the Dharmshala was inaugurated by seth Ram Rakh Dholkhedia, which was attended by a large number of delegates.[111] It is important to mention here that this Dharmshala is having about 22 rooms, 3 bathrooms and toilet facilities.

Just like Swami Gopal Ram Maharaj and Swami Ramanand Maharaj, Swami Balak Dass Maharaj, disciple of Swami Jiva Ram Maharaj, also took an initiative in constructing Dharmshala of Raigar community at Ram Devra (also called Runicha).

To discuss the proposed Dharamshala and its significance for the Raigar community, Swami Balak Dass Maharaj toured extensively and attempted to persuade the caste fellows for financial support. The mobilisation phase of Dharmshala movement under Swami Balak Das was gathering momentum and caste fellows expressed support for this plan. Finally, Swami Balak Dass Maharaj purchased a piece of land measuring 100 x 100 sq ft at Ram Devra on April 21, 1983. The foundation stone of the Dharmshala was laid down by Nikhwat Singh, the then Sarpanch of Ram Devra.[112] This consists of five rooms and all kinds of facilities.

Raigar Dharmshala at Runicha, Jaisalmer

Most of the initiative for construction of the Dharmshala and social work came from the male saints. However, it is significant to mention here that there was also Balak Dass (female saint) – a great social worker of Bhanpura village in district, Jaipur. She was married with Raigar man. After a few years of her marriage her husband died and thus she became a widow.[113] In the course of her wanderings, she came in contact with Swami Jiva Ramji Maharaj who was a well known Dharmguru in the Raigar community. She became his disciple.[114] Coming from poor Raigar family, she took the initiative in starting public utility establishments such as Dharmshalas and schools. She carried on her guru's tradition of social service.

She engaged herself in proving free boarding facilities to sadhus, sanyasis, social workers, activists and religious pilgrims during the Baba Ramdev religious mela, held every year at Runicha in Jaisalmer district. Balak Dass Maharaj felt acute need of Dharmshala for Raigars. For this purpose, in the year 1982-1983,[115] a formal request was made to the Panchayat Samiti, Ram Devra, Pokran, district Jaisalmer for allotment of a piece of land measuring 200 sq yards. The Panchayat Samiti also supported Balak Dass' proposal and sanctioned a piece of land measuring 200 sq yards. The foundation stone of the Dharmshala was laid down on Ram Navmi day, on April 21, 1983[116] by the then Sarpanch, Nikhat Singh. By 2001 Balak Dass got built a Dharmshala comprising of 61 rooms to provide boarding for Raigars and others.[117] For this purpose donations were collected from caste fellows. The total cost incurred on its construction was roughly Rs 13 lacs. On August 26, 2001,[118] Ashok Gehlot, Chief Minister, Rajasthan inaugurated Raigar Dharmshala at Runicha. The function was presided over by Chhoga Lal Bakolia, Transport Minister, Government of Rajasthan.[119] A large continent of Raigars from Delhi, Punjab, Haryana, Madhya Pradesh, Gujarat, Rajasthan and Maharashtra attended the function.[120] According to an account published in Raigar Rakshak Issue Raigar Samaj Dharmshala Ka Udghatan 26 Koo. The Akhil Bharatiya Raigar Dharmshala was registered on December 28, 1994.[121]

Raigar Dharmshala at Sanganer, Jaipur

The Raigars of Sanganer, Jaipur took inspiration from establishment of the Dharmshalas at various regions of the state and wanted to build their own Dharmshala for providing all kinds of facilities, such as free boarding facilities to sadhus, sanyasis, social workers, and activists. For this purpose a few years ago a meeting of the Raigar Panchayat, Sanganer was held to discuss the issue of land for building the Dharmshala named 'Raigar Dharmshala, Sanganer' at Sanganer (Jaipur district). The Raigar Panchayat, Sanganer unanimously decided to donate their own land measuring 1650 sq ft[122] at

Sanganer. On December 7, 2000 the foundation stone of the Dharmshala was laid by P.N. Rachhoiya, Inspector General of Police, Rajasthan.[123] Soon after this, the Raigar Samaj of Sanganer started construction work of Dharmshala with the financial support of Rs 4.50 lacs. According to Raigar Rakshak, the total expenditure of all kind on Dharmshala would roughly estimate Rs 30 lacs.[124] For this purpose donations will be collected from caste fellows. A large number of donors donated generously to build the Dharmshala. The construction work is now over.

Raigar Hostel at Jaipur

Socio-educational aspirations of the Raigars and other untouchable communities in Rajasthan are closely related to the increasing awareness of democratic principles based on the population strength in the state as a whole.

Nearly two decades ago the Raigars had put up an application duly signed by many community men requesting the then State Government to allot a piece of land for the construction of Community Hostel. But up till July 2001, the government did not accede to their request.

During this period the state remained under the Congress and BJP regimes. Both the governments did not allot a piece of land to fulfil their aspirations for construction of a hostel building. After an interval of nearly one decade, when Congress party formed the government in the State at the end of the year 1998. When Ashok Gehlot was installed as the Chief Minister of the State, the demand for allotment of a piece of land was again voiced forcefully by the Raigars. There were 3 Raigar MLAs and all were from Congress; out of which one is a Cabinet Minister. According to the pamphlet published and circulated amongst the caste fellows by the President and other members of the Executive Committee (date not mentioned), sincere efforts for allotment of land to the Samaj were made under the leadership of Chhoga Lal Bakolia, Cabinet Minister and Chhitar Mal Maurya, Sanghathan Mantri, ABRM, for which Committee Members expressed their gratitude to them. Thus, in the year 2001, the Raigars were able to get a piece of land marked Plot No. 5A measuring 1005.85 sq metre in front of Vidhyashram School on concessional rates near the office of Dainik Bhaskar, Jaipur.[125] The total cost of the plot was Rs 13,14,545.22.[126] In this connection a big meeting of the Raigars was held at Shiv Mandir, Sri Kalyan Nagar,

Kartarpura, Jaipur on September 22, 2001.[127] Since they did not want to mix the academic programmes with other programmes, a separate committee called Raigar Chhatrawas Prabandh Samiti was formed unanimously under the presidentship of T.R. Verma. It may be noted that Raigar leaders and workers who participated in the meeting requested the caste fellows for donation and they whole-heartedly contributed towards it as it was essential. According to the pamphlet, in the same meeting the Committee received over Rs 6.05 lakh as individual and collective donation.[128] The Committee deposited on September 24, 2001, a sum of Rs 3,28,655 in the office of the JDA against the total cost of the land.[129]

The Committee, which had released the charter of collected amount for hostel purpose had mentioned the names of individual donors.[130] Over Rs 1,53,000 had been collected from the collective financial assistance, while Ghasi Lal Dulara and Mrs and Mr Ganpati Lal each contributed Rs 51,000; S.P. Verma and Birdu Ram, Ram Lal Deegwal and Gorishan Deegwal and Tara Chand Jojoria, each group had contributed Rs 31,000 and Ram Swaroop Verma, K.L. Kamal, Baldev Prasad Hinngonia and B.L. Chomia each had contributed Rs 21,000; Girdhari Lal Verma, Brij Mohan Maurya, P.M. Jalutharia, Mangi Lal Badetia, Kalu Ram Kuldeep, Shankar Lal Kuldeep, Ratan Lal Jaju, Bhori Lal Shastri, Bhudharmal Verma, Hari Narain Nirmal, Mangi Lal Aaloria, Mool Chand Dotania and Chhitar Mal Maurya, each contributed Rs 11,000 and Arjun Lal Tongaria, Tara Chand Phoolwadia, Ganga Ram Phoolwadia, Arjun Ram Ujjenia, Rampal Uchenia, Gendi Lal Badotia, Babu Lal Jatolia, Bhagwan Sahai, Jagrawal and Smt Damyanti Bakolia, each contributed Rs 5,100.

Currently, the donation drive is in full swing in different localities, towns and cities of Rajasthan and other states as well.

A most significant event of Raigar Mahasabha movement which occurred at Jaipur under the leadership of Hon'ble Chhoga Lal Bakolia, Minister of Social Welfare, Government of Rajasthan, the foundation stone of Raigar Chhatrawas was laid on December 14, 2002 by Chief Minister Ashok Gehlot – Chhoga Lal Bakolia presided over the function. Speaking on this auspicious occasion the Chief Minister[131] impressed upon the people the need for education in order to be able to make progress in all spheres of life. Thus under

Chhoga Lal Bakolia's guidance the Raigar Mahasabha achieved all its goals.

Relationship with Other Movements and Communities

The change in attitude and strategy from submissiveness to assertion and from acquiescence to defiance, represented a direct challenge to the caste system or *jati vyavastha*, which sought to maintain it, as well as an assault on the ideology and principles which underlay that order. This change was supported among all sections of the untouchable community. The All India Bairwas Mahasabha for instance, launched a campaign against untouchability and caste disabilities for untouchable Bairwa in Rajputana, Madhya Pradesh, Delhi and Uttar Pradesh. The reason behind launching this reform movement for overall improvement in the conditions of untouchables was to demand equality in socio-educational and economic spheres.

Among the other untouchable communities in the then Rajputana princely states, such as Chamars, Meghwals, Bhambhis and Raigars developed their own association separate from Bairwa movements in 1940. The tone, style and kind of issues promoted by these associations are reminiscent of Bairwa movement in the early 1940s.

It is not surprising that each of the untouchable communities, however, small or large, had developed their own organisations, as the rivalry and distinctions among them are of long standing. It is testament to the potency and pervasiveness of the idea of caste that amongst the untouchable communities themselves notions of pollution and purity shape their interrelationship. Chamars consider themselves as the most 'pure' of the untouchables, and thus do not inter-dine or inter-marry with either the Raigars or the Bhambhis.[132] While the Chamars, Bhambhis and Raigars as well consider each other to be the same yet they have very limited commensality. The residential patterns of each of these communities are segregated, there being a Chamar Mohalla (or basti), Raigar Mohalla as well as Bhambhi Mohalla, in any given village.

These ritual differences among the untouchable communities were parallel to the socio-economic differences as well. The Chamars seemed to be economically secure. They had their own traditional occupation of removing the dead animals, skinning them and leather working which was essential to the villages. They were heavily represented in the ranks of agricultural labour as were the Meghwals and Bhambhis. They had direct connection with the village administration and thus were considered as village servants. The Raigars also had their own traditional occupations – they were skin or leather-dyers and their products were economically necessary to the village. The advent of British rule had an advantageous effect on these (leather communities such as Meghwal, Bhambhi, Balai and Raigar) communities as the establishment of leather factories in India improved the working conditions of these communities. By the 1940s, therefore, the Chamars, Meghwals, Bhambhis and Balais became the most advanced.

The Raigars had not produced a leader with education, political skills or stature of Amarat Lal Yadav. However, Raigar organisations developed the confrontational ideology and strategy of Bairwa (former Chamar community) movement in its early reform phase. The Dharmgurus of Raigar samaj called upon their community fellows to initiate a process of self-reform and modernisation, to cleanse themselves of baneful social practices and above all to educate themselves. In this endeavour both the Raigars and Chamars recognised the dearth of qualified leaders and educators in their own communities. Furthermore, neither the Chamars nor Raigars or Bairwas organisations developed the political thrust as of Mahar movement in Maharashtra but remained by and large, socio-cultural groups dedicated to the internal self-reform. Instead Chamars, Meghwals, Bhambhis and also Raigars gravitated towards the Congress realising their social and political interests and aspirations through this party.

The divergence in the political orientation of Chamar movement on the one hand and the Raigar movement on the other, may be explained by differing socio-economic development of the two communities under traditional caste systems. The Chamar community was far more affected by the process of socio-political mobilisation than were either the Raigars or Bhangis. This process expanded the range of politically aware and politically silent Chamars – a more or less modernised elite to a much greater extent than among other untouchable communities including the Raigars.

The development of Chamar elites which had been influenced by modern ideas (such as Prajamandal agitation, Rajputana Harijan Sewak Sangh's socio-cultural activities, national movements and political awakening (in the then princely states), subversive of the established social and religious order was certainly crucial in the early politicisation of Chamar movement and direction. It was to take under Babu Jagjivan Ram. The stunted development of Raigar movement reflects the slow and uneven progression of social mobilisation among the Raigars and the other untouchable communities.

The development of the Chamar movement occurred more or less in isolation from the other untouchable communities of Rajputana. It also did not form close ties with other untouchable movement. Despite their common heritage in the ideas and example of Dr Ambedkar, the Chamars and other untouchable communities came closer over some fundamental issues. Yet at an earlier period, Prajamandal agitation, Rajputana Harijan Sewak Sangh activities, National movement, etc., had been active in promoting the social and educational progress of the untouchables. The Maharaja of Jhalawar was the first in removing social disabilities imposed on untouchables. The Maharaja had also opened the temples and schools to untouchables in his state.[133]

In the earlier and later stages of the untouchable movement they elicited cooperation from Prajamandal, Rajputana Harijan Sewak Sangh, Social and political leaders attached with the national movement, Arya Samaj and other organisations against untouchability.

Indeed, during the reform movements of the following years, conflict between high caste Hindus and untouchable movements became quite evident. During this period there were attacks and pillage of homes and property of the Chamars, Meghwals, Balais and Raigars, in rural areas. The untouchables were also physically assaulted and their houses pillaged by the upper caste zealots, who were on rampage against the untouchables in the villages. All this revealed that the dominant castes in rural areas opposed the attempts made by the untouchables to alter their socio-economic status. The efforts made by untouchables to transform their position ran counter to the established interest and ideology of caste Hindus, that of the Jagirdars, Jamindars, Brahmins, Gujjars, Jats, Ahirs, Yadavs, Jatis – the resulting equation was one that was detrimental to the Chamars and Raigars communities as untouchable castes.

Notes and References

1. Karal Deutsch quoted by Jaya Shree Gokhale in *From Concession to Confrontation: The Politics of an Indian Untouchable Community*, Mumbai, Popular Prakashan, 1993, p. 65.
2. For a discussion of Raigar movement that stress the role of both Dharmgurus and ABRM (social organisation) in the pre- and post-independence period and socio-religious consequences of the movement, see in particular Chandanmal Naval, *Raigar-Jati-ka-Itihas*, Jodhpur, Shyam Printing Press, 1986 and Roop Chand Jalutharia, *Raigar-Jati-ka-Itihas*, Jaipur, Capital Printers, 2001.
3. Swami Chaitanya Keerti, "The Guru Awakens and Heals the Mind" in *The Times of India*, New Delhi, July 5, 2001.
4. Ibid.
5. Ibid.
6. Ibid.
7. Ibid.
8. Ibid.
9. Ibid.
10. Jiwan Ram Gunsaiwal, *Prachin Raigar Itihas*, Delhi, Gunsaiwal Smarak Nidhi, 1973, p. 31, Also see p. 32.
11. Ibid.
12. Ibid. Also see p. 36.
13. Ibid., p. 34.
14. Ibid.
15. Ibid., p. 35.
16. Ibid., pp. 35-36.
17. Ibid., p. 35.
18. Chandanmal Naval, op. cit., p. 85
19. Ibid., p. 86.
20. Ibid., p. 85.
21. Ibid., pp. 85-86.
22. Ibid., p. 86.
23. Saint and his contributions, especially see: *Smarika Sri Dharmguru Swami Gian Swaroop Janam Shatabdi avam Akhil Bharatiya Raigar Mahasabha Swaran Jayanti Samaroh 1995; 'Raigar samaj key pratah smarniya parak shradaspad pujya sant', Raigar Sudhar,* 15-29 February 2000. Dharmguru Swami Gian Swaroop ji Maharaj 106th *janam utasav samaroh,* on 21 October, *Raigar Rakshak,* 15 October 2001, Ibid., p. 87.

24. Ibid., p. 87.
25. Ibid.
26. Ibid.
27. Ibid., p. 88.
28. Ibid., p. 89.
29. Ibid., p. 88.
30. Ibid., p. 89.
31. Ibid., p. 88.
32. Ibid.
33. Ibid., p. 89.
34. Ibid.
35. Ibid.
36. Ibid., p. 96.
37. Ibid.
38. Ibid.
39. Ibid.
40. Ibid., p. 97.
41. Ibid.
42. Ibid.
43. Ibid.
44. Ibid.
45. Ibid., p. 89. Also see, *Swami Sri Atmaram ji Lakshaya ki Antim Abhilasha, Raigar Sudhar,* 15-31 August 2000.
46. Ibid., p. 89.
47. Ibid.
48. Ibid., p. 90.
49. Ibid.
50. Ibid.
51. Ibid., Also see, *Chiranji Lal Bakolia aur Rajendra Prasad Gadegaonlia, Raigar Kaun aur Kya?* 1964, New Delhi, Asian Printers, pp. 64-65.
52. Ibid., p. 90.
53. Ibid., p. 91.
54. Ibid.
55. Ibid.
56. Ibid.
57. *Raigar Sudhar,* Fatehabad, Haryana, August 15-31, 2000, p. 2.
58. Ibid.

59. Chandanmal Naval, op. cit., p. 94. Also see, 'Paramvandan Sant Shreshtha Ramanandji 'Jigyasu', *Raigar Rakshak*, August 1-15, 2000.
60. Ibid., p. 94.
61. Ibid.
62. Ibid.
63. Ibid.
64. Ibid., p. 95.
65. Ibid.
66. Ibid.
67. Ibid.
68. Ibid., p. 94.
69. Ibid., p. 94 and 96.
70. Ibid., p. 91.
71. Ibid.
72. Ibid.
73. Ibid., p. 92.
74. Ibid.
75. Ibid.
76. Ibid.
77. Ibid., p. 94.
78. Ibid., p. 93.
79. Ibid., p. 92.
80. Ibid., p. 93.
81. Ibid.
82. Ibid., p. 94.
83. Ibid.
84. Ibid.
85. Ibid., p. 98 and 106.
86. Ibid., p. 94 and 108.
87. Ibid., p. 98.
88. Ibid.
89. Ibid.
90. Ibid., p. 65.
91. Ibid., p. 66.
92. Ibid.
93. Ibid.
94. Ibid.

95. Ibid.
96. Ibid.
97. Ibid., p. 102.
98. Ibid., p. 103.
99. Ibid., p. 104.
100. Ibid.
101. Ibid.
102. Ibid.
103. Ibid., p. 105.
104. Ibid.
105. Ibid.
106. Ibid.
107. Ibid., p. 99.
108. Ibid.
109. Raigar Dharmshala, Birla Road, Haridwar, *Dandata Namawali avam Aaya-Vaya Vivran 1982-1983*, Raigar Dharmshala Trust, New Delhi, p. 4 'ka'.
110. Ibid.
111. *Smarika Dashak Samaroh 30-31 Mai 1993*, Raigar Dharmshala Trust.
112. Chandanmal Naval, op. cit., p. 101.
113. *Ramdevra Jila Jaisalmer mein Akhil Bharatiya Raigar Samaj Dharmshala ka Udghatan 26 Koo*, *Raigar Rakshak*, Jaipur, Year 1, No. 1, 15 August 2001.
114. Ibid.
115. Ibid.
116. Ibid.
117. Ibid.
118. Ibid.
119. Ibid.
120. Ibid.
121. Ibid.
122. *Sanganer Mein Raigar Dharmshala ka Nirman Yudh Istar par Jari*, *Raigar Rakshak*, Jaipur 15 August 2001, op. cit.
123. Ibid.
124. Ibid.
125. *Raigar Chhatrawas Nirman key Liye Arthik Sahyog ki Appeal*, *Raigar Rakshak*, Jaipur, Year 1, No. 3, 15 October 2001. Also see, *Raigar*

Chhatrawas Hetu Bhukhand Aavedan per Abhar avam Badhaei, Raigar Rakshak, 1-15 August 2002.

126. Ibid. Also see: publication of the same matter under different titles: See, *Raigar Chhatrawas Prabhandh Samiti, Jaipur, Rajasthan, Raigar Chhatrawas Nirman key liye Aarthik Sahyog ki Appeal,* published and released by T.R. Verma and K.L. Kamal (n.d.).
127. Ibid.
128. Ibid.
129. Ibid. Also see, *Chhatrawas Nirman ko Prarthamikta hoo: Naval, Raigar Sudhar,* 15-31 July 2001. *Raigar Chhatrawas Nirman Hetu Dandatayoo mein appar Utsaha – Bakolia, Raigar Rakshak,* 16-31 January 2002. *Raj Mukhya Mantri Ashok Gehlot ka Abhar Prakat, Raigar Chhatrawas avam Dharmshala hetu Aavantit Bhookhand ka Aavantan Patra, Kabja Patra avam Patta Prapt, Raigar Rakshak,* 16-31 July 2002, *Akhil Bharatiya Raigar Mahasabha (Panji) Dwara Samaj ki Aitahisk Uplabdhi, Raigar Sudhar,* 1-15 August 2002.
130. Ibid.
131. *Shiksha key bina koi samaj taraki nahiker sakta – Mukhya Mantri, Chhatrawas Shilaniyas – Raigar Gaurav ki Itihas ka Shilanniyas – Jalutharia', Raigar Sudhar,* 15-31 December 2002.
132. Munshi Hardayal Singh, *Marwar Census Report, 1891,* Jodhpur Government Press, 1896 (reprinted in 1970), p. 540.
133. P.S. Chaudhary, *Rajasthan between the two World Wars (1919-1939),* Agra, Sri Ram Mehra and Company, 1968, p. 110.

4

Emergence of Raigar Movement (1810-1993)

Delhi and Sindh Hyderabad

The Raigars of Delhi region presented a unique picture in many ways. There are old urban Raigar residents living in the city of Delhi from pre-independence days and the immigrant Raigars came in waves especially after independence from Rajasthan, Madhya Pradesh and Punjab. They were employed as white collar workers, teachers, government and corporation employees, policemen, drivers, contractors, labourers and office boys. After 1952 General Elections, professional Raigar politicians, who were elected as Members of Parliament from different parts of the country, came to Delhi. The Delhi Raigar Panchayat came into existence only in the year 1881.[1] The most notable active leaders were Chandra Bhan Tongaria, Khoob Chand Jajoria, Khushal Chand Mohanpuria, Kishan Lal Kurdia, Moti Lal Bakolia, Ram Chandra Khorwal, Kanwar Sen Maurya and Mela Ram Nogia.

In the following years the Raigar movement operated through several forms and in a variety of locals, primarily in Delhi and the Rajputana. Just as local leaders in Delhi took initiative in holding meetings for self-reforming of the Raigar community, they also took concrete measures for the purpose of educating their community.

In the year, 1900 an organisation called Delhi Prantiya Raigar Panchayat (DPRP)[2] was formed in order to effect the social and the educational awakening of the Raigar community. This organisation extended financial support and spent its own money in supporting

Raigar untouchable students who had come from economically uneducated poor family. The organisers offered to the students accommodation facilities and also helped them in their education. This organisation was registered during the year 1972-73, under the Societies Registration Act XXI of 1860 and its registration No. is 5613. Another local based organisation in Delhi called Shri Moji Ram Satsangh Sabha (SMSS), Delhi, started a free adult education centre at Vishnu Mandir.[3] Persons from nearby areas came there to study. During this period, a variety of the adult education organisations were formed in Delhi. The major objective of most of these organisations was the promotion of education amongst the Raigar community with emphasis on women's education. The first local educational organisations Delhi Prantiya Raigar Subchintak Parishad (DRSP) in Delhi was established. Similarly another organisation formed as Raigar Vidhyarthi Parishad (RVP)[4] appealed to the Raigar community to support education amongst the Raigar untouchable students and to make available, funds for that purpose. These organisations drew the attention of a few dedicated Raigars in the Delhi region, notably Dr Khoob Chand Jajoria, Naval Prabhakar, Devendra Nath Khatnawalia and Gotam Singh Sakkarwal who were the first educated leaders. Thus in the Delhi region, Raigar community had shown considerable vitality in forming numerous local organisations and took initiative in its social and educational development. Especially in the field of education, the Raigars of Delhi had made significant progress on their own.

In the section that follows we shall deal with the growth of various organisations with divergent aims and their impact on the Raigar community.

Delhi Prantiya Raigar Mandir Prabandhak Committee

In 1910, Raigarpura came into existence in Delhi.[5] The local members came mostly from Rajasthan. Soon after the establishment of the Raigarpura the Raigars constructed a temple called Shri Ganga Mandir in Raigarpura and became the centre of social reform activities. The meetings of the caste Panchayats, religious festivals, special functions and lectures were organised in this temple.[6] A spiritual programme of 'Bhajan Kirtan' to keep the men away from alcohol and social evils was also initiated at the temple.

Ganga Mandir was initially meant for Raigars of Raigarpura but later on it was also shared by the Raigars of Baidanpura and Dev

Nagar up to 1914 and 1936 respectively.[7] It may be noted that Raigars in Raigarpura were also progressive. In 1950 just after a few years of independence, the Raigars from Raigarpura constructed Sabha Bhawan. It has been organising meetings of caste Panchayat, debates, competitions, essay competitions, etc. It also provides lodging and boarding facilities to Raigars coming from outside Delhi.

In 1914, another big residential colony was established at Bidanpura. It was named in the memory of Bidan Saheb[8], the then British officer. In 1914 the next big work with the organisational efforts of the Raigar community, was the establishment of a temple called Baba Ram Dev Mandir.[9] This temple became the hub of Raigar's activities in Bidanpura. This temple also managed to administer a school and a physical training centre for Raigars. In the year 1914, the area of the temple was only 166 sq feet, but after more than five decades, efforts were made by local Raigars to procure additional land from the government. Thus, Raigars succeeded in procuring additional land measuring 112 sq feet from Urban Development Ministry, Government of India, in the year 1968.[10] In the year 1975, after an interval of 7 years, Chaudhary Padam Singh Sakkarwal, who was the Chairman of Mandir Prabandhak Committee and an enthusiastic social leader who worked in close cooperation with founder members of ABRM, laid down the foundation stone on March 2, 1975 for reconstruction of the temple building[11] and just after a few days, Chaudhary Padam Singh Sakkarwal passed away. After his death, the local Raigars of Delhi collected donations from caste fellows and completed the construction work of the temple but roof remained incomplete. Later on with the support mainly from Chaudhary Gotam Singh Sakkarwal, the Chairman of the Trust came for the completion of the roof work. He loaned Rs 9,000 for the said purpose. Thus, the entire temple building was completed. The trust later on repaid the total loan to Chaudhary Gotam Singh Sakkarwal with thanks.[12]

Over a period of time, especially during the British India Raj some social activists and reformists had emerged who took up the leadership position of the Raigars. In 1936, the local Raigars had built a 'Shiv Mandir' at Dev Nagar, New Delhi[13] which is considered to be a sacred place for Raigars and the priest of this temple is a Raigar. In the beginning of the year 1936, its area was spread over 10,000 sq feet but slowly and slowly during the British Raj people started encroaching upon the land. At present there is only about 3,600 sq feet[14] area in the possession of the temple.

Naval Prabhakar, a former congress MP was a very dynamic and influential leader and was very close to eminent Congress leaders including Pandit Jawaharlal Nehru. As a popular leader, he got the support of the community. In 1956, he succeeded in opening a Government Senior Higher Secondary School[15] in the campus of the temple and constructed the boundary walls of the temple for its protection.

In 1959, Chaudhary Padam Singh Sakarwal took the initiative and made strenuous efforts to establish a Trust with substantial bank balance under the name of Delhi Prantiya Raigar Mandir Prabandhak Committee[16] (DPRMPC), which is responsible for running the various reformative activities and maintenance of all the three major temples namely Sri Ganga Mandir, Raigarpura; Shri Shiv Mandir, Ratiawali Piou, Dev Nagar; and Baba Ram Dev Mandir, Bidanpura. This was also registered on June 14, 1959, under the Societies Registration Act 1860. Its registration number is S/1469, 1960-61. Others who also supported his efforts to establish the trust were: Kanhaiya Lal Ratawal, Chaudhary Gyirsha Ram Chandolia, Prabhu Dayal Ratawal, Nathu Ram Atal, Ram Swaroop Jajoria and Gyan Shyam Singh Sewalia. The Trust had promised to build a four storey building from its own resources in Delhi and to instal a statue of Baba Ram Dev. The construction work of ground floor has already been completed.[17] The remaining work is in progress. The Trust is mainly controlled by the Raigars from Delhi and Rajasthan. It operates on a daily basis, maintaining three major temples referred to above. From October 1972 to August 1979, the Trust had collected a sum of Rs 1,81,373.87.[18] The expenditure incurred on the construction work and other items was Rs 1,35,170.76[19] and Rs 41,239.33[20] were in balance in the bank account. After receiving donations from the members from Delhi, Rajasthan and Bombay the cash in hand was Rs 4,963.78.[21]

Sanatan Dharm Satsang Sabha, 1914

In the first decade of the twentieth century, attempts were made by certain Raigar saints to change traditional belief and practices in Delhi. For instance, Saint Moji Ram Maharaj took initiative in starting Sanatan Dharm Satsangh Sabha (SDSS).[22] The establishment of SDSS was supported mainly by late Jai Ram Mohanpuria, Late

Bhairu Ram Mohanpuria, Ram Swaroop Jajoria, Late Asha Ram Sewlia, Kanwar Sen Maurya, Khushal Chand Mohanpuria, Shambhu Dayal Gadegaonlia, Ganga Ram Rachhoya, Ram Sukh Sarsunia and others.[23] Thus, in 1914, the first organisation of SDSS came into existence for Delhi Raigars. The main object of the SDSS was to promote and encourage the community to follow the religious path and to develop good habits among the Raigar community.

At that time Raigars were suffering from social and religious disabilities. Upper caste Hindus in Delhi and elsewhere treated the Raigars and other untouchables with contempt. They maintained their social distance with Raigars and this made Raigars lose all hope of getting rid of discrimination. By 1918, Saint Moji Ram Maharaj's influence spread into far flung areas and his attempts to educate community men bore fruits. He offered a more satisfactory lifestyle but within the framework of Hinduism. He and his staunch supporters encouraged the activities of both social and religious reforms among the Raigars.

In order to run various activities Moji Ram Maharaj envisaged the need for a place and in the same year (1914), his old abode called 'Gurudwara' was converted into a temple. This is known as 'Vishnu Temple'.[24] Thus, under Saint Moji Ram Maharaj's guidance the temple became the main centre of activities.

While Moji Ram Maharaj encouraged the socio-religious reform activities, he also started a school in 1923[25] in order to spread the educational reformations that he had brought about. This educational institution meant for the Raigars continued to function for a few years but due to financial crunch, the school was handed over to the Municipal Committee, Delhi.[26] The school is still in existence. Besides Primary School, SDSS encouraged the activities of adult education in the year 1925. The number of students in the school increased to 90. Daya Ram Jalutharia and Maharaj Mangalanand started work in Delhi. Dr Khoob Chand Jajoria of Delhi took initiative in working for education welfare of Raigars. He was responsible for opening of 'Sadhna Pustkalaya' and 'Vanchnalaya'.

Birla families are most famous for their donation to various social and religious activities. Seth Jugal Kishor Birla donated and in stalled three idols of Bhagwan Ved Vyas, Bhagwan Shiv and Bhagwan Laxminarian.[27]

SDSS's campaign for religious discussion took a positive turn when Moji Ram Maharaj requested 'Sadhus', 'Sanyasis' and scholars to deliver a talk or 'Pravachan' on religious issues. Thus, for the first time a category of religious scholars emerged in the third decade of the twentieth century. At the beginning, it was known as 'Satsangh Dharmo-updesh Sabha' (SDUS). It was renamed as 'Sri Sanatan Dharm Satsangh Sabha' Raigarpura, Delhi (SDSSR) and now it is known as 'Sri Moji Ram Satsangh Sabha' (SMRSS)[28].

All these activities and programmes were able to attract a large number of Raigars. The Raigars of Delhi were undoubtedly aware of the advantage of reforms. They saw reform as a mechanism for upward social mobility. Moji Ram Maharaj received a request for establishing another organisation or Dal. This was known as Mahaveer Dal (MD)[29]. The most significant role played by volunteers of MD during the religious festivals and fairs at Haridwar, Gad Mukteshwar, Kurukshetra and other places were rendering their free services to people and pilgrims, which earned admiration. MD was becoming a popular organisation and its activities widely published.

In 1944, a big sammelan of Raigar caste was held at Dausa in Jaipur state. Thousands of Raigars from all over North India attended it. The services of volunteers of MD were utilised. They rendered their services with sincerity and honesty. Swami Atma Ram 'Lakshya', the main force behind the sammelan, was extremely happy and he on the request of the Raigar volunteers rechristianised the MD by Delhi Prantiya Raigar Swayam Sewak Sangh (DPRSSS)[30]. This was a manifestation of the glory of MD with respect to the services rendered to Raigar community by volunteers of MD.

One of the most significant events of the SDSS movement occurred in Delhi under the leadership of Saint Moji Ram Maharaj. For instance, Kanhaiya Lal was a popular 'Kabir Panthi' among the Raigars. Once he came to attend a religious gathering called Satsangh Mandali. Satsanghis reached the Gurudwara[31] from far and near areas in a large number. Here he held discussion on certain religious issues with the disciples of Moji Ram Maharaj. Kanhaiya Lal took leading part in it. In his discussion, he was assisted by his own men. Throughout the discussions, he successfully influenced the gathering. He not only impressed the gathering but also succeeded in winning the heart of Moji Ram Maharaj. Thus, a closeness was developed between them. Having attained closeness between Kanhaiya Lal and Moji Ram Maharaj in the field of religion, the disciples of Moji Ram Maharaj, namely Ram Swaroop Jajoria, Kanwar Sen Maurya, Asharam Sewlia, Shambhu Dayal Gadegaonlia, Khushal Chand Mohanpuria, etc., turned their attention to bring him (Kanhaiya Lal) to their side, namely, 'Sanatani' sect.[32]

The disciples of Moji Ram Maharaj achieved significant gains when he left the Kabir sect, and later became the disciple of Swami Gian Swaroop Maharaj.[33] Later on, he was known as Saint Atma Ram 'Lakshya' – a famous Raigar saint.

Arya Samaj Ideology and Raigars, 1914

As has been stated earlier, the Raigars attempted to introduce socio-religious reforms in 1914 with Moji Ram Maharaj's SDSS. Since other Raigars found it difficult to come out from traditional set of society under SDSS, a separate organisation 'Arya Samajist'[34] was formed in the same year (1914), with Mahatma Narain Swami as President. This group of Raigars started their efforts for socio-religious reforms under the guidance of Arya Samajists. The reaction of Raigar Arya Samajist to the socio-religious reforms of Moji Ram Maharaj in Delhi has to be seen in the context of SDSS Reforms of 1914. SDSS were conservatives and orthodox. The Raigar community was shocked by this move of SDSS. The main concern of Raigars now shifted from conservative traditional to modern, which the whole community realised and was concerned about. This was opposed by other Raigars in Delhi in the year 1915. At this point Choudhary Kanhaiya Lal Ratawal, Chaudhary Padam Singh Sakkarwal, Mohan Lal Patel, Chaudhary Giarsi Ram Chandolia, Prabhu Dayal Ratawal and others, perceived dangers to Raigars.[35] They had earned a reputation of being staunch supporters of Arya Samaj and opponents of the activities of SDSS.

Delhi Raigars excommunicated the volunteers of MD for wearing 'Nikkar avam Pyajama' (half-pant and trousers) during the religious festivals at Haridwar, Gad Mukteshwar, Kurukshetra, etc. This created a flutter among the Raigars towards SDSS in general[36] and Moji Ram Maharaj in particular. This further changed the whole attitude of SDSS and Arya Samajists towards each other. The leaders of SDSS never addressed the leaders of other organisations by name, but were called as Member of Arya Samaj.[37] So was the case with

Arya Samajists. They beat up and abused each other.[38] Some of the Raigars had stopped inter-dinning and commensal relations between SDSS and Arya Samajists.[39] A series of violent conflicts occurred between them.

With this, by the third decade of twentieth century the leaders of SDSS and Arya Samajists had fought against each other. Around this time fissiparous tendencies began to appear among the Raigar organisations; it had increasingly involved itself in ideological conflicts. The major rift was between Raigars who supported Moji Ram Maharaj and those who aligned themselves with growing Arya Samaj movement. The leaders of caste Panchayat intervened in the clashes between the two organisations and they encouraged compromise and pleaded for friendship between them, but failed.

The campaign for compromise took positive turn when caste Panchayat invited the leaders of both organisations to plead their case before them. The first meeting of Panchayat was held at Jaipur in 1932.[40] At this time, both organisers pleaded for their movement with forceful speeches. The meeting lasted few hours. After hearing both sides, caste Panchayat pronounced its decision. According to Chiranji Lal Bakolia and Rajendra Prasad Gadegaonlia, it was mentioned that 'Arya Samajists are at fault'.[41] This decision was not accepted by both and the situation remained as tense as it was.

However, this did not create any nervousness among the masses, which made them (the caste *Panchas*) realise that continuous efforts were needed to bring them round for compromise and therefore decided to work afresh and with vigour.

The leaders of the caste Panchayat gained self-confidence and began to assert their influence. In 1933, during the second attempt, the leaders of Panchayat again convened a 'vishal' very large community meeting at Alwar,[42] Rajasthan, appealing to both the organisations to dump their differences. Thousands of Raigars from all-over India again assembled here. The community Panchayat without hearing anything from both sides asked them to carry on their activities as usual and accepted the existence of both organisations. Thus, a long standing contentious issue was ultimately settled down amicably.[43] Raigar masses appreciated the leaders of caste Panchayat for this.

Similarly, there was one other development which contributed towards the removal of bitterness and tension among the Raigars who supported SDSS and those who aligned themselves with growing Arya Samaj movement. Swami Atma Ram 'Lakshya' met the leaders like Mohan Lal Patel,[44] Pradhan, Raigar Panchayat, Delhi and their supporters with the help of some religious gurus to resolve the issue. There was no religious guru of the community who was capable of checking this bitterness and tension. The public opinion among the Raigars was increasingly in favour of solution, as this conflict had seriously affected the harmony of the community as a whole.

With this, Swami achieved a major success. The amicable compromise was the result of continued efforts made by both under the leadership of Swami Atma Ram 'Lakshya' and caste Panchayat.[45]

Arya Kanya Pathshalla, 1929

Among the Raigars, educational awakening occurred in the third decade of the twentieth century under the influence of the Arya Samaj. It acquired the elements of opposition and protest against the upper castes in part of North India, which crystallised in sacred thread and anti-social evil movements. In Delhi the educational mobilisation of the Raigars under the leadership of Mahatma Narain Swami was part of the non-Brahmin movement. For instance, on January 13, 1929, at Basti Har Phool Singh, Pahari Dhiraj,[46] Arya Samajists opened the Arya Kanya Pathshalla (AKP) with five Raigar girl students[47] which worked for spreading awakening of educational importance among Raigars of Delhi. The first Head Mistress of the school was Shrimati Sumitra Jat. Thus, the foundation of this school was laid down by Mahatma Narain Swami. It continued its teaching activities for some years and later on in 1936 shifted to Bidanpura.[48] Again in 1951, after more than a decade it was shifted to Karol Bagh in a rented house.[49] It was recognised as Primary School by Education Department, Delhi.

It may be noted that Raigars of Delhi were interested in constructing their own school building. Thus, Late Goda Ram, son of Kanhaiya Lal Ratawal donated 557 sq feet of land for school building.[50] On January 7, 1951, Late Shankar Lal laid down the foundation stone of the building.[51] The Trust has now constructed two-storied building with 17 classrooms. It runs in two shifts.

After independence, the school was also upgraded to Middle School in 1954 and later on in 1966, it was elevated to High School.

Now it is Senior Higher Secondary School since 1987. The enrolment of girl students increased from 5 in 1929 to 800 in 2002.[52] The committee looking after the management of school was registered as 'Arya Kanya Pathsalla (Raigarpura) Trust' in 1957.

The most significant achievement in the school history is the completion of 75 years of its establishment during 2002-2003. Similarly, the old Raigar girl students of the school emerged as the most eminent Raigar women of Delhi. Shrimati Sundarvati Naval Prabhakar became the first Raigar woman councillor of Maha Nagar Parishad, Delhi and later on Member of Parliament from Karol Bagh. Shrimati Meira Kanwaria became first Raigar woman, Mayor of Delhi; Ms Kiran is serving as Deputy Press Secretary at Rashtrapati Bhawan; and Shrimati Shakuntla Pawadia became the Principal of the same school.[53]

Delhi Prantiya Raigar Swayam Sewak Mandal, 1938, Dev Nagar, New Delhi

The Raigars residing in Delhi, Sind Hyderabad and Rajasthan were among the first to realise the value of modern reforms and started to organise themselves and moved in the right direction of implementing the said reforms.

In 1938, in Delhi, the Raigars organised themselves, thanks to the efforts made by late Ram Lal Chandolia.[54] The others who also helped in the efforts to implement Chandolia's reforms programmes were: Khoob Chand Jajoria, Naval Prabhakar, Devendra Nath Khatnawalia, Puran Chand Rehadia, Jiwan Lal Bandhu (Maurya), Ram Pal Kurdia and Kishan Lal Sakkarwal.[55] Thus, Ram Lal Chandolia who was Arya Samajist took the lead and established Raigar Jati Swayam Sewak Mandal (RJSSM),[56] Dev Nagar, New Delhi, on January 14, 1938, and this was the beginning of caste awakening. This Mandal laid down its own aims and objects to reform caste customs, creating educational facilities, etc. Later on the name of this Mandal was changed to Delhi Prantiya Raigar Swayam Sewak Mandal.[57]

Arya Samaj had become popular by the turn of twentieth century in Punjab, Delhi, Madhya Pradesh and Rajasthan and many Raigars came under its influence and Ram Lal Chandolia was one of them who used Arya Samaj practices. This gave him an opportunity to participate in Vedic Hinduism and also gained self-respect and prestige in the eyes of others. His initiative in the Raigar Reform Movement provided social awakening.

From 1938 onwards the major ideas of the Mandal centred around three prominent issues, i.e., rendering free services to the Raigar community in organising socio-cultural activities, debate competition, essay writing, etc.[58] They emphasised the value of reforming customs to raise their social status and associated themselves with the propaganda with an appeal to eradicate social vices. The leaders and volunteers toured all-over Rajasthan, Delhi and other regions and in November 1944 rendered their valuable services in organising the first conference of ABRM at Dausa (in Jaipur state) under the leadership of Swami Atma Ram 'Lakshya'.[59] This was attended by Raigars from different parts of Rajasthan, Delhi, Madhya Pradesh, Punjab, etc. The second conference was held at Jaipur in April 1946 under the presidentship of Chaudhary Kanhaiya Lal Ratawal.[60] The office bearers and volunteers of the Mandal rendered their services and took leading part in organising the conference. After the successful completion of the conference the President of ABRM Chaudhary Kanhaiya Lal Ratawal held a special function at Shiv Mandir, Ratiawali Piou and Delhi and honoured each volunteer with a silver coin.[61] The third conference was held in November 1964 at Pushkar, District Ajmer, under the presidentship of Naval Prabhakar. In this conference the volunteers again rendered their services as watch-dogs during day and night and presented guard of honour at the time of inaugural function.[62] Its fourth conference was held in 1984 at Ram Niwas Bagh in Jaipur under the presidentship of Chhoga Lal Kanwaria.[63] In this conference volunteers of the Mandal were invited. On the first day of conference a procession was taken out which paraded through the Main Bazar, with 5 elephants, 11 horses and 11 camels, a band party, drum beaters, 'tamtams', cars, scooters and cycles with Raigar flags.[64] The procession was led by Nop Ram Deegwal – the Chief of the Mandal on a horse with Raigar flag.[65] Around 300 volunteers from Mandal were sent to this conference by Chandan Singh Chandolia – the Chief of Akhil Bharatiya Sewadal.[66] The conference addressed itself specifically to one issue, the reform programme for Raigar community. On the third and the Last day, Late Shrimati Indira Gandhi, the then Prime Minister of India, came to Jaipur and addressed the conference.[67]

It is important to note that Delhi Prantiya Raigar Swayam Sewak Mandal, completed 50 years on January 14, 1987 and has contributed in a significant way.[68] On May 30, 1987, the Mandal celebrated its Golden Jubilee at Shiv Mandir, Block 6, Dev Nagar, New Delhi, under the presidentship of Chandan Singh Chandolia.[69] On this occasion, leading figures of Raigar community praised the activities of Mandal and its contribution in improving community's image. The eminent personalities who praised the Mandal included Dharm Das Shastri – the President of ABRM, Kanwar Sen Maurya – an old and dedicated social worker, activist and founder member of ABRM, Gotam Singh Sakkarwal, Chairman, Delhi Prantiya Raigar Mandal Prabandhak Committee and Shrimati Meira Kanwaria, former Chairman Delhi Municipal Corporation and Chairman Mahila Pracost ABRM.[70]

Asamarth Sahayata Samiti, 1956[71]

The Raigars like other poor and untouchables suffered from certain diseases. These were serious ones such as TB, Asthama, Cardiac, etc. Since they belonged to poor Raigar families, they could not afford to pay heavy expenditure on their treatment. In many parts of Delhi, most of the Raigar families were economically poor and were performing the work of shoe repairing, field labourers and domestic servants which are low level occupations. They used to take meat and consumed alcohol. There was a need to provide them economic assistance. But this could be done by an independent organisation. Therefore, the Raigar community thought how they could overcome their miserable economic conditions and for this purpose they formed an 'Asmarath Sahayata Samiti' (ASS). Thus, this Samiti was founded by Kanwar Sen Maurya, a most eminent political elite. On April 1, 1956 at Vishnu Mandir, Raigarpura, and thereafter many more organisations were established independent of each other.

The first office bearers of the ASS were: Kanwar Sen Maurya (founding-father), Ram Narain Mohanpuria (Pradhan), Arjun Ram Sablania (Up-pradhan), Shambhu Dayal Gadegaonlia (Pradhan Mantri) and Lakmi Chand Kansotia (treasurer).One of the first accounts of ASS is given in first summary Annual Report (1957), published in Asamarath Sahayata Samiti Paper. In the beginning of ASS, the leaders were concerned with six basic objectives:

1. To help the poor and needy human beings by providing them moral and economic support,
2. To raise funds and provide them financial assistance,
3. To preach truth, 'ahinsa' non-violence love and unity,

4. To create an atmosphere of brotherhood amongst the human beings,
5. To serve the motherland, and
6. To ban the use of intoxicants.

As a founder member of ASS, Kanwar Sen Maurya did his best to raise the funds. Therefore by March 30, 1957, ASS had the strength of 142 members who paid the membership fees of paise 25 and 50 respectively. A payment of paise 25 was for ordinary membership and paise 50 for active membership. Thus, by March 1957, Rs 531 as membership fee was collected. They also took active interest in collecting donations. In the year 1956-1957, when the leaders of ASS approached their caste fellows with a request to donate, the donations collected from 37 persons was Rs 108. The minimum and maximum amount of membership was Re. 1 to Rs 11 respectively.

ASS served the cause of poor and needy Raigars, who were suffering from various diseases in two ways: first, the ASS provided financial assistance for their treatment and second, it worked for the welfare of the community. Kanwar Sen Maurya was also member of various organisations and as a founding-member, he championed the cause of Raigar's welfare. According to *Asarmarth Sahayata Samiti First Varshik Sanshipta Vivran Patrika (1957)*,[72] which gives the details of income and expenditure during 1956-57, it shows that Rs 256.25 were distributed among 37 Raigar patients for their treatment. The minimum and maximum amount given was Rs 4 and Rs 10.50 respectively. The total income during 1956-57 from all sources was Rs 639.50.

The positive approach of ASS to sufferers pacified the Raigars who were suffering from serious diseases. In 1957, Kanwar Sen Maurya got ASS registered in Delhi under Societies Registration Act XXI of 1860 and its registration number is S.1184.

Raigar Shikshit Samaj, 1963[73]

As noted earlier, the Raigars of Delhi played a significant role in spreading the education among the Raigars of Delhi and in early 1963, they formed Raigar Shikshit Samaj (RSS) at Karol Bagh, Delhi, which was managed by a committee and the educational activities were started as a result of sincere efforts of Raigars. RSS was made explicitly a socio-educational and cultural development of the Raigar community. This enabled government officials, employees and professionals to join the organisation in large numbers. There were members who took part in various activities especially the social awakening programmes. The first office bearers of this organisation were: Rajendra Nath Chandolia (Pradhan), Om Prakash Deegwal (Mantri), Parmanand Lavdia (Convenor, Research Cell), Ashok Kumar Ratawal (Convenor, Cultural Cell), Prithvi Chand Patel (Convenor, Library Cell), Tirth Ram Badalia (Convenor, Education Cell) and Sadhu Ram Sersia (Treasurer). There were 12 members: Kishan Lal Aaloria, Kishal Lal Mohanpuria, Kushhal Chand Sakkarwal, Gotam Chand Jajoria, Jaspat Girdhar, Nand Kishore Sabalnia, Prithvi Chand Alotia, Mohan Lal Dhulia, Mohan Lal Mohanpuria, Roop Ram Maurya, and Lakhpat Rai Atal. The main activities of the Samaj were:

1. To collect the data and information regarding origin and development of Raigar 'samaj' and ethnological evidences, if available,
2. To unite the Raigar samaj and promote the higher education among the Raigars,
3. To make efforts to improve the physical and mental health and spiritual development of young Raigar youths,
4. To inculcate national feelings among the Raigar youths,
5. To do something for the cultural development of the Samaj.

Donors were MPs, businessmen, government employees and rich Raigars from Delhi and the students who benefitted from this scheme were not confined to Delhi urban areas only, but were also drawn from rural areas. The income from all sources from 1969-1970 and 1970-1971 to 1971-1972 was Rs 14,594.21. From 1969 to 1972, the number of beneficiaries were 250 boys and girls.

A major programme of Delhi Raigar Samaj was to propagate education and sports activities with a view to establish schools, hostels, coaching centres for competitive examinations, evening classes, 'vachnalaya' debate, adult education centre, 'sangosthi', distribution of books, stationery, etc., to poor and needy Raigar students. Whenever, Raigar students were denied admission, there was agitation.

RSS had also started 'pustakalaya' library and vachnalaya in Vishnu Mandir to promote the reading habits among the Raigars. After 1963, RSS opened its branch in Dev Nagar and Bappa Nagar areas, New Delhi. In 1970 another vachnalaya of RSS was started at Madipur. This vachnalaya was formerly inaugurated on March 8, 1970 by Shiv Narain Sarsunia – the then Counsellor, DMC.

During the summer vacation and before the commencement of annual examination of middle classes, RSS had also arranged extra classes in the evening. This enabled the poor students to improve their performance in the annual examinations. Since 1963, the activities of RSS had increased considerably. Occasionally RSS held important debates on certain social issues. The office bearers of RSS felt that social activists and political elite should be drawn into debate and organised debates. In July 1969 the RSS arranged a debate on Gandhi Centenary and Upliftment of Harijans at Vishnu Mandir – Shiv Narain Sarsunia, the then Councillor, DMC delivered the Presidential address and said that Gandhi did a lot for the welfare and upliftment of down-trodden people. Another issue that caught the attention of RSS was 'Contribution of politics in the development of social and economic aspects of Harijans'. As a result of this, in February 1970, RSS organised another debate at Samaj Sadan Sarasavati Mandir, Raigarpura, under the presidentship of Puran Chand Peegonlia. The leading speakers were Shiv Narain Sarsunia, Naval Prabhakar and others. In December 1971, RSS held a debate at Sarsavati Mandir, which was attended by large number of Raigars from all-over Delhi. The topic was 'Why Political Malice in the Social Adjustment?' Several speakers stressed the fact that politics had created differences, hatred, jealousy and social distance among the Raigars. They pleaded for removal of all this in which the upper caste politicians exploited them and declared that ill feelings should come to an end. The leading speakers were: Chaudhary Giarsa Ram Chandolia, Chaudhary Padam Singh Sakkarwal, Prabhu Dayal Ratawal, Kanwar Sen Maurya, Ganga Prasad Dhudia, Laxman Prabhakar, Banshi Lal Khorwal and Parmanand Lavdia.

In 1970, RSS started taking an active interest in opening the 'Balbari' creche for Raigar children. On June 7, 1965, a branch of employment exchange centre was opened. Thus, it provided information about the job opportunities available in different government departments and also about the schemes of government for higher education.

The urban Raigars became aware of their poor economic conditions and got interested in the earning activities. RSS felt that women should be attracted to work for the movement and the work started from the tailoring activities. Thus, in April 1970 RSS established a tailoring centre in Raigar dominated bastis.

In order to propagate about the family planning programme for the community, RSS organised several programmes in Raigar dominated areas. In February 1969 and in March 1970, RSS organised a drama show, 'Makdi-ka-Jal' in Vishnu Mandir. On December 27,1969, another 'puppet' show was organised in Bidanpura. The Delhi Raigars also occasionally arranged to show the films particularly 'Mai Bhi Maa Hun', 'Upkar' and 'Parivar' under the auspices of RSS, where men, women and children met explaining the purpose of film and emphasising the need for family planning. In 1972, RSS started taking an active interest in mobilising public opinion for family planning in the community by broadcasting radio talks. Thus, on October 19, 1972, Rajendra Nath Chandolia, Jagdish Kumar Mohanpuria and Man Chand Tongaria delivered radio talks from AIR, New Delhi and on November 9, 1972, Om Prakash Deegwal and Parmanand Lavdia delivered talks on family planning. Besides, radio talks and organising of few selected dramas, etc., RSS also invited some well known doctors from Kapoor Matra Seva Sadan, Delhi, and some local medical officers to deliver the talk on family planning on March 14, 1970 at Vishnu Mandir. The doctors in their speeches explained advantages of family planning to the gathering. When the speeches were over, Raigars, who had come there from different parts of Delhi, started asking questions about family planning. It shows that consciousness among the Raigars of the necessity to adopt the family planning measures started growing in them.

It may be noted that RSS felt the need of a separate building for the Samaj. Thus, in September 1970, Kanwar Sen Maurya, a leading social leader laid the foundation stone of Sarasvati Mandir at Raigarpura. Soon after this, RSS started collection of donations from businessmen, government employees, social workers and activists and rich Raigars from Delhi region. According to RSS Smarika (1973), the donations so collected amounted to Rs 8,249 The total expenditure incurred on construction of the building was Rs 13,910.14. Shrimati Mota Devi wife of late Laxman Ram Kurdia, a rich Raigar of Delhi donated the highest amount of Rs 7,151. She did so only out of sentiment about the temple, which amidst all of its troubles can bring forth such men and women. Today one can only say that part of the credit goes to Shrimati Mota Devi Kurdia. On Tuesday, November 11, 1971, it was inaugurated by Chaudhary Giarsa Ram Chandolia. The idol of Sarasvati deity was established by her.

In order to make them familiar with the cultural diversity, Indian heritage, places of historical importance, RSS realised the importance of education-cum-cultural trips. Thus, a tour was arranged with a group of Raigar men, women, children and students in July 1970. The group toured Nainital, a hill station in Uttar Pradesh (now in Uttaranchal) and also visited nearby historical places such as Bheemtal, Astal and Bhuvali, and this gave the Raigars an opportunity to see the Himalayan kingdom. In October 1971, again they made another extensive tour visiting places of pilgrimage and historical importance in Rajasthan such as Jaipur, Ajmer, Udaipur, Chittorgarh and Pushkar and meeting social and political workers.

One of the most significant events of the movement occurred in Delhi region under the leadership of RSS. They organised social gathering on October 2, 1970, to promote inter-dinning between the Raigars and other low untouchable castes like Bhangis. More than 200 persons from different low castes/communities attended it. Orthodox Raigars considered the Bhangis and other untouchable castes as most degraded untouchable caste. RSS advocated castlessness and also started a programme of inter-dinning. The Raigars of Delhi had organised another get together at Delhi on October 2, 1971. This time more than 300 persons assembled. The credit of having started a movement of self correction among Raigars goes to RSS. RSS Smarika (1973) reported that the removal of restrictions on inter-dinning within lower castes had been widely appreciated and that there had also been a few instances of inter-marriages. The programme of inter-dinning with Bhangis marked the efforts of leaders to equalise by pulling up the bottom strata. It also gave the RSS movement wider appeal, identity and popularity.

These organisations drew the attention of a few dedicated Raigars notably Dr Khoob Chand Jajoria, Naval Prabhakar, Devendra Nath Khatnawalia and Gotam Singh Sakkarwal who were the first educated leaders in the Delhi region. Thus, in the Delhi region Raigar community had shown considerable vitality in forming numerous local organisations and took initiative in its social and educational development, especially in the field of education. The Raigars of Delhi had made significant progress on their own.

Raigar Shikshit Samaj (RSS) had a much wider popular support in Delhi, and many educated Raigars, social activists, political leaders, etc., patronised it and assumed leadership at the regional level.

Besides all this, the Raigars established various other Samiti and Sangh in Delhi region such as 'Raigar Sanyukta Agarjami Sangh', 'Delhi Prantiya Raigar Shubhchintak Parishad', 'Delhi Prantiya Raigar Yuvak Sangh', 'Sri Labhunath Satsang Sabha', 'Raigar Navyuvak Sangh', 'Gian Lakshya Nivriti Vidyapith'. All came into existence before 1964.

Raigar Dharmshala Trust, New Delhi

Swami Kewalanand Maharaj was a very influential personality. As a popular Swami, he got the full support of the Raigar Samaj. In the year 1980s, he toured Bombay, Gujarat, Rajasthan and Delhi. During his visit he collected a sum of Rs 1.50 lacs.[74] The donors were from Bombay, Delhi, Bikaner, Nagaur, Jaipur, Jobner, Ajmer, Beawar, Jodhpur, Udaipur, Ahmedabad, Firozpur, Abohar, Faridkot, Bhatinda and Dabwali. Swami had promised to build a Dharmshala at Haridwar.

On November 21, 1981, a meeting was convened at Haridwar to establish the Raigar Dharmshala.[75] The members came mostly from Bombay, Madhya Pradesh, Rajasthan, Delhi and other regions. It was also attended by Panchas, Sarpanchas and representatives of various organisations. After prolonged discussions, it was decided to build a Dharmshala at Haridwar. Some of the Raigars who had come from Bombay to attend the meeting at Haridwar took the initiative in discussing the issue with Delhi Raigars.[76] For instance in Delhi they had a meeting with Dharm Das Shastri, congress MP and assured him of more and more financial support. Dharm Das Shastri had an active social and political career. The next big organisational efforts on the part of Dharm Das Shastri and others came in the same year (1981) with the set-up of a committee for preparing a draft proposal for the formation of a Trust. The committee prepared an extensive draft proposal on aims and objects of the trust, their membership, executive council and its powers, etc., and submitted it for registration under the name of 'Raigar Dharmshala Trust'. It was registered under registration Number S/12652/1982.[77] Thus, Raigar Dharmshala Trust came into existence in 1981 with Rama Nand 'Jigyasu' as Pradhan,[78] Lala Ram Kurdia as 'varist-up-pradhan', Chiranji Lal Bakolia as 'up-pradhan', Swami Gopal Ram as 'mahamantri', Kishan Lal Kurdia as 'mantri', Dharm Das Phalwadia as 'up-mantri', Uda Ram Kurdia as 'prachar mantri', Punam Chand Dholkhedia as 'sanghatan mantri', Bhagirath Dholkhedia as

Treasurer and Ram Chand as 'lekha nirikshak'. Besides all these there were 18 members also.[79]

Some of the founding members, particularly Lala Ram Kurdia, from Delhi, Chiranji Lal Bakolia from Bombay and Kalyan Das Peepliwal from Delhi helped in all possible way in the collection of more and more donations. It is also important to note that there had been a good contribution and financial support from places like Bombay, Bikaner, Delhi, Kota, Jaipur, Ajmer, Beawar, Nagaur, Barmer, Punjab and Agra Raigars.[80]

In 1982, Jaipur Raigars made valiant efforts to contribute a substantial amount to increase the funds for Raigar Dharmshala Trust, Haridwar. They had collected a sum of Rs 50-60 thousand and promised to collect a sum of Rs 1 lac.[81]

In 1936 Ram Rakh Dholkhedia, son of Nanu Ram, started supporting poor Raigars from his savings in his business in an informal way. Nanu Ram Dholkhedia and his sons are one of the oldest and most rich men of Shivwadi, Bikaner, Rajasthan.[82] Nanu Ram's sons who were well placed and influential were social activists of the Raigar movement in Rajasthan and in India also. In 1936, Nanu Ram's third son, Ram Rakh Dholkhedia went to Kasur and Lahore (now in Pakistan) alone for his leather business.[83] Later he toured Ahmedabad and Bombay also for expanding his business. In the leather business he earned a name and fame. In 1944,[84] when his business was well established in Bombay, he went to Madras to start his leather business there. In 1948, he went to Calcutta to start his new business of 'kuram' leather in which he earned a lot.[85] He was from Bikaner and emerged as one of the biggest wholesale kuram leather dealer in Calcutta.[86]

Ram Rakh Dholkhedia of Bikaner involved himself in education, cultural and economic activities. In the educational field he established a Raigar's hostel. For instance, in 1951, Ram Rakh and his sons built a few rooms in Government School, at Shivwadi, Bikaner, his native place.[87] In 1963 a caste hostel building called Gyan Ganga Hostel was built at Jodhpur to provide boarding and lodging facilities for poor Raigar students.[88] In Bikaner he also built an Ashram Bhawan and at Ramalwara in Nagaur district he built a Satsangh Bhawan.[89] Thus, Ram Rakh Dholkhedia, his brothers and sons, the rich Raigar businessmen, were also active in reform movement and welfare activities. Similarly in 1981 when Raigar

Dharmshala was established by Lala Ram Kurdia and others, Ram Rakh Dholkhedia donated Rs 51,111.[90] Thus, Ram Rakh Dholkhedia became prominent in Bikaner region.

There was another rich man, Manohar Lal Mosalpuria, who received greater attention within and outside the region, was born on May 9, 1951 in Bhopalgarh, Jodhpur district.[91] His father's name was Kuma Ram and his mother was Chak Devi. Manohar Lal got his education at Bhopalgarh. He passed his higher secondary examination from Umaid School,[92] Jodhpur. He got his BE degree in 1974 from Jodhpur University[93] (now JNV University) and worked as an engineer in Coal India Pradhikaran in the year 1974-1975.[94]

He left his job and got his marine engineering degree in 1976 from Calcutta University[95] and worked as an Executive Engineer in Shipping Corporation of India, Bombay.[96] Later, he joined as Chief Engineer in Viliyam Ship Management Ltd.,[97] Hongkong. Manohar Lal's whole family has associated with the activities of the community. They also donated liberally for construction of rooms in Gian Ganga Hostel at Jodhpur. It is also important to note that at the 10th annual meeting held at Raigar Dharmshala, Haridwar, Manohar Lal donated Rs 61,000.[98]

Year-wise detailed figures of the membership are not available for all the years. The only figures available in *Smarika*, 1993 related to the years 1983 to 1993 which revealed the following facts regarding membership.

Table 4.1

Year-wise Membership

Year	1983	1993
Member	390	600

Source: Maha-mantri-ki-Report gives a detailed account of Raigar Dharmshala Trust, in Smarika: Dasak Samaroh, 30-31 May 1993, Page not mentioned.

Table 4.1 does not provide enough data to arrive at any generalisation regarding the Trust's membership. It only indicates that a large number of Raigars were not interested in getting themselves enrolled as members of the Trust. In order to get more details about the membership, we consulted Smarika 1993 and from that following two points emerged:

1. 22 donors each paid Rs 5,100. Thus in all 22 donors donated Rs 1,12,200.

2. Before his death Late Puran Chand Jagarwal of Abohar, Punjab declared to donate Rs 1 lac to Raigar Dharmshala, Haridwar, from his property.

In 1982-1983 the Trust had collected a sum of Rs 8,53,336 and the same was spent. Table 4.2 taken from Smarika Dasak Samaroh, May 30-31, 1993 gives a broad picture of their income and expenditure.

Table 4.2

Year-wise Income and Expenditure of Raigar Dharmshala Trust, since 1982-1993

Year	*Name of the Dharmshala*	*Income*	*Expenditure*
1981-86	Delhi	9,19,582.48	9,19,582.48
1986-87	Haridwar	24,122.53	24,122.53
1986-87	Delhi	9,11,715.30	9,11,715.30
1987-88	Haridwar	30,154.77	30,154.77
1987-88	Delhi	9,18,240.24	9,18,240.24
1988-89	Delhi and Haridwar	35,714.35	35,714.35
1989-90	Delhi and Haridwar	34,510.67	34,510.67
1990-91	Delhi and Haridwar	49,589.30	49,589.30
1991-92	Delhi and Haridwar	59,901.13	59,901.13
1992-93	Delhi and Haridwar	1,07,444.65	1,07,444.65
	Total	30,91,035.42	30,91,035.42

Source: Smarika, Dasak Samaroh, 30-31 May 1993. Published by Raigar Dharmshala Trust, New Delhi, 1993. Page number not mentioned.

Shri Raigar Shubhchintak Sabha, Sindh Hyderabad (now in Pakistan)

The Raigars of Sindh Hyderabad started to organise themselves to eradicate the social evils and emphasised the value for reform in raising their low social status, thanks to the efforts of Jaspat Rao, son of Girdhari Lal of Sindh, Hyderabad. His father, Girdhari Lal Heera Nand Phoolwadia was a government servant in the Railway at Sindh Hyderabad. He evinced keen interest in working for his caste when he was serving the railways. In addition to his active participation in the social programmes, he got all his four sons educated in spite of his poor economic condition.

In the year, 1946, Jaspat Rao formed 'Shri Raigar Shubhchintak Sabha' during British India which was the beginning of caste awakening.[99] It laid down its aims to reform caste customs and creating educational consciousness, work as honest, sincere and dedicated caste leaders; and as disciplined workers as also to prepare the history of the Raigar community. He intensified the efforts to spread the benefits of girl education among the Raigars and in the year 1946 took the lead in establishing, 'Shubhchintak Hindi Kanya Pathshalla' at Sindh Hyderabad.[100] It should be noted that Jaspat Rao was the first Raigar who passed his matriculation examination from Bombay University and worked as a clerk in Municipality, Sindh Hyderabad.[101] Thus, most of the leaders for collective mobilisation of the Raigars came from poor family.

Notes

1. A full account is provided in "Delhi Prantiya Raigar Panchayat: Aay Vyaya Vivran Avam Varshik Prativedan, 1979-80", New Delhi, Shi Ganga Mandir 53, Raigarpura, Karol Bagh, p. 4.
2. The most important sources for early movement and situation of Raigars in Delhi and the other regions is Chandanmal Naval's, *Raigar Jati-ka-Itihas*, Jodhpur, Shyam Printing Press, 1986, p. 54.
3. Ibid.
4. Ibid.
5. The most important sources for the early movement and the situation of Raigars in Delhi is Delhi Prantiya Raigar Mandir Prabandhak Committee (Registered) Ka Aay Vyaya Prativedan, 1972-1979. New Delhi, Baba Ramdev Mandir, Bidanpura, Karol Bagh, (Publication year and page number not mentioned.)
6. Ibid.
7. Ibid.
8. Ibid.
9. Ibid.
10. Ibid.
11. Ibid.
12. Ibid.
13. Ibid.
14. Ibid.
15. Ibid.
16. Ibid.

17. Ibid.
18. Ibid.
19. Ibid.
20. Ibid.
21. Ibid.
22. Bakolia, Chiranji Lal and Gadegaonlia, Rajendra Prasad, *Raigar Kaun Aur Kya*? New Delhi, Asian Printers, 1964, p. 47.
23. Ibid., p. 48.
24. Ibid. See also, "Sri Sanatan Dharm Satsang Sabha Raigarpura avam Bhagwan Sri Vishnu Mandir ka Sanshipt Vivran Patrika, published by Pradhan Mantri Sri Sanatan Dharm Satsang Sabha", Raigarpura, Delhi (year of publication not mentioned), p. 4.
25. Ibid.
26. Ibid., p. 49. Also "Sri Sanatan Dharm Satsang Sabha", Raigarpura, p. 3.
27. Ibid., p. 49. Also, "Sri Sanatan Dharm Satsang Sabha", Raigarpura., pp. 8-9.
28. Ibid., p. 47-48.
29. Ibid., p. 49. Also "Sri Sanatan Dharm Satsang Sabha", Raigarpura, p. 5.
30. Ibid., p. 49.
31. Ibid., p. 63.
32. Ibid.
33. Ibid.
34. Ibid., p. 50.
35. Ibid.
36. Ibid., p. 51.
37. Ibid.
38. Ibid.
39. Ibid., pp. 51-52.
40. Ibid., p. 52
41. Ibid.
42. Ibid.
43. Ibid.
44. Ibid., p.67.
45. Ibid., p. 64.
46. Arya Kanya Pathshalla Platinum Jayanti *Smarika* 2003, p. 25.
47. Ibid.

48. Conversation with Kishan Lal Kurdia, Karol Bagh, Delhi on 30 May, 2003.
49. Arya Kanya Pathshalla, op. cit., p. 25.
50. Ibid., p.26.
51. Ibid., p. 51.
52. Ibid., p. 26.
53. Ibid., p. 28.
54. Swaran Jayanti 1938-1987, *Smarika*, 30 May 1987, gives detailed account of Delhi Prantiya Raigar Swayam Sewak Mandals' (DPRSSM) activities, published by DPRSSM, New Delhi, 1987 (page number not mentioned).
55. Delhi Prantiya Raigar Swayam Sewak Mandal in Swarn Jayanti 1938-1987 *Smarika*, 30 May, 1987.
56. Ibid.
57. Ibid.
58. Ibid.
59. Ibid.
60. Ibid.
61. Ibid.
62. Ibid.
63. Ibid.
64. Ibid.
65. Ibid.
66. Ibid.
67. Chandanmal Naval, *Raigar Jati-ka-Itihas*, 1986, op. cit., p. 146.
68. Swaran Jayanti 1937-1987, *Smarika*, 30 May, 1987, op. cit.
69. Ibid.
70. Ibid.
71. For main contemporary analysis, see particularly *Asamarth Sahayata Samiti's Pratham Varshik Sanshipt Vivran Patrika*, Satya Printing Press, Delhi, 1957. Also see, *Vidhan: Asamarth Sahayata Samiti*, Delhi, Gopal Electric Press, 1958.
72. Ibid. *Asamarth Sahayata Samiti ki Pratham Varshik Sankshipta Vivran Patrika*.
73. For most important source for educational and other activities in Delhi is *Raigar Shikshit Samaj: Smarika* (year of publication not mentioned).
74. The most authoritative account of the Raigar Dharmshala Trust is given in Raigar Dharmshala, Birla Road, Haridwar, *Aay-Vyaya Vivran*

1982-1983, New Delhi, published by Prabhandhak Raigar Dharmshala Trust (Regd) (publication year not mentioned), p. 4 Ka. Also see 'Ek Parichya', in *Smarika: Dasak Samaroh*, 30-31 May 1993 (page number not mentioned).

75. Ibid., p. 4 Ka.
76. Ibid.
77. Details reported in pamphlet, "Raigar Dharmshala Trust (Regd)", published by Swami Rama Nand Jigyasu, Pradhan and Swami Gopal Ram, Maha Mantri, dated 5 September 1982, 1939/8 Sant Nagar, Karol Bagh, Delhi
78. Raigar Dharmshala, Birla Road, Haridwar, op. cit., p. 2.
79. Ibid.
80. Ibid., pp. 4 Ka – 4 Kh.
81. A full account is provided in a pamphlet published by Moti Lal Balotia, President, Raigar Dharmshala Trust, Branch Rajasthan, dated 17 November 1982, Jaipur, City Printers, Jaipur.
82. For a discussion of Dholkhedia's contribution that account Dholkhedia family's involvement with social activities, see in particular Seth Ram Rakhji Dholkhedia-ka-Sankshipt Jiwan Parichaya, in Raigar Dharmshala, pp. 4-1 to 4-11.
83. Ibid, p. 4-1.
84. Ibid., p. 4-11.
85. Ibid.
86. Ibid.
87. Ibid.
88. Ibid.
89. Ibid.
90. Ibid., p. 14.
91. The detailed coverage is given in *Ek Parichaya* in Smarika, Dasak Samaroh, 30-31 May 1993, Delhi Raigar Dharmshala Trust, 1993.
92. Ibid.
93. Ibid.
94. Ibid.
95. Ibid.
96. Ibid.
97. Ibid.
98. Ibid.

99. For most important sources for early movement and situation of Raigars in Sindh Hyderabad is Jaspat Rao, *Unnati Path Pradarshan* Aathwa Dhan Ka Duryopayog Hyderabad (Sindh) 30 March, 1947. See in particular back portion of Samalochana by Atma Ram 'Lakshya', Suryamal, Maurya and Rama Nand Sanyasi (page number not mentioned).
100. Ibid.
101. Ibid.

5

The Raigar Mahasabha

Reform and Authority

An examination of the early Raigar movement reveals that during this period no unified leadership or organisation emerged, whereas the movement was quite decentralised.[1] The impetus for agitation and mobilisation among the Raigars arose largely in response to local forces and at the behest of the local community leaders. These leaders were literate and studied at vernacular primary.

The earlier reformist character of Raigar movement was however, modified and an alternate strategy for socio-political organisation of the Raigar community came into existence. This strategy was based on the premise that mere socio-religious reforms were not sufficient for support and solidarity in their political movement but had to develop an independent organisation which would be concerned almost exclusively with their problems. The assumption was that Raigars all over India shared a set of common interests despite the peculiarity of regions.

The formation of the caste model organisation as All-India Raigar Mahasabha was related to the socio-political situation at that time. In the early 1940s, the other untouchable communities took concrete measures to improve the socio-educational and political awakening in their respective communities and had formed their all-India level organisations which represented their special point of view, the most prominent example being, of course, Akhil Bharatiya Raigar Mahasabha. Under these circumstances, Raigars felt that they had to have their own organisation through which they could agitate and speak with one voice. The earlier reform movement could not be converted into an all-India body and the task of forgoing an effective social alliance between the scattered and poor Raigars was one which would take many long years to complete. In view of the social and political urgency therefore, it was decided to form an organisation which would be exclusively for Raigars in composition and which would represent primarily Raigars and uphold their interests. Hence, reforms focused on Raigars of Rajasthan and thereafter shifted to caste thrust of the All-India Raigar Mahasabha.

With regard to the formation of the caste organisation, it should be noted that after a few years or so, Swami Atma Ram 'Lakshya' and others succeeded in propagating the reforms and creating consciousness among the Raigars. But Swamiji was not satisfied in conforming himself to the limited area and activities. In the course of his visit, when Swamiji reached Aandhi Tholai village, the local Raigars expressed their desire to Swamiji for holding a huge satsang sammelan at Aandhi Tholai for reform activities among the Raigars.[2] They also proposed that Raigars of neighbouring regions should also be invited. Thus, Swamiji proceeded further in his plan of holding a 'visal satsang sammelan'. Swamiji in order to build rapport with some eminent Raigars and went to Delhi and discussed the issue with some of his caste fellows namely, Ram Swaroop Jajoria, Kanwar Sen Maurya, Khushal Chand Mohanpuria, Shambhu Dayal Gadegaonlia and others.[3] They appreciated Swamiji's proposal for holding 'visal satsang sammelan'. While suggesting a concrete scheme, they added that instead of holding visal satsangh sammelan, they could arrange a big caste sammelan and then they could start or form an all-India organisation. They felt that a large organisation of Raigars might help to transform his dream into reality. Thus, Swamiji found a solution of their expectations and proceeded further in his plan of forming an organisation with the help and cooperation of their caste fellows. In addition to his active discussion with some of the caste-men, Swamiji also had meeting with other eminent figures of the Raigar community particularly – Mohan Lal Patel Kansotia, Nathu Ram Atal, Dr Khoob Chand Jajoria, Bihari Lal Jajoria and Naval Prabhakar.[4] Its agenda was to bring together the scattered Raigars by merging them into a single organisation at all-India level. The venue of the meeting was Dausa (Rajasthan).

Following this exchange of ideas, a committee of six members was constituted.[5] They included: Swami Atma Ram ('swagat-adhyaksh'), Naval Prabhakar ('up-swagat-adhyaksh'), Suryamal Maurya ('pradhan mantri'), Dr Khoob Chand Jajoria ('Publication mantri') and Jai Chand Mohil and Kanwar Sen Maurya (both 'prachar mantri'). The committee concentrated its efforts on various fronts. The representatives of the committee went to various places and regions of the country and also organised several meetings with local Raigars for seeking their social and economic support. Besides, Raigars were also requested for their active participation in the sammelan. For instance Swami Atma Ram visited Punjab, Marwar, Mewar and Ajmer regions and collected Rs 1,500.[6] Surya Mal Maurya toured Hyderabad and its neighbouring areas. During his tour he collected a sum of Rs 1,200.[7] Likewise, Kanwar Sen Maurya and Jai Chand Mohil too went on tour of the various places of Rajasthan. Everywhere, these leaders were welcomed by caste fellows and they promised to extend their full support for this noble cause. Thus they could enrol a large number of volunteers and could collect large funds for the sammelans.

As has been mentioned above, the pioneer of the sabha had therefore made an attempt in the early days of the organisation to foster 'consciousness and unity' for building the organisation. One of the attempts in this direction was pad-yatra, i.e., pilgrimage on foot.

Pad-yatra was the most important activity of the organisers during the early 1944. They adopted the device for creating consciousness among the Raigars of Rajasthan. They found that through personal contact with the village Raigars, the pad-yatra could develop the spirit, instil confidence for socio-economic development and popularise the organisation over a larger area.

The most active Raigar leader and first pad-yatri who worked round the clock for organising the scattered Raigars was Kanwar Sen Maurya. The team of pad-yatra consisted of two: Maurya himself and harmonium the symbol of religious songs. Everyday from the early morning he started his journey on foot with harmonium on his back. During his pad-yatra, he covered large number of villages. In each village, the Raigar inhabitants welcomed Maurya. The tour on foot and his express simplicity was an impressive affair. The zeal of Maurya, his colloquial language and his pitiable description of their poor socio-economic conditions through religious songs impressed the rural masses. Furthermore, he also appealed for social reforms and abolition of evil customs and vices. Similarly, he emphasised on imparting education. It created a stir and developed the movement among Raigars. In one of the songs[8] Maurya described the miserable condition of Raigars:

Joo jati ka beyhal hai, unhey yad
Kutoo ki tarah thukrah diya,
Dukh hal sabkoo bana diya,
Sheroo sey gigad bana diya,
Tumhey yad hoo key na yad hoo
Kuoo talab pyiu per aur motor erail per, chatey
amay bhi sadak per
Tumhey yad hoo key nayad hoo !!2!!
Aab dhyan sey kuch sooch loo, nidra sey ankhey kholo
Kuch muhasey jara tumm bollo, tumhey yad hoo key na hoo !!3!!
Aab jati ko jagrat karoo, aur vir bhav dil mein daro
Tumhey yad hoo key na yad hoo

In another song[9] he tried to stir and spread the message that plight was not a divine creation but was instead a social artifact:

Sansar uth chukka hai, tum kaisey soo rahe hoo
Bhagya key bhrosey, baithey kyo roo rahe hoo
Sabhi sampatti khoo chukeyhoo, oh unchi shan walon
Aab too jagoo abhagoo, bigdi koo phir sey bana loo
Duniya ki jatiya sab, gaflat sey jag uthi hai
Sab kam soch apna, tan dhan sey juta chuki hai
Alasya abhiman mad mein, ham sab beykhabar padey hai
Joo amullya jiwan, bekar khoo rahey hai
Jis jati mein karodoo, dharmavir na huhai hoo
Desh jati hit mein, pranoo ko kho chukey hoo
Ab khub durdasa hoo, is prakar aaj uski
Dukh sey baheyga kyo na, akhoo sey nir kiski
Bahano aur betio ki, ijjat gava rahey hai
Sari sharam ko khokar, sabko dikha rahey hoo
Is kadar durdasa mein, jiwan koo rakh sakoogey
Raksha kahi aab sabki, kis bhanti ker sakoogey
Dharma aur satya koo, sara hi kho chukey hoo
Badnam bhi jagat mein, bahut hoo chukey hoo
Aab phir bhi so rahe hoo, suntey nahi hoo koye
Aab too jagoo sab milkar, yaha sochta na koyi

Naram hoo rahey hoo, shero key putra hokar
Kayi bar lut chokey hoo, kayer aur bhiru banker
Phal burey hei chkhogey, aab phut braksha boo ker
Yadi jati mata ka, uddhar chahate hoo
Aur matrabhoomi ka kalian chahate hoo
Aur pahley sa jagat mein, samman chahate hoo
Aur jati ko banana vidwan chahate hoo
Sab dwaesh bhav tyago, aapas mein prem joodoo
Sab sangatith hookar, sab nichta koo toodoo
Aapas ka bhed viro, kabhi na layoo man mein
"Kanwar" uddhar hooga, utthan ek shan mein.

Similarly, in the early 1994, the Raigars of Punjab organised a big meeting in Amritsar for the same purpose under the presidentship of Ganga Ram Rachhoya.[10] In this meeting Swami Atma Ram 'Lakshya' was invited to deliver a lecture on social issues. The meeting widened the ethnic consciousness of the Raigars, making the Punjab Raigars aware of their castes in different parts of the country. The linguistic boundaries, however, were not formidable barriers in promoting continued interrelationship at the organisational level . The Raigars of Punjab contributed a sum of Rs 200 towards forthcoming sammelan.[11]

While the pad-yatra was an important source of awakening and mobility for the Raigars – the composition and publication of songs by the Raigar reformers were becoming more and more popular – was also an important factor in the development of socio-cultural movement.

Portraying of the miserable social, economic and educational condition of the Raigars began to be a feature of Raigar songs from 1940 onwards. During the year 1940[12] a small booklet published by Kanwar Sen Maurya entitled *Shri Raigar Bandhu Bhajnawali,* Do Shabad, a few words made their appearance and entire book was devoted to miserable conditions and also past glory of the Raigars community. A few years later in 1942 another Raigar reformer Chandmal Maurya alias Chand published a booklet *Gar Khastriopadesh Gayan.*[13] In other respect as well, Chandmal Maurya also attempted to point out 29 rules or characteristics of the traditional Raigar Kshatriyas.[14] Similarly, another Raigar reformer was Bhagat Bhagirath who also published a small booklet after 1947.The book was *Jati bijak mool prashan: Raigar Samaj.*[15] All the books were dedicated to the eradication of social evils and generated message to discard them.

Dausa Sammelan, 1944

With all these preparations, stage was set for the sammelan to begin on November 2 to 4, 1944.

The first Akhil Bharatiya Raigar Mahasabha Sammelan was convened at Dausa (in Jaipur) on November 2, 3, and 4, 1944.[16] According to Naval, it was attended by roughly ten thousand Raigars of various regions of the country.[17] On the first day November 2, 1944 the sammelan was inaugurated by Nathu Ram Atal.[18] Chand Karan Sharda, a well known social reformer and freedom fighter from Ajmer presided over the function.[19] An Executive Committee of seven members was formed for carrying out the functions. Thus, on November 2, 1944, the Akhil Bharatiya Raigar Mahasabha (ABRM) came into existence with Bhola Ram Tongaria as President, Pandit Ghisu Lal Shanswasia as Vice-President, Dr Khoob Chand Jajoria as Pradhan mantri, Kanwar Sen Maurya and Jai Chand Mohil as Prachar mantri and Prabhu Dayal as Swayam Sewak mantri. Lala Ram Jalutharia was elected as the Treasurer.[20]

On this occasion the following song was sung[21] and the Raigar flag was unfurled by Swami Gian Swaroopanand Maharaj:

Ek eitihasik prastha bhoomi jhanda uucha rahey hamara
Om swastika kesaria pyara, shiksha koo bal deney wala
Jati jagrat karney wala, hemein sadaiv rahey yeh pyara !! om!!
Bujurgoo ney tha isey pharharaya, matrabhhomi per bali chadaya
Punha palat dega yeh kaya, karney ko hai phir ujiyara !! om !!
Ravi vanshi harichand ney uthaya, phook dai sarvasva maya
Raghyjoo dasrath ka jaya, tha sagar bhagirath koo pyara
Chand udaya hua hai aaoo, tan man dhan sarvasya lutaoo
Jati mein prajati phalayoo, sangathit hoo jayo sara !! om !!

It is important to stress that Raigars asserted their claim of being 'Kshatriya' Rajput. In order to strengthen their claim the Raigars used the saffron coloured flag. This suited them best as they were warriors previously. As Kanwar Sen Maurya indicated in one of the songs[22] that Raigars could progress provided they follow the path of kshatriyaisation.

In his address, Naval Prabhakar asserted the need for unity and solidarity amongst Raigars to fight against the social evils and atrocities of upper caste people:

Vidya bin raigar jati, aaj teri hui khawari !! ter !!
Khuman aur chandragupta key yug mein, tumney kari ladayee
Gar kshtriyo ki dhak jagat mein tej sei baithai
Aab bhi kami kyoi na tum mein, dekho aankh uthai
Aapas mein sab prem badhaoo, vidya ki tyari
Vivah sanskar mein bhayoo, yagyapavit pahnavey
Kawach pahan ker kamar bandhker, hatoo talwar dilavey
Ghooda chadkey karoo chadhai, dhaus khub bajavey
Koi baat mein kami nahi hai, karoo unnati ki taiyari
Bhawaj ko mata saam jano, raghukul ki pahachan
Sab batoo mein atishesta hoo, yahi hai uchan gyan
Ram krapan ki bhakti kartey, dhartey bhagwat dhyan!
Joo koi tumko chota samjhey, unki buddi gae mari
Ved padho aur padhaoo bhai, sandhya havan karoo !
Ram Krishna aur Vishnu ki murti, mandir mein padraoo
Apna swaroop aaphi bhool, nahak kyo pachtao
Duniya koo phir sey dikha doo, "Kanwar ban vidyadhari !![23]

The sammelan stressed the importance of forming a few panel groups for the different socio-economic issues and suggested some remedial measures.[24] Thus, Bhola Ram Tongaria of Hyderabad was elected Chairman of the Panel for 'Social Reforms'. Likewise, Jai Narain Vyas of Jodhpur was elected Chairman for 'Social Boycott of Begar (forced labour), Mohan Lal Kansotia Patel (Delhi) for 'Defence of Raigars'. Pandit Ghisu Lal Shanwasia (Beawar) for 'Social History of Raigar'. Dr Khoob Chand Jajoria (Delhi) for 'Raigar Youths'.

During the three-day discussions, the Mahasabha showed great interest in the programme of social reforms, especially those concerned with eradication of untouchability and prohibition. The Mahasabha stressed the need of spreading education amongst the children in different regions and the necessity to make progress in economic activities. In addition to all this, the Mahasabha also passed a few resolutions for eradication of social evils. Thus the Mahasabha was seen as a part of socio-political consciousness.

An analysis of the various resolutions passed by ABRM at its first annual meeting shows that there were four major points to be focussed:[25]

1. A number of resolutions concerning reformatory measures, such as ban on eating meat and to serving alcohol on certain occasions was passed.

2. ABRM supported the rejection or refusal of the traditional tasks and made a strong plea to stop the removal of the dead animals with immediate effect. The ABRM directed that Raigars should not take out the skin of the dead animals and repair old shoes.
3. The ABRM in its 1944 Dausa sammelan passed resolution urging the caste-fellows to send their children to school, which was essential to raise the social status, which is below the line.
4. The ABRM encouraged inter-regional interaction among the Raigars.

In order to attain the goal the ABRM approved the following resolutions:[26]

1. The ABRM decided to send the Raigar students to schools and the needy Raigar students should be financially helped in their studies.
2. In order to eradicate social evils and vices, it decided to launch a campaign which can provide the necessary background to the Raigars for their all-round development.
3. It should initiate socio-religious reforms.
4. It should foster caste consciousness and unity in order to fight the atrocities perpetrated on them and to assert social solidarity.

Here it suffices to note that the sammelan succeeded in propagating organisation (ABRM) and creating consciousness 'WE' feeling among the Raigars. It gave expression to the national identity and ABRM emerged as a pivotal organisation enlisting the cooperation of Raigars from Delhi, Punjab, Uttar Pradesh, Rajasthan, Maharashtra and Gujarat. Delhi is also the place where Raigar leaders from different parts of India converged. They attained a high degree of political mobilisation.

Jaipur Sammelan, 1946

The formation of ABRM and its intense agitation against the practices of untouchability, socio-religious disabilities and to gain access to schools, wells, temples, etc., were whipped up by the opposition like Thakurs, Jagirdars, Jamindars, Brahmins, Baniyas and others, who were seen as the exploiters of low untouchable castes/communities. They were ill-treated by them and threatened that for their attempts on social reformation, economic restrictions would be imposed; their atrocities increased against this caste group. In an attempt to suppress the reform movement, they let loose some anti-social elements to even beat up the Raigars. These upper caste people were irritated and due to this several violent confrontations took place at Raisar (1945), Balesar (1945), Markeda (1945), Karana (1946), Parbatsar and Badi (Tonk)[27], all in Rajasthan. The news was widely published. Swami Atma Ram 'Lakshya' bitterly criticised and condemned all this action of upper castes.

The reaction of upper caste Hindus in Rajputana and else-where to social reform was so intense that the Raigars had to be seen in the context of Raigar Mahasabha Sammelan of 1944. Swamiji soon realised its repercussions. Thus, on October 31, 1945 an urgent joint meeting of the representatives of the Mahasabha was convened at Ghat Gate, Jaipur.[28] The meeting was chaired by swamiji. In this meeting it was decided that next sammelan be held at Jaipur in 1946.

Subsequently, on December 23-24, 1945, the Mahasabha under the leadership of Mohan Lal Kansontia Patel (Delhi) convened a big meeting of workers and representatives at Lala Ram Jalutharia's residence at Jaipur.[29] In this meeting more than 100 active workers and representatives from all-over the country participated. It is noteworthy that on this occasion Swami Atma Ram 'Lakshya' was also present. Thus, it was decided to hold the second Annual Convention on April 12 to 14, 1946. For this purpose a reception committee under the chairmanship of Dr Khoob Chand Jajoria as 'Swagat-Adhyaksh' and Chaudhary Asha Ram Sevila as 'Swagat Mantri' was constituted.

The first meeting of the above reception committee took place at Lala Ram Jalutharia's residence at Ghat Gate, Jaipur, under the convenorship of Swami Gian Swaroop Maharaj. A large number of representatives from Delhi, Hyderabad (Sindh), Phulera, Dausa, Lahore, Punjab, Udaipur, Bikaner, Marwar, Ajmer, Jaipur and other places attended the meeting.[30] In this meeting Chaudhari Kanhaiya Lal Ratawal was elected chairman of the reception committee. However, Dr Khoob Chand Jajoria was replaced by Gotam Singh Sakkarwal as Jajoria kept himself away from all this because of serious differences of opinion with other office bearers. Next day again a meeting was held under the chairmanship of Gotam Singh Sakkarwal at Ganga Mandir Ghat Darwaja, Jaipur, for constitution of a few sub-committees. A sub-committee was constituted with an aim to collect donations. Another sub-committee was formed under convenorship of Kanwar Sen Maurya, the prachar mantri of ABRM for giving wide publicity of the sammelan.

The representatives of the committee toured various places and regions of the country and had also organised several meetings with local Raigars for seeking their social, economic and financial support. For instance, 'Raigar Navyuvak Sabha, Karachi' donated Rs 565 for the sammelan.

With all these preparations, a stage was set for the sammelan to be held on April 12, 13, and 14, 1946, when Kanhaiya Lal Ratawal arrived at Jaipur railway station from Delhi, a grand warm welcome was accorded to him. Under his presidentship, the procession of Mahasabha started from Chandpole Gate, where a large number of members were present. Kanhaiya Lal Ratawal, the President of ABRM was sitting in the Victoria Coach. Other eminent Raigars who accompanied were: Gotam Singh Sakkarwal, swagat adhyaksh, Asha Ram Sevlia, Swami Gian Swaroopanand Maharaj and Swami Atma Ram 'Lakshya'. Throughout the procession, Raigars were shouting slogans in the praise of Mahasabha and extending warm welcome to delegates attending the sammelan from far and near.

After an interval of a few hours, the procession reached Ghat Gate, where it was converted into a vishal meeting. On the first day April 12, 1946, a warm welcome was accorded to Kanhaiya Lal Ratawal. On this occasion Gotam Singh Sakkarwal , swagat adhyaksh, reading out from his prepared text, asserted the need of education amongst the Raigars for all-round development of the community. In addition to all this, he emphasised for eradication of social evils such as use of alcohol, dowry, child marriage[31], etc. Chaudhary Asha Ram presented the account of various activities carried out by Mahasabha during the last year. Swami Gian Swaroop Maharaj, Swami Atma Ram 'Lakshya' and Kanwar Sen Maurya showed keen interest in the programme of social reform, especially those concerned with eradication of social evils and prohibition.

On April 13, 1946 the Raigar flag was unfurled by Swami Gian Swaroop Maharaj which was followed by performance of 'havan'. Soon after this, a meeting of the subject committee was held. The members discussed several proposals in the meeting. As narrated in the book written by Chiranji Lal and Rajendra Prasad, in all, 11 proposals[32] were recommended by the subject committee for approval in the open session. The afternoon open session on the same day, was held under the presidentship of Kanhaiya Lal Ratawal, where social, economic and educational issues were discussed in details. The proposals approved and recommended by the subject committee were discussed in the open session. After long discussions, the proposals were accepted in toto. Some eminent caste fellows, namely, Swami Gian Swaroop Maharaj, Swami Atma Ram 'Lakshya', Naval Prabhakar, Kanwar Sen Maurya, Surya Mal Maurya, Chhoga Lal Kanwaria, Ghisu Lal Siwania, Jai Chand Mohil, Ram Swaroop Jajoria, Mohan Lal Patel, Chaudhary Giarsha Ram Chandolia, Mohan Lal Patel and many more participated actively in the discourse.

In his presidential address Kanhaiya Lal Ratawal stressed the need to ban alcohol, death feast and other social evils. He also bitterly criticised and condemned the atrocities perpetrated by upper caste Hindus on the Raigar community.

On the third and last day, on April 14, 1946, a special programme of 'bhajno-updesh'[33] was arranged in which the main persons who sang religious songs were Pandit Chhedi Ram, Kanwar Sen Maurya and Pandit Ghisu Lal Siwania. Through religious songs and sermons they persuaded the community to get rid of social evils. It is important to note that in the Jaipur sammelan, under the leadership of Kanhaiya Lal Ratawal, the Raigar Mahasabha, which was founded by Swami Atma Ram 'Lakshya' in 1944, took a memorable decision and declared to present a Gold Medal[34] (weighing one tola – nearly 10 gm) to the leading reformer Swami Atma Ram 'Lakshya'.

On April 14, 1946, a new executive committee of 31 members came into existence with Kanhaiya Lal Ratawal as Pradhan, Ghisu Lal Siwania as up-pradhan, Naval Prabhakar as pradhan mantri, Asha Ram Sevlia as mantri, Ghanshyam Singh Sevlia as up-mantri, Kanwar Sen Maurya as prachar mantri, Ram Swaroop as Treasury Officer and Prabhu Dayal Ratawal as swayam sewak mantri.[35] Details about the annual meetings of ABRM held since 1944 onwards are presented in Table 5.1.

The formation of the executive committee of ABRM provides the landmark in the development of the Raigar movement.

In the light of the resolutions passed in Jaipur sammelan on April 13, 1946, we will now discuss some general major points. It shows that there were eight major points to focus. First, a number of resolutions concerned reformatory measures such as the ban on death feast, abolition of gift given to drum beaters and Jalani on the occasion of marriage, ban on drinking water from a pipe (nalia) at

Table 5.1

Annual Meetings (sammelans) of Akhil Bharatiya Raigar Mahasabha Held since 1944

Name of the place and state	*Year*	*Date*	*Duration*	*Presided by*	*Inaugurated by*	*Remarks*
Dausa, Jaipur, Rajputana	1944	November 1, 2, 3	3 days	Chand Karan Shah	Nathuram Atal	Raigar flag was unfurled by Swami Gian Swaroop Maharaj
Jaipur, Rajputana	1946	April 12, 13, 14	3 days	Chaudhary Kanhaiya Lal Ratawal	Swami Atma Ram Lakshya'	Raigar flag was unfurled by Swami Atma Ram 'Lakshya'
Pushkar, Ajmer, Rajasthan	1964	November 18, 19	2 days	Naval Prabhakar	-	-
Jaipur, Rajasthan	1984	October 6, 7	2 days	Chhoga Lal Kanwaria former Health Minister, Rajasthan	-	Smt Indira Gandhi, the then Prime Minister of India, came from Delhi particularly for this Sammelan and addressed on October 7. Chief Guest: Shiv Charan Mathur Chief Minister, Rajasthan
Vigyan Bhawan, New Delhi	1986	September 27	1 day	Dharm Dass Shastri	His Excellency Gyani Jail Singh, the then President of India	This was the special sammelan in which dedicated Raigar social workers were honoured. The total expenditure occurred on this occasion was borne by Gian Chand Ratawal s/o Chaudhary Kanhaiya Lal Ratawal of Delhi
Jaipur, Rajasthan	2000	October 30	1 day	P.N. Rachhoya	-	-

Source: 1. Chandanmal Naval, *Raigar Jati-ka-Itihas*, Jodhpur, Shyam Printing Press, 1986, pp. 139-146.
2. Roop Chand Jalutharia, *Raigar Jati-ka-Itihas*, Jaipur, Capital Printers, 2001, p. 80.

water huts (piao) meant for Raigars and other untouchables particularly. Second, the ABRM directed that at the time of marriage (boy), the Raigar family should donate Rs 5 to 'Education Fund' for spreading the education programme among Raigars. Also accepted education as the key, for all-round development of the community. Third, they again reiterated and supported the three resolutions passed previously at Dausa sammelan held in 1944. Fourth, ABRM in its 1946 Jaipur sammelan passed a resolution urging Raigars to detain the Barat for not more than 3 days. Fifth, in Rajputana particularly, the services of untouchable castes such as Meghwals, Chamars, Bhambhis, Raigars, etc., were utilised forceably as Begar (forced labour) by Thakurs, Jagirdars, Jamindars and others. In Jaipur sammelan, ABRM criticised it bitterly and passed a resolution urging the Thakurs, Jagirdars and Jamindars to stop it immediately. ABRM also encouraged caste fellows to discard this practice and face the consequences boldly. Sixth, the resolution strongly criticised and condemned the atrocities perpetrated by the upper caste Hindus in rural areas, particularly at Raisar, Parbatsar, Markeda, Karana and also appealed to the Government of Jodhpur, Ajmer, Udaipur and Jaipur, as stipulated in the Jaipur sammelan to stop the repetition of such incidents in future. Seventh, ABRM also opposed the division of the country on Hindu-Muslim basis and strongly supported unified India. Lastly, ABRM also supported Col. Tod and other historians' findings regarding the origin of Raigars and claimed that their origin was from 'suryavanshi rajputs'.

As has been stated earlier, in 1944, a major socio-religious change came with the passing of the resolutions in Dausa Raigar Mahasabha. ABRM introduced a number of reforms which annoyed the upper caste sections in villages in rural areas which inhabited most of the Raigars who boycotted traditional work. For instance, in Karana[36], a village in the then Alwar state, the Raigars refused to remove the dead animals and skin them, also refused for the Begar (forced labour). These activities of Raigars were not liked by the upper caste Hindus. Therefore, they imposed several socio-economic restrictions on Raigars for the oppression of their reform movement:

1. The caste Hindu villagers would not sell goods, vegetables and other essential commodities to these people.
2. No Raigar would be paid money as loan at the time of emergency.

3. Their (Raigars) animals would not be allowed to graze in the fields of upper caste people.

When this news reached Jaipur and Delhi, a delegation was sent from Delhi. The delegation visited the villages. Some attempts were made by the members of the delegation to settle the issue amicably but they all proved futile. ABRM in Rajasthan became the strength of Raigars and they backed the Raigars in their agitation. Another high powered delegation from Delhi was sent in 1946 under the leadership of Chaudhary Kanhaiya Lal Ratawal,[37] Kanwar Sen Maurya and Gotam Singh Sakkarwar, which met the then Prime Minister of Alwar state[38] and submitted a memorandum appealing to arrest the accused. Accordingly, the state government immediately ordered to send a group of 40-50 officials to the village to make an on-the-spot enquiry and verify the facts. The Raigars were, however, supported by the government officials at the local level, especially in filing a court case against the 27 upper caste[39] persons.

It is interesting to note here that soon after this, the initiative for settlement came from Rajput leaders of the village. Rajputs of the village held a meeting and took the initiative to reach an, out of court, amicable settlement of the issue with Raigars. Rajputs, who were exploiting and harassing the poor Raigars appealed to Raigars for compromise. They authorised Bhanwar Singh, son of Arjun Singh, and Pratap Singh, son of Phool Singh, for this purpose. Rajputs assured the Raigars that they would not repeat the same. On August 14, 1946, on this assurance given by the Rajputs, a compromise deed was signed between the Raigars and Rajputs.[40] We get an idea from the accounts of Chiranji Lal Bakolia and Rajendra Prasad Gadegaonlia how the Rajputs at local level compromised with Raigars,[41] with the growth of Raigar movements:

> *Dinak 14.8.1946 koo gaon karana key kul thakran ki aur sey Bhanwar Singh putra Phool Singh ney jimveydari detey huye tahrir likh di. Joo ki niman prakar sey hai:*
>
> *Ham ki Bhanwar Singh suputra ArjunSingh, Sardar Singh suputra Dalel Singh, Govind Singh suputra Sagar Singh, Bhenru Singh suputra Shri Phool Singh, Pratap Singh putra Phool Singh, Maktul Singh putra Bhanwar Sigh, Baney Singh putra Harnam Singh Thakur Karana, thana gazi key hai, joo ki gram karana, thana gazi mein thakuran va raigran key parasper jhagda chal raha hai. Jhagdey ki soorat yahan tak badh gai hai ki adalat mein mukadmey bazi hoo*

gai. Aab iyenda jhada samapat kartey hai aur shanti kayam rakney ki garaj sey aapas mey nimna likhit rooyatey karar pai:

1. Raigran koo thakran murda maveshyan uthaney key liye majboor nahi kar sakeygey.
2. Raigran sey beggar nahi lee jayegi.
3. Raigran sey koi kam liya jayega too uska bajib muaabza diya jayega. Jabardasti kaam nahi karaya jayega.
4. Maveyshiyan charaney key raigran koo vahi hak kayam hoogey joo auroo ko gaon mein hai.
5. Darkhataan aabadi thakran va raigran vakat jaroorat kateygey koi bech nahi sakeygey.
6. Basunda jamin ko kasta mein koi rookawat nahi dali jayegi. Jin raigran majkuran ney marusiyat hasil nahi ki vah bajariye patta kasta ker sakeygey.
7. Raigaran ki murda maveshi koo vahi shaksa uthaiga joo ki gaun ki shesh murda maveshi uthaiga. Yadi koi murda maveshi thakran key intajam sey raigran key yahan padi rahi too uski kanooni jimmeydari thakran per hoogi.

Aangutha nishani:	Gavah:
1. Bhanwar Singh	1. Ram Lal suputra Mangey Lal Mahajan
2. Pratap Singh	2. Raghunath Singh Thakur Badigau
3. Bhairon Singh	va Munshi Kalyan Brahman thana gazi
4. Maktul Singh	
5. Govind Singh	
6. Baney Singh	
7. Samar Singh	

Chaksu and Hindu-Muslim Incident, 1947

From 1940 onwards the question of temple entry agitation never became a social and political issue that involved not only the Raigars, but also Bairwa and other untouchables as well. The Raigar community never called upon the then government to solve this issue. The question that still begs for an answer is: Why did Raigars not launch temple entry agitation in the state? Regarding the non-initiation of temple entry agitation of Raigar untouchables, Roop Chand Jalutharia,[42] who had been associated with Raigar movement from his early age, states:

> The untouchable communities including the Raigars were allowed to enter the temple of Baba Ram Dev. Baba Ram Dev was a great social reformer and saint of 14th century in Rajasthan. The social and religious philosophy of Baba Ram Dev had a great influence on the life of untouchable communities. Baba Ram Dev was a Tanwar Rajput, though much of his works were dedicated to upliftment of downtrodden and untouchable communities. The untouchable communities expressed their gratitude to the great social reformer for freeing them from Hindu tyranny and bondage. The social and religious aspects of Baba Ram Dev's thoughts perhaps had greater effect on untouchables. The doors of Baba Ram Dev temple at Runiche in Jaisalmer district were thrown open for the lower untouchable castes centuries ago.
>
> The teachings of Baba Ram Dev had a deep impact on the social and religious life of the untouchable castes, who indeed acknowledged Baba as their massiha/saviour and inspirer. Many untouchables' argument regarding the removal of untouchability can be traced to Baba Ram Dev. The example of Baba Ram Dev is also an inspiration for many untouchables and non-Brahmins alike. He was the first non-Brahmin saint to preach that all human beings are the creatures of God and equal in all respects. The social reform movement which Baba Ram Dev initiated had an impact on the depressed communities, even today and therefore, the Raigars and Bairwas as well, did not feel the necessity of agitation for their entry in caste Hindu temples.

In this way Jalutharia tried to rationally analyse the theory of not to initiate temple entry movements. In addition, Jalutharia has narrated two such noteworthy instances[43] which also occurred in Chaksu and Jaipur involving Raigars' participation.

It was after the partition of the country in 1947 that, a Pathan and a few Muslims of Chaksu town threatened the Brahmin priest to stop the worship at Shiv temple adjoining the mosque. The emergence of such a tense situation caused by a few Muslims was particularly a crucial development in the Hindu community. The new situation which was the product of communal tension is a single important example of the untouchables' entry in the caste Hindus temples.

Soon after the Muslims' threat a few higher caste Hindus approached the untouchables, particularly Raigars, requesting that this issue should be taken up by them and the Muslims be persuaded to allow the priest to worship at Shiv temple again. Raigars, no doubt, live in large number in Chaksu.

Significantly, the untouchables had found that socio-economic and religious disabilities on untouchables and especially on Raigars in the rural areas of Chaksu continued to increase and by 1947, the atrocities of high caste Hindus on untouchables in rural areas was increased. The impact of the atrocities, denial of admission in schools, temples, etc., to untouchables was significant as Jalutharia observes; with such bitter experiences, a meeting was held by local Raigars at Chaksu and they refused to take up the issue with Muslims. An examination of the incident further revealed that Jalutharia who had been working for reform of his community, came to Chaksu and stayed at his relative's residence. Here he came to know about the incidence.

Just as a social activist as in Jaipur, Jalutharia took the initiative in holding again a meeting attended by a large gathering for resolving the dispute between caste Hindus and Muslims. He also took concrete measures for the removal of social disabilities related to untouchables.

Another significant feature of Jalutharia's strategy was to hold a meeting of untouchables. The unanimous decision taken in the meeting, which was virtually a tough decision and included the specific call meant for caste Hindus to open the doors of local temples and remove the social disabilities for the untouchable communities. To a great surprise, the local caste Hindu-leaders accepted their call. They agreed to allow the untouchables to enter in their community temples with the condition that they (untouchables) would come in a neat and clean dress. As regards the acceptance of untouchables' demand, it was due to caste Hindus being under stress of hard times in their own native place, that Jalutharia had been able to capitalise on the situation. It could be interpreted to mean that untouchables were trying to take maximum mileage of the caste Hindus's discomfiture over Muslim threat.

Jalutharia a social activist from Jaipur with his own men approached Pathan for allowing the priest who was stopped to perform 'puja' to restart the same. Pathan and other Muslims not only agreed to allow priest without any resistance or hindrance but also helped them in removing the misunderstanding between Hindus and Muslims. Jalutharia remarked on the unusual solidarity evinced by the untouchables, which he attributed to their common suffering and to the fact that untouchables were tortured by caste Hindus individually and collectively.

Another important thing that could have been made possible for the entry into the temples by the untouchables was done by the local Thakur of Jaipur Thikana. A few years later in 1948, the private temples of Jhalai Thakur situated in Gangori Bazar near Chhoti Chaupar, Jaipur were opened for untouchable communities, as if all opportunity was given to the untouchables to think of equality. The efforts made by the Thakur were instrumental in creating a climate of friendly atmosphere and a sense of reform within upper caste society. Therefore, the initiative taken by the Thakur Sahib was catalytic in giving impetus to the reforms movement amongst the Hindus.[44]

Salient Features of ABRM Constitution

Though the Raigar's Mahasabha had a written constitution[45] which prescribed objectives, functions, organisational set-up, procedures, etc., yet the leaders hardly took it seriously. Except a few, most of the Raigars did not even know the specific aim of the Mahasabha as mentioned in the constitution. To them, it was an organisation for the development of the Raigars.

According to the constitution, the organisation was divided into district, tehsil, city and village unit with elected executive committees having president, vice-president and secretary at each level. State units were formed in Rajasthan, Punjab, Haryana, Gujarat, Madhya Pradesh, Maharashtra and Delhi. However, they hardly met even once a year except on occasions when Mahasabha's conferences were held. Except a few district leaders who enjoyed state level positions, none cared to enrol members or to send reports of the units regarding their activities to the state office. A regular office with well maintained records was run only by the Jaipur district. Even at the state level, office records were not kept properly.

Year-wise detailed figures of membership are not available for all the years. This only indicates that a larger number of Raigars were not interested in getting themselves enrolled as members of the Mahasabha. In order to know more about the nature of membership, the author collected the information through conversation with social and political leaders and, the following points emerged:[46]

1. Membership of the Mahasabha was not constant, both in terms of members and individuals. Sometimes, it enrolled more than thousand members and at other times, it hardly registered hundred members. Similarly, some individuals usually did not continue their membership from year to year. This was so, because the Raigars took their membership very casually. They paid membership fee only when approached by a leader.
2. Decision making and executive powers of the Mahasabha were highly concentrated in the president and secretary – the core positions. These omnipotent offices had so far been occupied by eight male leaders. For the first fifty-seven years, the offices were held by four leaders – Bhola Ram Tongaria (1944-1946), Kanhaiya Lal Ratawal (1946-1964), Naval Prabhakar (1964-1984) and Dharm Das Shastri (1984-2001). The other office bearers of the Mahasabha at state level were the president, vice-president, maha mantri, organising mantri, treasurer, auditors and legal advisor. These chairs were occupied by several Raigars at a time.
3. An analysis of various resolutions passed by the ABRM at its annual meetings shows that there were many issues which were to be highlighted. First, a number of resolutions concerned reformative measures such as the abolition of dowry, ban on death feast, strong plea for eradication of the use of liquor and child marriage. The ABRM directed that Raigars should promote the widow remarriage. Second, there was a concern about the untouchability, particularly in the rural areas, and they encouraged the anti-untouchability movement. Third, they supported issues that the regional sabhas were interested in, for instance, the problem of inadequate educational facilities and job opportunities for scheduled castes which was a matter of concern to many scheduled castes (including Raigars) in different part of the state. In Rajasthan, this issue gained a regional focus and ABRM in its conference held at Jaipur in the year 1984 passed a resolution urging the government to provide more and more facilities to scheduled castes candidates. Fourth, the resolution urged the caste fellows to donate money for the construction of Dharmshala and caste 'sabha bhavan' and also appealed to the government to provide a piece of land at nominal rate. Finally, ABRM strongly pleaded for the girls' education among the Raigar caste.

4. From 1944 onwards the ABRM remained very active. On November 20, 1946, Atma Ram 'Lakshya' breathed his last. Since then ABRM remained inactive for some period. However, ABRM has since then been energised, gaining wide recognition and has emerged as the soul of Raigars.

Notes

1. For detailed discussion of Raigar Movement that stress the role of both Dharmgurus and ABRM (social organisation) in the pre- and post-independence period and socio-religious consequences of the movement, see, in particular, Chandanmal Naval, *Raigar Jati ka Itihas*, Jodhpur, Shyam Printing Press, 1986, and Roop Chand Jalutharia, *Raigar Jati ka Itihas*, Jaipur, Capital Printers, 2001. Also see, "Swami Sri Atmaramji Lakshya ki Antim Abhilasha" in *Raigar Sudhar*, Fatehabad (Haryana), August 2000, No. 13, pp. 1-4.
2. Chandanmal Naval, Ibid., p. 139.
3. Ibid.
4. *Raigar Sudhar*, op. cit., p. 139.
5. Chandanmal Naval, op. cit., p. 140.
6. *Raigar Sudhar*, op. cit., p. 2.
7. Ibid., pp. 2-3.
8. Kanwar Sen Maurya, *Do Shabad*, p. 5.
9. Ibid., p. 15.
10. *Raigar Sudhar*, op. cit., p. 2.
11. Ibid.
12. Kanwar Sen Maurya, op. cit.
13. *Gar Kshtriyaupadesh Gian* by Chandanmal Maurya. Beawar, Gar Hitaishi Sahitya Mandal, Shri Saligram Mandir, 1942.
14. Ibid., pp. 14-18.
15. Bhagat Bhagirath, *Jati Beejak Mool Prakash: Raigar Samaj*. Ajmer, published by Ramnath Maharaj.
16. Ibid., pp. 14-18.
17. Ibid., p. 141.
18. Ibid.
19. Ibid.
20. Ibid., p. 140.

21. Suryamal Maurya, "Swasthik Kesaria Dhawaj: Ek Mahatavpooran Prateek", in *Smarika: Dasak Samaroh,* May 30-31, 1993 (page number not mentioned).
22. Kanwar Sen Maurya, op. cit.
23. Ibid., p. 17.
24. Chandanmal Naval, op. cit., p. 141. Also see, *Raigar Sudhar,* op. cit., p. 3.
25. Roop Chand Jalutharia, op. cit., p. 65. Also see, *Raigar Sudhar,* op. cit., p. 3.
26. Ibid., p. 65. Also see, Chandanmal Naval, op. cit., p. 141.
27. Bakolia, Chiranjilal and Gandegaonlia, Rajendra Prasad on *Raigar Kaun aur Kya?* New Delhi, Asian Printers, 1964, pp. 112-117.
28. Ibid., p. 100.
29. Ibid.
30. Ibid.
31. Ibid., pp. 102-103.
32. Ibid., pp. 106-107.
33. Ibid., p. 107.
34. Ibid., p. 108.
35. Ibid.
36. Ibid., p. 109.
37. Ibid., p. 112.
38. Ibid., p. 110.
39. Ibid.
40. Ibid.
41. Ibid., p. 110-112.
42. Conversation with Roop Chand Jalutharia, Jaipur, February 24, 2002.
43. Ibid.
44. Ibid.
45. *Akhil Bharatiya Raigar Mahasabha, Vidhan 1965,* circulated by Prachar Mantri of the Akhil Bharatiya Raigar Mahasabha, Maurya Bhawan, Beawar.
46. Conversation with prominent Raigar social activists and workers.

6

Participation of Raigars in National Movement

It is necessary at this stage to mention about the social and political awakening of the untouchables from 1938 to 1947 in order to realise the contribution made by the scheduled castes in the freedom struggle or 'the participation of the grassroots – so-called untouchables in Northern India.

It was not until the early twentieth century that the Congress movement took root in the then princely states of Rajputana, though some of the educated and nationalists had got momentum through 'swadeshi' movement and by introduction of the activities of the press. In Ajmer, the first issue of the *Rajasthan Times*, an English weekly, was published on Thursday, August 8, 1885.[1] Along with these activities the 'swadeshi' movement was also endeavouring to awaken the masses in the last quarter of the 19th century. Swami Dayanand Saraswati was the first social worker, who had long before, stressed on assumption of swadeshi.[2] Rajputana became politicised only after 1938. Praja Mandal – a political organisation – was formed with branches practically in all princely states.

In the twentieth century the involvement of Raigars in the national movement was nil. Those who were agitating, opposing the British rule and demanding the freedom, were the Brahmins and other higher castes and that they neglected the issue of caste discrimination.

The value of 'satyagraha' as political weapon invented by Gandhi, became an important instrument in bringing the untouchable castes into the main stream of the national movement. At that time the upper caste people were compelled to involve the lower caste people.

We may now consider the involvement or participation of Raigars of different regions over a period of one decade in Rajasthan.

In Rajasthan

When the national movement was going on in Rajputana, the situation took a new turn because of the involvement of the untouchable castes/communities. The causes of their involvement in national movement and its allied activities, were an attempt of Congress to inculcate the social and political consciousness among the untouchables and to remove the social evils and vices and to bring the socio-cultural changes. In this context, the untouchables in general and Raigars in particular involved themselves in the national movement and participated in various agitations, demonstrations and 'dharnas'. All this created a social and political consciousness amongst untouchables.[3]

In the year 1920-1921, Gandhiji announced to launch an agitation for social boycott of foreign clothes, goods, etc. A number of public meetings were organised. Simultaneously, social boycott agitation was also started in various regions of Rajputana in the same year (1920-1921). A number of Congress workers started an agitation persuading people to boycott foreign goods. Lala Ram Jalutharia, Mahadevanuwal, Bheru Bax Jaginia, Raghunath Jalutharia, Dhanna Karadia (all residents of Jaipur) and Chetan Kabadi (Barmer) actively participated in the agitation, demonstration and dharna.[4] The state adopted a policy of repression and a number of persons were arrested which also included all the Raigar agitators[5] (as mentioned above). In this context, Raigar agitators were beaten mercilessly, harassed and tortured by the police.[6] A large number of agitators including the Raigars gathered in the streets and burnt the foreign clothes, goods, etc., in support of 'swadeshi aandolan'.[7] The agitators staged a dharna before the liquor shops which resulted in closing of the shops.[8] Police lathi-charged on the agitators. This led to clashes between police and agitators. The agitators were taken into custody and left in the forest.[9]

Throughout Rajputana some Raigar agitators which included Surya Mal Maurya, Hira Lal Panwar, Manu Ram Badaria and Jai Chand Mohil were arrested by the police and were sentenced to six months rigorous imprisonment.[10] Thus, when the national movement and various political activities were going on in the state from 1920-1921 onwards, the untouchables participated under the leadership of nationalist organisations.[11]

In the year 1934, political atmosphere in Mewar was very much tense. The people were demanding right to speech, liberty and to form an association[12] but state administration was not prepared to accede to their demands.[13] As such in the year 1937-1938, a 'satyagraha' movement was launched under the dynamic leadership of Manikya Lal Verma.[14] Manikya Lal Verma and his associates established Mewar Praja Mandal in April 1938.[15] Balwant Singh Mehta and Bhura Lal Baya were elected President and Vice-President respectively.[16] Verma was elected 'mahamantri' of the Mandal.[17]

Jai Chand Mohil was born in the year 1916, at Chhoti Sadari in Chittorgarh district.[18] His father's name was Dhanraj Mohil. Jai Chand Mohil received his early education at Chhoti Sadari and Delhi. He passed Prabhakar in Hindi and also High School examination. He was married to two ladies,[19] first in the year 1927 with Subhra Devi and again in the year 1947 with Tanku Devi. During the national movement he came in contact with 'satyagrahis' and freedom fighters. They made real impression on this young untouchable Raigar boy. Thus in 1938, his political career as a social worker in the national movement started in Chhoti Sadari, but later he became an active member of Mewar Praja Mandal.[20] Mohil drew inspiration from satyagraha and freedom movement and became an ardent follower of Mahatma Gandhi. In the meeting held in the year 1940 at Chhoti Sadari, Jai Chand Mohil was unanimously elected the President of the Pragana Praja Mandal[21] and in 1942, he took an active part in 'Bharat Chhodo Aandolan' and aroused political a wakening amongst the low untouchable communities.[22]

Another significant feature of Jai Chand's role was that he organised Harijan agitation popularly known as Kathju Kand in Mewar,[23] the then princely state.

From 1938 to 1947, just as a local political leader in Chhoti Sadari, Udaipur, he took an initiative in holding meetings, agitations, protests and dharnas against the government. He also took active part in the freedom movement. Because of such an active involvement, he was arrested by the police and lodged into jail, where he remained for about seven months.[24]

He was mainly responsible for creating a national consciousness amongst the untouchables in the region. From 1942 onward due to the emergence of powerful leader like Jai Chand Mohil some graceful events took place. His socio-political activities were vehemently opposed by the Jagirdars, Jamindars and upper caste Hindus, who were seen as exploiters of the untouchables. A bitter political rivalry developed between Jai Chand Mohil and the Jagirdars, Jamindars and others, which resulted in beating and torturing mercilessly of Mohil.[25] Not only beaten and tortured but hot iron rods were pierced in both his eyes[26]. In this way, they tried to destroy his eyesight forever. What is particularly noteworthy about Mohil's case was that, looking to his political stature, Thakkar Bapa and Manakya Lal Verma took him to Delhi for medical treatment.[27] Thus, Mohil's eyes were saved. This highlighted the contribution made by Mohil to national movement.[28]

With such rich experience and background Mohil became President of Dalit Jatiya Sangh, Udaipur region and later Chittorgarh also.[29] He was the Mantri of Congress Committee at Chhoti Sadri and member of Rajasthan Pradesh Congress committee.[30]

In the first General Election held in the year 1952, he was elected MLA from Chhoti Sadari, Kapasan, Chittorgarh[31] on a Congress ticket. Similarly, in second General Election held in the year 1957, he was again elected as a Congress candidate from reserved constituency of Kapasan, Chittorgarh.[32]

Lastly, it is important to note that after the independence, government declared him a freedom fighter and honoured with a Tamra Patra.[33]

Not only did some Raigars such as Jai Chand Mohil take part in national movement and Satyagraha but there were some other Raigars as well, who advocated participation in the national movement. Another case in point is Surya Mal Maurya (1928-1947), a native of Beawar, in Ajmer district.[34] During the national movement, he came in contact with freedom fighters. They made a real impression on this young boy. Thus, in 1928 his political life started with his association with the Congress movement in the country.[35] He played an important role in 1930 Salt Agitation against the British government and supported agitators at Ajmer.[36]

While the historical meeting held on August 7-9, 1942 regarding the Quit India Movement of the Congress was going on at Bombay, in which thousands of Congress leaders, members and workers attended, the government reacted in varied ways to such agitation.[37] The government arrested a large number of Congress workers throughout the country and they were put behind the bars and this marked the beginning of agitations throughout the country. On August 10, 1942, the students of Government College, Ajmer declared strike on the campus against the arrest.[38] On this occasion Bhanwar Lal Arya a leading Congress leader proclaimed agitation for immediate release of the workers from the jails. Maurya supported Bhanwar Lal Arya's agitation at Ajmer and procession was taken out which passed through the main bazar. Slogans were raised against the British. Seven persons were arrested but Maurya escaped the police arrest.[39] Maurya wanted to continue this agitation and for this purpose a secret meeting of selected agitators was summoned at the graveyard but except Seth Mathuram Khandelwai and Maurya himself, no other person turned up. [40] Even then Maurya was not disheartened.

Over a period of time, especially after Bhanwar Lal Arya's arrest, Maurya had emerged as the one who had taken up leadership position of agitation. According to Naval, to divert the attention of the police, Maurya floated a news amongst the natives of Ajmer that students of Government College, Ajmer had gone on strike again.[41] The police immediately rushed to the campus. During this period, the agitators protested against the government's decision of keeping the workers in the jail and also took a procession to the market shouting slogans. It may be noted that Maurya along with nearly 13 agitating members including Paras Ram Bakolia were arrested by the police. When they were produced in the court, the magistrate sentenced them to six months of rigorous imprisonment and sent them to Central Jail, Ajmer.[42]

In the jail, the agitators or the freedom fighters were compelled to grind grams and other food grains by grinding mill[43] ('ghati'). Maurya and his colleagues did so for nearly one month, but later on refused to do so. It is pertinent to mention here that Gandhi pressurised the government to stop it and appealed for providing the agitators cotton for spinning thread.[44]

In 1940, Maurya started a Hindi weekly called *Jagrati*,[45] with himself as the Chief Editor. This became the forum of the socio-political workers to propagate its activities and to bring out greater awareness amongst untouchables spread all over Rajputana.

In the year 1947-1948, especially after independence, Hindu-Muslim communal riots had started at Ajmer and Chief Commissioner of Ajmer had constituted a committee to stop the riots and to restore peace.[46] There were several Hindu-Muslim members nominated to the Committee and Maurya was taken from the untouchable communities.[47]

After independence, Maurya became the President of Raigar Mahasabha, Rajasthan and Mantri of Raghuvansh Hitkarani Sabha.[48] He was also a member of the committee for abolition of Jamindari system in the State.[49] He was the Chairman of the Harijan Welfare Board,[50] Hindaun Kanya Shiksha Vidyalaya and STC School, Hindaun.[51] He was the Chairman of Rajasthan Charm Kala Sangh[52] and was member of Rajasthan Khadi Gramoudyog Board.[53] Lastly, he became the member of Ajmer State Legislative Assembly.[54]

Naval observes that several untouchables including Raigars had been inspired by the freedom fighters, particularly for promotion of national movement. One such figure was Bhura Lal Aaloria (also known as Bhagat) a resident of Ram Nagar Colony, Sanganer, district Jaipur.[55] Bhura Lal was an active member after he had joined the Praja Mandal[56] in 1939. In the following years, Bhura Lal and other untouchables, notably Har Lal Singh Balai and Jivan Singh Dhanka took part in the protests and agitations.[57] Processions were taken out through the main bazar. Slogans were raised. During this period, Bhura Lal, Jiwan Singh Dhanka, Har Lal Singh Balai along with others were arrested and sent to Jaipur central jail for 9 days only.[58]

After 1947, Bhura Lal remained in the Congress party and became the member of the District Congress Committee, Jaipur.[59] In 1950 he was the member of Gram Panchayat, Sanganer Jaipur.[60] In the year 1939 he was instrumental in establishing the 'Prachar Raigar Mahasabha' and became its Chairman.[61] The main aim of this organisation was to promote education amongst the untouchable Raigars, with a particular emphasis on girls' education. He was also instrumental in establishing a large number of untouchable colonies, particularly at Lakhesara, Baddeviri, Kundanpura and Ramnagar.[62] In the year 1944, when the first convention of All India Raigar Mahasabha was held at Dausa, Bhura Lal was the member of the management committee.

As seen in the political sphere in Mewar, Jaipur as well as in Ajmer political awakening amongst the untouchable youths was radicalised after 1937.

Another notable freedom fighter Paras Ram Bakolia from Raigar Community was born in the year 1915 at Sindh Hyderabad (now in Pakistan).[63] His father's name was Ganga Ram. He passed his matriculation examination from Sindh, and was also well-versed in Sindhi and Gujarati.[64] In 1942, he took part in 'Quit India Movement' and was sent to jail for six months rigorous imprisonment.[65]

Over a period of time, especially after the partition, he came to Ajmer and settled down here permanently. In 1952, he became the member of Ajmer Legislative Assembly[66] and in 1967-1972 he was also elected to the Rajasthan Assembly.[67] Up to 1956, he was the Pradhan of Harijan Refugees, Raigar Panchayat and Ajmer Dalit Warg Sangh.[68] From 1947-1966, he was an active member of Rajasthan Pradesh Congress Committee.[69] Similarly, from 1954-1956, he was the editor of weekly magazine called 'Harijan',[70] In 1967, he left the Congress party and joined another party.[71]

This could be viewed as one of the routes that led to the political awakening and became popular amongst the Raigars. Thus, a stage for Raigars led socio-religious and political movement had already been prepared in the course of 'satyagraha' and national movement.

Another notable Gandhian follower and freedom fighter was Mool Chand Maurya from Raigar caste, born in 1919 at Sikar. His father's name was Dhana Ram Maurya. Mool Chand Maurya passed Sudhakar examination in Hindi literature.

Like Jodhpur State, when the suppression of the political activities was openly being crushed in the Jaipur State in the year 1937, the nationalists organised themselves under an institution called Jaipur Praja Mandal. The primary objective of the Praja Mandal was "to establish responsible governments, to secure elementary rights of citizenship for the people and to bring about an all-round improvement of the Jaipur State".[72] But, the state adopted the policy of suppression, the result of which was that people were forced to launch a civil disobedience movement. The state, in order to crush the satyagraha movement, imposed a ban on the entry of Seth Jamna Lal Bajaj into the state territory. But Bajaj was prepared to disobey the imposed ban and to launch satyagraha on February 1, 1939.[73] It is believed that about 500 persons were arrested including Seth Bajaj and other executive members of the Praja Mandal.

During the national movement, peasant movements, and Praja Mandal agitation, Maurya came in contact with satyagrahis and freedom fighters. They made real impression on this 19 year old young untouchable fighter Raigar boy. Thus, in the year 1937 his political career as social worker in Praja Mandal movement started in Sikar and he took active part in the peasant movement. In 1939, when Seth Bajaj was arrested, Maurya became an active member of Praja Mandal. He derived inspiration from Bajaj and Gandhi and became an ardent follower of Mahatma Gandhi.

Since then, he took an active part in 'Bharat Chhodo Aandolan' and aroused a socio-political awakening amongst untouchable castes in the rural areas of Sikar.[74] Maurya used to wear Gandhi cap till he died in 2001.

From 1937 to 1945, just as a social activist, he took initiative in holding meetings, agitations and protests against jagirdars, jamindars and upper castes. Because of such an active involvement, in 1945 he was tortured, harassed, humiliated and beaten by jagirdars, jamindars and others mercilessly in the village Nivana in Chomu. He was beaten and tortured not only in village Nivana but also in Prithipura.[75] In this way, they tried to terrorise him.

In the following years Maurya became instrumental in initiating the socio-religious and educational reform movement among the untouchables. The main aim of this initiative was to promote education amongst the untouchable Raigars. Another significant feature of Maurya's role was that he started persuading Raigars to boycott the socio-religious evils and bad habits by means of agitation.

Over a period of time, especially after independence, the progress made by Raigars in Sikar district and its surrounding areas was not considered satisfactory by Maurya, who was dedicated to the welfare work of the Raigars in Sikar. According to him, the main obstacle to the progress was illiteracy among the Raigars. So, in 1960, he established a hostel called Atma Ram Lakshya Hostel,[76] at Ringas town, Sikar district. The main aim behind establishing this hostel was to promote education amongst the poor and needy Raigars of rural areas. In the same year Raigars of Rajasthan formed a Rajasthan level organisation called the Rajasthan Raigar Sudhar Sangh and Maurya became its first President of Rajasthan Raigar Sudhar Sangh.[77] Lastly, in 1986 he was given the title Raigar Bhushan by Giani Jail Singh, the then President of India for his services rendered to Raigar Samaj.

A true Gandhian follower, freedom fighter and social activist, Mool Chand Maurya, 82, breathed his last on April 4, 2001 at Sawai Man Singh Hospital, Jaipur, after prolonged illness.

Nobody would expect that such a low and untouchable caste, which counted small in numbers before the independence, could produce such a few freedom fighters. In fact, a reference was made to them in some ways in Rajasthan. Rajasthani Raigars would feel proud of the fact that their caste could produce four freedom fighters. For instance – Surya Mal Maurya and Hazari Lal Panwar both from Beawar and Ajmer respectively, Jai Chand Mohil from Chhoti Sadri, Chittorgarh and Maya Ram Bathariya from Mohi, Udaipur. They suffered considerably as they took active part in the freedom movement. Even during the freedom movement they were sent to jail for six months rigorous imprisonment by the then government. Looking to their sufferings, it should be mentioned that these Raigars in Rajasthan were declared 'Freedom Fighters' by the government. However, the government not only recognised them as freedom fighters but also honoured them by awarding Tamra Patra (citation) and sanctioned political pension too. Apart from this, the active participation of few more Raigars in the freedom movement continued.

After independence the government declared Khoob Chand Jajoria and Naval Prabhakar (both from Delhi), Beej Raj Ujirpuria, Narain Das Maurya, Kishan Lal Dolia and Chandan Mal Maurya (all from Beawar and Ajmer), Bodu Lal Udriwal (from Srinagar, Ajmer) and Kanwar Lal Jelia (from Kota) as freedom fighters.[78] Besides, Lala Ram Jalutharia, Maha Devananual, Bheru Bax Jajinia, Raghu Nath Jalutharia, Dhanna Karadia (Jaipur) and Chetan Kabadi (Barmer) took active part in national movement and were arrested.[79]

In Delhi

Besides Rajasthan, Raigars of Delhi were also involved in 'Salt Satyagraha', 'Quit India' and 'National Movement'. It was only during this period that they became more active. Those who participated were Naval Prabhakar, Kanwar Sen Maurya, Dr Khoob Chand Jajoria, Chaudhary Padam Singh, Prabhu Dayal Ratawal, Gotam Singh Sakarwal, Asha Ram Sewalia, Shambhu Dayal Gadegaonlia, Khushal Chand Mohanpuria, Daya Ram Jalutharia[80], etc. Table 6.1 below shows the nature of participation in the freedom movement by Raigars:

Table 6.1

Nature of Participation in the Freedom Movement by Raigars

Nature of Participation					
During the Freedom Movement those who remained imprisoned for six months or more, treated as Freedom Fighters and enjoyed due privileges (such as pension and other fringe benefits)			*Those who participated for more than ten years and declared Freedom Fighters and honoured*		
Name of Participant	*Place*	*District/ State*	*Name of the participant*	*Place*	*District/ State*
Surya Mal Maurya	Beawar	Ajmer	Beej Raj Ujirpuria	Beawar	Ajmer
Hazari Lal Panwar (Dholpuria)	Beawar	Ajmer	Narain Das	Beawar	Ajmer
Jai Chand Mohil	Chhoti Sadri	Chittor-garh	Chand Mal Maurya	Beawar	Ajmer
Manu Ram Badaria	Mohi	Udaipur	Bodu Lal Uanriwal	Srinagar	Ajmer
			Kishan Lal Dolia	Ajmer	Ajmer
			Kanwar Lal Jelia	Kota	Kota
			Khoob Chand Jajoria	Delhi	Delhi
			Naval Prabhakar	Delhi	Delhi

Sources: 1. Chandanmal Naval, *Raigar Jati-ka-Itihas*, 1986, p. 77.
2. Chiranji Lal Bakolia and Rajendra Prasad Gadegaonlia, *Raigar Kaun aur Kya*? New Delhi, Asian Printers, 1964.

Notes

1. K.S. Saxena, *Political Movements and Awakening in Rajasthan (1857 to 1947)*, New Delhi, S. Chand and Company, 1971, p. 118.
2. Ibid., p.120.
3. For a discussion on the participation of Raigars in the freedom movement that stress the role of Raigar freedom fighters and socio-political consequences of the freedom movement. See, Chandanmal Naval, *Raigar Jati-ka-Itihas*, Jodhpur, Shyam Printing Press, 1986, pp. 71-72.
4. Ibid.
5. Ibid.
6. Ibid., p. 72.
7. Ibid.
8. Ibid.
9. Ibid.
10. Ibid.
11. Ibid.
12. K.S. Saxena, op. cit., p. 216.
13. Ibid.
14. Ibid.
15. Ibid.
16. B.L. Pangadia, *Rajasthan Mein Swantantra Sangram*, Jaipur, Rajasthan Hindi Granth Academy, 1988, p. 50.
17. Ibid.
18. Chandanmal Naval, op. cit., p. 72.
19. Ibid.
20. Ibid.
21. Ibid.
22. Ibid., pp. 72-73.
23. Ibid., p. 73.
24. Ibid. Also see, B.L. Pangadia, op. cit., p. 52 and 57.
25. Ibid., p. 73.
26. Ibid.
27. Ibid.
28. Ibid.
29. Ibid.
30. Ibid.

31. Ibid., p. 81.
32. Ibid., p. 82.
33. Ibid., p. 73.
34. Ibid.
35. Ibid.
36. Ibid.
37. Ibid.
38. Ibid., p. 74.
39. Ibid.
40. Ibid.
41. Ibid.
42. Ibid.
43. Ibid.
44. Ibid.
45. Ibid., p. 75.
46. Ibid., pp. 74-75.
47. Ibid., p. 75.
48. Ibid.
49. Ibid.
50. Ibid.
51. Ibid.
52. Ibid.
53. Ibid.
54. Ibid.
55. Ibid.
56. Ibid.
57. Ibid.
58. Ibid.
59. Ibid., p. 76.
60. Ibid.
61. Ibid.
62. Ibid.
63. Ibid.
64. Ibid.
65. Ibid.
66. Ibid.
67. Ibid.

68. Ibid.
69. Ibid.
70. Ibid.
71. Ibid.
72. K.S. Saxena, op. cit.
73. Ibid.
74. 'Freedom Fighter Late Mool Chand Maurya', *Raigar Sudhar,* 15-31 July, 2001.
75. Ibid.
76. Ibid.
77. Ibid.
78. Chandanmal Naval, op. cit., p. 71.
79. Ibid.
80. Ibid.

7

Decline of the Raigar Mahasabha

Facts and Factions

Active to Inactive: Growth of Discontentment

Roop Chand Jalutharia (2001) aptly summarises the different reasons for the inactiveness of the Akhil Bharatiya Raigar Mahasabha (ABRM) after the death of Atma Ram 'Lakshya' in the year 1946. Between the years 1947 and 1949, the Mahasabha remained active in terms of the membership and organisational diverse activities, but after that it became inactive. The strength of ABRM decreased day by day because of the following reasons: First, many young, active, sincere and dedicated workers had now become physically weak and old. Second, some of them were running after power, and therefore split occurred within the Mahasabha. Third, Naval Prabhakar, three times Member of Parliament from Delhi and National President of the Mahasabha also did not take active part in the struggle of the Mahasabha against social vices. Fourth, there was the opinion that Mahasabha, (which was responsible for presenting the account of income and expenditure) was not interested in presenting the budget. Fifth, the Pradhan Mantri of the Mahasabha had also resigned and in his place an ad hoc Pradhan Mantri had been appointed to carry out day-to-day functions but he too showed a lukewarm attitude towards the functioning of the Mahasabha. Sixth, the records of the Mahasabha were also not traceable. Seventh, the regular visits or trips of the office bearers of the Mahasabha to Rajasthan for discussion of various issues, were minimised. Lastly, soon after independence of the country, most of the active workers and political leaders had involved themselves in party politics actively. This line of thinking was adopted by the Raigars and their leaders. Hence, the Mahasabha became inactive.[1]

There was a debate amongst the Raigars about the inactiveness of the Mahasabha. A few attempts were made by the Raigars to reactivate the Mahasabha and they were successful in reactivating it. In 1958, a meeting of Raigar social workers and representatives of Mahasabha was held at Kangeti, Madhya Pradesh[2] which appealed to the Raigars to revive the Mahasabha controlled by inactive Raigar leaders, who were exploiting the poor. It is interesting to note that in 1958, the Raigars of Jaipur too appealed to the Mahasabha's President and others to give a new life to the organisation. Thus, we get an idea as to how the reform activities of Mahasabha were relegated to the background, with the growth of political interest as per the version of Roop Chand Jalutharia.

Subsequently, the Mahasabha, under the leadership of Chaudhary Kanhaiya Lal Ratawal decided to convene a big meeting of the workers and representatives at Ghatgate, Jaipur. Sometime in the year 1958, a vishal sammelan was held at Ghatgate, Jaipur, in which more than 100 active workers and representatives participated. The main aim of this meeting was to reactivate the Mahasabha. For this purpose, a reception committee under the chairmanship of Jai Dev Chaudhary along with few a members was also constituted.[3]

With the sincere efforts of the representatives and active workers of Rajasthan, the Mahasabha organised a big meeting on March 27, 1958 at Ganga Mata Mandir at Ghatgate, Jaipur, under the presidentship of Chaudhary Kanhaiya Lal Ratawal. In this sammelan the Mahasabha aimed at several radical points. First, there was the opinion that diverse activities be revived and the programme of social reform be taken up to encourage them further. This line of thinking was adopted by representatives and social activists. Second, many Raigar representatives bitterly criticised and condemned the negative attitude of the leadership. Third, they emphasised the need to strengthen the organisation and demanded early Mahasabha elections. Fourth, the initiative to start branches in the state came from the Raigar leaders of the states and also to build an office for the association. Fifth, they decided that the Mahasabha should start the publication of their own monthly paper. Sixth, to bring harmony and solidarity in the community. Seventh, to bring a major social change to unite both the Jatiya and the Bola communities in Raigar caste was initiated. Eighth, the need to oppose the use of liquor was emphasised and to get the Mahasabha registered under the Company's Act. Ninth, and last to request the state governments for allocation of agriculture land to Raigar caste members.[4]

Beside all these decisions, the subcommittees of the Mahasabha were constituted in the Jaipur sammelan. A committee was also constituted with the aim to review the Mahasabha's constitution. The Mahasabha formed another committee under the leadership of Ghisu Lal Sawansiya to write the history of the community. The notable members were: Jai Chand Mohil, MLA, Roop Chand Jalutharia, Prabhu Dayal Ratawal (all from Rajasthan) and Ram Swaroop Jajoria (from Delhi). On December 28, 1958, the first meeting of the committee was held at the residence of Ram Swaroop Jajoria at Delhi. This meeting led to a series of discussions on the issue.[5] On January 25, 1959 the next meeting was also held at Delhi and that too at Ram Swaroop's residence. During the discussions, there were serious differences of opinion among the members of the committee regarding writing of the history of the community. Thus, when serious differences emerged amongst the members, the meeting of the committee came to an end abruptly.[6]

The foregoing account shows that at the Jaipur convention, the social workers, activists and representatives of Raigar community made constant and sincere efforts to revive the activities of the Mahasabha by taking several important decisions. They extended full support to the Mahasabha in implementing the decisions already taken. They even persuaded the committee members to go ahead, but to no avail, and left the entire community in lurch. There were many factors which contributed to such a situation.

Social workers and representatives intensified their struggle against the inactiveness of the present leadership. They, however, succeeded in pressing the social workers for the early launch of the programmes and to activate it vigorously. Due to external pressure and resentment of the representatives, on August 15, 1964, again, a big meeting of workers, representatives and activists was held at Delhi. Roop Chand Jalutharia, Lala Ram Jalutharia and Jai Chand Mohil from Jaipur participated in it. The meeting discussed reforms to be implemented at length and ways and means for its revival in the state. On September 19-20, 1964, when they met at the annual function of Raigar hostel at Ringas,[7] they were particularly interested in implementing the economic, educational and social programmes of the community and decided to hold the annual meeting of Mahasabha on November 18-19, 1964 at Pushkar, Ajmer. Besides this, Naval Prabhakar was elected the President of the Mahasabha and a Reception Committee was also formed.[8]

Subsequently, on November 18, 1964, under the presidentship of Naval Prabhakar, the third annual convention of the Mahasabha was held at Raigar Mandir, Pushkar, Ajmer, where a large number of members were present. The main objective of the convention was to resolve the dispute between varying factions and to avoid open hostility at the convention. At this convention the internal cleavage in the Mahasabha which was based on a clash of personalities was resolved. This was resented by many members of the Mahasabha. The chief of them being Shiv Narain Sarsunia and his colleagues.[9] He opposed the Mahasabha's policy. Roop Chand Jalutharia also raised before the Mahasabha sammelan meeting, the issue of fund collection for construction of a 'samadhi' in the memory of late Swami Atmaramji Maharaj and everybody supported that Mahasabha should present the entire account immediately.[10] Likewise, Jai Narain Salodia, Sukh Raj Singh Arya and others raised several questions for clarification. There were also questions which were responsible for the upliftment of the community in regard to the inactiveness of the Mahasabha. In fact, the entire atmosphere became tense. There were many reasons which contributed to such an odd situation. It was because of this tense and uproarious scene that the major issues remained unresolved. Some members tried to bring about cordial atmosphere in the working of the Mahasabha. At this convention Devendra Chandolia from Delhi was appointed Pradhan Mantri of Mahasabha and Boduram Kanwaria from Ajmer, Rajasthan, was appointed Treasurer.[11]

After this, the Mahasabha, to some extent, revived its activities and this time with a firm commitment. This development can also be seen in the context of continuing agitation and stress on the Mahasabha. The Mahasabha's activities were restarted in 1964 but they continued for one year only. During this year the main issue before the Mahasabha was the revival of diverse activities for the benefit of Raigars, in the sphere of education and public service based on caste criterion. But still the Raigar masses realised that the main issue remained unresolved. Since the majority opinion was for an annual meeting of the Mahasabha, it was decided that the next annual meeting will be held at Ajmer. It was also generally felt that the Mahasabha had become ineffective because of several factors and that Raigars were being neglected in every sphere of social and public life. Around 1965, the next annual convention to elect the new President and its executive committee was held at Ajmer. In this convention Chhoga Lal Kanwaria was elected President of the Mahasabha and a new executive committee was also formed in 1981; Chhoga Lal Kanwaria, being an important congress leader, was inducted in Shiv Charan Mathur's cabinet. Although in principle Chhoga Lal Kanwaria was President of the Mahasabha but in practice, he did nothing for the Mahasabha. This was again resented by many of its members.

It would be noted that, since 1964, the only notable leader was Chhoga Lal Kanwaria, who was the President of the Mahasabha for a quite long time – say two decades (1964-1984). The Mahasabha had grown into an all-India organisation over a period of nearly forty years and had spearheaded so many agitations and implemented several programmes which came to a halt between 1950 and 1984, due to various reasons.

After an interval of two decades in 1984, the Mahasabha decided to hold the Fourth Annual Convention at Jaipur. It formed a reception committee as well as some other subcommittees. Before the commencement of the annual convention, the leaders toured various places to collect funds for the convention. The annual convention became very popular in which Dharm Das Shastri played an important role in fund collection. An appeal was issued to Raigar caste fellows, in which it was stated that they (Raigars) should contribute as much as possible. It should also be noted that Shrimati Indira Gandhi, the then Prime Minister of India, gave her consent to address the annual convention at Jaipur, mainly due to the efforts of Shastri and other leaders.[12]

Subsequently, Raigar Mahasabha convention was held on October 6, 1984 at Ram Niwas Bagh, Jaipur, under the presidentship of Chhoga Lal Kanwaria. The next day, i.e., on October 7, 1984, Prime Minister Indira Gandhi came to Jaipur and addressed the annual convention at Medical College grounds, Jaipur. At this convention Dharm Das Shastri from Delhi was nominated President of the Mahasabha as it was felt that Shastri had a dynamic personality and would be able to deliver the goods, as he himself was an active social leader and would also uplift the community.[13]

The scenario of the Mahasabha did not change even after Shastri became President of the Mahasabha in 1984. In fact, the Mahasabha which was inactive and ineffective till the time of Chhoga Lal Kanwaria's tenure, still remained the same. This development should also be seen in the context of continuing political change at the national level – particularly after the assassination of Shrimati Indira Gandhi. Shastri, being an important Congress leader, pursued an informal policy of eliminating himself from the active presidentship of the Mahasabha. This was resented by many of its leaders. Thus, the activities of the Mahasabha again came to a halt for one decade. Several attempts were made to pursue Shastri to hold elections but to no avail. It was because of this inactiveness of Shastri that the Mahasabha was put in the hand of Pradhan Mantri of the Mahasabha – Bhagwan Das Khorwal. It is alleged that Bhagwan Das, fearing the domination of other leaders over the Mahasabha, deferred the election for an indefinite period. With the death of Bhagwan Das Khorwal, elections could not take place.

ABRM under Kanhaiya Lal Ratawal

Having seen the dynamics of the movement regarding social and political dimensions, we shall now discuss the changes brought about in respect of social and political aspects of the movement. The major changes had been the growth of indifferent attitude of the ABRM office bearers and members. The main issue before the Raigars after 1946 was the revival of its (ABRM) activities as it was not so active as it ought to have been. The character of ABRM changed with the death of Swami Atma Ram 'Lakshya' in 1946. ABRM had now become inactive. Thus, ABRM which was so active till the time of Atma Ram 'Lakshya's death, had now moved away from its goals. This development should also be seen in the context of continuing rift between Naval Prabhakar and Raigars. He aligned himself with the Congress party. It was also generally felt that ABRM had become ineffective because of serious difference of opinion and that the Raigars were being neglected in every sphere of social life.

This is the story of the genesis, growth and dynamics of ABRM movement over a period of nearly fourteen years. The indifferent attitude of leaders, ineffectiveness of ABRM, individual rivalry and internal cleavage had adversely affected the socio-political dimension of the ABRM movement.

Thus, ABRM which had established its offices in various states all over the country over a period of nearly fourteen years and which had spearheaded so many violent confrontations and agitations, had implemented several programmes which came to a halt after 1946, mainly due to a clash of personalities.

In the beginning of 1958, Raigars had approached the President and Members of the Executive Committee of ABRM pressing them to convene a meeting of the Executive Committee and to constitute a committee to come out with new legislation for all-round development of the community.

As a result of this, on March 27, 1958, a convention of the Raigar workers and activists was held at Ganga Mandir, Ghatgate, Kothi Raigran, Jaipur.[14] The meeting was chaired by Kanhaiya Lal Ratawal. Besides executive members, the meeting was also attended by more than 50 representatives from all over the country. The main objective of the meeting was to revive its activities. At this meeting, representatives and workers reviewed its (ABRM) activities. They criticised ABRM bitterly for ineffectiveness and this was resented by many of its leaders. Issue of election to be held in the ABRM organisation also came up before the representatives and everyone agreed that ABRM should hold the election immediately. The criticism, to a great extent was also an expression of resentment for not presenting the accounts of the income and expenditure since 1946.

It may be noted that in the meeting, several issues and proposals were discussed. After long discussions, the meeting approved 15 resolutions:[15]

1. To pay rich tribute to their departed leaders.
2. To open branches in each state.
3. To review the proposals passed at Dausa and Jaipur annual conventions and expressed their regret over not implementing the proposals so far. Measures to be taken to implement them immediately.
4. To publish the history of Raigar caste.
5. To take initiative to publish its own paper fortnightly or monthly.
6. To send to central office a sum of Rs 5 collected at the time of marriage of a boy under Resolution No. 5 passed earlier at Jaipur.

7. To request the State Governments to allot fertile land to the Raigars.
8. To persuade caste fellows to take the advantages of various government schemes meant for their welfare and betterment.
9. To ban the use of alcohol.
10. To persuade all the community fellows to use the word 'Raigar' only after their names and not to any other word.
11. To prohibit serving of non-vegetarian dishes on occasion of marriages and other festivals.
12. To constitute a committee consisting of 11 members to make necessary amendments in the constitution of the ABRM.
13. To hold election to elect members of the ABRM within one year as per the new constitution.
14. To get ABRM registered as early as possible.
15. To send statement showing the income and expenditure of ABRM to all concerned.

At this meeting Daya Ram Jalutharia, son of Mangal Sen Jalutharia was appointed Pradhan Mantri, because it was felt that Naval Prabhakar as an MP could not spare much of his time for the forthcoming convention, as also he himself was responsible for his inactiveness.

From time to time several attempts had been made to revive the working of the ABRM. Thus, again after a long period of six years, ABRM called for a meeting on August 1, 1964. The meeting was held in Ganga Mandir, Raigarpura, Delhi[16] where most of the executive members were present. The main objective of the meeting was to fix the date for the next annual convention. In this meeting it was approved that the next executive meeting be held on August 15-16, 1964. Besides this it also approved a six-point agenda:[17]

1. To enquire about the account of income and expenditure.
2. To approve the proceedings of the meeting of ABRM.
3. To elect a new President of ABRM.
4. To approve the new constitution of ABRM.
5. To think about the socio-economic development of the caste.
6. To think about establishing the branches of ABRM throughout the country.

Subsequently, on August 16, 1964, an executive meeting was held at Ganga Mandir, Delhi, under the chairmanship of Kanhaiya Lal Ratawal, where 18 members out of 31 were present.[18] Shambhu

Dayal, as already decided presented the details of income and expenditure since 1946 to 1964, which was approved.

Kanhaiya Lal Ratawal, who had been a notable leader amongst the Raigars since 1964 and who had been the President of the ABRM – remaining its leader for 18 long years – declared the holding of the annual election. As a result on August 16, 1964, Bhola Ram Tongaria proposed the name of Naval Prabhakar, MP, for the post of President of ABRM and it was seconded by Kanwar Sen Maurya. Thus, at this meeting Naval Prabhakar was elected unanimously President of ABRM.[19] Similarly, Surya Mal Maurya was elected the Swagata-Adhyaksh for the next annual convention. The meeting also approved November 18-19, 1964 for the next annual convention to be held at Pushkar, Ajmer.

ABRM under Naval Prabhakar

Since 1940 and onward, the need for a powerful central organisation to propagate the philosophy of social reforms and to motivate the Raigar masses became apparent. Therefore, attempts were made by Raigar leaders to organise an all-India level organisation to work out a programme of action for fighting against various kinds of discrimination and deprivation. Thus, in 1944, a small committee headed by Swami Atma Ram 'Lakshya' Swagat-Adhyaksh and Naval Prabhakar as Up-Swagat-Adhyaksh came into existence. The main object of this committee was to form a strong organisational base all over North India to unite the Raigars. Thus, the establishment of ABRM at Dausa Maha Sammelan in 1944 provides the first land-mark picture of the development of the Raigar movement – the first being the agitation led by Swami Atma Ram 'Lakshya' before independence of the country and second, the emergence of a dynamic leader like Naval Prabhakar who gave it an ideology. The first phase of ABRM was associated with leadership of Swami Atma Ram 'Lakshya' and Naval Prabhakar, the well-known leaders of Raigars.

In 1946, the second annual convention of ABRM was held at Jaipur. It was at this meeting that he was elected Pradhan Mantri[20] next to Pradhan in the organisational hierarchy. During this period, the leaders were concerned with four basic issues: to boycott the 'begar' (i.e., forced labour) for higher castes, to abandon the traditional unclean jobs and repairing their old shoes, to ban the use of alcohol and eating the dead animals, to send their children to school, etc. As an elected office bearer of ABRM, he voiced the grievances of Raigars.

As has been stated earlier that a series of violent conflicts occurred in 1944, and thereafter between high castes and low untouchable Raigars. This was a manifestation of deep-rooted jealousy and hatred of upper caste Hindus to the emerging trend of reform initiated by the ABRM. The Raigars were now agitating for the right of entry into the public schools. ABRM intervened in the clashes between high castes and untouchable Raigars, encouraged compromise and pleaded for brotherhood. For instance the Hindus[21] of Dausa in 1944, Hindus of Parbatsar and Jawla in 1945, were angry with (due to) the resolutions passed in Dausa Maha Sammelan in 1944. Similarly in 1947, the upper caste people of Nimbahera, Chittorgarh[22] were angry with stoppage of 'begar' by Raigars. So the upper caste Hindus, in anger, robbed and set fire to the Raigar houses and beat them up mercilessly. The incidence of Raigar high castes conflict continued, which made ABRM to send a delegation under the leadership of Naval Prabhakar to tour the trouble-torne villages and to meet the Thakurs, Jagirdars, Jamindars and Brahmins appealing to them for compromise and protection.

In 1945, ABRM representatives first went to Parbatsar.[23] They had a meeting with Thakurs and Brahmins and appealed to them not to compel Raigars for removal of the dead animals. However, the upper castes did not agree. Even when ABRM's appeal to upper castes were stubbornly rejected by caste Hindus, Prabhakar continued his efforts in this direction.

Next day, the representatives met Jai Narain Vyas[24] – the President of Jodhpur Praja Mandal at Jodhpur. Naval Prabhakar, the leader of ABRM delegation narrated in detail the humiliation, torture and harassment meted out to the Raigars in village Parbatsar. The reply by Vyas indicated about the positive approach of the Praja Mandal. The representatives of ABRM under the leadership of Naval Prabhakar also met the Prime Minister of Jodhpur State at Jodhpur.[25] An application addressed to him was prepared and was submitted to him. It demanded for an enquiry regarding the atrocities committed on the Raigars of village Parbatsar. Thus, an enquiry was instituted. It was because of Prime Minister's intervention that Raigars were made free from upper castes clutches. Similarly, as regards the harassment of Raigars in Dausa, Jaipur State and Nimbahera, Chittorgarh, it was because of the sincere efforts of Naval Prabhakar that an amicable compromise was reached between Raigars and upper-caste Hindus. Thus, they achieved a big success in 1947, under the leadership of Naval Prabhakar.

As an elected Pradhan of ABRM, he voiced the grievances of Raigars. He took a leading part in the agitation in 1944 and thereafter demanded equality of citizenship. It was this agitation in which thousands of Raigars participated. Naval Prabhakar launched a campaign claiming equality of opportunity in education and abolition of all kinds of rituals and civic disabilities. As a result of all this, a third annual convention was held at Pushkar, Ajmer in November 1964, in which he was elected and elevated to the post of Pradhan[26] (Chairman) of ABRM and he remained in chair up to 1984.

The Congress was preparing itself for consolidating its position in 1952 General Election. So far it had gained the support of the dominant Delhi Raigar caste. Local Raigar bosses, therefore, remained in close touch with Congress leaders and tried to persuade them for Congress ticket. For instance, Naval Prabhakar, a leading Raigar leader of Delhi and Pradhan Mantri of ABRM was nominated as party candidate in parliamentary election 1952 from Karol Bagh reserved constituency and was declared elected and had the honour of being the first Raigar MP.[27] He was again elected in 1957. When third general elections were held in 1962, he was again nominated as Congress candidate and was elected to Parliament. Thus, Naval Prabhakar was active as a political leader from 1952 to 1967. He was the first Raigar to have shown political ability. He had more closeness with Congress leaders than any other Raigars because he was an efficient organiser. During a period of fifteen years, as a member of parliament he pointed out the pitiable conditions of untouchables with regard to social, educational and economic conditions. Naval Prabhakar remained active as socio-political reformer till 1967 and died on October 28, 1970. During a period of thirty years, the kind of changes he ushered in were remarkable.

Naval Prabhakar had attained a high political position among the Raigars and did not, however, lose its political grip even after his term expired in Parliament in 1967 after serving fifteen years. In the history of his family achievements in political field, 1984 was an important year. His wife Sundarvati Prabhakar was nominated as Congress candidate from Karol Bagh and was declared elected.

Thus like her husband, she also had the honour of being the first Raigar woman parliamentarian.

Soon after his election as President, a meeting was held on August 17, 1964, at Ganga Mandir, Delhi. The members of ABRM found that the main difficulties in convening the third annual meeting was its preparations, hence they tried to start working in advance. The ABRM wanted to hold the meeting of workers at the time of annual function of the Atma Ram 'Lakshya' hostel at Ringas, in which all the active workers and representatives from all over the country could assemble. Subsequently, all workers convention was held on September 19-20, 1964.[28] Besides 15 executive members, more than 100 representatives from all over the country attended it. It was generally appreciated that after an interval of nearly eighteen years, the third annual convention was going to be held at Pushkar, Ajmer, from November 17-19, 1964. Having remained inactive for many years, ABRM was reactivated in 1964 under his leadership.

It was felt that every worker and leader would help in making the annual convention, a success. This was the main concern of the Raigar leaders particularly, Kanhaiya Lal Ratawal, Surya Mal Maurya, Kanwar Sen Maurya, Chhoga Lal Kanwaria, Chaudhary Padam Singh Sakkarwal, Gautam Singh Sakkarwal and Bihari Lal Gagrat. On the same day a committee consisting of fourteen members under the chairmanship of Surya Mal Maurya was constituted. The main purpose of this committee was to chalk-out a detailed programme for the Third Annual Convention.

On September 20, 1964,[29] the ABRM held a meeting at Delhi and elected a few new members against the vacant posts. The meeting was chaired by Naval Prabhakar and Moti Lal Balotia (Jaipur), Hazari Lal Bakolia (Beawar), Khushal Chand Mohanpuria (Delhi), Devendra Kumar Chandolia (Delhi) and Pyare Lal Kansotia (Deeg) were elected as members.

A delegation consisting of Bhola Ram Tongaria, Chaudhary Padam Singh Sakkarwal, Chaudhary Giarsha Ram and Kanwar Sen Maurya made extensive tours to meet the Raigar brethren. On October 19, 1964 they visited Jaipur. They were welcomed by Moti Lal Balotia and his colleagues. The delegates concentrated mainly on community activities, the most important being the holding of Pushkar convention.

On October 20, 1964 they visited Ajmer and were invited by Raigar Panchayat leaders to visit Pushkar to participate in the proceedings of the Panchayats. They attracted the attention of their caste fellows towards the Pushkar sammelan and explained the purpose of undertaking such a long tour. In their speeches to community fellows at Pushkar, they stressed the need for their social and economic support.[30]

Besides Jaipur and Ajmer, the delegates also visited Beawar. The Raigars of Beawar were undoubtedly aware of the importance of the annual conference. Therefore, Shivlal Jatolia, Pradhan, Raigran Panchayat Samiti, Badabash, welcomed the delegates for their visit to this place and assured them of all kind of support and help. Later on a press note was released.

A few members of the delegation namely, Kanwar Sen Maurya and Chaudhary Padam Singh Sakkarwal toured Ringas from Beawar. The Raigars were so impressed that they also assured of all kind of assistance for the convention. While Kanwar Sen Maurya and his colleague Chaudhary Padam Singh Sakkarwal reached Delhi from Ringas, Bhola Ram Tongaria and Giarsha Ram Chaudhary toured from Beawar to Sojat City, Jodhpur, Peepad City and Nagaur. Again, after a few months, on November 8, 1964, Bhola Ram Tongaria toured Bikaner and Jodhpur. Throughout the 'yatra' Raigars shouted slogans in favour of the annual convention at the meetings held at Jodhpur, Bikaner and other places. They were successful in influencing the people by talking about social, educational, economic issues and unemployment among the youth of the community. The 'yatra' received the best response in Jaipur, Jodhpur, Ajmer, Beawar and Bikaner.[31]

The delegates toured all over the regions and collected a large number of volunteers and funds for the convention. With all these preparations, a stage was set for convention to begin on November 18, 1964. A large number of workers, representatives, etc., were assembled near the temple. It was mainly due to the efforts of the leaders and workers that third convention of ABRM was held at Pushkar, Ajmer, although amidst a lot of criticism and controversy.

The foregoing account of the achievements of the touring leaders of ABRM showed that they had provided a new life to the Raigar community and their charismatic leadership had brought about a social and political regeneration and given their caste-fellows self-confidence and respect. With this the leaders of ABRM movement had achieved a major success in reviving the ABRM.

Since the second phase of ABRM was associated with the leadership of Naval Prabhakar, it is necessary to assess his contribution to ABRM movement.

Naval Prabhakar was associated with the activities of ABRM during its early days in Delhi and Rajasthan. He was a man with progressive ideas. He also took a leading part in the agitation against the atrocities perpetrated on untouchables in rural areas in general and Raigars in particular. He along with Raigar leaders cooperated with Swami Gian Swaroopanand Maharaj and Swami Atma Ram 'Lakshya' in their socio-religious reform agitation and activities, and also played a leading role in establishing the ABRM. In his early days as a Congress worker, he took part in national movement. In response to Gandhi's call *'Bharat Chhodoo Aandolan'* (Quit India Movement) in 1942, he participated actively in rallies, dharnas and protests. Therefore, thousands of agitators were arrested and sent to jail. Naval Prabhakar was also arrested and sent to jail for a few days in 1942.

Soon after the country became independent, he was thrice elected to parliament in the years 1952, 1957 and 1962, and as a Member of Parliament he pointed out the miserable conditions of the Raigars with regard to education, untouchability and unemployment. He continued his attack on caste Hindus.

In this connection, however, it may be noted that majority of people held the view that between 1964 and 1984, no programmes were taken up by him such as building of new Dharmshala, hostels, prohibition on social evils, discontinuance of death feast and the child marriage and abolition of traditional occupations, promotion of education, stopping the use of alcohol on the occasion of marriage, diverting Raigars from traditional occupation to other craft and agitation to secure jobs in the government – activities that concerned the Raigars. Similarly, he never encouraged the Raigars to reform their way of life by the process of self-withdrawal and protest. Thus, during his twenty years' long tenure, the leaders of the movement and caste-fellows did not achieve any significant gain. Being inactive and ineffective in all the fields, most of the ABRM leaders began to question the leadership of Naval Prabhakar and thought of a change in the leadership to overcome their social, educational and political deprivation.

In the teeth of severe criticism about inactivity and ineffectiveness of the leadership of Naval Prabhakar, ABRM decided to hold a two-day sammelan on October 6-7, 1984 at Jaipur. The spirit of the sammelan was not to argue and win, but to change the leadership. The political personality was Shrimati Indira Gandhi, the then Prime Minister of India. Chief Minister, Shiv Charan Mathur, presided over the function. Dharm Das Shastri presented a memorandum to Prime Minister, Indira Gandhi. She addressed the convention and impressed the Raigars who wanted support from Congress leadership in Rajasthan for Raigars. Soon after the leaving of the dais by Shrimati Gandhi and other VIPs, Dharm Das Shastri's name was proposed and seconded by someone for the post of President of ABRM and it engaged the attention of the Raigar masses. Thus, on the next day, i.e., October 7, 1984, the ABRM elected Dharm Das Shastri as its next President.[32]

ABRM under Chhoga Lal Kanwaria

Another notable leader who was associated with the activities of Reform Movement during its early phase in Beawar (Ajmer), Rajasthan was Chhoga Lal Kanwaria. Kanwaria was born on April 12,1922 and from his childhood was directly affected by inequalities and status of untouchables. His father Pratap Mal Kanwaria was a poor Raigar. He encouraged his children for modern education. It may be noted that his father died when he was hardly seven or eight years old. However, his widowed mother supported him by doing work as a labourer here and there. They were passing their life in very miserable conditions. He was an intelligent boy and had influenced the school teachers. Looking at his active academic attitude, a few school teachers patronised Kanwaria and supported and encouraged him at the school level and awarded scholarships to such poor and needy students studying in the school. This helped him considerably and to a great extent solved the financial problem which was a serious one in an untouchable caste like Raigar.[33]

A Sardarji, Sikh the owner of a carpenter shop, who lived in Beawar was also the main helper of Kanwaria. Sardarji took the lead in providing him part-time job at his shop. He started carpentry work at his shop in early 1930s and earned money.[34] Owing to the helping attitude of the school teachers and administration, he passed his matriculation examination with first division from Mohammad Ali Memorial High School, Beawar, (now Higher Secondary) in 1940.

Kanwaria did his B.Sc. in 1944 from Government College, Ajmer, and later on LL.B. in 1956 from the same institute. He was not interested in practising law and he took to government service. In 1952, he appeared in RAS (Rajasthan Administrative Services) examination and was selected as the first Raigar RAS officer. He was general secretary of depressed classes association, Ajmer and was also member of Akhil Bharatiya Depressed Classes league and Congress even before he became an RAS officer.[35]

When he was selected as RAS officer, first, he was posted as Tehsildar for nearly two years. Later, he also worked in various capacities such as First Class Magistrate, Block Development Officer, Sub-Divisional Magistrate, Deputy Director – Local Self Government, Deputy Director – Social Welfare Department, Deputy Commissioner – Development and Commerce and Settlement Officer. Thus, as an administrator, he succeeded in carrying out his responsibilities with sincerity and earned a good reputation in the government.

After completion of twenty-five years service as an able administrator, in 1977, he submitted an application, seeking voluntary retirement from the government service and took active membership of Congress party in the same year. As an active member of the Congress party, he became the general secretary of District Dehat Congress. In 1980 he became the member of state enterprise committee. As a nominated Chairman of Rajasthan State Tannery Limited, he did a lot. Later, in 1980, he contested the election as a Congress candidate from Dudu reserved constituency and entered the Rajasthan Legislative Council in 1980.[36] In July 1981, Kanwaria became Medical and Health Minister, when Shiv Charan Mathur was heading the state as Chief Minister. When Chief Minister Mathur inducted Kanwaria in his ministry as a cabinet minister the Raigar community expressed their gratitude to the Chief Minister for this act. He remained a minister from 19 July, 1981 to 16 October, 1982.[37]

During 1983-84, he was nominated a member to Privilege Committee and here also he played an important role in solving the problems.

The first generation of leaders, besides Chhoga Lal Kanwaria at the all-India level were: Suwa Lal Tanwar, Gheesu Lal, Sukh Raj Singh Arya (Nogia), Mool Chand Maurya, Maga Ram Bakolia, Ram Swaroop Nidar, Ram Lal Karodia, Moti Lal Balotia and at Rajasthan levels: Hazari Lal Panwar, Hazari Lal Bakolia, Ganeshi Lal

Dholpuria, Ghewar Chand Phoolwaria, Amar Chand Sanwaria (Patel), Sant Dhula Ram Dholpuria, Sant Bhura Lal Singaria and Udai Ram Mehant (all from Bada Bas, Raigran and Chhota Bas, Raigran, Beawar).

The organising of a general body meeting is the major activity of ABRM. An MP or a minister was usually invited to preside over the National Executive Committee meeting, which was on November 8-9, 1981 at Panchayat Bhawan, Raigar Mohalla, Bada Bas in Beawar,[38] a tehsil headquarters. The conference was presided over by Chhoga Lal Kanwaria, the then Health and Medical Minister, Government of Rajasthan, as also the President of ABRM. Besides the social workers and political activists from Rajasthan, many more delegates from all over North India participated in it. Speeches were given and the sammelan also created a general awakening among the Raigars of North India. The meeting made a distinct contribution to the cause of untouchable Raigars. The different kinds of changes that were noticed amongst the Raigars can be characterised as a silent revolution. It was a revolt against the arrogance and brutality of upper-caste Hindus and the caste system. There are evidences that it was not entirely confined to Raigar caste, but was also spreading among the lower untouchable castes within untouchable castes.

The sammelan passed many resolutions,[39] the main of which was that ban should be imposed on social evils, that each family must send their children to school compulsorily and that each family on auspicious occasion should donate at least Rs 21 to the Mahasabha for strengthening its financial position. Besides passing several resolutions, for the first time, in different states of the country, President, Vice-President and General secretary were nominated for socio-educational and welfare activities by the President, ABRM.[40] Thus, nine-state Raigar Sabhas were formed in 1981 under the leadership of various social activists, who were affiliated to ABRM. The formation of the statewise Raigar Mahasabha in the country in 1981 is given in Table 7.1.

Similarly, to organise the Raigars in different districts of Rajasthan, President and General Secretary were nominated for the socio-educational and welfare programmes by the national President.[41] Thus, 23 district Raigar Mahasabhas came into existence in the year 1981 which were affiliated to ABRM. The formation of districtwise Raigar Mahasabha in Rajasthan in 1981 is given in Table 7.2.

Table 7.1

The Formation of Statewise Raigar Mahasabha in the Country, 1981

Name of the State	*Name of the Person*	*Designation*	*Place of Residence*
Rajasthan	1. Surya Mal Maurya	President	Beawar
	2. Prabhu Dayal Maurya	Vice-President	Lalsot
	3. K.M. Peepliwal	General Secretary	Jaipur
Delhi Pradesh	1. Kishan Lal Kurdia	President	New Delhi
	2. Bhagwan Das Khorwal	General Secretary	New Delhi
	3. Bihari Lal Jagrat	General Secretary	New Delhi
Madhya Pradesh	1. Nand Ram Jabdolia	President	Kangeti, Mandsor
	2. Onkar Mal Bakolia	General Secretary	Kangeti, Mandsor
Maharashtra	1. Lala Ram Kurdia	President	Chambur, Bombay
	2. Bhag Chand Deva Ram	General Secretary	Chambur, Bombay
Punjab	1. Udai Ram Chandolia	President	Amritsar
	2. Narain Lal Khatumaria	General Secretary	Bhatinda
Uttar Pradesh	1. Girdhari Lal Bachhabadha	President	Vrandavan
	2. Umrao Singh Kundara	General Secretary	Mathura
Gujarat	1. Udai Lal Barolia	President	Ganganagar, Ahmedabad
	2. Aasu Lal Kurdia	General Secretary	Sabarmati, Ahmedabad
Haryana	1. Bhori Lal Jagarwal	President	Bhiwani
	2. RamChand Balotia	General Secretary	Narnaul
West Bengal	1. Keshri Chand Dhawal	President	Calcutta
	2. Subhash Chandra Dholkheria	General Secretary	Calcutta

Source: Akhil Bharatiya Raigar Mahasabha Karyakarni Samiti Avam Karyakarta Sammelan, Raigar Panchayat Bhawan, Beawar, Rajasthan, November 8-9, 1981, pp. 14-16.

Table 7.2
The Formation of Districtwise Raigar Mahasabha in the Rajasthan, 1981

District	*Name of the Person*	*Designation*
Jaipur	1. Lekh Raj Balotia	President
	2. Badri Prasad Kankhedia	General Secretary
Ajmer	1. Hazari Lal Bakolia	President
	2. Mangi Lal Jatolia	President
	3. Kishan Lal Khetawat	General Secretary
Kota	1. Modu Lal Verma	President
	2. Puran Chand Toshniwal	General Secretary
Udaipur and Dungarpur	1. Kalu Lal Kurdia	President
	2. Kishan Lal Jatolia	General Secretary
Sawai Madhopur	1. Chuni Lal Jelia, MLA	President
	2. Peeru Ram Tongaria	General Secretary
Sikar	1. Mool Chand Maurya	President
	2. Kalu Ram Kuldeep	General Secretary
Jhunjhunu	1. Bhagwan Sahay Masalpuria	President
	2. Gopal Lal Deegwal	General Secretary
Bikaner	1. Ram Rikh Dholkhedia	President
	2. Prabhu Dayal Dholkhedia, Ex-MLA	General Secretary
Jodhpur	1. Aasu Lal Kanwaria	President
	2. Pokhar Das Khatnawalia	General Secretary
Tonk	1. Jai Narain Salodia	President
	2. Khoob Chand Gunsaria	General Secretary
Churu	1. Tulsi Ram Bakolia	President
	2. Nanu Ram Gadegaonlia	General Secretary
Jalore	1. Barda Ram, MP	President
	2. Dhana Ram Sonkaria	General Secretary
Nagaur	1. Gopal Ram	President
	2. Udai Ram Kurdia	General Secretary
Pali	1. Bhoma Ram Singaria	President
	2. Guman Chand Singaria	General Secretary
Chittorgarh	1. Jai Chand Mohil, Ex-MLA	President
and Banswara	2. Ganesh Ram Palia, Ex-MLA	General Secretary
Barmer	1. Dharam Ram	President
	2. Keshri Chand Singaria	General Secretary

Contd...

Contd...

Bhilwara	1. Babu Lal Jelia	President
	2. Raj Mal Naval	General Secretary
Bundi	1. Nathu Lal Master	President
	2. Ram Kumar Tigonia	General Secretary
Alwar	1. Sohan Lal Deegwal	President
	2. Sedu Ram Deegwal	General Secretary
Ganganagar	1. Ganesh Ram Jatolia	President
	2. Bal Raj Jatolia	General Secretary
Sirohi	1. Mukhitula Ram	President
	2. Mangi Lal Masalpuria	General Secretary
Bharatpur	1. Pyare Lal Kansotia	President
	2. Nathu Lal Bichhawandia	General Secretary
Jaisalmer	1. Laxman Ram Tongaria	President

Source: Akhil Bharatiya Raigar Mahasabha Karyakarni Samiti Avam Karyakarta Sammelan, Raigar Panchayat Bhawan, Beawar, Rajasthan, November 8-9, 1981, pp. 16-19.

According to the provisions of the Act, the ABRM became more representative body covering 15 different districts of Rajasthan and five states of northern India. It had also fixed the number of the members to be included from each districts/state in the executive committee. Thus members who were included in executive committee from different districts were: Ajmer – 100, Alwar – 100, Udaipur – 50, Kota – 50, Churu – 50, Chittorgarh – 50, Jaipur –150, Jodhpur – 100, Tonk – 50, Deeg – 25, Barmer – 50, Bikaner – 50, Shekhawati – 50, Sawai Madhopur – 50, Sirohi – 25, all in Rajasthan, Delhi – 200, Punjab – 50, Madhya Pradesh – 50, Gujarat – 20, and Maharashtra (Bombay) – 20.[42]

In 1964, the leadership changed from stalwarts like Naval Prabhakar to well-known social activists and staunch supporter of Congress like Chhoga Lal Kanwaria, who later on was elected as Congress MLA. The next big organisational efforts on the part of Chhoga Lal Kanwaria came in November, 1981, with the formation of new Executive Committee at the Beawar sammelan. Some of the office-bearers of the Executive Committee were: Chhoga Lal Kanwaria as President (Beawar),[43] Hazari Lal Bakolia (Beawar), Dharm Das Phoolwaria (New Delhi), Champa Lal Arya, MLA (Mandsor, Madhya Pradesh), Khushal Chand Mohanpuria (New

Delhi), Mangha Ram Bakolia (Churu), and Gopi Ram Salodia (Jaipur) all as Upadhiyaks (6); Dev Kumar Chandolia (Bidanpura, Delhi), Suwa Lal Tanwar (Beawar), Ram Chandra Dolia (Jaipur), and Poonam Chand Dholkheria (Chembur, Bombay), – all as Mahamantries (4); Surya Mal Maurya and Chuni Lal Jalutharia (Jaipur), as Prachar and Prasar Mantri (2); Madan Lal Dolia (Ajmer), Khushal Chand Lavadia (Jaipur), P.K. Maurya (Bikaner) and Bheema Ram Khatnawalia (Pali), as Mantri (4); Hardeen Lal Kamal (Ajmer), as Treasurer (1). Besides, there were 142 Executive Members from all over the country.[44] The statewise members of the Executive Committee were: Delhi (17), Rajasthan (106), Madhya Pradesh (3), Maharashtra (Bombay) (5), Punjab (3), Uttar Pradesh (2), Gujarat (Ahmedabad) (2), and Haryana (4).

It is interesting to note that out of 18 top officials, there were 13 from Rajasthan, 3 from Delhi, one each from Madhya Pradesh and Maharashtra. Likewise, the nomination of the executive members shows that here again Rajasthan dominated, they were 106 in number. The executive committee included members from Delhi – 17, Maharashtra – 5, Haryana – 4, Madhya Pradesh and Punjab – 3 each, Uttar Pradesh and Gujarat – 2 each respectively.[45] This explains how the local Rajasthanis dominated the Akhil Bharatiya Raigar Mahasabha.

ABRM under Dharm Das Shastri

Another notable leader who was associated with the activities of ABRM during its early days in Delhi, was Dharm Das Shastri of Delhi. His father, Nathu Ram Shastri, was a staunch Gandhian supporter, who became Chairman of Khadi Village Board in 1950.[46] His father had migrated from Sindh, Hyderabad (now in Pakistan) prior to independence and settled in Delhi. Dharm Das Shastri was born in 1937 and from his childhood he was directly affected by untouchability. While national movement was going on in the country, he came into contact with some eminent Congress leaders, namely,[47] J.K. Jain, H.K.L. Bhagat, Bansi Lal Mehta, etc., who were then leading the agitation against the British Raj. They were very popular leaders among the Congress. Shastri was attracted towards the national Congress movement and took keen interest in its activities and programmes. In response to Gandhi's call to 'Jail Bharo Andolan' in 1942, he participated actively in rallies, dharnas and protests. As a result, thousands of agitators were arrested and sent to jail. Shastri was also arrested and sent to central jail, Delhi, for ten days in 1942.[48] Similarly, after the independence of the country, he, as one of the leaders of weaker sections of the society, led a crusade against the government to settle the issue of 'Jhugi Jhopri' and pointed out the problems of the inhabitants with regard to their settlement. As a leader of the campaign, he was arrested and sent behind the bars in 1955. However, this time he remained in jail only for three-four days.[49]

Shastri did his MA in Hindi literature from Delhi University in 1955.[50] Around 1960, he published his book Nalanda Grammar from Sundar Pustak Bhandar, New Delhi.[51] In 1977, when Kalka Das was elected as BJP Chairman of Delhi Metropolitan Council, Shastri was appointed as Leader of Opposition (Congress) in that Council.[52] In 1977, parliamentary elections took place in the country and Shastri was elected to parliament from Karol Bagh reserved constituency on Congress ticket.[53] Since 1977 and thereafter he became more close to the then Prime Minister and National President of the Congress party Shrimati Indira Gandhi. In 1984, when Prime Minister, Indira Gandhi was assassinated, Shastri personally suffered a lot. He then occupied the back seat in the Congress.

Dharm Das Shastri as President of ABRM wanted the support of the Congress party and its leaders in Rajasthan and elsewhere for the betterment of the conditions of the Raigar community. Shastri, as the President of ABRM, paid a good deal of attention to its organisational problems. After two years, on September 27, 1986, under his leadership, ABRM held the historic Sammelan at Vigyan Bhawan,[54] New Delhi, where national and international conferences were being held and where, President, Prime Minister and other dignitaries used to preside over the functions. The function was chaired by Giani Jail Singh, the then President of India. According to Roop Chand Jalutharia, the main objective of this Sammelan was to honour those notable workers and leaders who were associated with the ABRM during its early days in different regions. In this sammelan, Roop Chand Jalutharia, Ghali Lal Peepliwal, Laxmi Narain Khorwal, Bansi Lal Arya, Mishri Lal Malviya, (all from Jaipur), Madan Lal Dolia, Daulat Ram Sablania, Surya Mal Maurya (posthumously) Hazari Lal Bakolia, Paras Ram Bakolia, Hazari Lal Panwar (all from Beawar, Ajmer), Jai Chand Mohil (Choti Sadri, Chittorgarh), Mool Chand Maurya and Kalu Ram Kuldeep (Sikar), Manga Ram (Churu), Champa Lal Arya (Mandsor, Madhya

Pradesh), Kishan Lal Kurdia, Bhagwan Das Khorwal (Delhi) and many more were honoured with the title of 'Raigar Bhusan'.[55]

Similarly, Swami Raman and Maharaj (Peepad), Swami Gian Swaroopanand Maharaj (Beawar), Swami Gopal Ram (Nagaur), (all three from Rajasthan), Lala Ram Kurdia (Bombay), Dr Khoob Chand Jajoria, Naval Prabhakar, Dharm Das Shastri, Kanwar Sen Maurya, Chaudhary Padam Singh Sakkerwal and Chaudhary Giarsa Ram, Bihari Lal Jagrat, Shambhu Dayal Gadegaonlia, Kushal Chand Mohanpuria and Kalyan Ram Peepliwal (all from Delhi) were honoured with the title of 'Raigar Ratan'.[56]

During his tenure as President of the ABRM (1984-2000), small and big Raigar sammelans were organised to consolidate the strength of the community. Another significant event was that a 'vishal' convention of Raigars of Bundi was organised in Bundi. A large number of workers, activists and representatives from Kota, Jaipur, Ajmer, Beawar, Delhi and Mumbai attended it. Similarly, another meeting was organised at Bisau in Jhunjhunu district. Thus, under Shastri's guidance the ABRM momentum got a thrust.

In the year 2000, after full fourteen years, the tide of inactive and ineffective persons again rose with full vigour and this time it was supported by most of the members of ABRM movement. The Raigars were no longer prepared to wait for further deterioration. Several letters were written to Shastri, requesting him to hold elections. Many Raigars personally met and appealed to him for early holding of the election. The inactive and indifferent attitude of Shastri once again rose the wave of controversy. All this resulted in an atmosphere of general resentment. At this point, Shastri perceived danger to his prestige. He had earned a reputation of being a staunch supporter of the Congress party. All this, which cost a shadow on Shastri's career and reputation led Shastri to reconsider the whole issue of holding the election and declared the election dates. This changed the whole attitude of Raigars towards him. The leaders of ABRM appreciated the decision of Shastri. Subsequently on October 30, 2000, the ABRM held the election at Government Hostel, Jaipur, under the Convenorship of P.N. Rachhoya, Inspector General Police, Rajasthan[57] and a proposal was moved by Jai Narain Salodia, former MLA that Shrimati Meira Kanwaria be nominated for the post of President of ABRM, and this proposal was seconded by Champa Lal Arya, a former MLA from Mandsor, Madhya Pradesh. Thus Shrimati Meira Kanwaria was declared as elected.

She was given a hero's welcome. The election victory is considered as a great victory by BJP group.

It was noticed that Raigars were divided on the election issue. In a communiqué issued on April 29, 2001, Bhori Lal Shastri was elected as President of ABRM.[58] The leadership of ABRM, had, since the beginning of the twenty-first century, divided in two major factions in fighting against each other. Around this time fissiparous tendencies began to appear in the ABRM organisation because it had increasingly involved itself in party politics. The major rift was between the leaders who supported the Congress and those who aligned themselves with growing rightist influence.

Both ABRM Presidents continued their activities and programmes even after the election. The leaders of Raigar community tried their best to resolve this contentious issue amicably. There were several state-wise meetings adopting resolution demanding the dissolution of both the organisations. The name and duration of president of ABRM since 1944 onward is given in Table 7.3.

Table 7.3

Presidents (Adhyaksha) of Akhil Bharatiya Raigar Mahasabha since 1944

S. No.	*Name of the President*	*State*	*Duration*		*Total Period*
			From	*To*	
1	Bhola Ram Tongaria	Sindh Hyderabad (now in Pakistan)	November 1944	April 1946	1 year 8 months
2	Chaudhary Kanhaiya Lal Ratawal	Delhi	August 1946	August 1964	18 years 9 months
3	Nawal Prabhakar MP	Delhi	August 1964	October 1984	20 years 5 months
4	Dharm Das Shastri, MP	Delhi	October 1984	October 2000	16 years 3 months
5	i. Shrimati Meira Kanwaria	Delhi	October 2000	Till today	
	ii. Bhori Lal Shastri	Delhi	October 2000	Till today	

Sources: 1. Chandanmal Naval, *Raigar Jati-ka-Itihas*, Jodhpur, Shyam Printing Press, 1986.

2. Roop Chand Jalutharia, *Raigar Jati-ka-Itihas*, Jaipur, Capital Printing Press, 2001, pp. 66-69.

Eminent Raigar Leaders

Chaudhary Padam Singh Sakkarwal[59]

In 1920s some educated Raigars emerged in Delhi, who provided a different kind of leadership and established an Akhil Bharatiya Raigar Mahasabha in 1944. One of the notable leaders during this period, who was one of the founders of the Mahasabha, was late Chaudhary Padam Singh.

He was born in Delhi in 1897 in the family of Sakkarwal of Godhbasi (also called Salyota) village in Alwar district of Rajasthan. He was one of the founders of Arya Kanya Pathshala in Delhi. Sakkarwal's public life started with his association with national movement and also Arya Samaj's reform movement in Delhi. Lala Deshbandhu Gupta was an eminent leader of the national movement and Chaudhary Padam Singh Sakkarwal took an active part in it.

With such rich experience and background Chaudhary Padam Singh Sakkarwal became one of the founder members of ABRM, and in 1946 was elected an executive member of it. He as an executive member toured several villages in Rajasthan. He was also responsible for spreading the beliefs of Arya Samaj among Raigars and encouraged the starting of educational institutions. Keeping in view his services to the Raigar community, one of the main roads in Karol Bagh, New Delhi was named after him – Chaudhary Padam Singh Road in 1961 by MCD.

Chaudhary Padam Singh was assisted by Gautam Singh Sakkarwal, his eldest son, who was well qualified with good command over English and Hindi. Gautam Singh Sakkarwal served the cause of Raigar Samaj in three ways: First, he worked as an active social worker and later on served the ABRM in various capacities. He played an important role in the early years of ABRMs and later on supported the agitation against the social disabilities and atrocities on the Raigars in rural areas of Rajasthan. Second, he was elected as Congress Municipal Councillor twice in 1952 and 1957 respectively. He was also chairman of various committees in MCD including education committee and in this capacity, he championed the cause of untouchables' right in general and Raigars in particular. Third, he worked as the Chairman of Arya Kanya Pathshala for several years, where he worked to promote the female education and welfare and progress of the community. He was elected as Chairman of the Reception Committee for Jaipur sammelan at Jaipur in 1945. On December 23-24, 1945, he presided over a meeting at Ganga Mandir, Ghat Darwaja, Jaipur, and also shared the dais with Swami Gian Swaroopanand Maharaj, Swami Atma Ram 'Lakshya' and others at the inaugural session of ABRM at Jaipur on April 12, 1946. Later on, he was elected as one of the executive members of ABRM in 1946.

Khoob Chand Jajoria[60]

Another notable leader in Delhi was Khoob Chand Jajoria, who also worked for Delhi Prantia Raigar Yuvak Sangh (DPRYS). He was born in 1914 in a well to do family of Jajoria and did his medical diploma/degree from Calcutta in 1937-38. He took a leading part in awakening socio-political consciousness among the Raigars of Delhi, Rajasthan and other regions of North India and bringing unity in the community.

Just before independence of the country, he was nominated as one of the members in the then Chief Commissioner's Advisory Committee by the British government. To be a member of this important committee, it was an award to legitimise his high status and 'good conduct'.

In the early years of the ABRM, he participated actively in all the social activities and programmes. Since the day the Dausa Maha Sammelan passed resolutions to discard the traditional occupation 'begar' and boycott of social evils, the atrocities by the upper castes had increased tremendously in the rural areas. As a member of several delegations, he toured several trouble-torne villages and heard the grievances of the Raigars and also about the atrocities committed on them in several villages by the upper caste Hindus. He prayed and pleaded the Raigars to have patience. For instance, in 1945, he was nominated by ABRM to make an enquiry about atrocities committed on the Raigars of the village Markeda, Kishangarh, Ajmer state. When he arrived in village Markeda, he met Durga Dutt Upadhyaya, a Settlement Officer of the Ajmer state and as a member of delegation, he pointed out the atrocities and restrictions imposed on the Raigars by the Jats and how Raigars were forced to leave the village. He pleaded for a change in the attitude of Jats towards the Raigars. With the sincere efforts of the Settlement Officer an amicable compromise was reached between Jats and Raigars. Khoob

Chand thanked the Settlement Officer and Jats for adopting a liberal attitude. The Jats not only compromised with Raigars, but also paid Rs 150 to Raigars as compensation to them for harassment.

In 1957, he was elected to Delhi Nagar Nigam, as a Congress candidate. He, as a Chairman of Jal Samiti tried his best to solve the public grievances with regard to the water problem.

The establishment of Delhi Prantia Raigar Yuvak Sangh in 1944 provided a landmark in the development of Raigar movement, the first being the agitation led by Mohan Lal Patel as Pradhan and second the emergence of Khoob Chand, who gave it an ideology.

When the Raigars were preparing for holding of the first Raigar Maha Sammelan at Dausa, Jaipur state in 1944, a delegation consisting of two persons namely Khoob Chand and Asha Ram Sevlia, was sent by Delhi Prantia Raigar Yuvak Sangh for ground work for the smooth conduct of the sammelan. A small committee came into existence in the same year (1944). The main object of the Committee was to manage and look after each and everything. The success of sammelan was associated with the leadership of Swami Atma Ram 'Lakshya', Naval Prabhakar, Khoob Chand and others.

Even before the Dausa Maha Sammelan (organised in 1944), the Raigars had formed five different Committees for different issues. Khoob Chand was made the Convenor of Raigar Navyuvak Sammelan. The credit of having started a movement for self-correction among Raigar youths goes to Khoob Chand.

Similarly, after the establishment of ABRM, an executive committee of six members was formed to implement the programmes. Thus, Bhola Ram Tongaria became the first Pradhan (Chairman), Shisu Lal Sevlia, Up-Pradhan (Vice Chairman) and Khoob Chand, Pradhan Mantri. Khoob Chand, *Pradhan Mantri* of ABRM led crusade against the discrimination and socio-economic disabilities imposed by the upper castes. During the early period of ABRM the leaders were concerned about the socio-religious change. As elected members of ABRM, they voiced these grievances. He took a leading part in 1946 Jaipur sammelan also. One of the parks, in Karol Bagh, New Delhi was named Dr Khoob Chand Jajoria Park in 1983 by MCD.

Surya Mal Maurya[61]

Besides Chaudhary Padam Singh Sakkarwal and Khoob Chand Jajoria, Surya Mal Maurya of Jaipur also took keen interest and participated in ABRM's activities and programmes. It may be noted that reaction of the upper-caste Hindus in the villages to the social reform of the Raigar caste has to be seen in the context of the resolutions passed in Dausa Maha Sammelan of 1944. As a result thereof in 1944 and onwards, several incidents of violence occurred in rural areas. Subsequently, attempts were made by ABRM to bring about a reconciliation between higher castes and low untouchable castes. For this purpose ABRM sent a delegation consisting of Naval Prabhakar, Khoob Chand Jajoria, Surya Mal Maurya and a few others as arbitrators to bring about a compromise. The following is an account of the circumstances under which the arbitrators were sent and the consequences of their efforts:

> A delegation of ABRM under the leadership of Swami Atma Ram 'Lakshya' and Surya Mal Maurya met with the high officials of Government of Jaipur on June 8, 1945. The representatives of the delegation also prepared a memorandum addressed to the Prime Minister and submitted it to the officials. It demanded that an enquiry be instituted for harassment, torture and humiliation perpetrated on Raigars of village Raisar by the upper castes. Since ABRM wanted to get social justice, the delegation also met Daya Shankar Bhargava, the President of Jaipur Praja Mandal at Jaipur and Thakur of Achrol. Under the leadership of Swami Atma Ram 'Lakshya' and Surya Mal Maurya, ABRM effectively fought for social justice and pressed for an enquiry. Thus, an enquiry was held and the upper caste people were found guilty.
>
> A combined meeting of the representatives of the two communities was held at the village which arrived at an amicable compromise.

In early first few years, several incidents of severe violence occurred. These issues came up before the ABRM meeting and everyone agreed that ABRM should send a delegation to support their own caste fellows in such a situation. It was because of ABRM decision of 1944 that it sent a delegation under the leadership of Naval Prabhakar along with Surya Mal Maurya and a few others to Dausa; in June 1945 to Makreda, Ajmer; in June 1947 to Nimbahera, Chittorgarh and in November 1949 to village Narwar, Kishangarh, Ajmer.

With the cooperation and support of police officials and local people, meetings of ABRM representatives were held in Dausa, Makreda, Nimbahera and Narwar, where upper caste members were also invited. The main objective of the meetings was to resolve the rivalry and to avoid open hostility in future. Thus, ABRM representatives succeeded in creating a friendly atmosphere in the working of upper castes and low untouchable castes.

Subsequently, ABRM conventions were held in 1946 at Phulera, Jaipur; in 1949 at Malpura, Tonk. At these conventions Surya Mal Maurya actively participated.

Kanwar Sen Maurya[62]

Since the very beginning of the ABRM movement, while most of the leaders used dialogues, speeches and press to fight against the social evils, Kanwar Sen Maurya led the movement with his poetic talents and powerful speeches from village to village and from 'Dhani' hamlet to Dhani to which he himself belonged and so was the main hero. He spearheaded the renaissance movement in local dialect and exposed the miserable conditions of the Raigars through his poems. His long narrative poem *Vir Uthoo* shows, why Raigars had fallen down to such a pitiable condition. He exposed the foolishness of drinking alcohol. At the same time he also exposed the cruelties of the upper castes through his poems and speeches. His book *Raigar Bandhu Bhajnawali* is a collection of 22 poems, in which he described the pitiable socio-cultural conditions of Raigar caste. He uses traditional lores in his poem; he was directly inspired by Raigar saints.

He believed like other Raigar saints, that leaving the evil customs, habits, child marriage, dowry, etc., that they were more important and hence he envisaged that Raigars by inculcating good habits, sanskars could attain the height that upper caste-persons had reached.

He, as the member of the delegation, met the members of Praja Mandal in 1948 at Tonk. The Praja Mandal members were informed of the atrocities, harassment and humiliation committed on Raigars by representatives who led the delegation to Praja Mandal. The delegation sought their help in releasing the arrested 18 Raigars. The members of the Praja Mandal assured them of their help in releasing the arrested Raigars. Since ABRM wanted to get social justice, the delegation and the members of Praja Mandal too met the Home member of Tonk. They demanded immediate release of arrested persons. The reply, by the Home member, showed the positive attitude of the government. It was stated that within three days suitable action would be taken.

A combined meeting of ABRM representatives, and the members of Praja Mandal was held at Tonk. In the meeting, it was unanimously decided that if the arrested 18 Raigars were not released by April 10, 1948, they would sit on hunger-strike for an indefinite period.

The positive response of the Home member to release all the 18 arrested persons pacified Kanwar Sen Maurya, who was fighting for social justice.

ABRM and the Congress

Soon after independence, the social and political activists who were well versed with current political process of the country, realised two things: (a) the Mahasabha was an important social reform organisation for the uplift of the untouchable Raigar masses, and (b) during the early days of Mahasabha, the pioneers sought 'good wishes' from the Congress for its activities. Everybody appreciated the pioneers in doing so. They felt that 'good wishes' by Congress might encourage their efforts in organising the caste Mahasabha. Some state Congress leaders of Rajasthan also appreciated their attempts towards strengthening the organisation. For instance Jai Narain Vyas, the pioneer freedom fighter, President of Jodhpur Praja Mandal and also former Chief Minister of the State, repeatedly supported the Sabha's activities in their reform campaign and other spheres from pre-independence to post-independence period.

Such an attitude of the Congress leaders encouraged Mahasabha office bearers and their fellow workers. They were conscious enough not to antagonise the party in power for three reasons: First, they knew that the Mahasabha did not have the capacity and resources to achieve socio-political objectives on its own strength. For that purpose they had to seek the support of the Congress party. Second, the Congress being a dominant party was the only party capable of doing something for their welfare and upliftment. Lastly, the Mahasabha was pro-Congress since its inception. The Mahasabha's leaders, therefore, made attempts to win over the sympathy of the Congressmen for the organisation. The Congress leaders also knew that an organised Raigars force was of much importance in the election for winning the seats. Therefore, they were soft towards the Mahasabha.

The Congress was preparing itself for consolidating its position in 1952 election. The competitive politics forced it to widen its base among the untouchable communities. Therefore, it turned to the numerically larger caste group. The local Congress appreciated numerical strength of Raigars in this direction. The local Sabha bosses, therefore, remained in close touch with Congress in Delhi. As has been noted earlier that even prior to independence, the Raigars were actively working in the Congress party, independently of the Sabha. They obviously put their claim for Congress tickets. As a gesture of goodwill towards Raigars, a few Raigars in Delhi and other states were nominated as party candidates in Delhi in the first general election. For instance, Naval Prabhakar, a leading Raigar leader of Delhi and most prominent leader of ABRM was given Congress ticket from Karol Bagh. In such circumstances, the Congress-minded Naval Prabhakar, who was also an ardent champion of Raigar cause, found himself in a very pleasant situation. He, therefore, worked for more closeness between Congress party and his caste fellows. The Raigar leaders appreciated the Congress-line of thinking.

The Raigar leaders, consequently had a free hand in pursuing their pro-Congress policy. In order to create pro-Congress opinion, the Raigars started a campaign. Congress leaders were invited to attend and address the public meetings of Raigars. The activities and programmes of the Congress were explained in colloquial language with analogies which could be understood by Raigars.

With the growth of ABRM under the leadership of Naval Prabhakar, Chhoga Lal Kanwaria and Dharm Das Shastri, the ABRM moved very close towards the Congress and decided that their best interest lay with the Congress. Thus, the longest period of fifty-seven years since ABRM came into existence in 1944, associated itself with the Congress. In 1982, Sundarvati Prabhakar, wife of Naval Prabhakar, was also elected as Member of Parliament from Karol Bagh. In 1977, the Congress party decided to give Congress-ticket to Dharm Das Shastri and he was also elected as a Member of Parliament. Congress party continuously tried to win the hearts of the Raigars by nominating them as Congress candidates in State Assembly, Delhi Mahanagar Parishad, Delhi Nagar Nigam, etc. It was because of the Congress that Dharm Das Shastri was elected to Delhi Nagar Nigam (DNN) and remained its member from 1967-75 and Delhi Mahanagar Parishad (DMP) (1977) respectively. Bhori Lal Shastri, DMP (1977-90); Khoob Chand Mohanpuria, DNN (1983-86); Hement Mohanpuria, DNN (1989-90) and Tulsi Sablania, DMP (2002).

Under the leadership of Naval Prabhakar, Chhoga Lal Kanwaria, Dharm Das Shastri since 1944 to 2001, the ABRM worked in close cooperation with Congress party. While the informal association of ABRM with Congress continues even today (2003), the leaders of ABRM in their individual capacity, remained also the leaders of Congress party and other parties. Naval Prabhakar, Chhoga Lal Kanwaria and Dharm Das Shastri continued to play important role in Congress. Similarly in 1980, when Congress party came into power, Chhoga Lal Kanwaria became the first minister of the Raigar community heading the Medical and Health Department in Rajasthan. In 1980, Chhoga Ram Bakolia was elected as Congress MLA and he became the Deputy Minister in the ministry headed by Shiv Charan Mathur. Again in 1998, when he was elected as Congress MLA, he became Transport Minister and later Social Welfare Minister in the ministry of Ashok Gehlot.

Rightist Movement (Jan Sangh, now BJP) among the Raigars and ABRM

In this section, we shall deal with the growth of the Rightist movement with divergent ideology and its repercussions on the ABRM.

Although the whole movement, described earlier, represented radicalism in terms of the departure it made from the traditional social and cultural system; there was a growth of rightist radicalism within caste and or movement, which was oriented towards Hinduism. The father of this trend was Shiv Narain Sarsunia of Delhi.[63] Sarsunia was born on November 11, 1930 at Delhi. He received his education in Delhi. From his childhood Sarsunia, along with a few other Raigar boys, took an active interest in Rastriya Swayam Sevak Sangh's activities. RSS made a real impression on this young boy along with Laxman Singh Atal, another young Raigar.[64] Both became formal members of RSS. At that time RSS launched a campaign to involve the untouchable boys and while RSS had a negative connotation about the caste, Sarsunia, Atal and other Raigar boys found a positive thinking in RSS' teaching of Hinduism. After his training as RSS volunteer on RSS' pattern, he (Sarsunia) started 'Raigar Swayam Sewak Sangh' (RSSS), 'Raigar

Swayam Sewak Mandal' (RSSM), 'Raigar Swayam Sewak Dal' (RSSD), and 'Krishna Mai Sewak Mandal' (KMSM) in Delhi,[65] which were devoted to integrate the Raigar interest for the good of the community. These organisations provided the forum for the reform movement and Sarsunia expounded his views on Jan Sangh. Thus, he became the chief organ of Jan Sangh ideology. Sarsunia while working as chief organ of Jan Sangh ideology, took active part in Kashmir agitation in the year 1953 and also participated in the movement against cow slaughter in the year 1966-1967.[66] On his active involvement in both the agitations, he was arrested and was lodged in jail.[67] Both Kashmir and anti-cow slaughter movements gave him boost; Jan Sangh (now BJP) had given him a ticket to fight the elections and according to Laxman Singh Atal's account in his essay "Sri Sarsuniji Bahumukhi Samajik Pratibha Key Dhani" in *Kalyan Sangh*, 1971; in 1954 he was elected to Nagar Palika, Delhi from the general seat; and in 1962 fought the Lok Sabha election from the reserved constituency, Karol Bagh, New Delhi.[68] Similarly, in 1966, Sarsunia was nominated by the party for the Mahanagar Parishad seat Delhi.[69] Sarsunia engaged himself in the welfare activities of the downtrodden. In this, he not only did the welfare programmes but created party organisational framework in different parts of Delhi, recruiting members of different castes or communities.

From the very beginning, Sarsunai was constantly watching the various activities of the ABRM and when he was not satisfied with what ABRM had been doing, he alienated himself from the organisation and on August 15, 1960, a group of a few young Raigars established an organisation called Kalyan Sangh under the leadership of Sarsunia.[70] Thus, Kalyan Sangh became the centre of socio-cultural reform movement. The objectives of this movement were as follow:[71]

1. To launch a campaign against those persons who have grabbed the community property in their individual names and to ban the death feasts, Gang Bhoj, use of liquor and other social evils and also to revive the dead Mahasabha once again.
2. To start Atma Ram Homeopathic Centre at Delhi to provide medical aid to poor and needy persons.
3. To start coaching classes for weak and poor Raigar students and to distribute books and stationery.
4. To open some centres to impart training of various trades such as cutting and tailoring, handicrafts, etc., to improve and make

the women folk economically independent. Also, to help the widows and aged women in providing the financial help from government.

5. To campaign for removal of untouchability and also to remove the feeling of inferiority complex amongst the untouchables and integrate them in the main stream of the society.

Sarsunia was a businessman dealing in spare parts and cycles and had a workshop to manufacture radio and electrical goods. One of the unique features of Sarsunia's functioning was to listen to the problems of the community and to solve them.

Thus, the Rightist movement in Delhi was associated with Shiv Narain Sarsunia. Sarsunia was the first person to start the programmes of Jan Sangh (now BJP) and the party (Jan Sangh) immediately after recognising the merits of the programme tried to encourage him further. Hence, he initiated a 'Hindutva movement'. The Rightist movement of Sarsunia attracted many youths, not only among the Raigars, but also from other untouchable castes, while most scheduled castes people who were not desirous of becoming members of RSS, Jan Sangh or BJP but talked only about Jan Sangh or BJP. Sarsunia praised the ideology of Jan Sangh or BJP. Due to his persuasion and proper guidance the Raigar youths were also attracted by Sarsunia's activities.

The Raigar youths organised meetings in Delhi, Rajasthan and in other regions of the country. The Kalyan Sangh was anti-caste but was committed to the value of humanness devoid of any kind of discrimination and exploitations. The youths considered Kalyan Sangh as reformatory and revolutionary which could spread mass movement. As stated earlier, the formation of ABRM and its intense agitation against the prevailing practices of untouchability and disabilities and to gain access to schools, temples, etc., incited the opposition against the Thakurs, Jagirdars, Jamindars, Brahmins, Baniyas and others who were considered as exploiters of untouchability; ill-treating and threatening their attempts towards the social reforms. Some socio-economic restrictions were imposed due to which atrocities increased in rural areas against this caste group.[72] The upper caste Hindus were irritated and one of the worst violent confrontation occurred in Dholai, Paldi Mudru, Dhanimal Pura, Pratapgarh, Harner, Dhani, Sendhu Singh, Suratgarh, Mazhipura, Gheeroad, Aangari villages.[73]

Since the inception of the reform movement atrocities on the Raigars had increased considerably. The rural Raigars became aware of their strength and got interested in the implementation of the social reforms of the ABRM. They had also encouraged the active members for the reform movement. Due to this the upper-caste Hindus were irritated and one of the worst violent confrontation again occurred in Mohanpura, Sujanpura, Dhudhli, Damodarpura, Shamria, Kajuta, Shanvasa, Buj and Chamjanpur villages.[74] Besides, on September 8, 1971, nearly 1,500 upper-caste Hindus attacked a Raigar basti in village Palwada Jat Bidi.[75] Ten Raigar huts were torched and thirty houses were ablazed and looted.[76] Many Raigars left the village due to fear. This news was widely published in papers. Subsequently a large number of complaints were received by Kalyan Sangh, New Delhi. As a result, a meeting of Kalyan Sangh workers was held at Delhi, where a large number of the members were present. The main objective of the meeting was to condemn the upper caste's action and to pass a resolution. Later on, the resolution was sent to the then President of India and the Prime Minister of India, and National Commissioner for Scheduled Castes and Scheduled Tribes.[77] An urgent, meeting of the Kalyan Sangh was convened at Delhi on August 15, 1971. It was decided in the meeting that a 'vishal sammelan' be organised at Alwar (Rajasthan) on August 28, 1971,[78] and according to Ramji Lal Shastri, roughly 2,500 representatives from 130 villages assembled.[79] After the sammelan was over, a detailed report portraying the various incidents which occurred in various rural areas of Rajasthan, was prepared and submitted to the then Chief Minister, Rajasthan.[80] A copy of the same report was also endorsed to the Government of India.[81]

A delegation of Kalyan Sangh, Delhi, visited almost all the riot affected rural areas, met the victims and expressed their solidarity with them. They also criticised and condemned bitterly the act of atrocities perpetrated by the upper caste Hindus.[82]

Subsequently, the delegation of Kalyan Sangh decided to hold a big demonstration on October 3, 1971 at Jaipur, the state capital, to attract the attention of the state government against the ongoing atrocities in the state.[83] A delegation of about 20 social workers made an extensive tour of various villages and propagated their message for attending the demonstration to show their solidarity.[84] After two months or so Kalyan Sangh did organise a 'vishal' rally at Jaipur. On the prescribed date (October 3) nearly 30,000 people assembled and demonstrated.[85] They went to Chief Minister's residence to submit a memorandum. Since the Chief Minister was out of capital, the memorandum was submitted to Punam Chand Vishnoi, the then Education Minister, Government of Rajasthan. The major demands were:[86]

1. To stop the atrocities on the untouchables in rural Rajasthan immediately.
2. To allot land to landless people.
3. To constitute an enquiry committee to assess the loss suffered by Raigars in riots.
4. To punish the culprits.
5. Government should bear the expenditure to be incurred in fighting the court cases related to land disputes.

The chief of the Kalyan Sangh, Shiv Narain Sarsunia wrote letters attracting the attention of the then Prime Minister Shrimati Indira Gandhi and Chief Minister of Rajasthan, Barkatullah Khan.[87] On September 10, 1971, Prime Minister acknowledged the receipt of letter stating that this letter had been sent to the Chief Minister of Rajasthan to look into the matter[88] and the Chief Minister informed on December 17 that the District Collector, Tonk had been directed to allot land to the Raigars.[89]

Rift in Mahasabha

The long time internal cleavage based on the clash of personalities between Naval Prabhakar or Dharm Das Shastri and his group on the one hand and Meira Kanwaria and her group on the other, emerged openly in the year 2000. The rift, to a great extent, was also an expression of the conflicting ideologies. Naval Prabhakar and Dharm Das Shastri being important Congress leaders pursued an informal policy of pro-Congress. Both were the presidents of the Mahasabha. In practice, they made Mahasabha the pressure group of Congress, a vote bank, although in theory, they declared that Mahasabha was non-political. They used the Mahasabha to propagate Congress ideas, which others opposed.

The issue of holding elections of executive members of the Mahasabha came up several times in the annual conventions as well as on other occasions and every one agreed that Mahasabha should hold elections. As stated earlier, workers, representatives and others of the Raigar community bitterly criticised and condemned the attitude of Dharm Das Shastri for not holding election and opposed him to use the platform of Mahasabha to support Congress. There were also no socio-educational and cultural activities regarding the upliftment of the Raigar community. It was in fact due to the inactiveness and ineffectiveness of the President that Mahasabha remained as it was earlier. It is alleged that Shastri fearing that the pro-BJP members may not dominate over the Mahasabha, deferred the election for decades together.

Several attempts were made for reconciliation between the varying factions. The following is an account of the circumstances under which elections were held and the result declared.

The foregoing account of the activities of the Mahasabha shows that there were various reasons that contributed to such an ugly situation. It was because of the tense situation and uproarious scene that intensified its agitation against the present president Dharm Das Shastri, the President agreed to hold the election to the Mahasabha. As a result, according to Roop Chand Jalutharia's account in his book *Raigar Jati Ka Itihas* (2001), Dharm Das Shastri the President of Mahasabha responding to the general feelings of the members agreed to hold the meeting on October 30, 2000 at Government Hostel, Jaipur. Accordingly, a notification was issued. In this meeting, most of the executive members were present. There were also a large number of workers, from Delhi, Punjab, Haryana, Uttar Pradesh, Madhya Pradesh, Gujarat and Maharashtra.[90]

Various issues came up before the Mahasabha executive meeting. The present president of the Mahasabha was criticised bitterly. It was because of all this that Shastri had to resign from presidentship.[91]

In the meeting held on October 30, 2000 at Government Hostel, Jaipur, elections to the Mahasabha under the chairmanship of Permanand Rachhoya, Inspector General of Police, Rajasthan, were held. Jai Narain Salodia, former MLA proposed the name of Shrimati Meira Kanwaria for the post of President of the Mahasabha and Champa Lal Arya, a resident of Mandsor (Madhya Pradesh) and also a former MLA, seconded it. Thus, Shrimati Meira Kanwaria, who is grand-daughter of Chaudhary Kanhaiya Lal Ratawal who was president of the Mahasabha for long time, was elected unanimously. She was also administered the oath of the office immediately. Thus, Shrimati Meira Kanwaria became the first Raigar woman President of the Mahasabha.[92]

Meira Kanwaria, daughter of late Dharm Pal Ratawal was born on March 1, 1950, at Delhi. Her husband Vashu Dev Kanwaria is Chief Accounts Officer in Central Secretariat, Government of India, New Delhi. She received her early education and higher education in Delhi. She did her M.A. in Hindi. After her B.Ed., she started her academic career as a school teacher. During her teaching job, she was honoured by several organisations. In 1997, she took voluntary retirement from service and joined the BJP party immediately. Soon after joining the BJP, she fought the election in 1997, and was declared elected as a member of Delhi Nagar Nigam and also became the Chairman of the Delhi Nagar Nigam.[93]

New Face of Mahasabha

The character of the Mahasabha changed with the election of Shrimati Meira Kanwaria as President in the year 2000. The Mahasabha had now become a part of a new political party, the Bharatiya Janta Party. Thus, the Mahasabha which was pro-Congress till Dharm Das Shastri's tenure, had now moved away from Congress ideologies. This development can also be seen in the context of the continuing rift between the pro-Congress and pro-BJP.

Thus, Mahasabha revived its ideology and that too with a definite commitment to a more radical change. However, with ruling party at centre becoming more radical in its stance, it seemed to win adherents. In any case, the Mahasabha movement is increasing and inevitably caught up with party politics to fight for increasing educational and economic benefits for the community.

We may now consider the other side of the coin. We have noted earlier that since the inception of the Mahasabha, there were always pro-Congress Presidents of the Raigar Mahasabha. Such affiliation or alignment with political party gave them certain privileges and legitimised their political elite status within the caste.

According to Yash Pal Singh Khorwal, Mahamantri, in his letter dated April 16, 2001,[94] circulated amongst the Raigars, Shastri, President of Mahasabha, realising the mistake, held a meeting on March 11, 2001, and dissolved the earlier executive committee. Shastri who was bitter and frustrated, alienated himself from organisation and declared his whole hearted support to Bhori Lal Shastri, the present President of Mahasabha. Thus, the disgruntled leaders were divided and they bifurcated the organisation in two parts.[95] They were working for the achievement of common goals and Swami Atma Ram 'Lakshya's' ideology provided a common basis of activity for different regions and programmes of activities through similar, but on varied emphasis.

It should be noted that a meeting of the Mahasabha workers was held at Jaipur, where most of the members were present. The main objective of the meeting was to resolve the rivalry and to avoid open hostility. In this meeting a coordination committee headed by Chiranji Lal Bakolia[96] was constituted to bring about a cordial atmosphere in the working of the Mahasabha. The first meeting of the coordination committee was held on April 16, 2001, at the residence of Chiranji Lal Bakolia in New Delhi. Since the first meeting of coordination committee was concerned particularly with leadership crisis of Mahasabha, it is necessary to discuss in brief the committee's efforts and its result. While a few persons represented Bhori Lal Shastri's groups, Chandra Bhan, Padam Singh and others represented Meira Kanwaria's group in the meeting. In the conversation that took place between both the groups, all were of the opinion that in Jaipur sammelan no proper procedure for election was followed.[97] They also agreed that both Bhori Lal Shastri and Meira Kanwaria, presidents of their respective Mahasabha, should resign.[98] Briefing the members, Puran Mal Jalutharia, Legal Adviser to the Mahasabha remarked that at present the Mahasabha is passing through a crisis.[99] He further remarked that, we are not pure at heart to encourage the issue of compromise for friendship. Since then the leadership crisis continued in the Mahasabha.

By such activities, individual interest may be served but it harms a large part of the community. It creates rivalries and bitterness amongst the caste fellows. This tendency hampers social and political unity.

Such feelings are expressed by the Raigars even today also. On July 29, 2001, in a caste meeting held at Khole-ke-Hanumanji Mandir, Jaipur, where a large number of caste fellows assembled, Hardev Patel, resident of Sanganer, moved the following resolution. Later, it was unanimously adopted. The resolution appealed:

> *Akhil bhartiya Raigar Mahasabha mein gutbazi honey sey samaj mein katuta badti ja rahi hai aur samaj ki sakti shin hoo rahi hai,atah gutbaji samapta kerkey naye chunav karvaey jave.*[100]

In this regard, Puranmal Jalutharia further narrated:

Dinak 26.4.2001 koo akhil bhartiya Raigar mahasabha key samanvaya hetu samanvaya samiti ki baithak Krishna nagar karol bagh nai dilli mein shri chiranji lal bakolia ki adhayakta, mein aayojit ki gai thi jismein nimna likhit prasthav sarv sammiti sey parit kiya gaya tha.[101]

Samast sadasyo ney yeh prastav parit kiya ki dinak 30.10.2000 ko government hostel, jaipur mein akhil bhartiya raigar mahasabha ka chunav hua jismey shrimati mira kanvaria avam shri bhonri lal shastri doney adhyaksha baney, vah chunav mahasabha key vidhan key anusar sampana nahi hua hai[102]

The paper further reported in details:

Is prastav ki anupalna mein dono paksho ki aur sey doney adhaksho key istiphey leney aur vidhan key anusar naye chunav karvaney key sujhav aaye.In sujhavo ko bhonri lal shastri ki aur sey upsthit sadasyoo ney smarthan kiya, lekin shrimati mira kanwaria ki aur sey upsthit shri lakshman dhanvadia ney is prastav koo maaney sey inkar kar diya. Natijan samanvaya samiti key dwara kiye janey valley ekta key prasyoo mein gatirodh paida hoo gaya[103]

Thus, in a year's time, efforts were made for compromise between Bhori Lal Shastri and Shrimati Meira Kanwaria's groups to foster the unity in order to assert political powers, but failed.

After more than two decades, on December 24, 2000, ABRM, headed by Bhori Lal Shastri passed social, political and organisational resolutions along with constitutional amendment, which K.L. Kamal, Member, Executive Committee, ABRM published and circulated amongst the Raigars.[104] Later, it became the authentic document of ABRM. The aim of the bulletin, as expressed in it, was to raise the consciousness of the Raigars for developing self-importance, reviving their socio-economic programmes and welfare activities through unity and mutual cooperation among the Raigars and thereby to defend their socio-economic interest. It further appealed:

Prarambha mein akhil bhartiya raigar mahasabha ney desh bher mein raigar samaj ko ekjut ker samaj ke tatsamya vyapta kuritioo, malin karyoo avam khan pan per pratibandh lagaker samaj koo unnat banaya tatha aanya samajo sey agarni honey ki prena di. Raigar mahasabha key teen mahasamamelano avam vibhinnas khestriya sammelanoo kcy madhyamo sey samaj sudhar ky karyo ko aagey budhaya aur samaj mein vikas ki ek nai chetana jagrat ki. Lekin pichley doo daskoo mein un prasoo mein shithilta si aah gai. Samaj

> *key vikas ki gati ko aagey badney key isthan per kewal dikhava aaur aupcharikta per bal diya gaya. Phalswaroop vikas ka rath ruk sa gaya, kaei jagah samajik vyavthyein tool si gei tatha jatiya gaurav samapt hoo gaya. Puraney rozgar dwastha hoo gaey, lekin naye rozgar avam udhog dhandhey nahai apnaney key phalswaropp hamrey samaj ki aarthik isthithi davadol hoo gai hai. Pahley kewal matra sawa rupye mein sagai hoo jaya karti thi aur aab sagai per vivah sey adhik kharcha kiya jata hai. Is sambandh mein mahasabha koo thos avam kathore nirnaye lekar is vaivahik phezol kharchi ko rookna chahiye. Is phezol kharchi ko rookney sey joo rashi bachey usey bachcho ki shiksha per vyaya kiya jana chahiye. Raigar mahasabha ko chahiyey ki vah samaj key aarthik uthan key liye ek samabadhya karyakram banavey taki hamara samaj aarthik pragati ki dagar per chal sakey.*[105]

Besides passing the socio-economic resolutions for the all round development of the Raigar community, the ABRM was also aiming at defending 'political rights'. In political resolution, it stated:

> *Bhartiya rajniti ney swatantra prapti key paschat sey kai mod aur padav par ker liye hein. Hamney sarvpratham sammelan mein puran swarajya ki mang ki thi. Pratham aur dusrey dasak mein vidhan sabhaoo mein hamarey samaj key vidhyakoo ki acchhi sankhiya thi. Sansad mein bhi hamarey sadasya the, parantoo iskey paschat jis rajnaitik party per ham aashrit the, vahan hamari pakad samapta si hoo gai aur iskey phalswaroop anya samaj key log is shetra mein hamey pichey chod gaye. Is sambandh mein mahasabha ko joo sakriya bhoomika ada karni chahiyey thi, vah nahi kar saki. Badalty huye paripreksha mein hamey bhi hamarey vyapak samajik hit ko dhyan mein rakhker hi khuley dil-dimak sey kam lena hooga. Gram panchayat, panchayat samiti, jila parishad,nagar palika, nagar parishad, nagar nigam, vidhan sabayaoo, aur sansad tak hamarey samaj key log adhik sey adhik sankhiya mein chahiyey. Iskey liye haemin vibhinn rajnaitik daloo key sath gatbhandhan kerna chahiye. Aatah hamey iin sab batoo koo madhyey nazar rakhtey huey samaj key sarvageen unnati per adharit rajniti apnani chahiya*[106]

Notes

1. Roop Chand Jalutharia, *Raigar Jati ka Itihas*, Jaipur, Capital Printers, 2001, p. 73.

2. Ibid.
3. Ibid., p. 74.
4. Ibid.
5. Ibid., p. 75.
6. Ibid.
7. Ibid.
8. Ibid.
9. Ibid.
10. Ibid., p. 76.
11. Ibid.
12. Ibid., p. 78.
13. Ibid.
14. Bakolia, Chiranji Lal and Gadegaonlia, Rajendra Prasad, *Raigar Kaun aur Kya ?* New Delhi, Asian Printers, Hardhyan Singh Road, Karol Bagh, 1964, p. 126.
15. Ibid., pp. 126-128.
16. Ibid., p. 158.
17. Ibid.
18. Ibid., p. 159.
19. Ibid., p. 161.
20. Ibid., p. 168.
21. Ibid., p. 115.
22. Ibid., p. 113.
23. Ibid., p. 92.
24. Ibid., p. 91.
25. Ibid., p. 92.
26. Ibid., p. 161.
27. Naval, op. cit., p. 80.
28. Bakolia and Gadegaonlia, op. cit., p. 162.
29. Ibid., p. 163.
30. Ibid., p. 165.
31. Ibid., pp. 165-166.
32. Naval, op. cit., p. 144. Resolution passed *Akhil Bharatiya Raigar Mahasabha, Karyakarini Samiti avam Karyakarta Sammelan, Raigar Panchayat Bhawan, Beawar,* dated 8-9 November 1981, (Publication year not mentioned).
33. Conversation with Sua Lal Tanwar and others, Beawar, July 2,2003.

34. Ibid.
35. Naval, op. cit., pp. 78-79.
36. Ibid.
37. Ibid.
38. Resolution passed *Akhil Bharatiya Raigar Mahasabha, Karyakarini Samiti avam Karyakarta Sammelan, Raigar Panchayat Bhawan, Beawar,* dated 8-9 November 1981 (publication year not mentioned).
39. Ibid., pp. 2-4
40. Ibid., pp. 14-16.
41. Ibid., pp. 16-19.
42. Constitution of the *Akhil Bharatiya Raigar Mahasabha,* p. 4.
43. Ibid., pp. 6-7.
44. Ibid., pp. 7-14.
45. Ibid., pp. 6-14.
46. Conservation with Dharm Das Shastri, Delhi, July 16, and 19, 2003.
47. Ibid.
48. Ibid.
49. Ibid.
50. Ibid.
51. Ibid.
52. Ibid.
53. Naval, op. cit., p. 80.
54. Jalutharia, op. cit., p. 78.
55. Conversation with Madan Lal Dolia, Beawar, July 6, 2003.
56. Ibid.
57. Jalutharia, op. cit., p. 80.
58. For detailed information, see, oath taking ceremony of the newly elected executive and Sammelan of the *Akhil Bharatiya Raigar Mahasabha* held on December 24, 2000. Also see, report of other achievements dated April 29, 2001.
59. Letter from Rudradev, son of Late Chaudhary Padam Singh Sakkerwal written to author (received on June 26,2003). Telephonic conversation from Delhi on July 17, 2003. For further details, see, Chiranji Lal Bakolia and Rajendra Prasad Gadegaonlia, *Raigar Kaun aur Kya?,* New Delhi, 1964.
60. Ibid.
61. Ibid.

62. Ibid. Also see, *Shri Raigar Bandhu Bhajanawali*, Part I, Kanwar Sen Maurya, Delhi, Vidya Bhoosan Press, Koocha Ghasiram, Samvat 2002.
63. For most important discussion of the origin of *Kalyan Sangh* in Delhi and other regions of the country, see in particular, *Sri Sarsuni ji, Bahumukhi Samajik Pratiba key Dhani* in Souvenir, Kalyan Sangh, New Delhi, Published by Kalyan Sangh 1971, p. 30.
64. Ibid.
65. Ibid., p. 14.
66. Ibid., p. 30.
67. Ibid.
68. Ibid., p. 31.
69. Ibid.
70. Ibid., p. 15.
71. Ibid., pp. 15-16.
72. Ibid., p. 18.
73. Ibid., p. 19.
74. Ibid.
75. Ibid.
76. Ibid.
77. Ibid.
78. Ibid.
79. Ibid.
80. Ibid.
81. Ibid.
82. Ibid.
83. Ibid.
84. Ibid.
85. Ibid.
86. Ibid.
87. Ibid.
88. Ibid., p. 20.
89. Ibid., p. 21.
90. Ibid., p. 80.
91. Ibid.
92. Ibid.
93. Ibid., pp. 80-81.

94. Letter published and circulated by Yashpal Singh Khorwal, Mahamantri, ABRM, New Delhi, dated 16 April 2001.
95. "Ek Nivedan Ekta key liye, Mahasabha key doo Pradhan Kyo?" *Raigar Sudhar, 15-31* July 2001, p.2. Also see Adhiyaksh avam Delhi Raigar Samaj: Samaj ko Atmachintanki Avaksyakta, *Raigar Joyti,* Barmer, June 1, 2001, p. 11 and 16.
96. "Akhil Bharatiya Raigar Mahasabha: Akhil Bharatiya Raigar Mahasabha ki Stithi ka Spastikaran", *Raigar Sudhar,* July 1-15, 2001, pp. 1-3.
97. Ibid.
98. Ibid.
99. Ibid.
100. For detailed information, see, "Akhil Bharatiya Raigar Mahasabha mey Ekta ka Niryanaya", *Raigar Rakshak,* Jaipur, August 15, 2001, p. 7 and 11.
101. Ibid., p. 7.
102. Ibid.
103. Ibid.
104. On the rift and specially in ABRM, see, Oath taking ceremony of the newly elected executive and sammelan of the *Akhil Bharatiya Raigar Mahasabha* held on December 24, 2000, by K.L. Kamal. Also see Report of other Achievements published and circulated by ABRM on April 29, 2001, pp. 1-8.
105. Ibid., p. 7.
106. Ibid., pp. 5-6.

8

Origin and Development of Raigar Organisations in Rajasthan (1950-2004)

Fight Against Disabilities

The formation of Akhil Bharatiya Raigar Mahasabha (ABRM) and its intense agitation against the practices of untouchability and disabilities, and to gain access to schools, temples, etc., whipped up opposition by the Thakurs, Jagirdars, Jamindars, Brahmins, Baniyas and others, who were seen as the exploiters of untouchability, ill-treating them and threatening their attempts for social reformation. Economic restrictions were imposed and atrocities increased against this caste group. In an attempt to suppress the reform movement, they let loose some anti-social elements to even beat up the Raigars. These upper-caste people were irritated and as a result, one of the worst violent confrontations took place at Raisar, Parabatsar and Makreda[1], all in Rajasthan. The news was widely published. Swami Atma Ram 'Lakshya' bitterly criticised and condemned this action of Savarnas.

The reaction of the upper-caste Hindus in Rajputana and elsewhere to social reform of the Raigars, has to be seen in the context of Raigar Maha Sammelan of 1944.[2] Swamiji soon realised its repercussions. An urgent joint meeting of the representatives of the Mahasabha was convened at Ghat Gate, on October 31, 1945. The meeting was presided over by Swamiji. In the meeting it was decided that the next conference be held at Jaipur. After five months, ABRM organised the second annual conference at Jaipur on April 12-13, 1946.[3] The main participants of this conference were Khoob Chand Jajoria (Swagata Adhiyaksh), and Chaudhary Asha Ram Sevlia (Swagat Mantri). On the first day on April 12, 1946 the conference took place under the presidentship of Kanhaiya Lal Ratawal.[4] The Raigar flag was unfurled by Swami Atam Ram. On this occasion, Gotam Singh asked Raigars to carry on social reforms without yielding before the pressure and atrocities of upper-caste people. The main issue of the conference was to organise annual conferences in different parts of the country, with a view to politicise and to gain the support of Raigars for the day-to-day working of its organisation. Thus, there was a zeal amongst the workers and from 1944 until 1984 the ABRM organised four conferences – three at Jaipur[5] and one at Pushkar[6], Ajmer. Most of the issues were similar to those already taken up by the ABRM.

Since the inception of the reform movements, atrocities on the Raigars had increased considerably. The rural Raigars became aware of their strength and got interested in the social reform of the ABRM. They also encouraged the community people to sincerely implement the reforms programmes. Jagirdars, Jamindars, Brahmins and others were irritated and similar violent confrontations again took place at Dausa (Jaipur, 1944), Makreda (Ajmer, 1945), Parbatsar (Nagaur, 1945), Raisar (Jaipur, June 1945), Balesar (Jaipur, July 1945), Karana (Alwar, June 1946), Badi – Tonk (Tonk, 1946-1947), Beted (Sawai Madhopur, January 1947), Nimbaheda (Chittorgarh, June 1947), Niwai – Tonk (Tonk 1948) and Navwar (Kishangarh, November 1949)[7]. This news was widely published. Subsequently a delegation of social workers of Delhi Raigars under the leadership of Naval Prabhakar and Kanwar Sen Maurya visited all these places,[8] met the victims and expressed their solidarity with them. They also criticised and condemned in strong words the acts of atrocities perpetrated by the upper-caste Hindus.[9]

The oppression of the untouchables including Raigars in the rural areas of Rajasthan by the upper castes is beyond description. The delegation submitted a representation to the then government officials concerned but was unable to help the aggrieved Raigars to secure redressal. Hitherto, the Raigars had to bear all this without murmur.

The position, the Raigar movement now adopted, was refusal to perform their traditional tasks as it involved the question of low social position, economic backwardness and illiteracy of the Raigars. Through refusal or rejection to perform their traditional occupation, the reformists transformed the traditional tasks into social issues. The elimination of the traditional tasks could have succeeded and had social significance as the traditional relationships which had been established between Raigar community and villagers would be overturned. Moreover, refusal to perform their traditional tasks constituted a rejection of their original status in the village society and hence invited conflict between the caste Hindu villagers and the Raigars. It also implied a question of the ideology on which the 'varna' order was based and the decision of labour which that order embodied.

Opposition and reprisals to perform their traditional tasks came from the caste Hindu villagers. These incidents confirmed from various sources occurred in large number of villages in Rajputana. For instance, it happened at village Jawla,[10] situated at a distance of 12 miles away from Degana Railway station in Nagaur district. The Raigars of the village collectively took the decision not to remove to dead animals and skinning them. They also refused to repair the old shoes. Thus, the Raigars of Jawla village showed the signs of refusal to their traditional work to revitalise and regenerate the Raigar community. In doing so, they came into direct conflict with the structures of the power in the villages. The caste Hindu villagers took the following decisions[11] regarding the Raigars for the oppression of their reform movement:

1. The upper-caste villagers warned its members against helping the Raigars in any manner and barred them from supplying food grains and water. It also imposed fine on any person breaking the restrictions.
2. The caste Hindu villagers would not sell goods, vegetables and other essential commodities to these people with immediate effect.
3. No Raigar would be paid money as loan at the time of emergency.
4. Their (Raigar's) animals would not be allowed to graze in the fields of upper caste people.
5. Like the sale of the essential commodities, medicines too would not be sold or provided to their patients.

We also learn from the report of the Sabha[12], that when Raigars of village Palawala Jarana, Bassi in district Jaipur decided to refuse the traditional work and started reform, their action roused the wrath of the dominant higher castes. This resulted in violence. Their 60 huts were torched and their property were destroyed and livestock were looted. They were beaten mercilessly. Consequently, several Raigars were seriously injured. Complaints were lodged and a few were arrested.

During the period of pre-independence, the Raigars of village Tholai Jamva Ramgarh in Jaipur refused to do the traditional work. This affronted the upper-caste Hindus, who beat the Raigars and their properties were destroyed and livestock looted.[13]

Similar incidents have been reported from other parts of rural Rajputana in pre- and post-independence period or so. The Rajasthan Prantiya Raigar Mahasabha mentions that whenever and wherever the Raigars of various villages refused to do the 'begar', a traditional task and took the initiative in the reform movement, upper-caste Hindus beat them and tore off their clothes, their huts were torched and residing places were demolished. Their standing crops were burnt or looted. Properties were looted, mango trees were cut down, their wells and water tanks were polluted by night soil and dirt. Raigar women were tortured and harassed. Caste Hindus tried to prevent Raigars from passing through their fields and roads. They also prevented them from the use of the public places.[14]

The Rajasthan Prantiya Raigar Mahasabha mentions the names of the several villages in which such incidents occurred. Some of the important villages where such incidents happened are as follows: Rajpura (Thana Jamva Ramgarh), Dhola and Ghatwadi (Thana Chandwaji), Madhosinghpura and Markhiya (Thana Chaksu), Raisar (Thana Jamva Ramgarh), Sawansha Salempur and Bichhiya (Thana Lalsot), Banen (District Tonk), Bhankhri, Shamodar and Chawdia (Thana Bassi), Khatipura and Kundanpura (Thana Sanganer), Surajgarh Baldevgarh and Gheerod (District Alwar), Sujanpura, Rohtashpura and Kankrel Khanyahalla (District Jaipur), Mundra (District Sikar) and Peeplai (Thana Gadmora).[15]

The picture that emerges from the above description is that throughout Rajasthan, the dominant castes then tried to maintain the structural distance between upper-caste Hindus and lower-caste untouchables living within their jurisdiction, but they failed. The members of the Prantiya Raigar Mahasabha toured the effected areas to study the prevailing law and order situation and did not find it satisfactory. A large number of Raigars marched to the district authorities in protest against atrocities, arson, harassment and insult perpetrated on them in rural areas. In Jaipur, Raigars held a protest rally and later submitted a memorandum to the then Chief Minister and Home Commissioner for CBI/CID enquiry and demanded that police protection should be provided to them.[16] They also demanded that stern action against the culprits should be taken and anti-social elements be arrested. Thus, there was a gradual change in the behaviour of the Raigars from traditional to modern, in about a span of 60 years.

The social activists and reformers for Raigar movement from 1944 onwards held that by eliminating the traditional tasks, they could initiate the process of reconstruction of themselves as free men, without which no progress was possible, as they thought that the present conditions in the villages were indeed like a living death for all the untouchables.

Hence, they gave an instant call to the community to immediately shun the traditional occupation. The reformers were of the view that, if the community had to progress and survive with dignity, they, both from the point of view of social relationship and the ideology imposed on them, would have to be discarded. The reformers, therefore, emphasised the need to the self-reformation in the community and to shun the traditional tasks so that the status of the untouchables could be elevated.

From Caste Struggle to Downfall of Untouchability Relief

During the last days of the princely rule, several things happened which upset the systems based on acquired sense and roused untouchables (including Raigars) consciousness to agitate against their low status and the discrimination against them. Tension started building up, paving the way for a massive movement, with a distinct ideology led by political leaders, all directed towards social transformation.

A notable feature during the princely rule was a grand success of the untouchability relief campaign in Rajputana. In 1947, the then Government of Jaipur finally issued orders of removing disabilities imposed on untouchable Dalits.[17] Consequently, public schools, wells, tanks, temples, etc., were thrown open to the untouchables by the then State government in 1947.[18] The untouchables of Rajputana were happy. With this the untouchables achieved a major success in fighting against the deprivation in social, educational and religious spheres. But high-caste Hindus were angry with this move and so they beat them up and destroyed or torched their huts in rural areas.[19]

Even after 58 years of independence such atrocities still exist and in some spheres they have increased manifold. For instance on October 3, 2000, the leading regional daily newspaper *Dainik Bhasker*[20] (Jaipur) reported a case of untouchability under caption *'Chatro ney pani manga too school sey nikal diya'*. According to the report which appeared in the paper, the students of upper caste imposed prohibition on 38 untouchable students, who were studying in the government primary school, Navoda Bera, a village in Panchayat Samiti Balotara, District Barmer, in western Rajasthan, not to drink water from common water pots placed for students in the school campus. The untouchable students lodged a complaint against this restriction to the headmaster. Instead of supporting the untouchable students the headmaster became furious and expelled all the 38 untouchable students from the school. This action of the headmaster led to a row of resentment in the village when a non-government organisation called 'Unnati' interfered in the matter – all the expelled students were taken back. But the issue did not end there. The village Panchayat issued a show cause notice to NGO for interfering in the working of the government institution. Now the NGO reported the entire case to both, District Education Officer and Tehsildar, Barmer respectively. But the exercise of both the officers was seen as a more formality and they brushed aside the incident. When the case was not settled amicably the NGO further lodged a complaint with the Education Minister, Government of Rajasthan. Consequently, government sent the Deputy Director, Primary Education to investigate the case. Similarly the district Collector (Barmer) also conducted an independent enquiry and sent his report to the authority concerned in which headmaster was found guilty, for necessary action. When the case was brought to the notice of National Commission for SCs and STs and Human Rights Commission, both asked the authorities to submit their factual report immediately.

Similarly, after one year, on 22 August 2001, the same regional paper (*Dainik Bhaskar*, Jaipur) reported another case of untouchability.[21] This time the case was from Pali district in western Rajasthan. According to the paper, when the untouchable boys of Government Primary School, Shivansh village, felt thirsty, they took the courage to drink the water from a public tap. When this happened, some villagers saw them. They created an unruly scene in the entire village. In support of the agitators, the villagers immediately called an urgent meeting of the village panchayat. Panchayat felt frustrated and such violation hurt the ego of the 'Savarnas'. Consequently, the Gram Panchayat issued a 'Fatwah' expelling half a dozen untouchable families who were residing in the village for a long time from the village immediately.

Besides, village panchayat propounded three restrictions as follows:[22]

1. That the expelled untouchable families shall not be allowed to interact with upper caste people.
2. That shopkeepers shall not sell the goods to untouchables.
3. That no Sahukars, i.e., moneylenders (Baniyas) shall lend money or give financial support or any kind of help to these untouchables.

The decision was implemented in the village with immediate effect and untouchables were affected severely by this act. What is important is that such incidents are still widely prevailing in rural areas of Rajasthan.

Atrocities Against Untouchables in Rajasthan[23]

Having described the two incidents, now, we shall cite a few more cases. In doing so, we draw attention to the treatment meted out to the untouchables by the upper castes.

The incident took place at village Mauza Guthakar, Police Station Weir, district Bharatpur nearly six years ago. Mohini Devi Jatav, wife of Laxman Singh Jatav, was gangraped by the upper caste Hindus of Mauza Guthakar namely Nathu Singh, Mahinder Singh and Shri Ram on April 10, 1999. FIR No. 46/99 was lodged in the Police Station Weir on April 14, 1999 under Section 376 IPC. After the FIR was lodged the accused started harassing and torturing her and her husband for not to pursue the complaint. The case is too well known to all and need no detailed description. Another instance occurred in village of Jasrajpur in Khetri tehsil, district Jhunjhunu in Rajasthan. On September 6, 2000, all the family members of untouchables Om Prakash, Bajrang and Prahlad were attacked by the powerful Jat community of the village. FIR No.106

was lodged on February 6, 2000 with police station Khetri under Section 3 of the SC/ST Act 1989 against Phoola Ram, Moola Ram, Rameshwar and Khyali. It was also brought to the notice of the National Human Rights Commission. A Memorandum was sent to Chief Minister Ashok Gehlot, Home Minister L.K. Advani and Dalip Singh Bhuria, the then Chairman, National Commission for SC/ST, New Delhi.

Similarly, untouchable Pappu and his brother of Ghetada village, District Alwar, lodged FIR No. 137/98 dated September 1, 1998 against Mandasada, Birbal, Lalan, Mangala, Chhotu and Kailash belonging to a dominant caste for destroying their standing crops and illegally occupying their lands. There was another notable incident which happened 35 years ago. In 1972 Jinsi Ram Bairwa purchased a plot of land and got it registered. The dominant Gujjar community looked upon with an eye to use the fertile land in and around their field as an affront to their dignity and ordered the untouchables not to cultivate the land. They also sued him based on the forged and fabricated documents. The Bairwas family was beaten up bitterly several times and his wife and daughter were molested on various occasions. The victim was harassed and tortured by the police too.

The tyranny practised by the Hindus on the Bairwas an untouchable community in village Chakwara in Jaipur state was mentioned by Ambedkar in 1936 and is so typical of upper castes' attitude that we venture to quote from it the following extract. Ambedkar mentioned:

> It seems from the reports that have also appeared in the newspaper that an untouchable of Chakwara who had returned from pilgrimage had arranged to give a dinner to his fellow untouchables of the village as an act of religious piety. The host desired to treat the guests to a sumptuous meal and the items served included pure ghee (butter) also. But while the assembly of untouchables was engaged in partaking of food, the Hindus in hundreds, armed with lathis, rushed to the scene, despoiled the food and belaboured the untouchables who left the food which they were served with and ran away for their lives. At the moment it was not clear, why this murderous assault was committed on the defenceless untouchables? The reasons given was that the untouchable host was impudent enough to serve pure ghee and his untouchable guests were foolish enough to taste it. Ghee is

> undoubtedly a luxury for the rich. But no one would think that consumption of Ghee was a mark of high social status. The Hindus of Chakwara thought otherwise and in righteous indignation avenged themselves for the wrong done to them by the untouchables, who insulted them by treating Ghee as an item of their food which they ought to have known could not be theirs, consistently with dignity of the Hindus. This means that an untouchable must not use Ghee even if he can afford to buy it, since it is an act of arrogance towards the Hindus. This happened on or about the April 1, 1936.[24]

Sixty-six years ago, the Chakwara event led by the untouchables in the Jaipur state to claim access to use desi ghee was greeted with stones and lathis while eating the meal – matters do not seem to have changed much in some places of the country in general and Chakwara in particular.[25] This is a coincidence that his stark truth dawned upon the untouchables of the very Chakwara village, in Jaipur's Phagi tehsil when Bairwa – the very untouchable community planned to take out a 'Sadbhavna Yatra' to expose the caste discrimination. The untouchables of Chakwara to this day, barred from bathing at the public pond or entry to Hindu temples, planned a march from Chaksu to Chakwara to challenge the oppression of the Hindu upper castes. As news about the Yatra spread, the upper castes started forming illegal assemblies near the pond and blocked access to the venue. This culminated in a violent confrontation between the Savarnas and the police on September 21, 2002, in which more than 50 people including 44 policemen were injured. The immediate decisive issue in Chakwara goes beyond politics and local power equations. It involves access to common village pond, where stepped ghats have been built and maintained over the years with the state funds and contributions raised by the entire village including the untouchable Bairwas. But they have been barred from using the common ghats for decades. Caste-based 'purity' demands they be treated lower than the buffaloes, cows and pigs which have virtually unrestrained access to the pond.

On December 14, 2001, Babu Lal and Radhey Shyam Bairwa decided to defy the hallowed 'parampara' and took a dip in the pond. All hell broke loose.

The Savarnas led by the Jats who form about two-fifths of Chakwara's 500 household population held menacing public meeting that evening. There were blood curdling speeches. A severed social and economic boycott of Bairwas was enforced. They are:

1. The untouchables can no longer buy tea or vegetables in Chakwara or hire farm implements.
2. The fair-price shop ostracised them.
3. The local mechanic would not repair their bicycles.
4. The local doctors would not treat them.
5. Filthy abuse greeted them everywhere – their men were stalked, women abused, their main basti besieged.
6. The upper castes publicly threatened a 'blood bath' unless the Bairwas paid a fine of Rs 51,000 and worse, signed a 'compromise document' promising willingly to maintain caste apartheid in the use of the pond.

Intimidation, fear and lynch ruled Chakwara. This was the worst kind of terrorism in slow motion for the untouchables.

The police were amazingly perseverant with their mature advice and with rebukes and insults to the untouchables for breaking tradition. Despite this Babu Lal and Radhy Shyam lodged their First Information Report (FIR) at Phagi police station on December 22, 2001. The police took no action – a clear case of dereliction of duty is a cognisable offence under the SC/ST Prevention of Atrocities Act (POA), 1989 and the Indian Penal Code.

Within less than two weeks, the case was declared closed. Another compromise had been thrust upon the terrorised Bairwas and they had been administered a bitter pill down the throat by the administration who refused to physically protect them or invoke the POA to deter/punish Savarnas.

The police and district authorities, at least until two months ago have been studiedly callous towards the Bairwas's plight in the face of Savarna's oppression

By and large, the authorities have been themselves not as an enforcing agency of the law but as an upholder of conventional, hierarchical, caste-ridden social order. The State Human Rights Commission, a statutory body had, in some ways, been an even greater 'disappointment'. It received a complaint from Babu Lal and Radhey Shyam on December 28, 2001. It could have initiated an independent inquiry but it ordered the Superintendent of Police to investigate. Once the police reported that a compromise agreement had been reached, HRC too closed the file after issuing some pro-forma notices to the complainants presumably through the police (which Babu Lal says he never received).

It was more than a decade ago that Rajasthan witnessed the Kumhar carnage in Bharatpur, in which 17 Jatavs were burnt alive and quartered by a lynch mob, including public servants.

Atrocities against the untouchable women persist and many a time are used as tools to punish those who 'dare' raise their voice to get justice in society. The *Hindustan Times* reported that in the past three years, Rajasthan alone had recorded 15,072 cases of crimes against the SCs/STs including an annual average of 46 killings, 134 rapes and 93 cases of grievous injury.

The issue in Chakwara is not merely access to a pond. It is systematic, entrenched discrimination against the untouchables. An untouchable woman cannot wear a pair of sandals in the main village. Untouchable children can sit only at the back of the classroom and drink water from separate pot. The bridegroom riding a horse at a wedding 'baraat' risks being roasted alive. Droitde Seigneur (the upper caste landlord's right to 'deflower' an untouchable bride - to be) was prevalent.

As stated earlier, Chakwara was mentioned by Ambedkar way back, more than six decades ago. The Bairwas then defied the Savarnas by making Desi Ghee, a 'privilege' denied to them. Caste Hindus retaliated by pouring dirt into the Ghee. Bairwas have asserted themselves again after decades with greater resources – most people are literate and no longer submissive.

They have the law explicitly on their side. But so long as guardians of law, driven by Parampara based on obscurantism, continue to make a travesty of it, the untouchables struggle for elementary human dignity will face heavy odds.

The journey of the untouchables quest for social equality, which began with the movements initiated by Jyotirao Phule has traversed a long and painful path. Their strongest articulation came during the life time of Ambedkar. His Chavdar Talab agitation, Kalram Mandir entry effort and burning of the Manu Smiriti are the three major landmarks in this arduous task, which apparently remains incomplete till date. The denial of these "identity related practices" is the surface phenomenon hiding the deeper deprivation of justice of these "children of a lesser God" the failure of land reform and the persistence of Brahminical values in society. During the freedom struggle Ambedkar's emphasis on issues related to social justice forced the leaders of the national movement to take these up as part of the agenda associated with the main demand for unshackling the country from the chain of colonialism.

To ride on a mare on an auspicious occasion like marriage is the right of every caste Hindu. It is also in evidence that the community, which enjoys this right, is accepted as a respectable community. The untouchables have no such right. But they have been seeking to establish such right by riding on a mare at the time of marriage with the object of establishing their social status. The following incidents which have been reported from time to time in the newspapers show how the Hindus have dealt with this claim.

The correspondent of *Tathya Bharti* (A Hindi fortnightly magazine) reported the following incident which appeared in the issue of *Tathya Bharti* of March 2, 2003:[26]

> On the 5th Day of March, 2003 the marriages of two daughters of Chhitar Bairwa of village Bharthalla was to take place. On the same day at 9.00 p.m. when the baraat of sons of Bhura Bairwa (both bridegrooms – Ram Kishore and Nanag Ram respectively) reached Bharthalla from nearby village Ramnagar, the baratis were lodged in a village school for the time being till other baratis arrive. Just at that moment, a band party (music party) composed of lightmen and mares started beating the drums. The marriage procession of Bairwas of which the greater portion was composed of boys, girls and women was setting out for bride's house on its usual way. When Gujjars, Meenas, Kumavats and others heard that marriage party of an untouchable Bairwa was coming and grooms were sitting on the mare, they took offence at this for they thought it to be an insult to them. The marriage procession was just to start, when the Gujjars, Meenas, Kumavats and others started pelting stones. The baratis were belaured. Not only this, the groom – Ram Kishore also received a stone at his back. At that time another groom Nanag Ram, the elder brother of Ram Kishore was trying to protect his younger brother. The Gujjars, Meenas etc. gave him also thorough beating. Both the grooms along with some baratis ran away in the fields and reached safely to clusters of Dhanies belonging to Bairwa community. The general situation now was that baratis had to run away to safer places. When this news reached amongst the family members of Chittar Bairwa, they were shocked. Miscreants have run away taking the advantage of darkness. They informed the police authorities at Niwai about this episode.

> At last on March 6th, at 1.00 a.m. (night) SP, SDM, and Tehsildar along with police force reached the village Bharthalla. At that time all the villagers were sleeping and at that time (on of March 6th at midnight) in the presence of the district authorities, the marriage procession was taken out. It was reported that the marriage was performed and farewell was given to baratis in the presence of SDM and police party. FIR was lodged in this connection.
>
> Some other instances of similar nature are given below:

The correspondent of *Hindustan Times* reported the following incidents which appeared in the issue of *Hindustan Time* of March 11, 2003.[27]

> Alwar, March 10. According to the FIR lodged at Mundawar Police Station by the victim's brother, when the Nikasi of Dalit bridegroom Rajendra in Khund Road village under Mundawar Police Sation in Behron Tehsil, District Alwar, reached the Rajput Mohalla, Gajraj Singh dismounted Rajendra from the mare. Gajraj Singh and his family members started pelting stones, breaking the glass panes of Tata Sumo moving along with the *baraat*. *Baratis* after passing through Rajput Mohalla again mounted the groom on the mare. After reaching the bus stand, the *baraat* left for Badali village in Mundawar Tehsil.
>
> The police on Monday arrested Gajraj Singh and Hukam Singh under Section 341, 323, 336 and 3 SC/ST Act.
>
> The atrocities committed by the caste Hindus on the untouchable – Bhangi of village Darda Hind in Tonk District was reported in the issue of *Dainik Bhaskar*, Jaipur, on Thursday, April 17, 2003.[28]

According to newspaper, when Nikasi of bridegroom Mukesh Kumar s/o Ladu Lal Bhangi was passing through the village, Radha Kishan Jat started throwing water from the roof of his house on the procession. Apprehending any untoward incident on the marriage day (just after a few days) the terrorised Ladu Lal approached District Collector and Superintendent of Police to provide security to him. Consequently, the marriage procession was taken out in the presence of the local authorities and it was performed in the presence of a police party.

From 1944 onwards several other organisations came into existence: Raigar Society Ravivans Hitkarini Sabha, at Beawar, founded by Gheesu Lal; Raigar Sewak Sangh at Jaipur, founded by Ghasi Lal Peepliwal, Roop Chand Jalutharia, Gopal Mahoria and Kanhaiya Lal Palia; Kshatriya Raigar Vikas Mahasabha Bikaner at Bikaner, founded by Pana Lal Sakkarwal, Gopal Chand Singadia and Praveen Kumar Sukhadia; Shri Raigar Sudharak Karyakarini Sangh at Ajmer, founded by Sukhraj Singh (Arya) Nogia; Shat Patti Raigar Panchayat Ajmer, founded by Raigars of the Ajmer regions; Rajasthan Raigar Pragatisheel Sabha Jaipur, founded by Naval Kishore 'Nidar', Ram Narain Gusaiwal; Raigar Navyuwak Sangh at Bagdi, District Tonk, founded by Vikram Kumar Bansiwal; Akhil Rajasthan Raigar Yuva Mahasabha, founded by Anil Jalutharia, Mahesh Chandra Karadia and Sohan Lal Dudia and Raigar Vikar Sansthan Rajasthan at Jaipur, founded by K.L. Kamal, Baldev Prasad Hingonia and Man Mohan Jalutharia.

In the Section that follows, we shall deal with the growth of these organisations with divergent objectives and their effects on the socio-economic conditions of the community.

Origin of Raigar Caste and Bahi Bhatt

In many major towns and cities such as Nagaur, Pali, Ajmer, Beawar, Jodhpur and Jaipur in Rajasthan, the Raigars have shown a high capacity for social and political mobilisation. The leaders of Ajmer-Beawar occupy the leading position. The poor Raigars, religious saints, freedom fighters and social activists in Ajmer and Beawar towns have started organising themselves for welfare activities and mobilised the resources to build hostels, Dharmashala, etc. Gheesu Lal, a resident of Beawar took the initiative in working out plan for the educational welfare and social upliftment of the Raigars, Thus, in the year 1927, a Raigar association was established in the city of Beawar called Raigar Society Ravivans Hitkarini Sabha, Beawar.[29] Gheesu Lal became the President. The main programme of the association was to propagate the social reforms. The association also pressed for the education of Raigars and for sending the boys and girls in large numbers to the schools. In the same year the association also published a small booklet of 38 pages for propagation of reforms in their caste customs, and for socio-cultural reformation. It was reformative in its orientation and encouraged programmes of upliftment.

In the same year, Gheesu Lal issued a notice to 19 Bhatts (Raigar caste geneologists) of the different areas in Rajasthan, who had been serving the Raigar community for generations asking 12 questions[30] and demanded for submission of their replies. The major agitation of the Raigar community centred around the following prominent issues:

1. What are the proofs of the origin of Raigar caste with you? Was the caste already in existence or how was it linked with Saint Ravidas?
2. What things were given to you (Bhatts) as gifts by Saint Ravidas and how many times? Let us know about the date of gifts.
3. Tell, the name of the place where Ravidas was born and breathed his last. What was his age at the time of death.
4. Who was his God? Where did he show his miracle.
5. What are the evidences with you that show that Ravidas skinned?
6. In your records, it is said that Ravidas had two wives namely Agarwalin and Loonde Chamri. There were 12 sons and one daughter of Ravidas.
7. Tell us how Agarwalin married with him. Tell us, how many children were born by Agarwalin and Chamarin respectively? Also tell where these children were married and with whom you link the Raigar community.
8. It has already been proved from your records, that there were 12 disciples of Ravidas belonging to Dabgar, Jat, Telli, Kumhar, Dhobi, Brahmin and few other castes. If there is any legal dispute about it, then you would be held responsible.
9. It is alleged that the Bhatts cheated the Raigars, exploiting their ignorance. Explain.[31]

After a few months, in the same year, a large contingent of Raigars attended the meeting of caste Panchas, Sarpanchas, Chaudhary, Patels, etc., held at Beawar on Sudhi 2, Samvat 1984 and replied received from Bhatts were placed before the Caste Panchayat.[32] The Samaj also asked the Bhatts to submit their oldest records. While the bulk of the records with Bhatts were three hundred year old, the oldest of them was 350 years old.[33] The replies made by the Bhatts was not considered satisfactory by Gheesu Lal, who was dedicated to the welfare work of the Raigars in Rajasthan. According to him the chief obstacle to the progress is the traditional 'Bhatt system'[34] among the Raigars. The Bhatts misguided Raigars regarding their origin, customs, rituals, etc. The Bhatts in the cities and villages did not bring to their notice the right things, but they exploited them economically and mentally by demanding more and more money and benefits. In this way the Bhatts were the exploiters of the community and while the traditional 'Bhatt system' did not fulfil any important function, it has no relevance because the Bhatts exploited the people demanding customary payments on several occasions.

Not only did the association raise the questions for their origin, but it also agitated for poor socio-economic conditions and asked the caste men to minimise their expenditure on marriage, birth of male child, death feast and ban on serving of liquor on certain occasions.[35]

Lastly, it composed a few songs on their economic and social conditions and educational backwardness which were played on public announcement system in the large gatherings of Raigars in cities and villages. The songs depict why they were socially backward and their economic condition poor, and educationally no where. One such song is as under:

Martak ausar per barbadi ki ek mahima gaye sunatey hai
Nugta auusar mauusar karkey, ham kya kya kast uthatey hai
Ghar mein maaut mari padi sab, kutumb roodan yu kartey hai
Kal key gal mein jaya basey, assu ki ghunt pitey hai
Awwaj maut ki sunney per, ham bhojan karna pap samajtey hai
Mratakk bhojan ka jeeman jeem ker, kya nahi doosh baratey hai
Lokachari panth baith,kar aapas mein kana phusi kartey hai
Slahkar panchoo ki niti, alag bitha samajtey hai
Janam maran aur maut jindgi, dukh sukh sab mein aatey hai
Sartan pas mein sab kuch terey, uchit rai batlatey hai
Goodtey ghar ko bhog bataker, shram per dand dikhatey hai
Malpuwa ter mal mithai, koi panch pakwan banatey hai
Jaat jeeman ganga nahaan, aisa punhah batatey hai
Phirto chahey banoo bhikhari, yeh punah pavitra ker detey hai
Panch sammelan karkey ikkatha, ver thithi sey muhrat kaayam kartey hei
Aagey ki kuch bhool hoyey too, iis avsar per puri kartey hai[36]

Shri Raigar Sudharak Karya Karini Sabha and Sukhraj Singh 'Arya' Nogia

The agitation for banning untouchability and atrocities perpetrated on Raigar caste in the state of Rajasthan forms the fourth phase of the history of this movement.

The three earlier phases of this movement discussed in the previous chapters were: (1) spiritual reformation ushered in by Dharmgurus, (2) the social awakening created by ABRM, and (3) the phase that was characterised by fighting against the social disabilities. The main leader of the agitation for fighting against untouchability and atrocities of upper castes, was Sukhraj Singh 'Arya' Nogia. He was born in the year 1929 in a village called Dorai, in District Ajmer.[37] His father Bhagirath Nogia was from a poor Raigar family. Sukhraj Singh Nogia had studied up to middle-school and was employed as Amin (Patwari) in the Revenue Department in the erstwhile Ajmer State.

The main problem which attracted the attention of Sukhraj Singh Nogia in the earlier years of independence was the increasing atrocities on untouchable communities in general, and Raigars in particular, in rural Rajasthan.

During the 1940s, a few major untouchable communities connected with leather occupations, particularly Chamars, Bhambi, Meghwals and Raigars announced to discard their traditional occupations and this was enthusiastically followed by their respective caste-men all over Rajasthan.[38] It attracted the attention of Thakurs and Brahmins. As a result of this, the upper-caste Hindus from 1940 onwards increased the atrocities on untouchable communities in rural Rajasthan. Thus, there were violent riots due to boycott of traditional work in the villages by untouchable castes. The upper castes opposed the Raigars and Chamars and invaded the Raigars with 'lathis' and swords. Here mention can be made of some trouble-torn areas[39]: Hadoti, Mewar, Merwada, Shekhawati, Toravati and Rajavati regions. In this regard the Meenas, Gujjars and Ahirs in north-eastern regions of Rajasthan joined hands with upper castes against the Raigars, Bairwas and Chamars. It will be noted that Meenas, Gujjars, Ahirs were financially well-to-do and socially dominant castes. It were the Meenas, Gujjars and Ahirs, in rural areas who were the first to oppose their reform movement. Being numerically dominant and socially superior, they harassed and tortured the untouchables. Hence, for Raigars and Chamars (now Bairwas), in rural Rajasthan, the main opposition caste groups in their reform movement were the Meenas, Gujjars and Ahirs.[40]

Since the independence, Babu Jagjiwan Ram emerged as a powerful leader of scheduled castes at the national level. He belonged to a Chamar community from Bihar. He was known for his political leadership, Massiha of Harijans and took an active interest in the welfare of downtrodden. The harassed and tortured Chamars of Rajasthan met Babuji in Delhi to bring to his notice their grievances, problems and atrocities committed by the upper-caste Hindus.[41] He was mainly responsible for protecting the interest of untouchables in general, and chamars in particular. But the social security and protection of Raigars had become a particular problem with the increase of atrocities in earlier years after independence. The leaders of ABRM were indifferent and no attempts were made to protect against all this happening with savarnas. Thus harassment, torture and atrocities posed a serious problem in the history of Raigar movement.[42]

Around middle of twentieth century, Sukh Raj Singh Nogia was aware of such miserable conditions of his caste-men in several regions. Another problem which attracted the attention of Nogia was the passive role of political leaders. Three MLAs, for instance in Ajmer Assembly, did not help in solving their genuine problems.[43] Most of political leaders were running after the political power and ABRM was inactive.

With such sad experiences and background, Nogia left his government job[44] and became the founder of Shri Raigar Sudharak Karyakarini Sabha (SRSKS).[45] SRSKS had emerged as a pivotal organisation enlisting the cooperation of Raigars from rural Ajmer. The establishment of SRSKS in the year 1950 was a great event in the history of Raigar movement. This organisation made the Raigars aware of their pitiable conditions, their low social status as untouchables and the necessity of social reform for social change and fighting against the atrocities in order to make progress. This organisation supported the opening of the branches of SRSKS, whose main activity was to agitate and fight against the atrocities, untouchability and disabilities in different areas of Rajasthan. This was the means of social mobilisation. Thus, this organisation got a separate identity due to the development of the activities of the Raigar movement. An application for registering of SRSKS was submitted in Ajmer by the Management of the Sabha and registration licence was granted by the government. The main objective of Sabha was to promote and encourage the young generation to implement reforms and to educate and to inculcate industrious habits amongst them.

It is significant to note that Nogia's whole family was associated with the activities of the Sabha and his wife Sushila Devi took an active interest in the affairs of the Sabha.[46] In addition to his active participation in the Sabha, Nogia was also associated with the court litigations and since his resignation from government job, he started working as 'Petition Writer' in the court and fought occasionally small cases related with land disputes of his caste-men for which he charged a nominal fee.[47]

Since Nogia did not have his own house in Ajmer town, he started living in a rented house at Ramganj area, Ajmer. Here, the grievances and other problems of Raigars who came from far-flung areas were heard by him and he tried his best to solve them through the police and court.[48] He was known for his organisational abilities, oratory in Hindi, honesty and sincerity of purpose.

SRSKS introduced certain positive programmes of reforms. It encouraged education and stressed the importance of construction of hostels for the poor and needy Raigar students in different regions and the necessity to make progress in diverse economic activities and the need to secure jobs. The Sabha was also interested in the programmes of the social reforms, especially those concerned with eradication of child marriage, eating of meat, dowry, drinking of liquor, etc. The Sabha pointed out the undesirability of such practices and also condemned the death feasts which besides being expensive were seen as instances of backwardness.

The Sabha, in the earlier years concentrated its attention on two issues, the whipped-up opposition to upper-caste Hindus who were seen as the exploiters of untouchables, ill-treating them and thwarting their attempts for progress and social mobilisation. The agitations were directed against these groups. In this, Raigars joined hands with other cognate castes which were making similar attempts for progress in spite of opposition from the Meenas, Gujjars, Ahirs and others.

Nogia made extensive tours, propagating his message, by visiting some important cities and towns in east and southern Rajasthan and meeting activists, social workers and political leaders. He visited Tonk, Bundi, Sawai Madhopur, Niwai, Chaksu, Sanganer and Jaipur to seek the cooperation of the people and to involve them in the campaign.[49] Nogia also attracted the attention of the rural Raigars and was invited by them to visit and hold meetings in their villages. From 1950 onwards, he addressed several meetings at many places notably Peeplu, Jamdoli, Bhagatgarh, Siwad, Sawai Madhopur, Agarpur, Nader, Karvar, Pander, Narvar, Sawaria, Diggi, Phagi, Kota, Chaksu, Bagru, Sawansha, Bali and Aluda.[50] In all his speeches, Nogia emphasised specially on three issues – increasing educational facilities for Raigars and eradicating social vices for change. He impressed on the value of reform in raising their ritual status and boycott of traditional occupation. Besides meeting, he started organising 'satsang mandali', which was another major source in the caste awakening. Likewise, he started performing stage programmes in different areas of Rajasthan from 1960 onwards. Thanks to the efforts of Nogia and his colleagues, through stage programmes they portrayed the real socio-cultural conditions of the Raigar community.

As a result of all this, a large number of caste fellows were attracted by Nogia's teachings and became his followers. Contemptuous curiosity prompted Raigars to eradicate their social vices. The Sabha became popular among Raigars in Rajasthan from 1950 onward. A notable feature of the spread of Nogia's teachings among the Raigars in Rajasthan was adoption of social reforms. It led to violent riots due to boycott of traditional work by Raigars. The worst violence occurred at Gotor, Marot, Ajmer, Chaksu and Chawdia. Upper-caste Hindus also filed false criminal and civil cases against Raigars in law courts, with a view to harass them.

Nogia was active as socio-religious reformer,[51] in the 1950s and he died on January 13, 1983. During the period of about thirty-three years, the kind of radical changes he ushered in, were remarkable. He formulated his system of thought, oriented towards social transformation, and maintained that the reformation of community was necessary for the upliftment of the masses.

Raigar Sewak Sangh

As have already been mentioned earlier, that from 1940, Raigars in the rural areas had started boycotting the traditional work and since then violent confrontation occurred in many parts of north-eastern Rajasthan. During this period a lot of Raigars arrived in Jaipur to seek the support of Raigar leaders. Roop Chand Jalutharia claims that there was nobody to listen and guide them and they were dissatisfied with the unmethodical way in which ABRM functioned. Roop Chand Jalutharia (a resident of Chandpole) and his other colleagues evinced interest in working for his caste-men when they met such helpless persons in Jaipur in 1950.[52] The other colleagues were: Ram Lal Karadia (Kotri), Gopal Chanwal, Moti Lal Mandawaria, Dhanna Lal Dewatwal and Prabhu Dayal Pigolia (all from Ghatgate).[53] As in the case of SRSKS, Raigar youths of Jaipur were also involved in the social activities of community.

Thus, Raigar youths who provided a different kind of leadership and established a Raigar Sewak Sangh in 1950 emerged in Jaipur. The most notable leader in this period, who founded the Sangh was Ghasi Lal Peepliwal.[54] The other members of the Sangh were: Roop Chand Jalutharia, Gopal Mahoria, Kanhaiya Lal Palia, Ram Chandra Dudia, Ramdhan and Shalig Ram Jalutharia.[55] In Jaipur they established an Ashram called Gandhi Ashram[56] and also taught the Raigar students. They used to help the poor Raigar boys coming from the rural areas in their admission to government schools and hostels and filling up their scholarship forms.

Thus, the Raigar Sewak Sangh acquired a mass character in Jaipur region, where Raigars came into open conflict with upper-caste Hindus in their agitation to boycott the traditional work and to abolish the custom of 'begar'. While the former was an attempt to remove social disability, the latter was an effort to abrogate an economic disability. Raigars were attacking the monopoly of the upper castes both in social and economic domains. The Raigars Sewak Sangh centred around two prominent issues: the filling of criminal and civil cases against the upper castes in law courts for their harassment and atrocities on them, and to carrying out a programme of social reforms.

Roop Chand Jalutharia was one of the founders of Raigar Sewak Sangh in Jaipur. He was born in Jaipur on November 25, 1930,[57] in the family of Raigar of Jalutharia. He started his career as a school teacher in Jaipur. Later, he took his M.A. in history and B.Ed. and became the Principal of Senior Government Secondary School, Narena, a small town in Jaipur district[58] and wrote a few books in Hindi. His two younger brothers Ramdhan and Shalig Ram Jalutharia had been Deputy Director, Agriculture Department, Government of Rajasthan and Assistant Secretary at Government Secretariat, Jaipur, respectively and his third brother Rati Kant was a Bank Manager in Rajasthan.[59] Roop Chand Jaluthari's eldest daughter Savitri was the first girl candidate who did her M.A. in 1976 in second division. His three daughters namely Vidya, Vimal and Anjurani also did M.A., B.Sc. and B.A. respectively. His two sons Davendra Kumar and Pawan Kumar did B.E. from Rajasthan.[60]

Roop Chand Jalutharia's public life started with his association with Raigar movement in Rajasthan and he took an active interest in it.

As stated above, Jalutharia started teaching at school level and later went to Sawai Madhopur district for further studies. Besides his professional achievement, Jalutharia was a keen social worker and launched the reform activities in the rural areas of Sawai Madhopur district and succeeded in organising the Raigar youths from villages. Later in 1953, he established Raigar Sewak Sangh in Sawai Madhopur.[61] The main activity of the Raigar Sewak Sangh was to organise meetings with a view to popularise the reform programmes and gaining the support of the community fellows for its execution.

Campaign for Eradication of Social Vices and Its Effects

A meeting of the Panchas of Raigar Panchayat Shatpatti, Ajmer took place around early 1976, at Pushkar Mandir, Ajmer. During the course of the meeting, it was decided to immediately ban the use of liquor, giving death feast along with other social evils in the community.[62] At the conclusion of the meeting it was urged that Raigars should wholeheartedly implement the decisions taken by the Panchayat and so a campaign was launched. At this place a decision was published by the Panchas, which appealed to the Raigars to discard the use of liquor and death feast. A large number of Raigars took the lead in eradicating the social evils in the surroundings of the Ajmer region. Some Panchas, however, opposed it. On March 27, 1976, when such news reached Ajmer, a big meeting of the Panchas of Shatpatti Panchayat, Ajmer was summoned at Pushkar Mandir, Ajmer,[63] where 125 Panchas were present.[64] Opposition to eradication of social evils had far-reaching implications, as it involved the whole question of improving the socio-economic position of the Raigars. The Panchayat concentrated its attention in discussing the question of opposition to the Panchayat decision. It argued that eradication of evils was essential as it affected the condition of the community as well as Raigars' socio-cultural development.

The Panchayat, therefore, took a decision to expel Panchas, particularly Mohan Lal Patel and Ramji Lal Sarawandia, Ajmer, from community of violating the Panchayat decision.[65] This decision was supported largely by Raigar community.

As a result of this, expelled Panchas filed a civil suit on April 11, 1977 and May 12, 1977 against the decision of the Raigar Panchayat, Ajmer region, in the courts of First Class Munsif and Judicial Magistrate,[66] Ajmer respectively. The total number of the Panchas against whom case was filed was nineteen.[67] Their names were: Gopi Lal Karawlia, Chhagan Lal Mandravlia, Arjun Lal Maurya, Jagat Ram Detwal, Hazari Lal Balotia, Ram Kishan Sivasia, Madan Lal Dolia, Kishan Lal Khetawat, Suryamal Maurya, Ganga Ram Balotia, Ram Lal Mandravlia, Hari Ram Charotia, Ram Dev Kanwaria, Hari Ram Sarvad, Panchu Ram Dholpuria, Chhoga Lal Bakolia, Laxman Bakolia, Ugam Chand Beer, and Ram Pal Dholpuria.

After a lapse of nearly four months, on August 23, 1977 Chand Mal Totla, Munsif Magistrate dismissed the case by pronouncing the following decision:[68]

> *Vidhavaan adhivakta abhiyogi ney tarak diya hai ki dhara 500 bhartiya dand sanhita ka abhiyogi daraj kiya jana chahiya, vichar kiya gaya. Abhiyogi mohan lal key vayanoo tatha gavah madan lal key bayanoo sey bhi pramanit hai ki abhigogi is panchayat ka sadasya hai tatha puri panchayat bulakar 27 march 1976 ko abh;iyogi ko samaj sey nikala gaya tatha parcha egji-1 chapvayagaya. Parcha egji – 1 saat patti ki virat panchayat ka nirya hai, is parchey key pahaley para sey ispata hai ki pushkar key mandir mein saatoo patti kei vishal panchayat hui, jismey sau sava sau panch upasthit they. Is parchey ko dekhaney per paata chalta hai ki panchayat ney vichar kerkey jaati virodhi karyahiyo key liye abhiyogi to jati bahar kiya tatha yeh parcha panchayat key nirnaya ko prakashit kerta hai. Is tarah yeh manney mein koi sandesh nahi haiki panchayat ki sabha ki jakar is per vichar karey key bad panchayat dwara abhiyoti ko jati sey bahar karney ka nirnaya kiya gaya.Dhara 499 antargat 'exceptiono mein' yah mamla manhani ka nahi mana ja sakta. Law of crime lekh ka Rattan Lal dhirajlal addition 22 peg 1333 per is sambandh mein ispatast hai ki yadi panchayat ya sabha key nirnayao ko prakshit kiya jata hai too kewal matra yeh prakashit kiyey janey sey man hani nahi mani ja sakti kyoki jati key tamam sadasio ka issey hit hai. Yadi kisi vyakti to vastav mein jati sey bahar ker diya gaya hai too iskey prakashit honey sey maanhani nahi hogi. Yeh ispast hai ki jab tak panchayat aapni jati key hitco ko dekhtey huaye kishi sadasya key virudha nirnaye leti hai too issey dhara 500 key antargat dandniya apradh nahi mana ja sakta. Parcha egji 1 dekhney per yeh ispat hai ki panchayat ney sharab piney va mritayu bhojan na karney key panchayat key nirnaya ka virodh*

karney tatha aanya karnoo sey vichar kerkey abhiyogi ko jati sey bahar nikala. Egji-2 dwara kewal matra panchayat mein hui nirnayo ka palan karney key liye kaha gaya. Vidhavaan adhivakta abhiyogi ney aey. ie. aar 1939 madras, page – 382, aey. ie. aar 1940, nagpur, page 283, aey. ie. aar 1932 nagpur page 97, tatha aey. ie. aar 1930 calcutta page 645 mein di gagye vyasthayoo pesh ki hai. In vyasthayoo ka dhyanpurvark avlokan kiya jakar prastut abhiyog per vichar kiya gaya. Prastut abhiyog mein abhiyogi key vayanoo va egji-1 sey yeh ispast hai ki abhiyogi ko jaati sey bahar ker diya gaya hai, aatha uprokta vyasthaye abhiyogi ki madad nahi karti hai. Nyayalaya ki raaya mein dhara 500 bhartiya dand sanhita key antargat ya Anaya koi apradh nahi banta hai. Dhara 211 bhartiya dand sanhita ka apradh banney ka prashna hi nahi hai, aatah dhara 203 da. Pra. Sanhita key antargat istagasa kharij kiya jana chahiye.

Aadesh

Istagasa dhara 203 da. Pra. Sanhita key antargat kharij kiya jata hai. Aadesh aaj dinaka 23 august 1977 ko type karaya jakar sunya gaya.

s.d. Chandmal
Munsif avam Nyayik Magistrate
Pratham Verga Ajmer, Jila – Ajmer

The Raigar Panchayat Shatpatti's venture into organisational aspects of the Raigar movement, however was not essentially different from earlier organisations within the movement. Thus, the Raigar Panchayat showed signs of being more than a socio-cultural body devoted to the amelioration and uplift of Raigars in Ajmer region. The pamphlets published and circulated from 1977 onwards by Raigar Panchayat amongst the Raigars suggest that, it was beginning to take more interest in socio-economic conditions of the Raigar community in rural areas, and in doing so, was coming into conflict with caste fellows in the villages.

The Raigars of the villages of Sarmalia, Raigar Lamana, Rajiawas and Chhota Bas, Beawar complained to the Raigar Panchayat Shatpatti of certain violation of caste men in the matter of their social issues. The Raigar Panchayat took a serious note of it and took the decision to ex-communicate them immediately. The matter of Raigar's ex-communication became a prime issue, with the pamphlets warning for its violation.[69] The expelling issue had far reaching implications. This had ensured to obey the Raigar Panchayat Shatpatti's decision. Through pamphlets Raigar

Panchayat urged therefore that Raigars must reject and ban the social evils which they had been following in the community.

Rajasthan Raigar Pragatisheel Sabha, Jaipur

In 1978, a few educated young Raigar youths in Jaipur took the initiative to bring together their caste men. The first meeting of their like-minded progressive people was convened on April 9, 1978 at Ram Niwas Bagh, under the leadership of two Raigars – Naval Kishore Nidar (advocate) and Puran Mal Jalutharia.[70] In this meeting, a committee consisting of 7 members was constituted to formulate a scheme for an all-round development of the society. Naval Kishore Nidar became the convenor. On December 17, again a meeting of the committee was held. Some of the active members of the Rajasthan Raigar Prantiya Mahasabha were also invited in this meeting. It presented its report which was approved.[71] It also requested the Rajasthan Raigar Prantiya Mahasabha (RRPM) to initiate the process of holding elections of the Mahasabha but the RRPM was not interested in the election.

Due to the organisational efforts made by Nidar and Jalutharia, a meeting of the like-minded people of the community was held on January 7, 1978 on the lawns of Ravindra Manch in Ram Niwas Bagh under the Presidentship of Moti Lal Balotia. In this meeting it was unanimously decided to form a separate sabha to be called Rajasthan Raigar Pragatisheel Sabha (later to be called RRPS). Thus, RRPS came into existence on that day with Nidar as President, Ram Narain Gusaiwal as Vice-President; Puranmal Jalutharia as General Secretary; Bhagwan Sahai Jagrawal as Mantri; Brij Mohan Verma as the Joint Mantri; Hira Lal as Organisational Mantri; Bhagwan Sahai Kankhedia as Treasurer and Ram Lal Dewat as the Office Mantri.[72]

On January 28, 1978 RRPS constituted a draft Committee for framing its constitution with Prayag Chand Verma as its Chairman.[73] Besides, there were about 12 members in the Committee. The Committee made sincere efforts in preparing its constitution under the name of RRPS which was approved in the meeting held on May 2, 1979 for registration. It was registered under Registration No. 371/79-80.[74] The Sabha had promised to ameliorate the lot as also all-round development of the community.

The aim of the organisation was to propagate and spread education among the Raigars. In order to attain the goal, the organisation laid down the following agendas:[75]

1. In order to fulfil the aims of the organisation it decided to launch a campaign against the social vices such as the use of the liquor, death feast, child marriage, gang bhoj, dowry, divorce and also inculcate self confidence amongst the caste fellows.
2. Needy Raigar students should be helped morally and financially in their studies.
3. Organisation should take the initiative to apprise the various welfare schemes launched by government for the economic development of the weaker section.

In December 1981, the RRPS started a Hindi monthly paper called *Raigar Pragatisheel Patrika* (monthly) in Jaipur with Kalu Ram Jajoria, Sita Ram Maurya and Smt Meera Jajoria as Chief Editor, Assistant Editor and the Managing Editor, respectively.[76] Naval Kishore Nidar became Patron and Legal Advisor.[77] This became the forum of the Sabha to propagate its activities and bring about great consciousness among the Raigars spread all over Rajasthan.

Raigar Nav Yuwak Sangh, Bagdi

In 1980, the rural Raigars of the village Bagdi, District Tonk started taking an active interest in order to propagate the reform activities among the caste men. The villagers established a new organisation called Raigar Navyuwak Sangh, Bagdi on November 19, 1980 with Vikram Kumar Bansiwal as President.[78] They decided to hold meetings in different villages, promote interaction between urban and rural Raigars. Rural Raigars became aware of their strength and got interested in the activities of Raigar Navyuwak Sangh. The Sangh established Ambedkar Bal Parishad in Raigar dominated villages.[79] They also started taking active part in eradication of social evils and vices. The Sangh activities became more social, cultural and educational. In order to propagate the religious activities the Sangh occasionally arranged religious discourses, where men, women and children met at one place.

In the same year, the Raigar Samaj Welfare Sansthan in Tonk district came into existence.[80] Tonk district has a large number of Raigar population where this welfare Sansthan was organised for the educational and reformatory activities. The Welfare Sansthan is affiliated to Rajasthan Raigar Prantiya Mahasabha.

Some of the educated Raigars of Tonk district started a Hindi quarterly patrika called *Vikas Kiran* in Tonk with Babu Lal Khamokharia (Bank Officer, Tonk); Kishan Lal Bakolia (District

Udyog Officer, Tonk) and Ram Avatar Dularia (Development Officer, Tonk) as editor and co-editor. The woman editor of the patrika was Jaishri Thangria (Project Director, DRDA, Tonk). Bhushan Salodia, Deputy Chief Medical Officer, Tonk was its patron.[81] These persons formed the forum of Welfare Sansthan to propagate its activities and bring about a greater consciousness among the Raigars spread in rural areas of Tonk district.

Having seen the dynamics of the Mahasabha, with respect to socio-political dimensions, we shall now discuss the change in the leadership, internal cleavage and ideological aspect of the Mahasabha.

Akhil Rajasthan Raigar Yuva Mahasabha

As stated earlier, there was a growth of internal dissension, cleavage and conflict within the Raigar movement. Since 1990 onwards, Anil Jalutharia, along with a few other educated Raigar youth, realised the plight of the community.[82] This realisation aroused the consciousness of the educated Raigar youth. Consequently, Jalutharia launched a campaign in the state. He organised the Raigar youth with a view to discuss the socio-economic and political conditions of the community. For this purpose, he toured different places in Rajasthan propagating his views and sought their cooperation.

Anil Jalutharia and his colleagues realised the following facts about the miserable conditions of the community:[83] First, there was a general opinion that since more than two decades or so, there have been no social, educational, cultural and political activities in the community. Second, leadership of Raigars adopted indifferent attitude towards the youth and third, there was no organisation for youth in Raigar community. Hence, Raigar youths were kept away from their involvement in the community programmes and activities. This line of thinking was adopted by Jalutharia and his group. Hence, youths supported Jalutharia.

The Raigar youths wanted to fight for their rights and privileges by actively participating in the movement and opposed the social vices and took a vow to infuse a new social and political consciousness in the community. This group of the Raigars emerged with a view to unify the caste-fellows. Hence, Jalutharia initiated a youth movement. Around 1997, a youth movement came into existence amongst the Raigars called Akhil Rajasthan Raigar Yuva Mahasabha. This was led by Anil Jalutharia, Mahesh Chandra

Karadia, Shankar Lal Dudia, Phool Chand Bilonia and Jugnu Kumar Jalutharia. The objective of this organisation was to infuse new consciousness to ameliorate and to uplift the community, to eradicate the social evils and to bring unity in the community. This organisation attracted many youths among the Raigars. On April 19, 1998 the Raigar youths organised the first Raigar Youth Mahasabha Sammelan at Ram Lila Ground, Jaipur.[84] The organisation made significant gains in terms of membership and organisation of social and cultural activities in diverse areas.

Re-christanisation of the Name 'Raigar' to 'Raghuvanshi'

By the end of the twentieth century, attempts were made by a few educated youths to change their traditional name Raigars, but these attempts did not acquire the character of movement. For instance in 1998, Ram Pal Uchenia, President Akhil Rajasthan Raigar Yuva Mahasabha, Kartarpura Area, Jaipur, advocated to adopt the world Raghuvanshi[85] for Raigars. It is significant that Raigars' origins were centered around Kshatriyas. He saw the change to Raghuvanshi as mechanism of upward social mobility and thus in future the community would get rid of the stigma of untouchability, but Raigars were ambivalent in regard to adopting the word 'Raghuvanshi'. The lack of enthusiasm for adopting the word 'Raghuvanshi' for Raigars of North India can be explained in terms of certain interrelated factors. First, the benefits of reservation policy offered a more satisfactory lifestyle and world view within the framework of the untouchable communities, that is scheduled castes. It was this fear of loss which largely contributed in adopting this process. Second, and lastly they maintained the traditional name and did not associate with Raghuvanshi and this made Raigars gainers of all kind of benefits of reservation. Hence, they were more attracted by the educational and employment benefits of reservation rather than the improvement of social status.

Swami Gian Swaroop Birth Centenary and Golden Jubilee of ABRM

ABRM was formed on November 2, 1944 as a result of a resolution passed at the first All India Conference of Raigars in Dausa in the then princely state of Jaipur. There it was decided to form an organisation which would devote itself exclusively to the amelioration and upliftment of Raigars in the country. Indeed, ABRM was to function only in Rajputana. The aims of the organisation were educational, cultural and economic upliftment. Its motto was Educate, Agitate and Organise.

The moving spirit behind this organisation was Swami Gian Swaroop Maharaj and other Dharmgurus. Swami Gian Swaroop Maharaj in many respects was a unique phenomena, both in his personality and social and cultural style, in the history of Raigar community.

From the year 1917 onwards Swami assumed an active role vigorously in the social and cultural affairs of his people. He created a number of organisations to mobilise the Raigars into viable and assertive community, increasingly conscious of its human, social, economic and political rights.

The birth centenary of Swami and successful completion of 50 years of ABRM in arousing the Raigars, encouraged the Swami's disciples and ABRM's office bearers, social workers and activists to celebrate both Swami's birth centenary and Golden Jubilee of Mahasabha at Ganga Mata Mandir, Karol Bagh, New Delhi.

Swami's disciples and Mahasabha's office bearers discussed the issue of celebration of birth centenary and Golden Jubilee with all other Raigars. Subsequently, on Sunday, July 11, 1993, a meeting was convened at Delhi where birth centenary and golden jubilee celebration committee was formed under the convenorship of Shiv Narain Sarsunia.[86] As many as 41 active members were included.[87] In the Committee some of the members included were: Kalyan Das Peepliwal, Chandra Bhan Tongaria, Shambhu Dayal Gadegaonwalia, Man Singh Lavadia, Heera Lal Khatumbaria, Yashpal Aluria, Chiranji Lal Tongaria and Prabhu Dayal Bakolia. The Committee was authorised to include more members as and when required. Dharam Das Shastri, President ABRM and former MP was the Chief Patron.

A long publicity campaign was conducted especially in Delhi, Rajasthan, Gujarat, Maharashtra and other states. In Delhi, Rajasthan, Gujarat and other states, celebration was made through pamphlets, small booklets, posters which urged the Raigars to contribute whatever amount they could and to attend the celebration in person as well. The cost of celebrations and making other arrangements could be more than one lakh rupees and the committee made vigorous efforts to collect the necessary funds.

The Committee could manage to collect a sum of Rs 4,51,345 in order to redress the grievances and problems of Raigars.[88] Shiv Narain Sarsunia, Convenor of the Celebration Committee adopted a novel method:[89]

1. To provide an occasion for direct education and the alteration of social customs and behaviour of Raigars who came to the celebration.
2. To raise the issue of their downfall and to know, how to come out from such miseries.
3. To urge their fellow Raigars to abandon old ways and follow the path marked out by their Dharmgurus.
4. To strengthen the community solidarity and unity and to contribute whatever amount they could.

However, some opposition/non-cooperation was noticed from segments of Raigar community itself who felt that its successful conduct would negate their social and political image. Partly in response to opposition and partly in order to educate Raigars to change their opinion in favour of this important celebration, the convenor of golden jubilee celebration left much space in the issue of *Smarika*, 1995 for this discussion.[90]

The golden jubilee celebration of ABRM was held at Ganga Mata Mandir, Karol Bagh, New Delhi, on October 6-7, 1995. Swami Govindanand Maharaj inaugurated the golden jubilee function by unfurling the flag.[91] Surya Mal Maurya – freedom fighter, an aged man, former Congress MLA and Chairman of the Reception Committee welcomed the dignitaries sitting on the dais and the audience as well.[92] Maurya in his speech narrated the ups and downs of ABRM in details and praised the activities of Mahasabha and its contribution in improving the society's image. Thus, the golden jubilee and birth centenary celebrations took place. In fact, it was a very happy day. The deliberation became an event of major significance in the history of Raigar movement. This incident captured the imagination of Raigars and was to become a central mobilisation issue in the political development of the movement. The celebration itself was quite a success and about 10,000 people attended. The importance of the celebration expanded into the socio-cultural areas in the life of Raigars as well.

On this occasion, the leading figure of the country praised the activities of Mahasabha and its contribution in improving the society's image. The eminent personalities in praising the

Mahasabha included Mata Prasad, Governor of Haryana; Atal Bihari Vajpayee, then leader of Opposition in Lok Sabha, Shankar Rao Chauhan, Home Minister, Government of India; Charti Lal Goel, Speaker, Delhi Vidhan Sabha; Sahib Singh, Minister for Development and Education, Government of Delhi; Surendra Pal Ratawal, Minister, Social Welfare, Tourism and Welfare of SC/ST, Government of Delhi; Jagdish Mukhi, Finance Minister, Government of Delhi; Dharm Das Shastri, President, ABRM; S.K. Das, Inspector General of Police, Bhilai and several MPs.[93]

Collective Marriages

The next big effort on the part of the Rajasthan Raigars for social reform came in 1998 with the establishment of the Collective Marriage Committee (CMC) as a socially approved body with rules and regulations. Such committees were formed in different regions such as Jaipur, Ajmer, Beawar, Tonk and Kota respectively. The reformatory measures were introduced in the collective celebration of weddings, instead of individual marriage. This would reduce the expenditure considerably and to a great extent solve the problem of searching suitable boys and girls, dowry, accommodation, which are considered serious problems in big cities like Jaipur. We shall now discuss the initiation and changes in the marriage aspect of the movement.

In 1998, the Raigars of Jaipur took the lead in organising collective marriages. The initiators were mostly from Jaipur district. The Raigars under the convenorship of K.L. Kamal formed a committee called Raigar Samaj Shamuhik Vivah Aayojan Samiti Jaipur (RSSVAS).[94] Kamal, who became the convenor, is a retired Additional Registrar, Cooperative Department, Government of Rajasthan and a very influential social person, who got the support of the samaj. Besides, other members were: Laxmi Narain Khorwal, Hardev Patel, Damodar Nogia and Sita Ram Jagarwal. Man Mohan Verma was the Treasurer. Chiranji Lal Bakolia, IRS, Member Income Tax Authority, Rajasthan, Jaipur and P.M. Rachhoya, Inspector General of Police, Rajasthan, Jaipur were the patrons.[95]

On July 7, 1998, RSSVAS, organised its first wedding function at Dr Ambedkar Mangal Bhawan Community Centre, Sanganer, Jaipur, under the presidentship of Sita Ram Mistri, an eminent social worker from Mumbai, Maharashtra. S.P. Ratawal, Minister for Labour, Tourism, SC and ST, Government of NCT of Delhi, was the chief guest of the function. The guest of honour were: Jaswant Barolia, JRS, Additional Commissioner, Income Tax Department, Ludhiana, Punjab; Keshav Lu, Freedom Fighter and former Minister, Government of Andhra Pradesh and Ghanshyam Sharma, Deputy Mayor, Nagar Nigam, Jaipur.[96] On this occasion, weddings were conducted in Sanganer.[97] RSSVAS has influence on both the rich and poor Raigar people in the community as well. The RSSVAS collected the donations/funds for this purpose. These activities were reported in the paper published by RSSVAS, Jaipur in 1998.

The second collective marriage was conducted on February 14, 1999 at Dr Ambedkar Mangal Bhawan, Sanganer, Jaipur under the presidentship of Babu Lal Singaria, Congress MLA from Kekri, Ajmer.[98] Chhoga Lal Bakolia, Minister of Transport, Government of Rajasthan was the chief guest. The guest of honour were: Indra Maya Ram, Dy. Finance Minister, Government of Rajasthan; S.P. Ratawal, Mohan Chauhan, MLA from Parbatsar; Bhudar Mal Verma, former MLA, Dausa; Dara Singh Basetia, Excise Officer and Muniraj Patel, Film Distributor.[99] Nearly 21 weddings were conducted in Sanganer. These activities were reported by RSSVAS, Jaipur in 1999.

The foregoing account of the RSSVAS, Jaipur and others shows that in the early days of arranging collective marriages, they functioned independently. However, they were working for the achievement of common goals and provided a common basis of the activity for the different regions and the programme of activities though similar in nature, yet varied in emphasis.

The collective marriage organisation, which had conducted so many wedding ceremonies and implemented several other programmes, had grown into an all-Rajasthan level, over a period of nearly three years. It was registered under No. 281/2000-2001 dated July 14, 2000.[100] Thus, Raigar Vikas Sansthan Rajasthan, Jaipur, came into existence with K.L. Kamal as President, Baldev Prasad Hingonia as Vice-President and Man Mohan Jalutharia as Secretary.[101] Two promoters C.L. Bakolia and P.N. Rachhoya became the Patrons. An Executive Committee of 21 members was constituted for carrying out the functions.[102] However, it is necessary to mention here that all leaders of other Raigar organisations whole-heartedly extended their cooperation for the collective marriages or providing financial help for the organisation.

The aim of the organisation was to propagate and spread education among the Raigars. In order to attain the socio-cultural and educational goals which this organisation had laid down earlier. Objectives of the organisation were discussed in the Raigar Vikas Sansthan, Rajasthan, Jaipur. Here, it will suffice to note a few selective objectives:

1. All-round development of the community in the field of economic, social and cultural, educational and academics and to unite the community.
2. To conduct collective marriages regularly.
3. To stop child marriage and to promote widow remarriage.
4. To impart education compulsorily to the boys and girls of the community.
5. To build community hostels and to run them properly. Also to build community dharmashalas.
6. To do something for the upliftment of the women-folk.
7. To honour the intelligent and meritorious boys and girls who secured positions in Board and University examinations. Also to encourage them for further higher education and if need be, provide them with financial assistance.
8. To support socially, economically, legally and morally at the time of crisis such as atrocities committed by the upper caste people.
9. To seek the help of other caste organisations for betterment.
10. To promote Dr Ambedkar's ideology.[103]

Besides launching reform activities for all-round development of Raigars, the organisation particularly framed 13 norms in order to give social and legal sanction for collective marriages.[104]

In the year 2000 the Raigar Vikas Sansthan Rajasthan, Jaipur launched a campaign of collective wedding. The aims of the campaign as expressed in the objectives was to prepare the Raigars for collective wedding, minimising the marriage expenditure and to arouse caste consciousness through collective marriages and mutual cooperation among the Raigars and thereby to fight social evils. On June 8, 2000, RVSR Jaipur conducted its third wedding function at Sanganer, under the presidentship of C.M. Chandolia, Joint Commissioner, Customs Department, Gujarat.[105] B.L. Atal, Director General of Police, Madhya Pradesh was the chief guest.[106] The function was attended by a large number of Raigars from Delhi, Gujarat, Madhya Pradesh, Haryana, Rajasthan, etc. This time, nearly

29 weddings were solemnised at Dr Ambedkar Mangal Bhawan, Sanganer, Jaipur.[107] These activities were published in RVSR, Jaipur in the issue of June 18, 2000. In the following Table 8.1, details of the collective marriages, donations collected, etc., are given:

Table 8.1

Showing Details of Raigar Collective Marriages, Donation Collected and Number of Donors

Name of the Region	*Year*	*Number of collective weddings*	*Donation*			*Total amount collected Rs*
			Number of donors	*Maximum and Minimum amount received as donation*		
				Max. in Rs	*Min. in Rs*	
Jaipur	1998	7	507	11,551	10	1,56,619.00
	1999	21	1157	21,000	5	4,29,751.00
	2000	29	1109	25,251	1	4,89,594.00
Ajmer	2001	15	389	15,000	51	4,62,394.00

Sources: 1. *Raigar Samaj Samuhik Vivah Aayojjan Samiti, Madhur Smiriti, Smarika, Pratham Samuhik Vivaha Samaroh,* 5 July, 1998, p. 1,9, and 32.

2. *Raigar Samaj Samuhik Vivah Aayojjan Samiti, Dutiya Samuhik Vivah Samaroh, Madhur Smiriti, Smarika,* dated 14 February, 1999.

3. *Raigar Vikas Sanstha Rajasthan, Jaipur, Tritiya Samuhik Vivah Samaroh, Madhur Smiriti, Smarika,* 18 June 2000, p. 4, 54, and 124.

4. *Surya Sagar – Ganga Smarika – Tritiya Raigar Samaj Samuhik Vivah Sammelan, Pushkar,* 29 January 2001, p. 8, 72, 77 and 78.

The Raigars of Ajmer are also progressive. On January 22, 1997 nearly 20 weddings were solemnised in Ajmer. The second collective marriages were performed on February 10, 2000. On January 29, 2001 collective marriage organisation performed its third wedding function at Pushkar Fair grounds, Ajmer under the presidentship of Kundan Lal Kurdia. Om Prakash Singaria, known as Bhamashah of Raigar community, was the chief guest of the function. The function was attended by a large number of Raigars from different areas including Jaipur Raigars and these activities were reported in the *Raigar Jyoti.*[108] On this occasion nearly 15 weddings were performed in Pushkar (Ajmer).[109] It should be noted that Raigar Samaj Samuhik Vivah Samiti, Pushkar (Ajmer), during its early days from 1998 to 2001 had performed so far more than 109 collective marriages[110] as done in other parts of Rajasthan. There are so many factors which had contributed to such a successful movement. Details have been presented in Table 8.1.

On February 18, 2001 nearly 30 weddings were solemnised in Devli, Tonk district. The initiative was taken collectively by Raigar Yuva Samiti Tonk, Raigar Samaj Vikas Samiti, Devli and Sakal Panch Raigar Samaj, Tonk.[111] The organisation had collected a handsome amount. The donors were from Niwai, Jaipur and other places. Damodar Shalodia, Niwai – a wealthy Raigar donated Rs 21,000.00.[112] Besides, 40 donors paid Rs 5,100 each and thus,[113] they donated Rs 20,400. It may be noted that Kota Raigars also organised collective weddings at Dr Ambedkar Nagar, Kulhadi Kota, where 12 weddings[114] were solemnised and these activities were reported in *Vikas Kiran*.

Hazari Mal Manohari Devi Charitable Trust and Collective Marriages

Bhanwar Lal Naval assumed the leadership to fight against the social evils prevailing amongst the Raigars in the field of education and marriages. This was the first set of events which sparked off a mass movement.

Bhanwar Lal is the illustrious son of Hazari Mal Naval, who was a poor Raigar and was passing his life in the traditional style, in the village Chhoti Khatu, tehsil Didwana, district Nagaur, Rajasthan. Hazari Mal had five sons and three daughters. Bhanwar Lal Naval is the eldest son. He was born in February 1947 (Basant Panchmi, Samvat 2004) in Chhoti Khatu, a village situated 54 kms from district headquarters. He received his primary education in Government Primary School, Chhoti Khatu and in 1964, secondary education from the same upgraded Government Higher Secondary School, Chhoti Khatu.[115] In 1964, Naval went to Jodhpur for higher education and was admitted in SMK College, Jodhpur. Here, for a brief period, he remained in Gian Ganga Chhatrawas (community hostel), Jodhpur.[116] However, throughout his childhood and youth he did not have a steady career and hence in 1965, he returned to his village and started living with the caste fellows. Soon, he could get the job with Government of Rajasthan and hence in 1966, he was appointed as Primary School Teacher at village Fardod in Nagaur district.[117] After serving the school nearly for six months or so, he left the job to join the post of a clerk in Rajasthan Rajya Kraya Vikraya Sangh, Jaipur, in 1966. In the course of his service, Naval came in contact with Dhana Ram Kurdia a resident of Aaldiyabas, in Merta city, Nagaur district who had settled down in Bombay.[118] Dhana Ram Kurdia was considered to be a well established businessman and exporter of leather goods to foreign countries. According to Dev Karan Naval,[119] in 1968 Naval eventually left the government job once again to join Dhana Ram Kurdia's business in Bombay and worked as a salesman. After he proved himself as a good salesman, hé also looked after the export section of the business. After two years' experience at Dhana Ram Kurdia's business organisation, Naval eventually left it and established his own independent business in 1970.

It should be mentioned here that at the initial stage, Naval had started his business as a supplier of raw material of leather goods. During the years 1973-1977, he had established himself well in export. He travelled to USA several times with regard to his business to establish personal rapport and eventually landed in USA in 1977 as one of the biggest wholesale leather goods dealer.[120]

Naval acquired business tactics and used to send business orders to his men in Bombay from USA and other big cities. Thus, he emerged as a charismatic businessman by the year 1980. During a period of about five years (from 1977-1981), Naval was active as a big businessman. In 1982-83, he applied to the USA government for granting him a Green Card. His application for Green Card was accepted.[121] Naval's eventful life started in USA. While he started his business in USA, the idea of purchasing old houses and to repair and renovate them for reselling as another weapon of business was exploited by him. This gave him an encouraging response.

This was the zeal with which Naval spearheaded his business and hence in 1977 he went to USA, where he rose from position of salesman to that of a leading businessman. In the social life among the Raigars, this is the first set of events of significance.

It is also true that Naval made tremendous progress in the field of business. Thus, during more than one decade, he earned lakh of rupees. In 1994, the members of his family persued Naval to form a Trust and appointed himself as the founder member of that trust when Hazari Mal Manohari Devi Charitable Trust (HMDC Trust) came into existence with a capital of lakh of rupees. The objective of the Trust were to promote social reform, to maintain and establish the educational institutions and to set up hostels. The Trust is run by a Board of Trustees and there are in all 11 members of the Board. The overall incharge of the Board is Naval himself and the Chairman is his mother. Other members are nominated by the Chairman. The headquarters of the Trust is located in Bombay and is registered body.

In a short span of time, the achievements of the Trust are incredible. It has conducted the collective marriages throughout India in different states. Although the trust is controlled mainly by Naval himself from USA, yet it operates on an all-India basis conducting collective marriages in different parts of India.

Naval is one of the first Raigar NRIs from New York who for the first time in the middle of 2000, held the telephonic conversation with Gian Chand Khatnawalia,[122] an eminent social activist of the Raigar Samaj at New Delhi and expressed his willingness to bear the total expenditure to be incurred on organising collective marriages at different places in the country. Both Gian Chand Khatnawalia and Kishan Lal Sokria, President of Ganga Mandir, Sat Nagar, New Delhi, and his other colleagues (such as Mohan Jatolia, Vijay Kumar Tongaria, Mohan Lal Balotia, Dev Das Kanvadia, Lala Ram Tongadia, Jugal Kishore Jatolia and Govind Kumar Dholkhedia) , welcomed his proposal and according to Raigar Sudhar's account published in its issue Shri Hazari Mal Manohari Devi Charitable Trust[123] after exchanging views with the organisers of arranging collective marriages at New Delhi, conveyed their consent. All the workers showed great enthusiasm in organising it and expressed its importance in regulating their lifestyle. They were also attracted by his ways of helping the poor caste fellows. Thus, the local activities with the cooperation of both the organisations namely Ganga Mandir, Sat Nagar and Kewala Nand Ashram Trust, Rameshwari Nagar, Karol Bagh, New Delhi, formed a Local Committee for this purpose with Gian Chand Khatnawalia as the Chairman. Naval introduced this social reform to keep the poor Raigar families away from debt and in the interest of general good. This programme also provided, a forum to integrate the Raigar community.

The organisers circulated the news about collective marriage programme activities in the local papers published from Delhi, Rajasthan and Maharashtra and it also sought help from individuals and local associations/organisations to promote it and support fully the campaign of collective marriages. Thus, it became the chief organ of the Hazari Mal Manohari Devi Charitable Trust and when Naval reached Delhi he saw that all preparations had already been made in this direction in a proper way. Naval realised that the organisers were already doing their job well. He felt pleasure to see all this and also involved himself deeply more to the basic problems of the Samaj in the light of the present day social and economic crisis. In this way Naval created an organisational framework in several parts of the country conducting collective marriages of Raigars.

In Delhi, on February 10, 2000, 21 collective marriages[124] were performed at Sundar Alfa Garden, Karol Bagh, New Delhi, under the leadership of Naval and Gian Chand Khatnawalia. It should be noted that on this occasion Shiela Dixit, Chief Minister, Government of NCT of Delhi was the chief guest. Prominent among those present were Surendra Pal Ratawal, former Minister, Government of NCT of Delhi; Meira Kanwaria Mahapor, Delhi Nagar Nigam; Moti Lal Bakolia, MLA; Narendra Malpuria, IAS; Muktesh Chandra Godgaonlia, IPS and others.[125]

The achievements of the Trust were incredible, looking to the short span of time. It had established a network and organised the collective marriage at different towns/cities. On November 7, 2000, 56 collective marriages were performed at Nagaur, Rajasthan under the leadership of Naval. Chief Minister, Ashok Gehlot, was the chief guest. Prominent amongst others present were: Chhoga Lal Bakolia, Minister, Government of Rajasthan; Swami Gopal Ram Maharaj, Chhitar Mal Maurya and Narain Kurdia.[126] It should be noted in this context that each couple was given the following items as dowry or donation by Naval: 1 bed, 1 centre table, 2 chairs, 1 stove, 1 choki, 31 utensils (including steel, brass and kansi), 1 sewing machine, 1 clock, 2 pillows, razai and gadda, 2 bed sheets, wedding clothes, gold ornaments weighing one and half tola, and silver ornaments worth 250 grams.[127] Besides this expenditure, the Trust also met the expenditure incurred on food served, lighting arrangement and other essential items.

On this occasion, Naval, the rich Raigar NRI, not only supported the social but also educational causes. For instance, to start a hostel for poor Raigar students, he publically announced to donate Rs 10 lac for the construction of a hostel building.[128] Finally, Naval presented a cheque of One lac to Chief Minister Ashok Gehlot, for famine relief works in Rajasthan.

Like collective marriages held in February and November 2000 at New Delhi and Rajasthan respectively, the Trust also performed 20 collective marriages at Mumbai on January 29, 2001. Thus, the mass movement led by Naval among the Raigars became a more popular movement.

The collective marriages for Raigar boys and girls in different states of the country formed the second phase in the history of collective marriage movement initiated by the Trust. The first phase of the movement had been discussed above and the second phase of organising collective marriages initiated by Naval during the year 2002 has been discussed in the following lines.

Jodhpur is the second among the six big towns/cities in the state. The Trust, in fulfilling its social obligations towards the poor community, increased their aspirations and hopes. The maximum number of collective marriages performed at one time were 56 so far. According to K.L. Kamal, on February 27, 2002, the trust solemnised the historic marriage at Jodhpur, in which 65 couples[129] tied nuptial knot under the presidentship of Bhori Lal Shãstri. Dharm Dass Shastri, a former Congress MP, was the chief guest. Similarly, on February 17, 2002, the Trust also organised the collective marriages at Chhoti Khatu in Nagaur district and 27 couples[130] were married. The function was chaired by B.L. Naval himself and Chhoga Ram Bakolia, Minister, Government of Rajasthan was the chief guest.

The Hazari Mal Manohar Devi Trust is dedicated in regulating the lifestyle of the poor caste fellows. The Trust helps in managing temples, ashrams, dharamshalas and schools. Every year, it organises the collective marriages in different regions of the country, which are attended by Raigar elites, political and social workers and other social elites belonging to different castes and communities. These reforms with regard to the domestic rituals has reduced costs and weeded out unnecessary procedure and given marriage a new symbolic significance.

Gaining confidence by his success in arranging collective marriages, B.L. Naval concentrated his efforts on construction of public hospitals, schools and hostels with a view to encouraging the modern education and relief work in rural areas and to help the poor and needy villagers during famine and drought period, making all this a part of social welfare movement. He considered schools the real temples which would educate youths and to come out of the caste differences. From an account of the activities and programmes of Naval given by one of his brothers Dev Karan Naval,[131] it may be noted that the first Girls' Secondary School was built by B.L. Naval in the year 2002 at Chhoti Khatu in Nagaur district, where he was born and spent his earlier childhood. Sarpanch, Chhoti Khatu, Nagaur, laid the foundation stone of this building. In 2004, when the building was completed, Naval handed it over to the Education Department, Government of Rajasthan. The Girls' Secondary School had been established under the name Shri Hazari Mal Bhanwar Lal Naval Government Higher Secondary Girls' School, Chhoti Khatu, which is now run by the Government of Rajasthan. Naval constructed 16 class rooms in the school for girls' students. The size of each room is 16 x 20 sq feet and well furnished. The total expenditure incurred so far according to Dev Karan Naval was 25 lakhs. The school is spread over an area of 315 x 150 sq feet.

On April 14, 2004, B.L. Naval provided 50 beds, 50 chairs and 50 tables in Gian Ganga Chhatravas, Jodhpur to provide better boarding facilities for Raigar hostellers. Earlier, in 2002, he also built a big hall, measuring 16 x 20 sq feet in Government Girls Higher Secondary School, Deh – a village in Nagaur district for academic purpose and expenses of the building were borne by him. According to Dev Karan Naval, the expenditure incurred was Rs 11 lakhs. On June 26, 2003, he donated a Maruti van too to Government Hospital, Chhoti Khatu for public use.

It is necessary to point out that in recent years the participation of B.L. Naval in the welfare programmes has increased. For instance during great famine and drought during the years 2001, 2002 and 2003 in Rajasthan, Naval distributed food grains among the poor and needy villagers. Those who benefited from this help were not merely confined to Nagaur region but were drawn from Churu and Bikaner districts also. Thus, distribution of wheat provided good relief to the villagers. The process of distribution of wheat continued for three consecutive years, i.e., from 2001 to 2003. Besides, Naval also distributed fodder for the animals in rural areas during the same critical period and saved the livestock. Thus, during 2001 to 2003, the total expenses on all these activities were Rs 30 lakhs and Rs 10 lakhs respectively (each year) and were totally borne by him. It was narrated by Dev Karan Naval. In June 2003, B.L. Naval also announced a donation of Rs 70 lakhs for establishing a public hospital at Chhoti Khatu, requesting the Government of Rajasthan to allot him a suitable piece of land for this purpose.

The drive for collective marriages among the Raigars took a positive turn when B.L. Naval gave financial assistance to poor upper-caste Hindus and other low-caste untouchables to arrange their own collective marriages. In this regard, Naval also took the lead in arranging collective marriages. He brought about a new social awakening among the Bhangis of Nagaur district by organising 15 collective marriages. Thus, for the first time, collective marriages of Bhangis were solemnised in the first decade of 21st century (2001-03) making a breakthrough and dropping the old orthodox traditions.

B.L. Naval not only encouraged collective marriages among low-caste untouchables but also the poor upper-caste Hindus. He had borne all the expenses incurred on two Brahmin marriages – one in Nagaur district and another in Deshnok in Bikaner district during the year 2002-03. Later, in 2004, in another instance narrated by Dev Karan Naval, B.L. Naval arranged four marriages of the followers of Nath sect in Nagaur district. As a result of all this, expenses incurred on 15 Bhangi marriages, two Brahmin marriages, and four followers of Nath sect were Rs 5.25 lakhs, Rs 70,000 and Rs 1.40 lakhs respectively which were borne by him.

The collective marriage campaign was launched by B.L. Naval and among the poor Raigars, low-caste untouchables and poor upper-caste Hindus to support them financially. It was launched on February 10, 2000 and is still continuing. During the last four years, Naval had arranged 586 marriages throughout the country as narrated by one of its organisers Dev Karan Naval. It is believed that Rs 35,000 was incurred on each marriage. Thus, Dev Karan Naval in his conversation with the author on May 1, 2004 said B.L. Naval had spent in all Rs 2.05 crores for this purpose.

Notes

1. Raigar writers have given many important incidents of violence which occurred in different regions in Rural Rajasthan. See particularly "*Mahasabha ka sanshipt parichaya avam mahasabha dwara gaun gaun mein Brahman ker unki madad ka beora*", Rajasthan Prantiya Raigar Mahasabha, Jaipur. On the eve of First Anniversary, release of first *Smarika*, 8 July 1972, pp.6-8. Also see, *Raigar Sudhar*, 15-31 August 2000, pp 2-3.

2. Ibid., pp.6-8.
3. Roop Chand Jalutharia, *Raigar Jati ka Itihas*, Jaipur, Capital Printers, 2001, p. 67.
4. Ibid., p. 68.
5. Ibid., pp. 66-69.
6. Ibid.
7. Ibid., p. 72. Also see, Chiranji Lal Bakolia and Rajendra Prasad Godegaon, *Raigar Kaun aur Kya?*, New Delhi, Asian Printer, 1964, pp. 91-95, 109-118.
8. *Raigar Sudhar*, 15-31 August, 2000, p.3.
9. Ibid., p.3.
10. Ibid., p. 2.
11. Ibid
12. Rajasthan Prantiya Raigar Mahasabha, op. cit., p. 7. Also see, Roop Chand Jalutharia, op. cit., pp. 71-72.
13. Rajasthan Prantiya Raigar Mahasabha, op. cit., p. 8.
14. Ibid.
15. Ibid.
16. Ibid., pp. 8-9.
17. Shyam Lal, *Untouchable Movement in India*, Jaipur, Sublime Publications, 2002, p. 66.
18. Ibid.
19. Ibid.
20. A full account of incident, reported in *Dainik Bhaskar*, Jaipur, dated 3 October, 2000. See in particular "*Chatro ney pani manga too school sey nikal diya*".
21. A full account of incident, reported in *Dainik Bhaskar*, Jaipur, dated 22 August, 2001.
22. Ibid.
23. Since untouchability, caste discrimination and atrocities on Dalits are directly concerned with our study, we have therefore discussed a few select cases of atrocities with substantive details attending to only those aspects that tell us something about the types of atrocities. We may note that incidents of atrocities on the Dalits are increasing day by day, particularly in Rajasthan and this phenomenon has got its significance in the face of social transformation. Centre for Dalit Human Rights (CDHR) Rajasthan's Study, "Few grave violations of Dalit Human Rights in Rajasthan", 2002 widely characterised

aspects of this issue. The centre noticed, "Violence against Dalit and women is normally treated as a marginal issue by the law enforcement machinery in Rajasthan.... It is, therefore, essential to sensitise this entire machinery to the problem of Dalits, particularly violence on Dalit women".

24. *Dr Babasaheb Ambedkar: Writings and Speeches*, Vol. I, Education Department, Government of Maharashtra, 1979, pp. 40-41.
25. The evidences readily available to us are from set of Ambedkar volumes and news, editorials and essays published in English national daily newspapers from Delhi and Lucknow and also published in Hindi from Rajasthan.

    In order to maintain the objectivity in the presentation of the facts on which this description is based, we have depended on English and Hindi newspapers. For example, see, *"Phagi mein ugra bhid per goliya"*, *Dainik Bhaskar*, Jaipur, September 22, 2000; Dalit Demonstrators Clash with Police, In *Sunday Times*, New Delhi, September 22, 2002. DIG among 30 hurt in Phagi Clash, in *Hindustan Times*, New Delhi, September 22, 2002; *"Dehshatja dalit aab dharma badalney ko taiyar hai"*, *Dainik Bhasker*, Jaipur, September 23, 2002; *"Ek ghat per nahayagey savaran aur dalit"*, *Dainik Bhasker*, Jaipur, September 24, 2002; *"Chakwada ka Sabak"* (editorial), *Dainik Bhasker*, Jaipur, September 24, 2002; *"sahmey dalitoo ney talab mein dubki lagai"*, *Dainik Bhaskar*, Jaipur, September 25, 2002; On Chakwara Issue, *"Rajasthan: vihip sey dalit naraj"*, *Outlook*, Delhi, October 28, 2002, p. 38; Sheoraj Singh, *"Hariyana mein panch dalito ki hatya sampradayak rajniti ka natija: hindu ugravad ko dalit bhi pasand nahi hai"*, *Danik Bhaskar*, Jaipur, Friday, October 25, 2002.

    These writings provide us with a background against which to examine the incidents presented in print media. The news, editorials and essays provided us facts, whether original or repetitive. Besides, we also discussed the issue with NGO, Centre for Dalit Human Right (CDHR), Rajasthan.

    We have also benefited from Ram Puniyani's essay in formulating this description. Ram Puniyani elaborately narrated how, "the rise of Hindutva politics is the reassertion of pre-modern hierarchies ... the main point being to push back any gains in the process of social transformation ..." This mode of thought becomes evident with Hindu thinkers as Puniyani remarked, "The rise of Hindu Right was most concentrated expression of opposition to the possibility of social transformation of caste ... The social space ..." For the problems related to "This world" started getting side tracked and the issues of temple and mosque were thrust upon an unsuspecting society. The core political agenda of this change of track was to curtail the development of the deprived section of society. For details see, Ram Puniyani, "Striving for Social Justice", in *The Hindu*, New Delhi, September 28, 2002.

The untouchables from Chakwara village in Phagi's tehsil find the caste Hindus opposing their efforts for social transformation. The caste Hindu ridicules the untouchables on the issue because, as Praful Bidwai, remarked, "If you saw that episode (Chakwara incident) on television, you couldn't have missed the near fascist inspiration of the rioting caste Hindus, driven by base passion, visceral prejudices and a consuming lust for power and (now threatened) privilege.

Recalling of Hari Shanker Bairwa, a political Savvoy village leader, President of local Ambedkar Janakalyan Parishad and once proud member of VHP, who even went to Ayodhya as Kar Sevak with two other Dalits from Chakwara, at this point is most appropriate and his sincere observations expose the caste Hindus. According to Bidwai, "He (Hari Shankar Bairwa) now accuses the VHP-BJP of having cynically 'used' the Dalits with the high sounding slogan of 'Hindu unity' only to betray that idea and contemptuously tell them they should observe Maryada (prescribed quasi-sacred norms) and parampara (tradition), that is, defer to rank casteism". For more details, see particularly Praful Bidwai "Dalits under Siege" in *Hindustan Times*, Lucknow, October 4, 2002.

26. For more details, see, particularly, Hemant Kala *"Bairwa dulhey ki barat per pathrav: phir dohrai kahanai"*, *Ta Thaya Bharti*, Jaipur, March 2, 2003, pp. 7-11. Also see, Vinod Sharma, *"Bharthala baneyga chakwada"*, *Ta Thathya Bharti*, op. cit., pp. 14-15.
27. "Dalit bridegroom forced to dismount from mare", *Hindustan Times*, New Delhi, March 11, 2003.
28. *"Dalit dulhey ki bandooko key sayey mein nikli baraat"*, *Dainik Bhaskar*, Jaipur, April 17, 2003.
29. The most authoritative account of the Bahi Bhatt debate regarding the origin of the Raigar caste is given by Gheesu Lal, p. 37.
30. Ibid., p. 3.
31. Ibid., pp. 6-10.
32. Ibid., p. 12.
33. Ibid.
34. Ibid., p. 25.
35. Ibid., pp. 25-26.

36. Ibid., pp. 33-34.
37. Roop Chand Jalutharia, op. cit., p. 86.
38. For more details, see Shyam Lal, *Untouchable Movement in India*, Jaipur, Sublime Publications, 2001.
39. Room Chand Jalutharia, op. cit., pp. 85-101.
40. Ibid.
41. Ibid., p. 85.
42. Ibid.
43. Ibid., p. 86.
44. Ibid.
45. Ibid., p. 87.
46. Ibid., pp. 86-87.
47. Ibid., p. 87.
48. Ibid.
49. Ibid., pp. 87-95.
50. Ibid., pp. 87-95.
51. Ibid., pp. 85-101.
52. For a discussion of Raigar Sewak Sangh Movement that stresses the role of Raigar youth and social consequences of sangh, see, "*Jaipur key navyuvak karyakartao dwara samaj sudhar karya*", Roop Chand Jaluthair, *Raigar Jati ka Itihas*, Jaipur, 2001, Chapter 13, pp. 82-84.
53. Ibid., p. 82.
54. Ibid.
55. Ibid., pp. 82-83.
56. Ibid., p. 83.
57. Ibid., p. V.
58. Ibid.
59. Ibid.
60. Ibid., pp. V-VI.
61. Ibid., p. 83.
62. *Raigar Panchayat Shat Patti key pancho per kiya gala mukadma kharij* gives an account of the meeting of the Panchas of Raigar Panchayat, Shat Patti, Ajmer, held at Pushkar Mandir, Ajmer, around early 1976 that banned the social vices. The pamphlet printed at Kamal Printing Works, Ajmer, August 23, 1977.
63. Ibid.
64. Ibid.
65. Ibid.

66. Ibid.
67. Ibid.
68. Ibid.
69. The most elaborate account of Raigars' ex-communication from the community is given in the pamphlet published and circulated by the Raigar Panchayat Shatpatti, Ajmer. See, *satoo patti ki vishal raigar panchayat ka nirnaya: pushkar mela,* date not mentioned. The meeting was held on November 29, 1982. On the basis of another meeting held on November 19, 1983 at Ganga Mai Mandir Pushkar, Ajmer, a pamphlet *satoo patti ki vishal raigar panchayat ka nirnaya: pushkar mela* was published. (date not mentioned). Also see, *Rajasthan prantiya raigar mahasabha jaipur (Regis): raigar samaj ko suchana.* Based on the meeting held on March 11, 1984 at Ram Niwas Bagh, Jaipur, published and circulated by Bhura Ram Bhagat, President, Rajasthan Prantiya Raigar Mahasabha, Ram Narain Gusaiwal, Mantri, Rajasthan Prantiya Raigar Mahasabha, Jaipur and others. Printed at Moti Printers, Hanuman ka Rasta, Kashinathji ki Gali, Jaipur.
70. For most important discussion of the origin of Pragatisheel Sabha in Rajasthan, see *"Rajasthan Raigar Pragatisheel sabha ka udgam, kiyo aur kisliye?" Raigar Pragatisheel Patrika,* December 1981, pp. 7-8.
71. Ibid., p. 7.
72. Ibid., p. 4.
73. Ibid., p. 8.
74. Ibid.
75. Ibid.
76. Ibid., p. 2.
77. Ibid.
78. *Gram Bagdi Vikas Kiran,* Tonk, April-July 2001, p. 11.
79. Ibid.
80. Ibid., p. 1.
81. Ibid.
82. *Akhil Rajasthan Raigar Yuva Mahasabha: Pratham Sammelan Smarika, April 19, 1998, Ram Lila Maidan, Jaipur, gives a detailed account of Akhil Rajasthan Raigar Yuva Mahasabha. See Raigar Samaj key Vikas Hetu Chintan,* p.5.
83. Ibid.
84. Ibid.
85. Ibid., p. 29.

86. For discussion of Swami Gian Swaroopanand Maharaj birth centenary and golden jubilee of ABRM, see, *Smarika, "Sri Dharmguru Swami Gian Swaroop Janam Satabdi Avam Akhil Bharatiya Raigar Mahasabha Swarna Jayanti Samaroh"*, dated October 6-7, 1995. Also see *"Kratagayata"* in *Smarika* 1995 (page number not mentioned.)
87. Ibid. (page number not mentioned).
88. Ibid., *Samaroh Samiti Aaya-Vaya Vivran.*
89. Ibid., Shiv Narain Sarsunia.
90. Ibid., also see *Narad Uowach: Ek gyatvya aapaki sewa mein* by Shiv Narain Sarsunia: *Pravas key anubhav: ek ispastikaran* by coordinated Janam Shatabdi Sararoh Samiti.
91. Ibid., *Kratagayata,* Shiv Narain Sarsunia.
92. Ibid., *Swagata Adhyaksha,* lecture by Shri Surya Mal Maurya, former MLA, Jaipur and Freedom Fighter.
93. Ibid., see *Subh Sandesh.*
94. *Raigar Samaj Samahuk vivah aayojan samiti, madhur smiriti smarika (pratham samuhik vivah samaroh) devshayani ekadash,* July 5, 1998, back page of the main page.
95. Ibid.
96. Ibid., p. 1.
97. Ibid.
98. *Raigar Samaj Samuhik Vivah Aayogan Samiti, Dwitiya Samuhik Vivah Samaroh, Madhur Samiti, Smarika Valentine Day,* 14 February, 1999, p. 3.
99. Ibid.
100. *Raigar Vikas Sansthan, Rajasthan, Jaipur, Tritiya Samuhik Vivah Samaroh, Madhur Smiriti Smarika,* June18, 2000, p. 1.
101. Ibid., p. 2.
102. Ibid.
103. Ibid., pp. 9-10.
104. Ibid., pp. 11-12.
105. Ibid., p. 6.
106. Ibid., p. 5.
107. Ibid., p. 4.
108. *Raigar Jyoti,* Barmer, February 1, 2001, p. 3.
109. *Surya-Sagar-Ganga-Smarika, Tritiya Raigar Samaj Samuhik Vivah Sammelan, Pushkar, Vasant Panchmi,* 29 January 2001, p. 8.
110. Ibid., p. 35.

111. *Vikas Kiran*, Tonk, April-July 2001, p. 17.
112. Ibid.
113. Ibid.
114. Ibid., p. 20.
115. Conversation with Dev Karan Naval on telephone, Jodhpur, 18 August 2002.
116. Ibid.
117. Ibid.
118. Ibid.
119. Ibid.
120. Ibid.
121. Ibid.
122. For detailed information, see Shri Hazari Lal Manohari Devi Charitable Trust, *Raigar Sudhar*, November 15-30, 2000.
123. Ibid.
124. Ibid.
125. Ibid.
126. Ibid.
127. Ibid.
128. *Raigar Sudhar*, 1-15 February 2001.
129. Conversation with K.L. Kamal, Jaipur, dated July 23, 2003. Also see, *Jodhpur mein samuhik vivah sampan, Raigar Sudhar*, 1-15 March 2002.
130. *Raigar Sudhar*, 1-15 March 2002.
131. Conversation with Dev Karan Naval, Jodhpur, May 1, 2004.

9

Social History of Raigar Agitation (1940-2004)

Rajasthan, Gujarat, Madhya Pradesh, Haryana, Uttar Pradesh and Punjab

Regional Raigar Associations

We shall discuss in this chapter the formation of the Raigar associations in different parts of India. This will serve two important purposes in understanding the building up of the movement. First, it will bring out the regional variations in the pursuit of diverse programmes to fight against the different kinds of discriminations in a degree of collective mobilisation and in the pattern of leadership. Second, it will enable us to analyse the nature of linkages and feedback between different levels of organisations – local, regional and all-India in the movement. For the purpose of describing the growth of Raigar associations, six regions were identified: Rajasthan, Gujarat, Madhya Pradesh, Haryana, Punjab and Uttar Pradesh.

Raigars in Rajasthan

The Raigars in Rajasthan, Delhi and Madhya Pradesh were among the first to respond to the modern forces of change. They realised the value of modern education and employment opportunities and started to organise themselves to establish the educational institutions and to exploit modern employment.

In Rajasthan, they started organising themselves in 1940, thanks to the efforts of Swami Atma Ram 'Lakshya' and others. They formed a 'Satsangh Mandali' in the year 1940 which was the beginning of caste awakening. They used to hold small meetings under the leadership of Swami Atma Ram, in which the Swami used to deliver socio-religious sermons to the Raigars. It laid down its aims to reform caste customs and creating educational facilities. Other leaders connected with the organisation of Mandali were Naval Prabhakar, Surya Mal Maurya, Jai Chand Mohil, Kanwar Sen Maurya, Ghisu Lal Sanwaria, etc. The leaders toured all-over Rajasthan and on April 14, 1971 organised its first meeting at village Sanganer, district Jaipur.[1] This meeting was attended by various Raigar representatives of village Panchayats and Chokhla Panchayats from different districts of Rajasthan. The first conference of the Rajasthan Raigar Mahasabha was held at Ghat Gate, Jaipur, on July 11, 1971. Since then, the Sabha has organised Rajasthan Raigar Mahasabha Conferences in various parts of the state. It was registered on May 14, 1972. From 1971 to 1984 the Rajasthan Raigar Mahasabha had (hereafter to be called RRM) organised eight conferences, one each in Chaksu, Data Ramgarh, Chomu, Shavarda, Niwai and three in Jaipur.

The eighth Annual Conference of RRM was held at Jaipur on August 1-2, 1984,[2] under the presidentship of Naval Kishore Nidar, a leading advocate. The first day of the conference, held on August 1, 1984, was inaugurated by Shiv Charan Mathur, the then Chief Minister of Rajasthan. Other chief guests and special invitees were:[3] Dharm Das Shastri, Member of Parliament; Chhoga Ram Bakolia, Deputy Minister, Government of Rajasthan; Chhoga Lal Kanwaria, former Minister; and Kushal Chand Mohanpuria, President, Education Committee, Nagar Nigam, Delhi. Moti Lal Bakolia, Sundarvati Naval Prabhakar and Bhori Lal Shastri – all members of the Maha Nagar Parishad, New Delhi. This conference was attended by nearly five thousand Raigars from different districts of Rajasthan, Madhya Pradesh and Delhi.[4] The meetings of RRM held since 1946 onwards are given in Table 9.1.

The major thrust of Rajasthan Raigar Mahasabha in 1984 centred around the social evils. The leaders emphasised the need to educate and to raise their social status through propaganda and to

Table 9.1

Annual Meetings (Sammelan) of Rajasthan Prantiya Raigar Mahasabha (since 1946)

Name of the Place and District	Year	Date	Duration	Presided over by	Inaugurated by	Remarks
Phulera (Jaipur)	1946	4, 5, 6 June	3 days	Lala Bansi Lal Luharia	Narain Aaloria	Attended and addressed by Gotam Singh Sakarwal, Surya Mal Maurya, Pandit Ghisu Lal, Narain Aaloria.
Malpura (Tonk)	1949	2, 3 March	2 days	-	-	Attended and addressed by Swami Gian Swaroopanand Maharaj, Naval Prabhakar, Chaudhary Padam Singh, Sakkarwal, Kanwar Sen Maurya, Bhola Ram Tongadia, Surya Mal Maurya, Bihari Lal Gagrat, Pandit Chhedi Lal
Masuda (Ajmer)	1951	25 May	1 day	Mukut Bihari Lal Bhargava, MP	Amarat Lal Yadav, Deputy Minister, Government of Rajasthan	Raigar flag was unfurled by Swami Gian Swaroopanand Maharaj. Three resolutions were passed
Ajmer	1955	-	-	Hari Bhau Upadhyaya, Chief Minister, Ajmer State	-	-
Kankatti (Madhya Pradesh)	1958	17 January	1 day	Nanu Ram Batadia 'Mohi'	Nathu Lal Naval	-
Ghat Gate (Jaipur)	1971	11 July	1 day	Uda Ram Narolia	-	Rajasthan Prantiya Raigar Mahasabha came into existence on April 14, 1971 at the Sammelan held at Sanganer, Jaipur. Registered on June 26, 1972. The first Sammelan held at Ghat Gate on July 11, 1971, in which nearly 10,000 Raigars gathered.

Contd..

Contd...

Ram Niwas Garden (Jaipur)	1971	3, 4 October	2 days	Barkat-Tullah Khan, the then Chief Minister of Rajasthan	-	Attended by 20,000. The Sammelan was attended and addressed by Poonam Chand Vishnoi, the then Education Minister, Government of Rajasthan. Jasraj former Minister and Shiv Charan Singh Gujjar.
Chaksu (Jaipur)	DA					
Data Ramgarh (Jaipur)	DA					
Chomu (Jaipur)	1972	10 February	1 day			
Shavarda (Jaipur)	DA					
Niwai (Tonk)						
Government Hostel (Jaipur)	1984	1, 2 August	2 days	Naval Kishore Nidar, Advocate	Shiv Charan Mathur, the then Chief Minister of Rajasthan	Chief Guest: Dharm Dass Shastri Special Guest: Chhoga Ram Bakolia, Chhoga Lal Kanwaria, Kushal Chand Mohanpuria, Moti Lal Bakolia, Smt Sundarvati, Naval Prabhakar, Bhure Lal Shastri Attended by 5,000 persons from Delhi, Madhya Pradesh and Rajasthan

Sources: Chandan Mal Naval, *Raigar Jati ka Itihas*, Jodhpur, Shyam Printing Press, 1986, pp. 146-48.
Roop Chand Jalutharia, *Raigar Jati ka Itihas*, Jaipur, Capital Printers, 2001, pp. 102-111.
Chiranji Lal Bakolia and Rajendra Prasad Gadegaonwalia, *Raigar Kaun Aur Qia*? Delhi. Asian Printer, Hardhyan Singh Road, 1964, p. 120-124.
NB: DA = Data not available.

discard the traditional occupation. The name and duration of the presidents of Rajasthan Prantiya Raigar Mahasabha is given in Table 9.2.

Table 9.2

President (Adhyaksh) of Rajasthan Prantiya Raigar Mahasabha (since 1971)

S. No.	Name of the President	District	Duration From – To	Total Period	Remarks
1	Uda Ram Narolia	Chaksu (Jaipur)	May 1971 – August 1984	13 years 8 months	
2	Bhudhar Mal Kankhedia	Dausa (Jaipur)	August 1984 – July 2001	17 years	
3	Tara Chand Jajoria	Jobner (Jaipur)	July 2001 – continued till today		

Sources: Chandan Mal Naval, *Raigar Jati ka Itihas*, Jodhpur, Shyam Printing Press, 1986, pp. 139-46.
Roop Chand Jalutharia, *Raigar Jati ka Itihas*, Jaipur, Capital Printers, 2001, pp. 66-79.
Rajasthan Prantiya Raigar Mahasabha-ka-Sadasya Abhiyan Suru, A pamphlet published and circulated by Tara Chand Jajoria and Brij Mohan Maurya, dated 26.2.2001.

Raigars in Gujarat

The Raigars of Gujarat state present a unique picture in many ways. There are old urban Raigar residents living in the city of Ahmedabad from Moghul days and the Raigar immigrants who came in waves, especially after independence from Sindh Hyderabad (now in Pakistan), Rajasthan, Maharashtra, Madhya Pradesh, Bihar and Uttar Pradesh to settle there.[5] They were employed as factory labourers, government employees and office boys there.[6] The Raigars of Rajasthan have close social links with those in Gujarat. There are approximately 1,948 families[7] of Raigars in Gujarat with 1,218 in the city of Ahmedabad.[8] It is interesting to note that in Gujarat, the Raigars are not active in Ahmedabad, which is considered to be one of the leading industrial cities of India. The Raigars of Gujarat for this reason are most backward in the Raigar society. Some of the migrants, who had settled in Ahmedabad, took the initiative in bringing together their caste-men. For instance, in Ahmedabad there resides a large number of families (1,218). Some families owned houses in Kandla (450), Gandhinagar (150), Baroda (20), Jamnagar (50) and Junagarh (10). While 30 families have also settled in Nariyad, Viramgaon, Rajkot and other places.[9] Majority of Raigars are engaged in small business such as 'chappal' manufacturing factory as labourers, and a few are working as clerks.[10]

Around 1997, the Raigars established Raigar Samaj Shiksha Samiti (RSSS) in Ahmedabad,[11] but before that there was an informal local organisation which was working for the welfare of the Raigars. The encouragement given by the educated Raigars of Ahmedabad led them to organise themselves at the district and State levels. Thus, they organised themselves into RSSS, Ahmedabad (1997), with Kastur Chand Nogia of Ahmedabad as President; Devendra Kumar Kurdia as Vice-President; Aashu Lal Kurdia as Mantri and Treasurer; both Ramesh Chandra Kunwaria and Durga Ram Sukhadia (Gandhinagar) as Sah-Mantri and Mohan Lal Phoolwaria as Prachar Mantri.[12] There is an executive committee of 13 members.[13]

There were a few educated and highly placed Raigars in the community who encouraged the local Raigars to form such social organisations and to initiate the welfare programmes. For instance, Gian Chand Raigar, IPS and C.M. Chandolia, IRS who became the patrons of the RSSS were posted as Additional DGP Ahmedabad and Joint Commissioner, Customs and Central Excise, Kandla respectively.[14] As very influential and popular Raigar officers, they extended full support for educational programmes and in organising adult literacy programmes for both men and women. Another educated Raigar officer who became the advisor, was the Manager, Reserve Bank of India, Ahmedabad[15] and the other person named as Ladhu Ram Gusaiwal was a very influential social worker.

The major programme of RSSS was the propagation of education,[16] with a view to establish hostel and grant scholarships to the needy and wherever Raigar students were denied admission, there was a public agitation. The RSSS also pressed the caste fellows to send more and more children to schools. The RSSS also called for reform in their caste customs and for spiritual reformation. It was nationalistic in its orientation and supported the policies of the national congress including the abolition of untouchability. In order to attain the goals, the RSSS laid down the following seven activities:[17]

1. Among the untouchable castes in Gujarat, Raigars are educationally the most backward community. According to Kastur Chand Nogia, who is the President of RSSS, it is very shameful

for the community. In order to fulfil the aims of the RSSS, it was decided that the children should be sent to schools.

2. The RSSS would provide financial support to the poor and needy Raigar students coming from the rural areas.
3. Secondary and Higher Secondary passed Raigar students should be helped and guided in their pre-medical and engineering examinations.
4. For the success of the Raigar candidates in the various competitive examinations, such as IAS, IPS and allied services, bank services and state services, the RSSS would provide coaching facilities to them, as per the financial norms fixed by the RSSS.
5. The RSSS would make available the costly books and other important literature to the caste students appearing in the various competitive examinations within the financial limits of the RSSS.
6. Reformatory measures were introduced in the community to limit the wedding expenditure. RSSS took the decision that each Raigar family would donate Rs 100 to the RSSS at the time of each wedding. This would collect a considerable amount that will be utilised to solve the problem of financial crunch which was prevalent in the community.
7. It was decided by the RSSS to make compulsory for each Raigar employee, small and big businessmen to contribute 10 per cent of his annual income to the RSSS so that it may be able to award the scholarship to deserving students and also help their caste-men.

Thus, RSSS became the forum of the Raigars to promote its activities and bring about greater consciousness among Raigars spread all over Gujarat.

In 1998, the RSSS made valiant efforts to bring out a book entitled *Raigar Samaj in Ahmedabad* with Aashu Lal Uma Ram Kurdia, Maha Mantri, ABRM, Ahmedabad, as its Editor. There are a few Gujarati writers among the Raigars who contributed small articles in the book. On the occasion of the inauguration of Ganga Mai Mandir, at Thakkar Bappa Nagar, Ahmedabad, C.M. Chandolia, Joint Commissioner (who supported the publication of the book) is a dedicated worker of a section of Gujarat Raigars, released it on November 3, 1998.[18] On this auspicious occasion, Chandolia donated Rs 15,000 for educational programmes and loaned Rs 10,000 to Ganga Mai Mandir.[19] The function was presided over by Swami Gopal Ram Maharaj. Among others who were present were: Kastur Chand Nogia, Aashu Lal Uma Ram Kurdia, Gian Chand and others. News regarding B.E. degree courses and MBBS degree colleges got circulated in *Smarika* (1999), as it concerned many Raigar students.

The Raigars of Gujarat were involved in social, cultural and educational activities. In the social field the RSSS took a special interest in welcoming the Raigar VIPs and apprising them about their various socio-cultural activities undertaken and the problems being faced by them. For instance, on May 23, 1998, when Satya Narain Jatiya, Labour Minister, Government of India visited Ahmedabad, a delegation of the Raigars of Gujarat under the leadership of Aashu Lal Kurdia, Maha Mantri, ABRM, Ahmedabad, went to the Circuit House to welcome and see him. The delegation attracted the attention of the Minister towards their pitiable socio-economic conditions and also submitted a memorandum requesting him for inclusion of the Raigars/Jatiya castes in the Scheduled Castes list of Gujarat state.[20] Among other leading leaders who participated in the delegation were: Govind Ram Gusaiwal, Ram Chandra Phoolwaria, Heera Lal Phoolwaria, Bharat Gusaiwal, Tara Chand Phoolwaria, Ramesh Phoolwaria and Mohan Lal Phoolwaria.[21]

The demand for inclusion of Raigar/Jatiya is still a live issue with ABRM. Meanwhile, Raigar leadership has earned more credit for strengthening their demand. Although the Government of India is not in favour of including any new castes in SC/ST list, yet it has introduced certain welfare schemes for weaker sections of the society in the state.

In recent years, the Raigars of Gujarat have started taking active interest in mobilising public opinion for their demands of inclusion of Raigar/Jatiya castes in the SC list of Gujarat state, with the support of Raigar leaders. The senior government officials could not openly be involved in political activities and Aashu Lal Kurdia, who is the Mahamantri of ABRM, Ahmedabad and Kashtur Chand Nogia assumed the leadership of Raigars. They have great organisational capacity which they direct towards socio-cultural activities. Nogia once told the author on phone that even 54 years after independence, the Raigars had not sent even a single MLA at the state level.[22]

The demand for Raigars/Jatias inclusion in SC/ST list as discussed above, had two significant effects on the Raigar movement. First, the ABRM revitalised and strengthened in many ways. While local and regional associations were affiliated to ABRM, important social workers and political leaders among the Raigars started taking interest in the new programme, as they considered the case genuine. As a result of this, ABRM emerged as a strong organisation representing Raigar population of India. Second, the demand for the SC status boosted self-image of Raigars as a Scheduled Caste and they gained recognition from central government in Rajasthan, Madhya Pradesh, Haryana, Punjab and Delhi. The central government has not yet accepted the demand. An indirect effect of the growing power of the Raigars has been that the Congress party has gathered the support of Raigars in different parts of India, so as to enlarge their political base and to increase their vote bank.

The foregoing account of the emergence of the Raigars educational organisation shows the miserable socio-educational conditions of the Raigars in Gujarat and participation of Raigars in creation of educational and other facilities for their caste-men.

The Gujarat Raigars also took lead in their contribution to the religious activities. Since this is relevant to the reform movement launched by ABRM for socio-cultural changes in the Raigar community, we shall now discuss religious activities of the Raigars in Gujarat with particular reference to Ganga Mai Mandir.

Before 1980, the Raigars in Gujarat had purchased a plot of land measuring 400 sq. feet in Ganganagar Society, Ahmedabad for construction of Ganga Mai temple[23] but only after a lapse of 20 years or so, they have been able to complete the temple in a significant way. The Raigars of Ahmedabad continued to provide financial support. The donors were from Thakkar Bappa Nagar, Kuber Nagar, Ishanpur, Jamalpur, Rakhialvada, Narianpura, Chanakyapuri, Shalagram and Ram Rajai Nagar. The Raigars of Ahmedabad laid the foundation stone of Ganga Mai Mandir building in Ahmedabad on June 26, 1980 at an estimated cost of some thousands of rupees.[24]

As noted earlier, the educated and highly placed Raigars played a significant role in bringing socio-cultural changes of Raigars, and round about in 1995, C.M. Chandolia came to Ahmedabad on transfer as Joint Commissioner, Customs and

Central Excise, Ahmedabad. He encouraged educational and reform activities at Ahmedabad and religious programmes were started with the support of Chandolia.[25] After his arrival, the spiritual programme and educational activities increased in Ahmedabad and eventually with the full support and encouragement of Chandolia and others, the dream of Ganga Mai Mandir turned into a reality. On November 4, 1998 (i.e., on Kartik Sud Purnima) the Raigars of Ahmedabad held a huge gathering at Thakkar Bappa Nagar which was attended by thousands of delegates from Rajasthan, Maharashtra and Gujarat. The chief guest of the function were Mrs and Mr C.M. Chandolia[26] and they also inaugurated the Ganga Mai Mandir. Among other delegates who attended the inauguration function and spoke on the occasion were Kashtur Chand Nogia, Aashu Lal Kurdia, Gian Chand, Swami Gopal Ram Maharaj, Swami Hari Narain, Bhanwar Lal Singharia (Rajasthan) and Govind Ram Chorotia (Mumbai).[27]

An executive committee was constituted in April 2001 in Ahmedabad, an industrial city of Gujarat. The initiative to start a branch came from National President of ABRM, who vide his letter dated January 2001 authorised General Secretary ABRM to visit Ahmedabad. As a result of this, he visited Ahmedabad and held a meeting under the Chairmanship of Govind Ram Gusaiwal, Upadhiyaksh, ABRM to elect the executive committee and also to initiate the socio-educational activities. Thus, the first state executive committee came into existence on April 8, 2001 with Devendra Kumar Kurdia as President; Heera Lal Phoolwaria, Ram Chandra Gusaiwal and Shankar Lal Mosalpuria as Vice Presidents; Ram Chandra Phoolwaria as State Mantri; Ram Chandra Bansiwal as Organising Mantri and Hari Ram Gusaiwal as Treasurer. In addition to the above members 21 Executive Members were also elected.[28]

Raigars in Madhya Pradesh

Raigars in different districts of Madhya Pradesh had intimate connections with the Raigars of Rajasthan and many Raigars from Rajasthan had migrated to Madhya Pradesh during the British Raj in search of work and later on to save themselves from the atrocities of the upper caste Hindus in the then princely states of Rajputana.[29] Thus, most of them who migrated to Madhya Pradesh from Rajasthan had settled down in many major towns and cities of Madhya Pradesh, such as Mandsor, Neemach, Indore, Ujjain,

Ratlam and Bhopal. The migrated Raigars still have their social linkage with their ancestors' villages in Rajasthan. In the section that follows, we shall discuss the consequences of the Raigar movement in Rajasthan, migration of Raigars from Rajasthan to Madhya Pradesh and present day socio-educational and political scenario of their conditions in different districts of Madhya Pradesh.

In Mandsor district there are about 150 families, who are mostly Peepalia Mando, Malhar, Menora, Kangato, Varkhedo Dago and Hingonia Raigars. Most of them migrated to Mandsor from Mewar region between 1700 and 1800 and the poor Raigars did the traditional work for their livelihood. Now the Raigars are found in a variety of occupations as agricultural labourers, factory workers and government servants.[30]

According to Puran Mal Verma, a social activist, there are about 200 families in Neemach district who are mostly Bakolia, Hindonia, Jawdelia, Ujjenia, Dhuria, Kartalia, Mardhalpuria, Indoria, Phoolwadia, Dholpuria and Bansiwal Raigars. Most of the Raigars are found in various government departments as school teachers and in white-collar jobs. Champa Lal Arya[31] (Hindonia gotra) had been a prominent leader. Champa Lal Arya an enthusiastic social worker was elected MLA on the ticket of Bharatiya Jan Sangh and Bharatiya Janata Party respectively for many years. It may be noted that from 1962 to 1972,[32] Arya was elected to Madhya Pradesh Legislative Assembly from Suwasara constituency, district Mandsor, Madhya Pradesh, on Bharatiya Jan Sangh ticket and later in 1977, he was elected MLA on the Janta Party ticket from the same constituency. In 1980[33] he was also elected as MLA on BJP ticket from Suwasara constituency. Thus, Champa Lal Arya had been the key leader of BJP and was elected to Madhya Pradesh Legislative Assembly for four consecutive terms.

Another educated person of the community is Shyam Arya, a doctor by profession, who took an active interest for the upliftment of Raigars. The other important persons of the community are: Mrs Shila Arya and Rajendra Arya as school lecturers; Parvati Arya, the first woman truck driver in whole of the country from Madhya Pradesh, is a Raigar and is currently member of Zila Panchayat. Babu Lal Machalpuria remained the Member of Municipal Council, Neemach. Geeta Ujjenia, who is taking an active interest in welfare of Neemach Raigars, is Councillor from Neemach and a Raigar. Mohan Lal Arya, Deputy Collector from Chitakhera, Neemach, is a

Raigar who has donated liberally in the construction of the building of Dharmshala at Bhodvamata Place at Neemach.[34]

In the first decade of twentieth century, there were about 250 Raigar families who migrated to Indore from Kota, Sawai Madhopur, Jaipur, Dausa (200 families) and Marwar (50 families) regions respectively to protect themselves from the atrocities of dominant castes and since then have been doing their traditional work. In Indore, most of the migrated poor Raigars were employed in various textile mills, factories, and industries. In Indore Kankheria, Jandolia, Tongitia, Maurya, Khamokharia, Hindonia and Gusaiwal Raigars are found in different professions as advocates (1), engineering students (2), university cricket players (3) and soldiers (1). Another important person of the community is Hasti Mal Dadwal, retired Commissioner, State Insurance, Madhya Pradesh. His two daughters are studying in the medical college, Madhya Pradesh. Similarly, another eminent person of the community who has earned name and fame for the community is Shrawan Kumar Das, Additional Inspector General of Police and he is also taking, an active interest in the reform of Indore Raigars. His daughter Rakhi got first position in Madhya Pradesh State Administrative Services examination and was posted as Deputy Collector, Indore. She is married to Dr Rakesh Bakolia, who has obtained a medical degree from Madhya Pradesh (is son-in-law of Shrawan Kumar Das). He was selected by Madhya Pradesh Public Service Commission, Bhopal as Deputy Superintendent of Police. It is interesting to note that there were some Raigars in Indore, who took courage to publish community paper. One such person of the community was Kanti Devi wife of Puran Mal Verma, who brought out *Raigar Uthan* a Hindi monthly from Indore with Kanta Devi herself as editor. The paper reported socio-educational and political conditions of the local Raigars and other activities.[35]

Similarly, Raigars in Ujjain district are negligible. There are about 15 families, a few of whom migrated to Ujjain from Ajmer and Jaipur region between 1970 and 1975 and have settled down in Ujjain, while the bulk of the Raigars in Indore-Ujjain are doing either traditional work or are daily wagers. Shiv Sahai Pingolia migrated from Rajasthan, was Class II Gazetted Officer who died a few years ago. His eldest son is now an engineer. Another son is a doctor (with medical degree) and has now been selected as the Deputy Superintendent of Police by Madhya Pradesh Public Service Commission,

Bhopal. Similarly, his youngest daughter is studying in medical college, Indore.[36]

Like Ujjain, Raigars in Bhopal district are also few in number. There are 8 families only, most of them are Bakolia Raigars. While the bulk of Raigars in Bhopal are engaged in manufacturing chappals, Balwant Rai Nirmal 'Nogia', a migrant from Rajasthan, was an IPS officer and retired as Inspector General of Police, Madhya Pradesh. He provided higher education to his sons. All the three sons are engineers. One son is serving in USA.[37]

Some of the 30 Raigar families of Rajasthan have migrated to Ratlam where they were also employed in textile factories. Only one family is residing in Nagda, that too which migrated from Rajasthan.[38]

The foregoing account highlights several important aspects of the Raigar movement. It is important to note that there was a concerned effort on the part of Raigars of Rajasthan, to gain self-respect by discarding the traditional work and also social evils. As a result, they strongly protested and refused to oblige to give forced labour (begar) to Jamindars, Jagirdars Brahmins, etc. They acted as domestic servants. They fought against untouchability, social injustice and atrocities perpetuated by upper-caste Hindus. They also organised themselves for educational and welfare activities and to accept the status of man. All this annoyed the Jagirdars, Jamindars and other dominant castes. Thus, there was a growing conflict between the upper-caste Hindus and Raigars. Atrocities on Raigars increased and a series of violent conflicts occurred in rural areas. Consequently, Raigars of Rajasthan migrated in large number to different districts of Madhya Pradesh for shelter. Whereas they had formed a sizeable social group especially in Rajasthan, but in Madhya Pradesh they had not emerged as a socially viable group. Being quite few in numbers, Raigars had been unable to wield decisive powers, although Raigars in Madhya Pradesh remained mainly traditional workers in the towns and cities, they to some extent, succeeded in altering the traditional work and they are also employed in the white-collar jobs.[39]

Over a period of time, especially after independence, not a single political, professional and business elite had emerged, who could take up the leadership of the Samaj. In the last few years, there were one MP, one MLA and a few Municipal Councillors from Neemach. There are a few doctors, engineers, IPS, IAS officers, etc.

The progress made by Raigars in Madhya Pradesh was not considered satisfactory by Puran Mal Verma.[40] The main obstacle for the progress was the lack of the numerical strength. There was also lack of education. They were not very conscious about the education of their children.

In early 1991, the Raigars made valiant efforts to organise the community sammelan and the first community sammelan was also held in Indore in 1992 and H.D.K. Das, IGP, Indore was the chief guest of the function. A large contingent of the Raigars from Ujjain, Mandsore, Neemach, Ratlam (all in Madhya Pradesh), Kota, Nagaur, Jaipur (all in Rajasthan) and Delhi attended the sammelan and they exchanged their views on the socio-economic and educational conditions of the Raigars of Madhya Pradesh.[41] And, similarly, the Raigars of Neemach took active interest in organising a one-day sammelan (1993) at Neemach.[42]

A notable leader who was associated with the activities of RSS and its allied organisations during his early days in district Mandsore, Madhya Pradesh was Satya Narain Jatiya of Jawad. Born on February 14, 1946 in a poor family of Jatiya community, he received his primary education in his village Jawad. After passing his primary education, he was selected as a talented student, by the State and was admitted in one of the leading educational institutes, known as Malhar Ashram at Indore for his Secondary School education. From his childhood Jatiya was under the influence of RSS directly.[43]

His father was a man of progressive ideas. He encouraged the members of his family to get higher education. Inspired by his father, Jatiya did his graduation with science. While studying LLB in Madhya Pradesh, he was arrested (as emergency was imposed during that period (1975-1977)) as he was a staunch RSS activist and was lodged in a Madhya Pradesh jail.[44] Even then, Jatiya was conscious about his study, he appeared in LLB examination from the jail and was declared successful.[45] He was not interested in practising law and turned to public service.

After obtaining his LLB degree, Jatiya was admitted in the University. He did his MA in sociology.[46] After obtaining MA degree in the subject with the help of his teacher, he did his Ph.D. in the same subject.[47]

According to the pamphlet published and circulated by Information Ministry, Government of India, New Delhi on November 10, 1999, Jatiya started his public career as labour leader of both organised and unorganised labour unions of electricity, textile mill, transportation, agriculture and the railway employees.[48] Several times intense agitations, demonstrations and Dharnas, etc., were organised against the social injustice under his leadership. He also took active part in the affairs of Bharatiya Mazdoor Sangh.[49] He offered satyagraha and courted arrest. During demonstrations, the workers were 'lathi charged' and were also arrested including Jatiya and put in the jail.[50]

He was an active Jansangh worker. In 1972, he was appointed Organising Secretary of the Bharatiya Yuva Sangh, Madhya Pradesh. Later on, he became district organising Mantri of Shahjapur of Bharatiya Jansangh, Bhopal; President of BJP, Ujjain city and Ujjain district; Mantri of BJP, Madhya Pradesh; Vice-President of BJP, Madhya Pradesh; Member of National Executive and National Council of BJP; Maha Mantri and President of Scheduled Castes Morcha, BJP and Secretary of the Parliamentary Group of BJP.[51] He was one of the leaders who agitated for the restoration of the traditional values. Between 1984 and 1989 several 'Padyatras' were organised by him. Jatiya played an important role in water purification movement of Shipra river in Madhya Pradesh.[52]

Jatiya took keen interest not only in political affairs but also in the affairs of social and cultural activities and was elected the President of Vivekanand Yuwa Kalyan Parishad.[53] Besides, he was also President of Dr Ambedkar Smriti Smarak Sansthan and in 1998 and 2000 he headed the Indian delegation to International Labour Conference held at Geneva.[54]

Thus, he gained much popularity. In 1977 he was for the first time elected an MLA to State Assembly from Aagar constituency in the district Shahjapur.[55] During his tenure as MLA Jatiya worked as a member in close cooperation with Chairman of the SC/ST Welfare Committee. In 1980, he was elected MP for the first time from Ujjain constituency.[56] Since then he was elected in 1989, 1991, 1996, 1998, 1999 and 2004.[57] In 1998[58] Jatiya became the Labour Minister at the centre and later on was also shifted to another ministry, i.e., Urban Employment and Poverty Eradication Ministry.[59] Again, in 1999, he became the Labour Minister and is currently Minister of Social Justice.[60]

Apart from the political activities, he also took a leading part in literary activities. As a writer, he wrote on contemporary issues from time to time in various periodicals and newspapers. He also wrote poetry. In 1995, the collection of his poetry called *Aalekh*, was released by Prime Minister Atal Behari Vajpayee.[61] He is also editor of *Labour Bulletin* and *Kranti Rath*.

Jatiya attended and participated in several conferences and meetings, held abroad, particularly in UK, France, Kenya, South Africa, Mauritius, Syria, Switzerland and United Arab Emirate[62] in various capacities.

Raigars in Haryana[63]

The Raigars of Haryana and Punjab regions present a unique picture in some way. There are the old urban Raigar residents living in different towns and cities of Haryana from pre-independence days, and Raigar immigrants came in waves especially after independence from Rajasthan. In the beginning, they sold readymade leather goods such as Rajasthani *juti*, etc. Some worked as labourers and shoes repairers. After independence, during different periods, the Raigar families who were residing in different districts and regions of Rajasthan such as Jhunjhunu, Ratangarh, Churu, Rajaldesar, Sardarshahar, Suratgarh, Mandawa, Bikaner, Nagaur, Ganganagar, Jaipur and Sikar belonging to different 'gotras' came to Haryana. Thus, Raigars settled down in different districts of Haryana, such as Hansi (in 1940), Dabwali Mandi, district Sirsa (in 1943), Siwani, district Bhiwani (in 1943), Fatehabad (in 1946), Hisar (in 1947) and Anandpur (in 1960). Thus, Raigars of Haryana have very close social link with those residing in Rajasthan.

Haryana has 20 districts and Raigars are thickly populated in four of them, namely, Sirsa, Fatehabad, Hissar and Bhiwani.

During 1980s, the Raigars started taking an active part in local body politics. According to Ashwini Kumar, in 1982, Kishan Lal Deegwal, the first Raigar and a resident of Raigar Basti, Fatehabad contested the election for Nagar Palika, Fatehabad from General Ward 9, and was elected. Later on he became the President of Nagar Palika. Similarly, Lila Ram Bakolia was elected to Nagar Palika, Hansi. One of the Raigars was elected as Councillor in Nagar Palika. Siwani. Thus, in 1982 the Raigars started taking an active part in local body politics. This is one of the most significant factors in the process of politicisation of Raigars of Haryana region.

Likewise, in 1980s, the Raigars of Haryana started taking an active interest in mobilising public opinion for educational, social reforms and welfare of Raigar community. It was during 1980s that Ashwini Kumar, MA, LLB, started an agitation for the establishment of Raigar organisation. However, the efforts to organise the Raigars of Haryana region date back to 1975, when there was a growing consciousness among some of its social activists and workers, of the need to initiate educational and other programmes for Raigars who had come from different parts of Rajasthan, could materialise.

Thus, in 1980, a Harijan Sudhar Samiti (HSS) was established aiming at the social and cultural development of Raigar community. The first office bearers were: Ashwini Kumar (President), Jagna Ram Gadegaonlia (Secretary), Poonam Chand Kurdia (Vice-President), Geeg Raj Deegwal and Mala Ram Kurdia (Patron) and 11 executive members.

The main activities of the HSS were to:

1. spread education amongst the Raigar boys and girls and also help the poor and needy students;
2. grow socio-political consciousness among the Raigars;
3. promote socio-cultural activities; and
4. impart training in various social spheres such as tailoring, preparation of food, etc., and maintenance of house, etc.

It may be noted that in the beginning, HSS took the services of 'Sewa Bharati', an organisation of Sangh Parivar, in holding the classes of Raigar girls but later on opened a centre of Sewa Bharati, at Raigar Basti, Fatehabad.

HSS also played an important part in the construction of the building for community Dharmshala. Thus, HSS purchased a piece of land and constructed Dharmshala in 1980. The total expenditure incurred according to Ashwini Kumar was Rs 10,000.

In recent years to awaken the social and political consciousness among the Raigars, Ashwini Kumar, Editor of *Raigar Sudhar* from Fatehabad, Haryana launched a campaign called 'Raigar Chetna Abhiyan' in January 2000. Its main objective was to create a social and political consciousness. He organised eight district-level meetings, three in Haryana and five in Rajasthan. The meeting started with the series of speeches explaining the purpose of the meetings and emphasising the need for social and political unity.

The speech by Raigar leaders was always the highlight of the meeting. Thus, the district-level 'Raigar Chetna Abhiyan' brought the Raigars from different states in contact with Rajasthan and Haryana Raigars. Thus, it provided a platform for Raigars belonging to diverse political parties to review their socio-economic context through frequent interaction with Raigar Chetna meetings. In 2000, Ashwini Kumar also started publication of a fortnightly magazine called *Raigar Sudhar* from Fatehabad, Haryana.

Another centre of Raigar's activity in Haryana is district Sirsa, where the Haryana State Raigar Mahasabha (HSRM) was established in 2001 under the leadership of Ganpat Ram Gadegaonlia, a resident of Dabwali. He was nominated by ABRM President, Bhore Lal Shastri as the President of the State Raigar Mahasabha and was authorised to form a State Executive Committee to launch the social, economic and political programmes in the state with immediate effect.

HSRM derives its support from Raigars of Rajasthan. Efforts have been made by the local Raigars for promoting education among women and children.

Raigars in Punjab[64]

Prior to independence, there had been waves of immigration of Raigar caste into Delhi, Uttar Pradesh, Gujarat, Madhya Pradesh, Haryana and Punjab, mainly from Rajasthan to protect themselves from the atrocities of Jagirdars, Jamindars and high caste Hindus and also as more economic opportunities became available to them in these states. The immigrant Raigars felt the need for an association and launched a campaign for awakening the masses. The attitude of the Raigar residents was lukewarm in the beginning although they participated in it later.

In order to initiate awakening of the social and political consciousness amongst the Raigars and also to promote educational, welfare and the social reforms, an attempt was made by the Chief, Rashtriya Raigar Samaj Prabandhak Committee (RRSPC) and Ashwini Kumar, a law graduate and Chief Editor of *Raigar Sudhar*.

Ashwini Kumar made extensive tours propagating his new message by visiting various places in Haryana and neighbouring state of Punjab and meeting social workers and political activists. He also visited Moga, Jira, Malla Walla, Makhu, Japani Mill,

Kotakhalta, Halgate, Chatipindu and others in Punjab and was invited by social activists to visit Kotmit Singh, Magita, Fatehgarh Chaudia, Ajnala and Khalda. In all, he visited 31 towns and cities.

During the first phase of his tour, the notable social activists, who were associated with the activities of social political awakening campaign in Punjab were: Suwa Lal Kanwadia and Om Prakash Bansiwal (resident of Jira), Mangtu Ram Kurdia, Khajan Singh Hingonia, Kukam Chand and Girish Bharati (all residents of Amritsar) and Radhe Shyam Kanwadia (resident of Magita).

One of the most significant events of Raigar movement, occurred in Amritsar city under the leadership of Gian Mohanpuria. A small committee 'Raigar Sabha' came into existence in 2001, which was object of caste awakening campaign. The main object of the committee was to propagate social reform and to give encouragement for socio-economic development and industrious habits among the Raigars of Hall Bazar Katra Sher Singh. Thus, Gian Mohanpuria was made President of the Committee, Raj Kumar Mundotia as Secretary and Raj Kumar Basotia as Treasurer along with a few members.

The local Raigars of Amritsar, Punjab realised the value of various socio-religious programmes and started their efforts to construct a Dharmshala and to run various activities from there. Around November-December 2001, Laxmi Kanta Chanwala,[65] an MLA donated a cheque of Rs 1 lac from her Development Fund to Gian Mohanpuria in the presence of a huge gathering at Hall Bazar, to be utilised for construction of a Dharmshala at Hall Bazar Katra Sher Singh. Other leaders connected with this function included: Gian Swaroop Jajoria, Tota Ram, Mohan Lal Basotia, Ganesh Ram Kurdia, etc.

There are about 410 Raigar families in Rama Mandi district Bhatinda. The earliest migrants who had settled in Rama Mandi came mostly from Jaipur district of Rajasthan in 1932.[66] Some of the Raigars who had also settled in Rama Mandi came after partition from Lahore in 1947.[67] There are 50 families of Tongaria and 40 families of Basetia respectively. Thus, they dominated among the Raigars who migrated to Punjab. The Raigars of Rama Mandi were the first to organise themselves for educational and other welfare activities. The Raigars had built their own Dharmshala and two temples: one each of Baba Ram Dev and Ganga Mai in Rama Mandi.

It is interesting to note that there had been a gradual growth of political elite among the Punjab Raigars. For instance, at present Maya Devi Tongaria is a Councillor in Nagar Palika from Ward 1. She also became the Vice Chairman of Nagar Palika and was responsible for welfare activities and programmes in Raigar Basti. It may be noted that Vishan Ram Basetia, Ruda Ram Sukaria, Govind Ram Basetia and Prabhu Dayal Basetia also became Councillors.[68]

Over a period of time especially after independence professional elite had emerged, who had taken up government jobs in various departments. According to *Raigar Sudhar*, a fortnightly Hindi paper published from Fatehabad, Haryana, there are: 1 Tehsildar, 1 Tehsil Welfare Officer, 2 LDC, 3 Food Inspectors, 3 in FCI, 2 in Treasury, 1 Cooperative Inspector, 1 NFC, 1 Overseer, 1 Octroi Inspector, 2 in Bank, 7 in Sales Tax Department, 1 in Post Office, 1 in Electricity Board, 7 in Agriculture Departments, 1 in B&R Department, 2 in Tube Well Corporation, 1 in Income Tax Department, 1 in Marketing Committee, 1 on Airport, 1 in Tele Communication Department, 1 in TV Tower, 1 in Army, 1 in Nagar Palika, 2 in LIC and 2 Postmen.[69]

The progress made by Raigars in Rama Mandi is considered satisfactory by Ashwini Kumar, who is dedicated to welfare work of Raigars in Haryana and Punjab. According to him, the main obstacle to progress is the problem of educated unemployment among the Raigars. There are some well educated Raigars in Rama Mandi who are unemployed. For instance, there are 100 Matriculates, 20 BAs, 2 BEs, 1 BSc, 3 ITI, 2 diploma holders and 5 ETT.[70]

While a small number of Raigars in Rama Mandi are in government service, majority of them are still following the traditional work. For instance, there are 400 persons who manufacture shoes, 3 families are engaged in skin dyeing, 200 are labourers, 3 are craftsmen, 6 do the work of polishing, 1 is store keeper, 1, has his own PCO, 6 are electricians, 5 are tailors, 5 are small shop owners and 7 are vegetable sellers.[71]

As mentioned earlier, in 2001 the Raigars in Punjab had organised themselves as a group for educational reforms and welfare purposes but in the early months of 2003, Raigars entered in local body politics in negligible number. In the beginning of 2003 a few Raigars contested the elections to Nagar Palikas in Punjab. According to Ashwini Kumar, 3 Raigars were elected to Abohar Nagar Palika.

The other Nagar Palikas in which one Raigar Councillor each was elected are: Firozpur Nagar Palika, Faridkot Nagar Palika, Moga Nagar Palika, Amritsar Nagar Palika and Vareta Nanagar Palika. Thus, there is an emergence of political elite among the Raigars of Punjab.

Afte1 independence, the Punjab gave one IAS officer. In 2000,[72] Ram Lal was selected for the first time as an IAS officer.

Raigars in Uttar Pradesh

Around 160 years back (year 1844), Raigars of Jaipur – the then princely state of Rajputana – exhibited unparalled courage.[73] The poor Raigars left Jaipur for Mathura in search of jobs. Thus, a group of five Raigars under the leadership of Mansha Ram Mohanpuria (village Peeplai), reached Dwarkadheesh Mandir, Chhata Bazar, Mathura. All the five Raigars stayed for sometime at Chamarwada and earned wages.

The five Raigars, viz., Mansha Ram Mohanpuria, Moola Maurya, Kripa and Balu (both brothers) of Peeplai village, Jaipur and Tota Kansotia stayed at Chamarwada for years together. Both Chamars and Raigars used to clean and dye the skins of the animals.

The number of Raigars increased further after a lapse of few years. Efforts were made by the Raigars of Chamarwada, Mathura to bring their relatives and caste-fellows from Jaipur. As a result of this, few more Raigars joined.

Till the year 1860, the Chamars and Raigars in Chamarwada did not face any problem. However, in the changing socio-religious scenario, the upper castes and pilgrims realised the problem of bad smell of skins of animals and they protested to the local administration to shift these untouchable communities to some other place. As a result of this, the Chamars were shifted to Mohanpura, near Bharatpur gate, while Raigars were rehabilitated at Khari Kauwa Sadar Mathura respectively.[74] Although the Khari Kauwa Sadar Mohalla was dominated by the Raigars, yet it was called Sadar Chamaran Mohalla. Now, it is popularly known as Raigar Mohalla.[75]

For the purpose of describing the dominant gotra of Raigars four gotras may be identified as told by Mansingh Phoolwaria, for the Raigars of Mathura: Mohanpuria, Maurya, Phoolwaria and

Kansotia. It is noteworthy to mention here that the immigrated Raigars of Rajasthan are called as Raigars but have not been able to establish their identity even today with Raigars of Mathura, its surrounding areas and also with the State Government. They are considered as Jatavas or Chamars. The Raigars provided an efficient leadership in leather works. Hence, the upper caste people and local untouchable communities namely Jatavs, Chamars and Mochis considered them to be the Jatavs, Chamars or Mochis respectively.

Raigar Associations

The immigrant Raigars felt the need of associations/organisations and formed various associations. In this section that follows, we shall deal with the formation of various associations with divergent objectives and its repercussions on the Raigar organisations.

Raigar Shikshit Yuva Kendra (RSYK), 1960[76]

In the history of Raigars in Mathura, 1960 was an important year. It is significant because the school-going Raigar boys and a few aged illiterate residents in Raigar Mohalla felt the need for educating their own caste boys and old Raigars and established Raigar Shikshit Yuva Kendra (RSYK). The attitude of older Raigar residents was encouraging and they participated in it. The founder members of RSYK were: Kundal Lal, Kishan Lal, Bhola Ram, Sundar Lal and Parmanand. All were school-going Raigar boys. Aged Raigar residents were: Bal Kishan Barotia, Gopal Maurya and Mathuradas Vasiwal. With this aim in mind, a night school was started in Narain Kansotia's residence in Raigar Mohalla. The School was attended by about 15-20 boys and girls.

The main programme of RSYK was to campaign against the social vices. It also stressed the need for reform in their caste customs. It was reformative in its orientation. Similarly, it took the initiative to awaken the socio-educational consciousness among the caste-fellows. They were persuaded to send their children to schools. It is worthwhile to mention here that, with the help of RSYK the aged Raigars learned to sign and to read the Hindi newspapers. Two local newspapers *Amar Ujjala* (Agra) and *Sainik* (Mathura) were subscribed by RSYK for Raigars. The Raigar boys going to day-school, worked as first Raigar teachers at night-schools. The first to work as teachers were: Kundal Lal, Kishan Lal and

Parmanand. The moving spirit working behind this campaign was Ram Dev Sokaria – a local Raigar.

Over a period of time, after the completion of their education the Raigar teachers-cum-boys joined the government jobs. As a result the educational activities of RSYK slackened after that and lost its effectiveness. Efforts were not made by Raigars for its revival.

Raigar Samaj Sevi School[77] *(Ratri Pathshala) (RSSS), 1971*

Another organisation of Raigars in Mathura was Raigar Samaj Sevi School (RSSS). The first to be appointed as teachers were: Dharampal Mohanpuria, Puran Kansotia, Gulab and Bhagwan Das Phoolwaria. The lady teacher was Prem Maurya. The aims of RSSS were to provide extra coaching facilities to poor and helpless Raigar boys. RSSS also encouraged girls education. RSSS was attended by Ram Prasad, Khayali Ram, Dhan Singh, Prabhu Dayal (all boys) and Sarbati, Gendo and Dropadi (all girls). RSSS used to run in Duli Chand Maurya's residence. The boys and girls were taught at night in the light of lanterns. From education point of view this was a good initiative. According to Arjun Mohanpuria, it may be noted that during 1971 India-Pakistan war (popularly known as Bangla Desh yudh) the night school had to be closed as burning of lanterns, lamps, Deepak, Diya, electricity, etc., were strictly prohibited throughout the country by the government and thus, the academic activities of RSSS slackened after that.

According to Prem Singh,[78] Senior Assistant in the State Bank of India, Refinary Nagar, Mathura, the drive for education was never launched. No socio-cultural awakening among the Raigars of Mathura and its surrounding areas was brought about by any individual or organisation. Thus, they did not create any enthusiasm among the masses for educational progress in a socially and financially most backward community.

Raigar Sudhar Samiti[79] *(RSS), 1976*

In 1976 the Raigars started taking an interest in arranging a meeting at Mohalla. The meeting was attended by 15-20 Raigars. Thus, Raigar Sudhar Samiti came into existence in 1976. The first office bearers of this Samiti were: Arjun Mohanpuria (President), Hukam Singh (Sangthan Mantri), Than Singh (Treasurer) and Laxman Sarsunia (Maha Sachiv). Besides, there were seven members. They were: Damodar Vasiwal, Babu Lal Khatnawalia, Ganesh Maurya, Banwari Lal Maurya, Chhagan Barotia, Amar Kansotia, and Khemchand Aaloria. All the office bearers and members were illiterate.

The main purposes of the Samiti were to:

1. assist financially the poor and needy Raigars at the time of marriages of their sons and daughters;
2. protect and maintain assets of Samaj such as Dharmshala, temples and Bagichi;
3. send the children to schools;
4. ban the use of liquor and gambling;
5. accept only Rs 11 at the time of marriage for Bhat; and

But, actually over a period of three years, the socio-educational activities of RSS slackened and lost its effectiveness.

Nav Yuvak Raigar Sudhar Samiti[80] *(NYRSS), 1976*

In Mathura, Raigars organised themselves once again in 1976, thanks to the efforts of Ram Prasad Barotia, Keshav Dev Nirana, Gulab, Chandralal Kansotia and a few others. A small meeting under the leadership of Ram Prasad Barotia was held in Ganga Mai Mandir, Raigar Mohalla. It was attended by nearly 50-60 Raigars. Thus, in 1976, the Nav Yuvak Raigar Sudhar Samiti (NYRSS) was formed aiming at the social and cultural development of the community. The main activities of NYRSS were to:

1. provide financial assistance to the poor, needy and helpless Raigars;
2. support the poor Raigars for solemnisation of the marriages of their children;
3. help them financially at the time of the crisis, such as flood, houses gutted in fire and for performing the last rites of the poor Raigars;
4. provide legal aid to the victims of upper castes atrocities, and to express caste solidarity and moral support with them; and
5. stop the working of young girls and married women outside home and thus save them from sexual harassment of the upper castes.

The first President was Chanda Lal Kansotia. Besides, there were eight members. They were: Keshav Dev Nirana, Arjun Mohanpuria, Narain Nirana, Hukam Vasiwal, Gulab, Leku Jajoria, Khayali Mohanpuria, and Laxman Sarsunia.

It may be noted that there had been some instances when NYRSS came forward for help at the time of crisis. For instance, in 1976, the house of widow Kalodai Dehatwal was burnt in a fire. NYRSS played an important part in the reconstruction of her house. Thus, according to Arjun Mohanpura, Rs 500 were given as financial help to the widow, Kalodai Dehatwal.

It was during 1976 onwards that NYRSS started collecting donations from caste-fellows. This process continued for some years and later on, it was stopped. Soon after the formation of NYRSS, factional division in Samiti occurred. In Raigar Mohalla the faction led by Shyam Lal Mohanpuria, Prabhu Dayal Kansotia, Net Ram Jajoria, etc., criticised and opposed NYRSS. Thus, within a few years, the socio-economic and reform activities of NYRSS slackened.

Raigar Samaj Coaching Centre[81] (RSCC), 1980

In 1980, Raigars formed another organisation called Raigar Samaj Coaching Centre (RSCC) in Raigar Mohalla. The founder members were: Prem Singh, Laxmi Narain, Babu Lal and Damodar.

The main programme of the Centre was to hold extra classes at night on the roof of Narain Nirana's House, with a view to remove the illiteracy of the poor and helpless Raigars boys and girls., The Centre was attended by 30-40 students. The founder members rendered their services to the Centre free of cost.

In the same year (1980), the educated Raigars started a small library called 'Ravidas Pustakalaya' in Raigar Dharmshala at the Raigar Mohalla, Mathura. The Hindi newspapers and literary magazines subscribed by it were: *Nav Bharat Times* (Delhi), *Amar Ujjala* (Agra), *Jansata* (Delhi), *Sandhya Times* (Mathura), *Bahujan Sanghatan* (BSP's paper), *Sarita, Satya Katha, Filmi Kalia,* children's book and *Manohar Kahania*. Besides, a large number of small books in Hindi on Ambedkar's life, mission, writings, speeches, etc., were purchased by way of donations. They also purchased *Bhagvat Geeta, Ramayan* and few other religious books. Laxman Sarsunia, Bhagwan Das Phoolwaria, Hukam Singh Vasiwal, Arjun Mohanpuria, Amar Singh Vasival and Babulal Khatnawalia took leading part in starting the library. The library facilities were utilised by the local Raigars and other untouchable castes. Later on, the library also served as a meeting place for Raigars. The library remained open both in the morning and evening. The library encouraged the reading habits among the Raigars. After an interval of four years or so the members, who used to pay membership fee regularly, stopped it immediately. As a result of this, one of the worst effect, was that the library had to be closed. The readers were disheartened and lost enthusiasm.

Over a period of time, especially after independence, some professional who had taken up government jobs in a few government departments emerged. According to Prem Singh,[82] Senior Assistant in the State Bank of India, Refinery Nagar, Mathura, there are 1 Deputy Commissioner, Income Tax, Government of India, Lucknow, Uttar Pradesh; 1 Class I officer, P&T Department, New Delhi; 1 Foreman (retired); 1 PRO, Northern Railway (retired), 1 Guard, Northern Railway (retired); 1 Engineer; 2 Junior Engineers; 3 LDC; 1 UDC; 2 in Bank; 2 in Uttar Pradesh Roadways; 1 in Civil Court, Mathura; 1 Telephone Operator; 1 Engine Driver, Railway (retired); 1 Constable; 1 Teacher, 3 Women Messengers (one in SBI and two in Supply Department), Ministry of Defence, Mathura and 4 Peons.

The progress made by Raigars in Mathura is not considered satisfactory by Raigars themselves. According to them, the main obstacle to the progress was problem of educated unemployment among the Raigars. There are some well educated Raigars in Mathura who are unemployed. For instance, there are 4 B Com, 4 BA (2 boys and 2 girls), 7 Intermediate including one girl, 1 B Sc, 2 MA; 2 M Com and 3 Matriculates.

While a small number of Raigars in Mathura are in government service, majority of them are still following the traditional work.[83] For instance, 99 per cent people repair old shoes on footpath, 1 is owner of lathe machine, 3 are running welding and denting shop, 1 is owner of scooter repair shop, 3 are 'mistry', 2 owners of refrigerator repair shops, 2 are TV mechanics, 1 has his own tyre service centre, 12 are tailors and have their own shops, 1 has his own electrical shop, 4 are small shop owners, 1 is TV and cooler repairer and motor binder, 1 is salesman of sarees, 6 are salesman of shoes, 1 is salesman of the gift item shop, 4 are shoe shop owners and 1 has his own PCO.

There are some well educated Raigars in Mathura who are notable professional elite. For purpose of illustration one notable professional elite, Keshav Dev Khatnawalia,[84] served Income Tax Department since 1981 at Maharashtra, Gujarat, Rajasthan and now serving in Uttar Pradesh. He passed High School Examination in

1964 from Subhash Inter College, Mathura. Later on, he passed his Intermediate Examination from the same institute in 1966 and joined K.R.College, Mathura, from where he did his B Com in 1968. After graduation, he joined Bata Shoe Company as a salesman at Bidanpura, New Delhi. He was paid Rs 5 per day. Thus, he served the company only for six months. Again, in 1968, he joined as UDC in AG Office, Shimla, where he remained for one and a half year. After this he was transferred to New Delhi. Soon he left the job and in September 1970, he joined Reserve Bank of India, New Delhi as LDC. In order to increase his qualification, he joined as regular student in the evening classes of the Law Faculty at Delhi University and passed LLB Examination in 1975.

In 1977 he appeared in the All India Administrative Services examination but failed. In 1978 he again appeared. This time he was selected by UPSC for allied services. This was a great achievement. In the same year (1978) he also appeared in the written examination conducted by the department and was declared successful. As a result of this he was promoted as Staff Officer Grade 'A' in Reserve Bank of India, New Delhi. But, due to certain internal conflict with bank authorities, he left the job. Meanwhile, he was informed by Government of India to proceed to Nagpur, Maharashtra for training. From 1978 to 1981, roughly four years, he remained at Nagpur. After training, he was first posted as Assistant Commissioner, Income Tax at Bombay. After eight years, he was promoted as the Deputy Commissioner, Income Tax in 1989 and was posted at Jamnagar, Gujarat. Thereafter, he was transferred to Baroda (remained there for three years), Ahmedabad (one year), Allahabad (four years), Gorakhpur (one year), Jodhpur (two years) and Barmer (one year). On October 25, 2004 he joined at Lucknow, Uttar Pradesh.

Another notable professional elite is Prem Singh Phoolwaria, Moti Kung Extension, Mathura. Prem Singh passed his B Com in 1983 from K.R. College, Mathura from Agra University, Agra (now Ambedkar University, Agra) and in the same year (1983) he joined M Com in the same institute. He obtained M Com degree in 1985 from the same University. After postgraduation, he appeared in Bank examination and was declared successful. In 1988 he was posted first at State Bank of India, Mathura. Currently, he is serving SBI as Senior Assistant at Mathura.

Raigar Dharmshallas and Mandirs[85]

Raigaron-Ki-Bagichi

During the British Raj significant efforts were made by the then Raigars in the social and cultural fields. In the social field the Raigars took special interest in purchasing a piece of land and constructed their own 'Bagichi'. For instance, as narrated by Arjun Mohanpuria, around 100 years back (year 1905), the Raigars of Mathura purchased piece of land from an upper caste person, which is located at Dada Mohalla, Kali Basti, near Jamna Bagh Road at Mathura. The size of Bagichi was 1000 sq. feet, for which according to Arjun Mohanpuria the Raigars paid roughly Rs 500. The Raigar Samaj built Shiv Mandir and Bheru Mandir also. It has one well, two handpumps, one tubewell and also electricity. It also has one room to provide boarding facilities to sadhus and sanyasis, etc. There is a 'Chaupal' meant to hold caste meeting. One sadhu is living here permanently who looks after the Bagichi. To protect and maintain assets of the Bagichi, caste-fellows donate liberally to it.

Raigar Dharmshala

In Raigar Mohalla, there was a very old Raigar Dharmshala. After selling the old one, Laxmi Narain Vasival, a well-to-do Raigar purchased a new piece of land which is also located in the same mohalla for which according to Arjun Mohanpuria he spent more than Rs 60,000 for constructing a room and its boundaries. The size of the room is 8 x 10 sq. feet. The total size of the plot of Dharmshala is 100 sq. feet.

Ganga Mai Mandir, Devi-Ma-Ka-Mandir and Baba Ram Dev-Ka-Mandir

Like Raigaron-ki-Bagichi, the poor Raigars of Mathura constructed three mandirs also during British India. They are Ganga Mai Mandir, Devi-Ma-ka-Mandir and Baba Ramdevji-ka-Mandir. All are located in Raigar Mohalla. After many years, the conditions of the Mandirs deteriorated due to floods in Yamuna river which washed away the idols and the boundary walls. At present, the mandirs are in a miserable condition.

The Raigars on the Frontiers of Politics: Local Level[86]

Like other untouchable communities in Uttar Pradesh, the Raigars of Mathura also came under the influence of Congress during the pre- and post-independence periods. The Congress influence had also increased more and more from 1947 onwards.

Raigars took active part in various social and political activities of the Congress. Girdhari Lal Vasival, Chet Ram Mohanpuria and Narain Maurya were the first Raigars who came in contact with Abdul Satar, the then Vice Chairman, Mathura Municipal Corporation, Kanhaiya Lal Jatav, the then Congress MLA from Goverdhan constituency, Mathura, Shiv Charan Vakil and Pandit Banwari Lal. These were eminent and influential Congress leaders of Mathura. They used to help the poor and helpless Raigars in various ways. In Uttar Pradesh Raigars have a positive reference group in Jatavs and Chamars who had entered into the state politics long back and also have their own political parties.

However, the Raigars in Mathura, for the first time, came under the influence of Roshan Lal Saini, the then Vice Chairman of Mathura Municipal Corporation.

Thus, Shyam Lal Mohanpuria from Raigar Mohalla took a leading part in bringing the Raigars under the influence of the then Bharatiya Jan Sangh.

Arjun Mohanpuria who was an active Congress worker at Raigar Mohalla, demanded a Party Ticket for Municipal Corporation Election to which the party did not responded favourably. As result, Mohanpuria fought the election as a BSP candidate. According to Mohanpuria, Telveer – Koly by caste was elected from Ward No. 3 on BJP ticket. The Congress supported candidates and others (including Mohanpuria himself) were defeated.

As mentioned earlier, the influence of the Congress amongst the untouchable communities was tremendous but after the emergence of BSP, the influence of Congress started declining.

There are two factions among the Raigars of Mathura – one led by Arjun Mohanpuria and his colleagues (BSP) and other by Narain Maurya (Congress) and when Arjun Mohanpuria was refused the Congress party ticket he switched to BSP.

Raigars in Vrandavan[87]

As narrated by Madanlal, son of Vasu Dev, aged 59, Purana Market, Vrandavan, Bhavani Bachhawada (Madanlal's grand-father), village Khudana, Jaipur, the then princely state of Rajputana with his wife, children, his Bhuva Ramkor (fathers' sister) and his younger brother Dalu Ram reached Vrandavan. Thus, a group consisting of ten Raigars headed by Bhavani Bachhawada reached Vrandavan in around 1930 in search of manual work/jobs. Here, they stayed near the Vrandavan bus stand. Raigars had a tremendous potential for manufacturing of leather goods. They earned their livelihood by doing repair work of old shoes and did boot polish.

The number of Raigars further increased after independence particularly during 1969 and 1971, when another group of Raigars consisting of Bindra Molia, Ram Lal Molia (both brothers) and a few other arrived at Vrandavan with a view to work as manual labourers. Later on, their third brother also joined them. These three brothers and their family members also remained near bus-stand, Vrandavan. After few years they settled permanently at Bagh Mohalla, Vrandavan.

For the purpose of describing the growth of Raigars, another Raigar group may be identified for the Raigars of Vrandavan, as told by Madan Lal Bachhamada. The poor Raigars of Kumher, Bharatpur district, Rajasthan left this place (Kumher) for Vrandavan to protect themselves from atrocities of upper castes. Thus, again, a group of Raigars headed by Bhola Ram Aatoria consisting of a few Raigars reached Vrandavan after the India-Pakistan war of 1971. During this period all Raigars stayed for some months at bus-stand, Vrandavan, earned money by performing traditional work and finally settled down at Radha Nivas area, Vrandavan.

As noted earlier, during our fieldwork we came across an old Raigar resident, aged 59, who was born in Vrandavan and is one of the eye witness of the incident – Madan Lal Bachhamada. He, in his conversation at his shop at Purana Market, Vrandavan, on November 1, 2004 spoke of the shop his grandfather Bhavani had established since 1938. For the purpose of mentioning the shop, detailed are given below:

During the British India period, the Devasthan Department, Udaipur, the then princely state of Rajputana, built their own commercial shops and other assets at Vrandavan. It was during 1938, that authorities of Devasthana Department, Udaipur, posted at Vrandavan allotted a shop to Bhavani Bachhamada in Purani

Market. In the beginning Rs. 1.4.0 (Re one and Anna four) was paid as rent per month. After some years it was increased to Rs 5 per month. This continued for decades together. In 1970 Bhavani Bachhamada died. Later on, the shop was inherited by Madan Lal Bachhamoda. At present, Madan Lal is the owner of the shop and pays Rs 90 per month as rent. At Vrandavan, the Raigars of Bachhamada gotra are in a large number (10 families) and are well known for their educational achievement. The number of families of the Raigars of Molia and Aatoria gotras is 3 and 2 respectively.

Over a period of 57 years, especially after independence, negligible Raigars have taken up government jobs. According to Mukesh Bachhamada,[88] son of Madan Lal Bachhamada and the first post-graduate Raigar (MSc, Chemistry) from Vrandavan, Rajesh Bachhamada, BCom is the only Raigar who is presently serving as Instructor at ITI, Shergarh, Mathura since 2001. Besides, there are one TV, fridge and electronic goods repairer, one has his own PCO, one is running his own coaching centre, one is in Civil Court, Mathura, and one is working in a private factory.

The progress made by Raigars in Vrandavan is not considered satisfactory by Mukesh Bachhamada.[89] According to him, the main hurdle to the progress is the problem of educated unemployment among the Raigars. There are some well-educated Raigars in Vrandavan, who are unemployed. For instance, there are 1 MSc (Chemistry) and MBA, 1 MCom, 3 BA (all girls), 4 Intermediate (3 girls and 1 boy), 1 BSc Final, and 1 LLB.

While a negligible number of Raigars in Vrandavan are in government job, majority of them are still following their traditional work, i.e., manufacturing of chappals and shoes.

There are some well educated Raigars in Vrandavan who are notable professional elites. For purpose of illustration, one such notable professional elite who is running his own coaching centre in Vrandavan since 1995 is Mukesh Bachhamada. He passed his BSc from K.R. College, Mathura with 1st Division in 1996 from Agra University, Agra. For further study, he moved to Agra in the same year and joined Saint John College, Agra. He passed his MSc (Chemistry) with first division from the same University. In 2000, he did MBA from P.D. Management College, Dehradoon and was placed in Grade 'B'.

Over a period of time, especially after 1990, private coaching centres have emerged. There are various kinds of coaching centres run by upper castes. The number of such centres at present in Vrandavan are more than 40, including Mukesh's Coaching Centre.

Raigars in Govardhan[90]

Raigar Dharmshala (RD) 1980-81

In the beginning of 1976, sincere efforts were made by local Raigars for donations to purchase a piece of land. Thus, in 1976 each Raigar household paid Rs 5 per month to the Samaj for purchasing the land and construction of Dharmshala. However, after some years the amount of donation was raised from Rs 5 to Rs 10. Forced by poor collection, Raigar Samaj decided to increase the donation fee from Rs 10 to Rs 90 per month. The process of collection continued till 1999.

The year 1980-81 is an important year in the history of Govardhan. It is significant because in that year (1980-81) Govardhan Raigar Samaj purchased a piece of agricultural land from Kishan Chand Saini – Mali by caste, which is located at Patwadi, Barsana Road, Govardhan, for which according to Kedarnath Khudala, Raigar Samaj paid Rs 7,000. The size of the plot is 60 x 60 sq. feet. After purchasing the land, in 1982, the Raigar Samaj submitted its documents for its registry in the office of the Registrar, District Mathura, Uttar Pradesh. The Registration Fee fixed by the Registrar office was very high. However, when Raigars were asked to deposit Rs 8,000 they paid the fee to Registrars' office immediately.

Narotam Lal Kachawata, the Office Bearer of Ganga Mandir Avam Dharmshala Nav Yuvak Raigar Samaj, Govardhan said the purchasing of land and construction of Dharmshala by Raigar Samaj has been a great achievement. The cooperation extended by the Samaj in monetary terms was appreciable. We are working for the betterment of the Samaj.

After purchasing of the land, the Raigar Samaj built 11 commercial shops, three rooms, one temple, and put up a handpump also. It also has toilet, bathrooms and electricity facilities. A total expenditure of six lac was incurred, which was borne by the Raigar Samaj.

It may be noted that Kedarnath, Tej Pal and Madan Lal, all Khudala brothers built a room in the memory of their late father Umrao Singh Khudala in the Dharmshala. According to Kedarnath Khudala, the elder son of Umrao Singh Khudala an expenditure of Rs 70,000 was incurred on it, which was borne by all brothers.

Ganga Mandir Avam Dharmshala Nav Yuvak Raigar Samaj, Govardhan[91] *(GMDNYRS) 1988-89*

The year 1988-89 is again an important and significant year in the history of Raigar Samaj Govardhan because Ganga Mandir Avam Dharmshala Nav Yuvak Raigar Samaj (GMDNYRS) had emerged as a pivotal organisation enlisting the cooperation of Raigars. There was a natural urge on the part of Raigars to form an organisation. With this aim, under the leadership of Kedarnath Khudala, a meeting was held which was attended by Raigars from Govardhan and Agra. Thus, in 1988-89, the modern political elite and professionals started assuming a leadership position. The first office bearers were: Kedar Nath (President), Jyoti Swaroop (Vice President), Tej Pal (Mantri), Gokul Chand (Up Mantri), Kali Charan (Prachar Mantri) and Narotam Lal (Treasurer). Besides, there were six members. They were: Mansingh, Prem Chand, Harish Chandra, Kundan Lal, Nathi Lal and Roshan Lal.

The main objects of GMDNYRS were:

1. To spread socio-political consciousness among the Raigars for social, educational and moral development.
2. To protect and maintain Ganga Mandir and Dharmshala. Also to arrange and perform religious puja, havan and kirtan from time to time.
3. To help the poor and helpless Raigars.
4. To open Pustakalaya and Vachanalaya.
5. To earn the money by renting out the Dharmshala for marriage purposes.
6. To help financially the poor and needy Raigars for solemnising the marriages of their children.
7. To open schools to spread education amongst the Raigar boys and girls and also help the poor and needy students.
8. To open a Sanskrit School too, to impart the knowledge of Sanskrit to Raigar boys and girls.
9. To organise from time to time the socio-cultural programmes such as Vichargoshti, Kavi Sammelan, etc.
10. To raise funds by donations.

It was registered in 1988-89 and its registration No. is 1294. It is worthwhile to mention here that GMDNYRS is not affiliated to ABRM and operates from Govardhan independently.

The organisational activities of GMDNYRS reached a climax soon after its registration. It made big organisational efforts in the year 1993 by submitting a memorandum for the first time to the Government of Uttar Pradesh and Government of India for inclusion of the Raigars in the Scheduled Castes list of Uttar Pradesh. During 1993 onwards the GMDNYRS submitted a memorandum for inclusion of Raigar community in the list of Scheduled Caste category to the following:[92]

1. President of India.
2. Prime Minister of India.
3. Chief Justice of India.
4. Chief Minister, Uttar Pradesh.
5. Welfare Minister, Government of Uttar Pradesh.
6. Chief Justice of Uttar Pradesh High Court, Allahabad.
7. Collector, Mathura.
8. Tehsildar, Mathura.

It is important to note here that President Secretariat,[93] New Delhi vide its acknowledgement letter No. 2118 PO-11 (7)/93 dated October 18, 1993 sent the memorandum to the Chief Secretary, Government of Uttar Pradesh for necessary action and copy endorsed to the organisation. Despite repeated efforts, the Government of Uttar Pradesh has not accepted the demand and the demand for inclusion of Raigars in Schedule Caste category is still pending.

Like Mathura and Vrandavan, the progress made by the Raigars in Govardhan is not satisfactory. According to Kedarnath Khudala the main hurdle to progress is problem of educated unemployment among the Raigars. There are some well educated Raigars in Govardhan who are unemployed. For instance, there are 2 Graduates, 3 Intermediate (2 boys and 1 girl), 1 Engineer, 1 is manufacturer of shoes and has his own shop at Govardhan, Deeg Gate, 2 Tej Pal and Madan Lal – both Khudala brothers – have their own tailoring shop at Bada Bazar, 2 are running their own tailoring shops at Deeg Gate.

There are some well educated Raigars in Govardhan, who are notable professional elite. For purpose of illustration, one such notable professional elite, who is an Engineer in Railways, is Hari Krishan son of Kedarnath Khudala.

Hari Krishan passed his Intermediate Examination from National Inter College, Govardhan, Mathura. After passing the Intermediate Examination, he moved to Hathras and completed three years Diploma Course and joined Railways at Delhi. However, he continued his study and obtained Engineering degree from Delhi.

For the last 10-12 years, he is serving Railways at Delhi. The achievement is very high.

Raigars in Agra

According to Narain Naglia[94] (aged 58 years, Janta Quarters, Kamla Nagar, Agra), a few Raigars residing in Karachi, Sindh and Hyderabad came in waves especially after the partition in 1947. Thus, a group of Raigars under the leadership of Sawant Ram Singaria, consisting of nearly 50-55 Raigars and their family members reached Agra. The first Raigar immigrants were: Sawant Ram Singaria, Gokul Chand Bakolia, Deva Ram Singaria, Bhanu Prakash Singaria, Chela Ram Savashia, Moti Lal and a few more. At Agra the Raigars stayed at Roshan Mohalla behind Mahaveer Cinema, for five or six years. Raigars had a tremendous potential for manufacturing the shoes, chappals and other leather goods. Hence during their stay, they did this job and earned money. Around 1953, the then Government of Uttar Pradesh introduced certain positive programmes for the development of poor people. It provided residential quarters to the poor masses on a very low/nominal rent. Such facilities were praised in the leading local daily newspapers. In pursuit of this, some Raigars of Rosan Mohalla, for instance, applied to the Government of Uttar Pradesh for the allotment of rented residential quarters in Balkeshwar. As a result of this, the Government issued the allotment orders to 16-18 Raigars in Sector 8/50 and 8/51 in Balkeshwar respectively. The rent paid for the quarters by each allottee was only Rs 10 per month. Thus, all the allottees took the possession of their respective quarters and started living in Balkeshwar.

Again in 1965, another group of Raigars came to Agra. During my fieldwork in Janta Colony, Kamla Nagar, I came across an old Raigar, who himself migrated from village Peelwa, District Nagaur, Rajasthan and was very active and is one of the living eye witness of incident – Narain Das Naglia. He was in conversation with the author on October 31, 2004 at his residence spoke of his happy memories of his close association with the Raigar immigrants for long a time. Thus, according to him a group of Raigars from village Peelwa, District Nagaur, first started living with Thakurdas Kanwadia, son of Pritam Das Kanwadia at Balkeshwar. They were: Narain Das Naglia, Bhanwar Lal Naglia and others. After few months, the Raigars staying with Thakur Das Kanwadia at

Balkeshwar, shifted to Lal Masjid, Goshala, Agra. Here they started living in few rented houses of Jatavs. One such house was No. 32/142 of Roshanlal Jatav, who paid Rs 7 per month.

Another most significant factor in the increase of population of Raigars in Agra was the migration of Raigars from various districts of Rajasthan. The Raigars who settled in Agra earlier took the initiative in bringing together their relatives and caste-fellows. The efforts to bring the Raigars of Rajasthan dates back to 1948, when there was a growing consciousness among the Raigars to initiate manufacturing business of chappals. The earlier Raigars came mostly from Nagaur, Ajmer, Pali, Jodhpur, Jaipur, Sikar, etc. Since independence there had been manifold increase in migration and Raigars category has become linguistically, socially and economically diversified.

During 1967-68, when another group of Raigars consisting of Hathi Ram, Banshi Ram, Bhanwar Lal, Kishan, Hauman, Deva Ram and a few more (all from Nagaur district, Rajasthan) arrived at Agra with a view to work as manufacturers of shoes, chappals and leather goods, majority of Raigars had been residing in Bodla in Agra. Others owned their houses in the Janta Colony, Taus Jamuna Colony and Prakash Nagar.

The progress made by Raigars in Agra is not considered satisfactory by Kundan Lal Trigaya, the President, Raigar Samaj Vikas Samiti, Agra. According to him, the main hurdle which came in the way of progress is the problem of educated unemployment among the Raigars. There are some well-educated Raigars in Agra, who are unemployed. For instance, there are 1 Junior Engineer, 2 BCom, 1 BA, 5 Intermediate (1 boy and 4 girls), and 10 Matriculates (4 boys and 6 girls).

Raigar Samaj Vikas Samiti[95] (RSVS), Agra 1995

Till the year 1994, the Raigars in Agra had no platform to elevate their voice, to have interaction with caste-fellows, listening to what they had to say, articulating their problems and mobilising them in mass social activities. Prabhulal Bhatt, Kundan Lal Trigaya, Naraindas Naglia, Kishan, Chittar, Bhanwar Lal, Deva Ram and others played a significant role in bringing the Raigars together and in June 1999, a meeting was held under the leadership of Prabhu Lal Bhatt at the residence of Kundanlal Trigaya (House No. 4547) at

Janta Colony, Kamla Nagar, Agra. It was attended by 60-70 community people. Thus, in 1995, the modern political and professional elites started assuming leadership position. The first office bearers were: Kundan Lal Trigaya (President), Narain Das Naglia (Vice President), Kishan Lal (Treasurer), Prabhu Lal Bhatt (Maha Mantri) and Dayal Chand Tungadia (Secretary). Besides, there were 11 Executive Members. Some of them were: Raghunath, Bhanwar Lal, Chittar Mal Jajoria, Kailash Kansotia, Deva Ram, etc.

The main programme of RSVS was to campaign against social vices and to settle family and property disputes among the Raigars. The RSVS also called for inclusion of Raigars in Scheduled Caste List of Uttar Pradesh. It also stressed the need for reform in their caste-customs and for the spiritual reformation. It was reformative in its orientation. Similarly, it took initiative to awaken the socio-political consciousness among the caste-men. It is worthwhile to mention here that RSVS was affiliated to ABRM and operated from Agra.[96] On December 24, 1995,[97] it was inaugurated by Ram Sanjivan, the Chief Development Officer, Agra, in the presence of a large gathering. The function was presided over by Kundan Lal Trigaya. Among the others present were: Darshan Singh Sikarwal, District Congress Committee President, Agra, Hukama Ram Khorwal (from Gachhipura, district Nagaur, Rajasthan). RSVS's office is located in House No. 471, Janta Quarters, Kamla Nagar, Agra.

RSVS derived its financial support from caste-fellows. For this RSVS appealed to the caste-men to donate liberally to it. Thus, as narrated by Kundan Lal Trigaya,[98] the RSVS also sent a two-men delegation consisting of Deva Ram and Jagdish to Mumbai, Maharashtra for collection of donations from caste-men. Thus, according to him, the leading Raigars businessmen, influential social workers donated Rs 40,000 to the delegation for RSVS.[99] But actually they (Deva Ram and Jagdish) handed over Rs 18,000 to RSVS. The remaining amount of Rs 22,000 was to be received from them as stated by Kundanlal Trigaya.

Sikandara Avas Vikas Yojana Colony, Bodla[100]

During Mayavati's tenure, efforts were made by the government to introduce certain positive and welfare measures for the development of poor masses. The main purpose of the scheme was to provide residential quarters to homeless, low income group and weaker sections of the society on most nominal instalments. Such facilities were published and praised in some leading local daily newspapers. In pursuit of this large number of Raigars of Kamla Nagar applied to the government for allotment of quarters measuring 10 x 18 sq. feet in Sikandara Avas Vikas Yojna Colony, Bodla. The application fee fixed by the government was very low, so that people interested to purchase the flats can do so. The government charged Rs 250 as application fee. As a result of this, in 1999, the government issued the allotment orders to more than 80 Raigars. It was not freehold, obviously. It was on nominal instalments. The total cost of a flat, according to Kundan Lal Trigaya was only Rs 48,000. The monthly instalment to be paid by each allottee was Rs 450 per month. This benefited Jatavs and other sections of the society too. The stipulated time period was 15 years.

Raigar Panchayat Bhavan[101]

In the history of Raigars of Agra, the year 1999 was very important. It is significant, because Agra Raigar Samaj purchased a constructed flat at Sikandara Avas Vikas Colony from a Raigar for which, according to Kundan Lal Trigaya, Raigar Samaj paid Rs 35,000 to the person concerned as the first installment and the remaining amount was paid in instalments by the Raigar Samaj. Agra Raigar Samaj appealed to the caste-fellows to donate liberally to it. The quarter popularly known as 'Raigar Panchayat Bhavan' is meant to hold caste meetings and also provide boarding facilities to guests, Sadus and Sanyasis. It has both toilet and bathroom facilities.

Raigars Launched a Campaign for Inclusion of the Community as Scheduled Caste Category[102] in the Schedule

The major problem which attracted the attention of Raigars was the inclusion of Raigars in the list of Scheduled Castes category.

The Raigars belonged to the broad category of the low untouchable caste, but since they are not designated as Scheduled Castes in Uttar Pradesh, they are not entitled to enjoy the benefits of an affirmative policy. For instance, in Rajasthan, Delhi, Haryana, Punjab and Madhya Pradesh, Raigars belonged to Scheduled Caste category. In Maharashtra, Gujarat and Uttar Pradesh, they do not belong to Scheduled Castes category and therefore suffer from political and educational privileges and government jobs.

The Raigars caste sought to overcome this problem by not only claiming Scheduled Castes status but also by social agitation. As pointed out, Raigars were referred to both Scheduled Castes or non-Scheduled Castes category.

It is significant to note that in the beginning of 1996, RSVS held its meeting in Kamla Nagar under the leadership of Kundan Lal Trigaya who was the founder member of RSVS and also its Chairman. The meeting passed many resolutions, the main was that 'Raigars' must be included in the list of Scheduled Castes of Uttar Pradesh. On July 18, 1996 Kundan Lal Trigaya and Prabhu Lal Bhatt went to Lucknow – the capital of Uttar Pradesh to meet Moti Lal Vohra, the then Governor of Uttar Pradesh for submission of memorandum to include Raigars in the Scheduled Castes list of Uttar Pradesh. Here, they remained for four days and on the fifth day they succeeded in meeting the Governor of Uttar Pradesh. During their five-day stay at Lucknow, they stayed with a friend who was Mochi by caste from Nava, district Nagaur, Rajasthan and used to take their lunch and dinner at local Dhaba. Similarly, they had also submitted a memorandum to Collector, Agra, for necessary action.

The next efforts came in July and August 1996 when Kunan Lal Trigaya, Prabhu Lal Bhatt and other colleagues met the political leaders and Members of Parliament at New Delhi, seeking their support for inclusion of Raigars in the list of Scheduled Castes category. They were: Ram Vilas Paswan, the then Railway Minister, Government of India, S.S. Ahluwalia, the then Minister, Government of India, Chairman, National Commission for SC/ST, New Delhi, Phoolan Devi, the then Member of Parliament, Dharm Das Shastri, President, ABRM, and Bhagwandas Khorwal, General Secretary, ABRM, New Delhi.

It is important to note that after sometime, a fax dated July 23, 1996 by Kundan Lal Trigaya and Prabhulal Bhatt was sent, reiterating the demand for inclusion in Scheduled Castes List and requested the Governor of Uttar Pradesh and Ahluwalia, Minister, Government of India, New Delhi, to take necessary steps to rectify the injustice as early as possible. After a month another fax dated August 5-6, 1996 was sent as a reminder. Despite repeated efforts the Government of Uttar Pradesh had not accepted the demand and the issue for inclusion of Raigars in Scheduled Castes category is still alive.

The demand for Scheduled Castes status, discussed above, had two effects on the Raigar agitation. First, social workers and activists among the Raigars started taking active interest in this matter, as they considered the case worth fighting for. Second, it is a fact that till today neither the State Government has accepted the demand for Scheduled Castes status nor the political parties (such as Congress, BJP, Samajwadi Party and BSP) directly or indirectly has supported the Raigar cause in the Uttar Pradesh. With the result, Raigars have been disheartened and lost hope. Under such circumstances, the ways and means to obtain the caste certificate from State Government has been changed. Now Raigars used to get Scheduled Castes certificate under category of Jatav caste.

Factional division in Raigar movement in Agra occurred after three years in 1998 and the organisation lost its effectiveness. Hence today it exists only on paper.

Raigars from Rajasthan who migrated to Mathura and Agra regions of Uttar Pradesh in 1844, 1930, 1947 and even in 1971 have been part of local system over the last several decades. The elder persons, now in their 90s and above, are in a state of shock. Majority of them follow traditional work. Conventional wisdom is that Raigars are like most other low untouchable castes of Uttar Pradesh as well. The above analysis disappoint those who think protective discrimination policy should have changed everything. Remarkably, not a single aspect of social life changed for the Raigars in 2004 compared with 1930. Why? The main reasons are:

1. It has become hazardous to get the benefit of reservation policy in Uttar Pradesh, because Raigars have not been recognised the status of Scheduled Castes. So Raigars have started moving steadily from Raigars to Jatavs. This has an unexpected socio-political consequences.
2. The thin population has been another reason, i.e., why Raigars could not become a pressure group. The meagre number of Raigars is still a major hurdle.
3. The absence of political leadership.

However, the biggest overarching reasons of all may be that Raigars have not yet overcome from the Scheduled Castes status hangover.

Thus, the Raigars of Uttar Pradesh represent a meagre level of achievement.

Salient Features of Regional Associations

The foregoing account of the regional associations of the Raigars highlights a few important aspects of the movement. First, there was a concerted effort on the part of the Raigars in the different regions to gain self-respect by popularising the Raigar solidarity. They held the sammelans and persuaded the caste fellows for eradication of vices which lowered their prestige. The Raigars used Arya Samaj ideology to acquire, by the reform, the right to wear the sacred thread and perform other rituals. Thus, they began to participate in the rituals of the vedic Hinduism from which they had been excluded for centuries.

Raigars also became aware of their deprived economic status. In Rajasthan they were obliged to give forced labour (begar) to locally dominant upper castes. The upper castes exploited this situation and demanded many feudal services. With the growth of social awareness and political mobilisation, through the regional association, which formed part of the all India movement, the Raigars and other untouchable castes asserted themselves and protested against economic exploitation and political subordination by the upper castes. In Rajasthan, in some cases, it resulted in violent conflict.

Not only did the Raigars in different regions organise themselves to protest against their economic exploitation but they also agitated against the social atrocities.

The regional associations were also concerned for gaining their due share in modern employment opportunities. They led deputations asking for the recruitment to various jobs in government departments. The Raigars in all the states were listed under the category of Scheduled Castes and as such, were entitled to employment and educational benefits.

The Raigars everywhere made special efforts to establish educational institutions, trusts and hostels. In some cases the Raigar associations supported their students in their fight to gain admission to professional courses and the networks of the political administrative and professional elite which was a great help in this regard.

It is necessary to stress that the Raigar associations have been especially active in the urban areas. Acting as interest groups, they maximised utilisation of economic and educational resources and welfare services and tried to compete for the political power in the city municipalities. In some cities and towns the Raigars do share political power which was crucial in the urban opportunity structure.

The regional and local associations were affiliated to ABRM. This gave rise to two federal structures which ensured the internal autonomy of the regional associations with a degree of external control by all-India associations. The regional leaders were recruited to the committees of the all India bodies, thus the gaining all-India status. The annual conferences of the all-India associations demonstrated caste solidarity at the national level. They provided an opportunity for the Raigars to come together to renew contacts and to demonstrate caste solidarity as a social force. They also supported the articulation of specific demands by the regional ones, and played an important part by establishing a communication system. The all India Hindi journal of *Raigar Sudhar* and *Raigar Rakshak* reported the activities of the regional associations.

Notes

1. Chandan Mal Naval, *Raigar Jati Ka Itihas*, Jodhpur, 1986, p. 146.
2. Ibid., p. 147.
3. Ibid.
4. Ibid.
5. Aasu Lal Umaji Kurdia (ed.), *Ahmedabad mein Raigar Samaj*, Ahmedabad, 1998, p. 2.
6. Aasu Lal Umaji Kurdia (ed.), Raigar Samaj Shiksha Samiti, Ahmedabad, *Smarika*, Ahmedabad, 1999, p. 6.
7. Aasu Lal Umaji Kurdia, op. cit., p. 62.
8. Ibid.
9. Ibid.
10. Raigar Samaj Shiksha Samiti, Ahmedabad, *Smarika*, op. cit., 1999, p. 6.
11. Ibid., p. 7.
12. Ibid.
13. Ibid.
14. Ibid., p. 2.
15. Ibid.
16. Ibid., p. 7.

17. For details, see *Ahmedabad mein Raigar Samaj*, especially *Shiksha aur Samaj*, op. cit., p. 5.
18. Raigar Samaj Shiksha Samiti, Ahmedabad, *Smarika*, 1999, op. cit., p. 20.
19. Ibid.
20. *Ahmedabad mein Raigar Samaj*, op. cit., p. 2. Also see, *Gujarat mein Raigar Jati ko Anusuchit Jati mein samlit karney ki Mang, Raigar Sudhar*, dated April 15-30, 2001.
21. Ibid., p. 17.
22. Conversation with Kasthur Chand Nogia on phone, Ahmedabad, on November 26, 2001.
23. *Ahmedabad mein Raigar Samaj*, op. cit., p. 1.
24. Ibid.
25. Ibid., p. 4.
26. Raigar Samaj Shiksha Samiti, Ahmedabad, *Smarika*, op. cit., p. 19.
27. Ibid., pp. 19-23.
28. Letter from President, ABRM to Maha Mantri, ABRM, Ahmedabad, No. 2001/9 dated April 14, 2001.
29. The most detailed account on the socio-economic and educational and political conditions of the Raigars in the different districts of Madhya Pradesh is given by Puran Mal Verma, a resident of Indore, in his 4-page letter dated January 4, 2002, submitted to Jai Narian, Collector, Rajgarh, Madhya Pradesh. This letter is with the author.
30. Ibid., p. 1.
31. Chandanmal Naval, op. cit., p. 82.
32. Ibid.
33. Ibid.
34. Puranmal Verma's letter dated January 4, 2002 to author.
35. Ibid., pp. 1-3.
36. Ibid., p. 3.
37. Ibid.
38. Ibid.
39. Ibid., p. 4.
40. Ibid.
41. Ibid., pp. 3.-4.
42. Ibid.
43. The most detailed account on Dr Satya Narain Jatiya, Labour Minister, Government of India is given in a pamphlet published and

circulated by Ministry of Labour, Government of India, New Delhi. (publication year and page number are not mentioned).

A short account on Dr Satya Narain Jatiya is also available in a pamphlet published by Ministry of Information, Government of India, New Delhi, dated November 10, 1999.

44. Ibid.
45. Ibid.
46. Ibid.
47. Ibid.
48. Ibid.
49. Ibid.
50. Ibid.
51. Ibid.
52. Ibid.
53. Ibid.
54. Ibid.
55. Ibid.
56. Ibid.
57. Ibid.
58. Ibid.
59. Ibid.
60. Ibid.
61. Ibid.
62. Ibid.
63. Conversation with Ashwini Kumar, Editor, *Raigar Sudhar*, Fatehabad (Haryana) camped at Jaipur, May 2003.
64. Ibid. Also see, *Raigar Sudhar*, May 15-31 and June 15-30, 2001.
65. Ibid, *Raigar Sudhar*, June 15-31, 2001.
66. Ibid, *Raigar Sudhar*, May 15-30, 2001.
67. Ibid.
68. Ibid.
69. *Raigar Sudhar*, May 15-31, 2001.
70. Ibid.
71. Ibid.
72. Conversation with Ashwini Kumar, Jaipur, May, 2003.
73. Conversation with Man Singh, Mathura, October 30, 2004.
74. Conversation with Arjun Mohanpuria, Mathura, October 30, 2004.
75. Ibid.

76. Conversation with Keshav Dev Khatnawalia, Mathura, November 1, 2004.
77. Conversation with Arjun Mohanpuria, Mathura, October 30, 2004.
78. Conversation with Prem Singh, Moti Kunj, Mathura, October 30, 2004.
79. Conversation with Arjun Singh, Mathura, October 30, 2004.
80. Ibid.
81. Ibid.
82. Conversation with Prem Singh, Bholu Ram Kansotia and Arjun Mohanpuria, Mathura, October 31, 2004.
83. Ibid.
84. Conversation with Keshav Dev Khatnawalia, Mathura, November 1, 2004.
85. As narrated by Arjun Mohanpuria, Mathura, November 1, 2004.
86. Ibid.
87. As narrated by the Madan Lal Bachhawada, Vrandavan, November 1, 2004.
88. As narrated by Mukesh Bachhamada, Vrandavan, October 30, 2004.
89. Ibid.
90. Conversation with Kedar Nath Khudala and Narotam Lal Kachavata, Govardhan, October 31, 2004.
91. Ibid. For more details, also see, particularly a 4-page document submitted by GMDNYRS to the Office of Registrar, Mathura, for its registration. The document is with Author.
92. Letters from GMDNYRS to the President of India, Prime Minister and others.
93. Acknowledgements letter dated October 18, 1993 from President's Secretariat, New Delhi to GMDNYRS.
94. As narrated by Narain Naglia, Agra, October 31, 2004.
95. As narrated by Kundanlal Trigaya, Agra, October 31, 2004.
96. Ibid. Also see, letter dated December 18, 1995 from Bhorilal Shastri, Vice President and Bhagwan Das Khorwal, Maha Mantri, ABRM to Kedar Nath Trigaya.
97. Ibid.
98. Ibid.
99. Ibid.
100. Ibid.
101. Ibid.
102. Ibid.

10

Raigars' Migration to Maharashtra

Second and Third Generation Rajasthani Raigars in the Process of Change (1926-2004)

Raigars in Dadar

As narrated by Mana Ram Rasgania[1], aged 80, 61-A, Gian Sagar, S.K. Bola Road, Dadar, around 1926-27 Raigars of Jhunjhunu, Rajasthan exhibited unparalleled courage. The poor Raigars left Jhunjhunu on foot for Bombay (now Mumbai) in search of jobs/manual work. Thus, a group of Raigars under the leadership of Ladu Ram Deegwal (Channana village) consisting of five Raigars reached Dadar after several months. During this long journey all Raigars stayed for some days at different places, earned money and walked towards their destination in spite of several hurdles. They not only survived these difficulties but also reached their destination safely. The arguments given for travelling on foot by the Raigars were: first, that the Raigars were so poor that they could not easily afford to pay the railway fare for such a long distance. Second and last, the Raigars as a mistrys had a tremendous potential for building-work. Hence, during their entire journey Raigars did jobs and earned money.

At Dadar the six Raigars, viz., Bhera Ram Kanwadia (Bada Gaon Ka), Moga Ram Sevania (Jhunjhunu city), Teeka Ram Deegwal, Khaya Ram Deegwal (both of Jhunjhunu city) Gadshi Ram Rasgania (Bada Gaon Ka) and Ladu Ram Deegwal (Channa village) stayed in Room No. 31 in the first floor at Etawar Building, Tulsi

Pipe Road[2] (now Senapati Bapat Road), Dadar. It is noteworthy to mention here that the Raigars stayed at Etawar Building without paying even a single penny to the owner. On the contrary, as narrated by Mana Ram Rasgania, the son of Gadshi Ram Rasgania, the owner of the building paid each one four or eight Anna for staying in his building. The argument for allowing free of cost accommodation facilities and paying a few Annas to them was that since the population of Dadar at that time was not as problematic as today, the building remained empty for sometime and thus it became a ghost-bungalow.

The number of Raigars were further increased during 1932-1935, when another group of Raigars[3] consisting of Dhanna Ram Kurdia, Ram Chandra Deegwal, Har Dev Deegwal, Tulshi Ram Ujjenia, Ganesh Ujjenia, Bhera Ram Sevania and Ghasi Ram Deegwal (all Channa village, Jhunjhunu) arrived at Dadar with a view to work as labourers in the construction work.

Till the year 1934, the Raigars in Dadar had no meeting place for a get-together, to have interaction with caste-men, listening to what they had to say, articulating their problems and mobilising them in mass social activities. Khema Ram Deegwal[4] played a significant role in bringing the Raigars closer and in 1935, he along with the other Raigars established their own small 'Than' (a place of worship) of God Hanuman under a tree at Kabutar Khana) which was managed by the Raigars themselves and made it a place for get-together activities and a worship place of God Hanumanji. However, in the changing scenario, the upper castes had altered the whole scenario and they constructed a big beautiful Hanuman Mandir at the circle called Kabutar Khana, Dadar. The upper castes continued to provide the religious leadership.

After India attained independence, significant efforts were made by Raigars of Dadar to bring their relatives and also caste fellows from Jhunjhunu and few more Raigars joined.

For the purpose of describing the growth of Raigars four locations may be identified as told by Shyam Lal Sevania, Corner U – 35, 3rd Floor, Gokhale Road (North) Dadar, for the Raigars of Dadar: (i) Dadar – Sevania (15 families), Rasgania (6 families), Deegwal (5 families); (ii) Matunga – Sevania (2 families); (iii) Mahim – Sevania (3 families); (iv) Elphiston – Ujjenia (5 families).[5] Thus, the Raigars of Jhunjhunu, Rajasthan, established an identity not only with Dadar and its surrounding areas, but also with the government. Raigars are considered to be good builders and contractors and Raigars' efficiency provide a leading leadership in construction work. Hence, the Raigars consider themselves to be the elite amongst the untouchable castes, which other caste categories conceded to, to a great extent. Some of the top Raigar builders of Dadar are: Mana Ram Rasgania, Sita Ram Rasgania, Shyam Lal Sevania (all Dadar); Mata Deen Ujjenia (Elphiston); Bhagwati Prasad Ujjenia (Andheri), Sat Lal Sevania (Matunga) and few more.[6] Thus, the Raigars are most famous for their contribution to construction work. All the Raigar builders come from Jhunjhunu. Since this is relevant to the achievement made by the Raigar caste, let us give more information about Raigars in building-work, with particular reference to Dadar. During our fieldwork in Dadar, and other places, we came across some retired builders and those who are still active.

Over a period of time, especially after independence, builders, professionals and business elites had emerged who had taken up leadership position of the builders. There are different kinds of builders among Raigars of Dadar: small contractors doing new and repair work and interior decorators. Radhe Shyam Phoolwadia, Om Prakash Kanva, Devi Lal Sunkaria, Babu Lal Kanwadia, Beg Raj Khamkhedia and Arjun Kumar Sevania are among 67 builders. Likewise Mana Ram, Sita Ram and Girdhari (all Rasgania brothers), Jas Raj and Raju (both Rasgania – nephew of Mana Ram Rasgania), Mata Deen, Ratan Lal and Anil (all Ujjenia), Surajmal, Shishupal, Nand Lal, Ratan Lal, Govind and Raju (all Deegwal); Shyam Lal, Chhagan Lal, Madan Lal, Sant Lal and Thana Ram (all Sevania) are the big builders and contractors of Dadar, Elphiston, Andheri, Matunga, Mahim and Bandra.

Mana Ram Rasgania in his personal conversation at this flat 61-A, Dadar on May 18, 2004 spoke of buildings he had constructed during the last 40 years. For purpose of mentioning the buildings constructed, a few buildings may be identified:

1. Goyal Mahal, Malin Lane, Bombay (1954).
2. Jai Shri Sadan Juna Nagardas Road, Andheri, Bombay (1958).
3. Bharatia Raigar Samaj Cooperative Housing Society, Chembur, Bombay (1967).
4. Jai Shri Sadan, Udna-Udyog Nagar, Surat, Gujarat (1971).
5. Saint Paul Church, Parel T.T., Bombay (1974).

In all more than 12 such multi-storey buildings were constructed.

Raigars of Rasgania gotra are most famous and well known for their construction work. Their role in building work and during our fieldwork in Dadar, came across another person, viz., Sita Ram Rasgania, younger brother of Mana Ram Rasgania, who is also an active builder. Sita Ram Rasgania[7] in his personal talk at his company office at Gokhale Road, Dadar, on May 18, 2004 spoke of the company his four brothers had established. The need to establish such a company in Dadar region was first felt by the Rasgania brothers, who were economically prosperous and had made some progress in education. It was during 1968 that Rasgania brothers established a company for construction of buildings in Bombay. Thus 'Mistry MGS and Company: Builders and Contractors' came into existence. The first office bearers were: Mana Ram (President), Sita Ram (Treasurer), Girdhari Lal (Secretary).

The main activity of the company was to construct multi-storey buildings on the basis of contract.

On some auspicious occasion such as marriage, the Raigars of Jhunjhunu in Dadar and the surrounding areas, met occasionally. The urban Raigars became aware of their strength and got interested in social gatherings. In 1984, the Raigars started taking interest in arranging a meeting at Shivaji Park, Chaupati, a picnic spot in Dadar and where they had a Holi Milan for Raigars and music, fun, food and speeches.[8] There was a free mixing of Raigars who came from Jhunjhunu and belonging to several suburb areas, mainly – Dadar, Andheri, Bandra, Matunga, Kandiwali, Mahim and Elphiston. Mana Ram Rasgania, a big builder from Dadar presided over the first Holi Milan, which was attended by 40-50 Raigars.

To provide residential accommodations to Raigars coming from Jhunjhunu district (newcomers), the Raigars of Dadar organised first meeting in Shivaji Park in the city of Dadar, under the leadership of Mana Ram Rasgania. The meeting started with a series of speeches explaining the purpose of the meeting and emphasised the need for a separate building exclusively for Raigars. It was during 1997, that the need to provide such accommodation at low cost in Dadar was first felt by Raigars who were financially sound. Thus, a 'Housing Society' came into existence in 1998.[9] The first office bearers of this Society were: Mana Ram Rasgania (President), Sita Ram Rasgania (Vice-President), both Shyam Lal Sevania and Mata Deen Ujjenia (Cashier). Besides, there were a large number of members. This society was active in raising funds for construction of a multi-storey building for poor and needy Raigars. The establishment of society was a significant event in providing the accommodation to Raigars who could not afford to pay exorbitant rent for a single room in the city of Mumbai. Thus, the Society started collection of funds from the members. The membership of the Society increased in the course of time and according to Ashok Kumar Sevania, up to the year 2000, the Society succeeded in collecting roughly Rs 9 lakh. During the first phase of the society, the office bearers (of whom Rasgania Brothers were no doubt the foremost) were concerned with the publication of a telephone Directory of Raigars residing in Dadar. Thus, in 1998 Society published Mistry Telephone Directory, Mumbai, 1998, nicknamed as Shekhawati Mistry, as a Raigar mouth-piece.

From the very beginning of this Society its functioning was obstructed because of the emergence of factions among the Raigars in Dadar. Thus, due to internal differences the dream of poor and needy Raigars could not be fulfilled. It is necessary to note that the ABRM had no branch in the Mumbai region.

As noted earlier, while not a single Raigar in Dadar is in government service, majority of them are doing independent construction business. For instance there are eight Raigars who had completed 3 years Certificate Course long back and are working as interior decorators. According to Nand Lal Rasgania, they are: Nand Lal M. Rasgania, Gajanand Rasgania, Vasant Rasgania, Harish Sevania, Ramesh Rasgania, Hem Chand Rasgania, Biju Rasgania and Dinesh Kumar Ujjenia.

There are some well-educated Raigars in Dadar who are notable architects. For purpose of illustration, one notable architect, who is associated with construction work since 1986 in Dadar, is Ramesh, son of Mana Ram Rasgania. Mana Ram Rasgania is a man of progressive ideas. He brought up his son Ramesh from village Gudagod ji Ka, Jhunjhunu to Dadar in 1965. Mana Ram Rasgania was a reputed builder and amassed wealth by doing the construction business. Ramesh was admitted in Salvation School, which was under the Portuguese Church, Dadar. Ramesh passed his 10th Class Examination in 1978 with distinction. He was admitted in Jai Hind College, Churchgate and passed his 12th class in 1980. In 1980 he was admitted in Academy of Architecture College at Prabha Devi, Mumbai for a five-year course in architecture and obtained his degree in architecture in the year 1985.

Another notable architect is Vijay Kumar, son of Sita Ram Rasgania, Gokhale Road, Dadar. Like Mana Ram Rasgania his younger brother Sita Ram Rasgania is also a man of progressive ideas. Sita Ram Rasgania is also a reputed builder and the richest man among the Raigars. His son Vijay Kumar[10] passed High School Examination in First Division with distinction in 1988 from Lady of Salvation High School, Dadar. He passed his 12th class examination in Science with First Division from Kishan Chand Chela Ram College, Churchgate, Mumbai, in 1990 and in the same year (1990), he joined L.S. Raheja School of Architecture. He did his three-year Diploma Course for interior decoration in the year 1993. From the same Institute, he did B. Architecture in 1997. Besides, B. Architecture, he also did one-year Diploma in Business Management (DBM) from NMIMS, Juhu, Mumbai, in 2nd Division in 2001. Besides, Ramesh Rasgania, Vijay Kumar Rasgania, Hem Chand Rasgania son of Girdhari Lal Rasgania, Dadar also did B. Architecture. Rasgania families are highly qualified in Architecture and they have used their expertise for construction of buildings. They believed that education is more important than caste and hence they thought that by educating themselves they could attain the heights that some upper castes have reached.

In this connection it may be noted that majority of the Raigars held the view that higher education amongst boys and girls of the Raigars in Dadar is not satisfactory. According to Shyam Lal Sevania, Dadar, there are only three girls, who did B.Com. Their names are: Shakuntala Sevania (1997, SNDT University, Mumbai), Saraswati Sevania (1999, Kirti College, Dadar, Bombay University) and Mamta Sevania (2003, R.A. Poddar College, Matunga, Bombay University). According to a rough estimate more than 80 Raigars have passed the matriculation/12th class examination from Maharashtra State Board of Secondary and Higher Secondary, Pune. From the education point of view this is a good number.

The Raigars have an access to construction work without much difficulty. The government colleges in Dadar are open to Raigar youths but it was not until 2000 that Raigar boys had passed BA/B Sc./B Com. Sita Ram Rasgania described lack of education as a great hurdle in social progress. Similarly Mana Ram Rasgania, a notable builder of Dadar, remarked that the Raigar boys and girls had no aptitude for education.

The drive for education was never launched. No socio-cultural awakening among the Raigars of Dadar was brought about by any individual or organisation. Thus, they did not create any enthusiasm among the masses for educational progress in a socially and economically most backward caste.

It is clear from the foregoing description that although the Raigars have some success in construction business, they have yet to get higher education in the other fields. It is not only Raigars of Dadar who are still away from modern education, but also the Raigars of Chembur and Vashi are sailing in the same boat.

As noted earlier, since his arrival in Dadar in 1946, Mana Ram Rasgania spearheaded the construction business in Dadar and showed excellence through his work. After his retirement from active business in 1998, he has recently published a small booklet called *Sri Guru Maharaj ka Bhav Prasad*[11] in 2004, Mumbai. It is a collection of Bhajans, i.e., religious songs, which he composed in praise of God Ganesh, Hanuman and the other deities. Although Rasgania composed Bhajans in his book, he has also composed poems, Geet, Shalok and Heli. The book is dedicated to Saint Swami Gopal Ram Maharaj, Nagaur, Rajasthan.

Raigars in Chembur

Chembur is the seat of atomic research for over four decades. It is the home of refineries and of different cultures.[12]

To be sure, Chembur is fairly cosmopolitan. If we look around, we can find parts of suburbs that are distinctly Sindhi, Punjabi, Catholic, Maharashtrian and South Indians. This does not mean that Chembur has been ghettoised. There is no dearth of Camaraderie among Chembur inhabitants.[13]

Thakkar Bappa Colony, which is Asia's biggest footwear centre, is dominated by the Raigars and presents a unique picture in many ways. There were a few old Raigar residents living in the city of Chembur, who came in waves especially after the partition in 1947, from Karachi and Sindh (Hyderabad). When news regarding their arrival reached, old Raigar residents living in Dadar, since 1927 from Shekhawati region, Rajasthan, a group of a few Raigars under the leadership of Mana Ram Rasgania went to Railway Station, Kurla, Bombay (now Mumbai) in 1947 to receive them.[14] Other Raigars who had gone there were: Dhanna Ram Kurdia, Ram Chandra Deegwal, Tara Chand Deegwal, Tulshi Ram Ujjenia,

Ganesh Ujjenia, Bhera Ram Sevania and Ghasi Ram Deegwal (all from Jhunjhunu, Rajasthan). Mana Ram Rasgania and his colleagues gave a warm welcome to them at Kurla Railway Station. According to Mana Ram Rasgania about 20-25 Raigars and their family members came from Karachi. As noted earlier, during our field-work in Dadar we came across an old Raigar resident who was an eye witness of the happening.

According to Mana Ram Rasgania, the first Raigar immigrants were: Lala Ram Kurdia, Kishan Lal Phoolwadia, Jai Ram Phoolwadia, Chetan Ram Jajoria, Dhanna Ram Kurdia, Ram Prasad Singhadia and few more.

Again in 1948, another group of Raigars came to Kurla. During my fieldwork in Thakkar Bappa Colony, Chembur (TBC), we came across another very old Raigar resident, aged 85 who had himself migrated from Karachi and was very active then and is one of the living eye witnesses of the incidents – Uda Ram Parbhuji Kurdia.[15] He in his conversation with the author spoke of happy memories he had of his close association with Raigar immigrants for a long time. Thus, according to him a group of Raigars from Karachi first started living in Janabai-ki-Chawl, Kurla (West). They were: Bhag Chand Phoolwadia, Kesha Ram Balotia, Govind Ram Bora, Kishan Chand Phoolwadia, Pushpa Ram Jatolia, Kana Ram Savasia, Lala Ram Kurdia and Hari Dev Ram Kurdia. While some were allowed to construct their own huts in a jungle near another Chawl called Shanti Bai Ki Chawl, Kurla. Those living here were: Khiya Ram Phoolwadia, Kiran Ram Jatolia, Moola Gusaiwal, Mangala Ram Jatolia, Kuba Ram Kurdia and Inda Ram Balotia. Some Raigars were staying in Hira Bai Ki Chawl. In 1948, the number of Raigars had increased considerably.

After India attained independence, efforts were made by the then government to build a Harijan Colony. The main purpose of the colony was to rehabilitate Harijans in particular. But actually the persons who benefited from this scheme were not the Harijan but the Raigar refugees from Pakistan. Thus, in 1948, the first batch of 11 Raigar families was shifted to TB Colony, Chembur from Jana Bai Ki Chawl, Kurla. Thus, Raigar migrating from Pakistan were the earlier settlers in TB Colony. Another most significant factor in the increase of Raigars in TB Colony was the migration of Raigars from Rajasthan. Those Raigars who settled in Mumbai earlier, took the initiative in bringing together their relatives and caste fellows. The efforts to bring the Raigars of Rajasthan dates back to 1948 when there was a growing consciousness among the Raigars to initiate manufacturing business of 'chappals'. The earlier Raigars came mostly from Nagaur, Ajmer, Pali, Bikaner, Jaipur, Sikar, Jodhpur, Churu, Bhilwara, Jhunjhunu and Barmer.

Since the year 1948, there had been different waves of immigration of Raigar caste into Mumbai from other regions mainly from Rajasthan and slightly from Delhi and Madhya Pradesh, as more economic opportunities became available. Since independence, there has been manifold increase in migration and Raigars' category has become linguistically, socially and economically diversified.

The Raigars belonging to three gotras, viz., Savasia, Balotia and Kurdia are dominant gotras.[16] Besides, Raigars also belong to other gotras. They are: Bora, Jajoria, Phoolwadia, Maurya, Choratia, Khatnawalia, Khorwal, Chauhan, Jatolia, etc. Thus, there are Raigars belonging to different gotras residing in Chembur and are mainly engaged in manufacturing of Chappals.

There are about twenty-five thousand Raigars in Chembur. Majority of Raigars reside in 224 big Chawls (rows of houses with common water and latrine facilities) in Chembur. Others owned houses in Shell colony, Aroli, Vashi, etc.

The Chembur Raigars are famous mostly for their contribution to the manufacture of chappals and leather goods, not only in India but also in European countries namely: Canada, Australia, Brazil, etc. Hundred per cent Raigars are in the business of manufacturing chappals. Since this is a most relevant aspect of their economic life let us give more information on their role in the manufacture of chappals with particular reference to Chembur.

There are three kinds of businessmen amongst the Raigars in Chappal Udyog. There are a few Raigars who are considered to be top dealers and businessmen. A few, of them are Heera Lal Balotia, Ashok Kudia, etc. The other Raigars are distributors. In addition to dealers, distributors, there are large number of Raigars who are retailers.

During the last two decades or so, Raigars are also rendering distinguished business services in export business. Those who had earned name in the export business are: Vishan Chand Kurdia (Vijay Leather Company), Shiv Kumar Kurdia (Amit Leather Company), Narain Chand Kurdia (Rajiv Leather Company), Suraj Mal Naval

(Kolkata Leather Company), and Mahaveer Naval (Perfect Leather Company). Their participation has reached a new height during the last two decades. Thus, there is a significant increase in the number of top businessmen and export elites among the Raigars.

Majority are in the business of manufacture of chappals. Some are manufacturers of furniture and some are photographers. Many Raigar youths are also employed as workers in chappal manufacturing factory in Chembur. Hardayal Chauhan is in white collar job (LDC in Union Bank of India, Fort, Mumbai). Amit Shiv Dayal is also employed as computer graphic designer in Balaji Tele Film Company. In 1995, Nand Kishore Balotia started his own electrical shop. Later on he widened its scope to include TV repairing and videography in 1999. It may be noted that Raigars in Chembur are also progressive. Durga Ram Phoolwadia is a famous shop keeper since 1990. He opened two Kirana shops at Adarsh Nagar, Chembur. The name of shops are Durga Kirana store. The next effort on the part of Ugam Chand Suvasia came in June 2003, with opening of Suvasis Medical and General Store at TB Colony, Chembur. Besides Chembur, there are Raigars in Aroli, Navi Mumbai, where Chhagan Lal Jajoria and Sukh Dev Choratia are businessmen and are contractor and supplier of marble stones as also flour respectively.

Among the Raigars in Mumbai, Chembur has highest number of professional Raigar doctors and engineers. There are 5 medical and dental doctors in Chembur from all over Mumbai and there are two software engineers.

Vishnu Kumar[17] son of Durga Shanker Suvasia passed his 12th class examination in 'A' grade with distinction. He was admitted in GS Medical College in 1986 and got his MBBS degree from Bombay University in 1991. Thus, he became the first doctor among the Raigars of Mumbai. He worked as a doctor at VN Desai Hospital, Mumbai, for a very short period in 1993. Later on he opened his own clinic 'Shri Clinic' at TB Colony, Chembur. He also did one year diploma course in HIV and Family Education from Indira Gandhi National Open University, New Delhi.

Another notable doctor is Paras Kumar[18] son of Ridha Ram Sunariwal, who has a medical degree from Rural Medical College, Ahmadnagar, Maharashtra (2000). Like Dr Vishnu Kumar, Dr Paras Kumar is also running his own clinic at TB Colony, Chembur. Among other doctors of Raigar community is Prakash Bhagwan Das

Suvasia, who is a nephew of Dr Vishnu Kumar Suvasia. He did his MBBS from MIMER Medical College, Pune. Besides physicians there are a few dental surgeons (BDS) also in Chembur. Dr C.R. Kurdia son of Ram Raj Kurdia has a BDS degree from Nayar Dental Hospital, Mumbai and opened his own clinic called 'Ram Raj Dental Clinic' located at 56 Shell Colony Road, Chembur. Hira Lal did his BDS from Government Central College VT, Mumbai and has his own clinic at Thana, Mumbai. Heemat was admitted in Dental College but had to leave it in the middle.

Besides MBBS, BDS, this community has a few software engineers. For instance Hemant Kumar[19] Kurdia son of Kishan Lal Kurdia passed his 12th class examination from National Sarvodaya School, Chembur in 1993 and was admitted in Vivekanand Educational Society's Institute of Technology (VESIT), Chembur from where he passed his final examination held in the year 1997. He was declared successful and thereafter obtained his BE degree (computer) from Bombay University. Hemant Kumar Kurdia is the first Raigar BE Computer in Mumbai.

In 1998 after getting the degree of BE, he appeared simultaneously in both examinations, viz., Graduate Record Examination (GRE) and Test of English as a Foreign Language (TOEFL) held at Andheri, Mumbai for admission in Master of Science (equivalent to ME) abroad. These examinations were conducted for US institutes. Subsequently, he was declared successful and was also admitted in University of Bridge Port, USA, near New York in 1998. He was shocked when he was not given a visa by US Embassy, New Delhi and was forced to miss the flight to US. No reasons were given. But he believed that strictness in issuing the visa to Indian students had created the problems. His name was cleared by other agencies.

In 1999, he was selected and between 1999 and 2003 worked as Programmer in a private company called Power Net Technology located at Andheri. In 2003 he was again selected as an associate for a foreign based company called DOLOITTE Consulting, located at Hiranandani, Powai, Mumbai. The company deputed him to US from March 27 to April 10, 2004.

Another Raigar boy of TB Colony, Chembur is Kailash Khorwal, who is also doing his BE Computer at Mumbai.

Besides doctors and engineers, there are a few graduates and diploma holders among them. For instance, Rajesh Jajoria[20] son of Om Prakash points out some of the names of commerce graduates in TB colony where their strength is to be reckoned with. They are: Har

Dayal, Bhanwar Lal Chauhan, Hans Raj, Ratan Lal Jajoria, Hans Raj Hari, Phoolwa Kurdia and Rajeev Vishnu Kurdia. Rajesh Jajoria is a science graduate and is residing in Bharatiya Raigar Cooperative Housing Society, which is located in Chembur. In 2002 he did his graduation with first division with specialisation in Industrial Chemistry from the Vivekanand Educational Society of Arts, Commerce and Science, Chembur and has B.Sc degree from Bombay University. He also did one year diploma course in import and export from Indian Institute of Export Management, Bangalore. There are two more diploma holders (both in textiles) among the Raigars and both are brothers. They are Devraj Bhag Chand Tigya and Bharat Tigya.

Raigars in Vashi, Navi Mumbai[21]

In 1976-77, the City and Industrial Development Corporation of Maharashtra (CIDCM), introduced certain positive programmes for the development of Navi Mumbai. It provided more than 70 per cent loan to the masses on nominal rate of interest. Such facilities were published and praised in leading local daily newspapers. In pursuit of this, some Raigars of Thakkar Bappa Colony (TBC), Chembur, for instance, applied to CIDCO for allotment of a flat in Vashi, Navi Mumbai.

The CIDCM in 1978-79 issued the allotment order to Raigars in Sector Nos. 2, 3, 15 and also in Narol area of Vashi. It has been noticed that there were the Raigars of TB Colony, who were the first to take advantage of this scheme. Being economically prosperous, they had access to other avenues of progress. The allottees of Raigars of TB Colony were: Dhanna Ram Kurdia, Govind Ram Kurdia, Chhagan Lal Jatolia, Ram Deen Retadia, Prahlad Balotia, Deva Ram Balotia, Harji Ram Jatolia, Madhu Ram Kurdia, Jai Ram Retadia, Hansraj Phoolwadia, Sukh Dev Chorotia, Bhanwar Lal Chorotia and others.

The cost of a flat paid by each allottee was Rs 18,000 only. Thus, during the 1979, all the allottees took the possession of their respective flats and started living in Vashi.

In addition to allotment of flats, CIDCM also allotted bungalows to the applicants in Vashi with a view to popularise the scheme and to gain the support of public for its development. A few Raigars from TB Colony applied for allotment of bungalows. Thus, Dhanna Ram Kurdia and Chhagan Lal Jatolia got the bungalows measuring 25 x 40 sq feet at Vashi. The cost of each bungalow, according to Ashok Kurdia was Rs 45,000.

Similarly, during the same period Maharashtra Industrial Development Corporation (MIDC) also introduced a new scheme of allotment of plots in different areas of Vashi. It further introduced certain positive programmes of development. This time attempts were also made by Raigars of TB colony to purchase the plots of general categories, as was the case with the flats and bungalows. Sohan Lal and Chanda Lal Sevania both brothers of TB Colony were among the first to get the plots measuring 40 x 100 sq feet in MICD area, Vashi. These efforts were complimentary to their attempts to improve their social status through modern residential opportunities.

Chembur is a major source of employment for Raigars and this is also a source of business leading to their economic prosperity. After, few years Raigars in Vashi started to realise the major difficulties faced by them in travelling a distance of 15 kms from work place and business opportunities at TB Colony, Chembur and started to go back to TB Colony, Chembur. Around the 1992s the owners of the flats, bungalows and plots started selling their properties on marginal profits. While the former was an attempt to move from traditional basti to flats and bungalow, the latter was an effort to go back to traditional basti.

In the year 2004 in Vashi, Navi Mumbai, there are also a few persons who have excelled in export, furniture and interior decoration. Some of the professional businessmen may be listed for the sake of illustration. Jagdish Deegwal was an officer in ONGC, Panvel, Mumbai. In 2000, he took VRS and started his own business of export. He supplied electronic items to various companies. Prakash Dholkhedia is supplier of raw material for Chappal Udyog in Chembur. Jagdish Maurya is a famous manufacturer of furniture at Chembur. Chela Ram Phoolwadia[22] son of Puran Chand Phoolwadia passed Matriculation examination and had the honour of being the first Raigar matriculate. In 1962, he appeared in written test conducted by Railway for selecting TTE in which he was declared successful. He joined the railway service as TTE at Bombay (now Mumbai) in the same year. After serving 30 years in railway, in 1992, he took VRS and eventually engaged himself in social activities. Sita Ram Rasgania is an interior decorator. Only one girl is serving in Reliance establishment. She is Meena Maurya, B.Com. Lalit did his B.Com. in 2000.

Thus, the Raigars of Vashi represent a meagre level of achievement and they have to achieve a good position at district level.

Raigar Associations

The immigrant Raigars felt the need of associations/organisations and formed various associations. In the section that follows, we shall deal with the growth of different associations with divergent objectives and its repercussions on the Raigar organisations.

Bharatiya Raigar Cooperative Housing Society, 1967[23]

Nearly four decades ago, the Raigars in Chembur felt the need for their own residential flats and in the sixth decade of twentieth century, founded the Bharatiya Raigar Cooperative Housing Society (BRCHS). The attitude of older Raigar residents was luke warm in the beginning, although they participated in it later. The founder of BRCHS was Gokul Ram Choratia. Other members were: Bachan Lal Inda, Shiv Karan and Shiv Dan Dholpuria. BRCHS is a registered body with its own constitution. Its Registration No. is BOM/HSG/1311/1967.

The organisational activities of BRCHS reached a climax soon after its registration, when BRCHS applied for allocation of a piece of land for Raigars. The part played by BRCHS in pursuing the matter with the then government, was a significant event. Attempts were made to promote their new interest. At last, after a long struggle, they met with great success when government sanctioned the land to BRCHS at Shiv Shrastri Kurla (East) and that too free of cost for the welfare of the Scheduled Castes.

Soon, preparations for construction of 35 flats were made and members of BRCHS visited Mana Ram Rasgania and requested him to build the flats. Consequently, Mana Ram Rasgania, who was the leading builder in Dadar, readily agreed to do so for his caste-men. Thus, BRCHS built its own building in Kurla (East) Mumbai in 1984 at the cost of Rs 26 Lacs. There are two wings; each wing has 17 and 18 flats respectively. All the 35 flats were distributed among 35 Raigars. However, it is important to note that in some cases, the original owners of the flats have recently transferred their flats to non-Raigars. In 2004, Harish Kurdia and Om Prakash Jajoria became the President and Secretary of BRCHS respectively.

Maharashtra Raigar Samaj, 1980[24]

In the history of Raigars in Chembur, 1980 was an important year. It is significant because Maharashtra Raigar Samaj (MRS) had emerged as a pivotal organisation enlisting the cooperation of all Raigars. There was a natural urge on the part of Raigars to form an organisation. With this aim in mind under the leadership of Kesh Ram Balotia, a meeting was held which was attended by about 50-60 representatives from TB colony of which Bhag Chand Phoolwadia was Secretary. Thus, in 1980 the modern political elite and professionals started assuming leadership position. The first office bearers were: Kesha Ram Balotia, President, Govind Ram Jajoria, Vice-President, Bhag Chand Phoolwadia, Secretary and Narain Das Jatolia, Treasurer. All the office bearers and Members were illiterate.

The main programme of the MRS was to campaign against the social vices and to settle family disputes, divorce cases and arranging marriages and settlement of property disputes among the Raigars. The MRS also called for inclusion of Raigars into Scheduled Castes lists of Maharashtra. It also stressed the need for reforms in their caste customs and for the spiritual reformation. It was reformative in its orientation. Similarly, it took the initiative to awaken socio-political consciousness among the caste. It was registered in 1981, and its registration No. is BOM. No. 256/8/GBBSD/30.4.1981, No. F. 6745/10.6.81. It is worth while to mention here that MRS is not affiliated to the ABRM and operates from Chembur independently.

Rajasthan Trijan-Mitra Mandal, 1980[25]

Another organisation of Raigars in Chembur was Rajasthan Trijan-Mitra Mandal (RTMM). RTMM was established around 1980. The first office-bearers were: Prabhu Ram, President; Jiwan Ram Kurdia, Secretary and Mangla Ram Jatolia, Treasurer. Members were: Kesha Ram, Moola Ram Retadia and Purkha Retadia. The aim of the RTMM was to provide financial assistance in a secret manner to poor and helpless Raigars, especially at the time of death for performing the last rites. RTMM also took lead in carrying the serious patients suffering from TB, Cancer, etc., to specialists for their diagnosis and treatment and whenever necessity arose, RTMM also provided financial assistance to them for their treatment.

Similarly, RTMM also supported financially to poor parents for solemnisation of the marriage of their children. The RTMM derived its financial support from commercial establishments.

Over a period of time after the death of Jiwan Ram Kurdia, Madhu Ram Kurdia became Secretary of RTMM and the activities of RTMM slackened after that. Efforts were not made by the local Raigars for its revival.

Shiv Shankar Seva Sansthan, 1984[26]

In 1984, the Raigars established the Shiv Shankar Seva Sansthan (SSSS) in Chembur. The founder Members were: Dharma Ram Kurdia, Madan Lal Jajoria, Pancha Ram Singharia, Ugam Chand Naval, Shiv Ram Jajoria, Khetar Ram Kurdia, Ram Chandra Khorwal and Jagannath Mordharia. The first office bearers were: Dharma Ram Kurdia, President; Madan Lal Jajoria, Mantri; Ugam Chand Naval, Treasurer; Ram Chandra Khorwal, Secretary and Shiv Ram Jajoria, Adviser.

The major programme of Sansthan was the propagation of education among the Raigar children. The Sansthan also called for Socio-religious reform in their caste customs and spiritual reformation. The Sansthan also pressed for formation of social organisations for socio-economic development. It was registered on October 31, 1986 and its Registration No. is F. 9856. But over a period of time this registered body lost its effectiveness. Hence, today it is not in existence.

Maharashtra Raigar Trust, 1994[27]

Maharashtra Raigar Trust (MRT) was established in 1994 at a meeting held under the leadership of Poonam Chand Dholkhedia, Jagdish Kurdia and others and they were appointed as President, General Secretary and Treasurer respectively of MRT.

A major programme of MRT was propagation of education, with a view to establish Bal Vidyalaya, Schools, Vachnalayas, Adult Education Centres, Balbadi and to provide the books, pencils and other stationery articles to poor and needy Raigar students. MRT also emphasised for help to the widow, poor and aged men and women. It also wanted to protect and maintain the movable and non-movable assets of the Samaj. Like MRS, MRT is also not affiliated to ABRM – both of which operate from Chembur area independently.

Factional division in Raigar movement in Chembur occurred in 1980. It split into MRS, MRT and Shri Saint Ravidas Seva Samiti and this produced factions at the local levels. In Chembur the faction led by Jagdish Kurdia, businessman, who had been a social activist for several years supported the MRT. Most of the Raigars in Chembur supported the MRT and activities of this Trust are reported in the local papers.

The MRT is lead by Jagdish Kurdia. MRT which became the centre of Chembur Raigars was involved in social activities. In the social field, MRT built a community hall. For instance, MRT purchased a constructed house from Ganga Ram Savasia which is located at Chawl No. 1, Room No. 6, TB Colony, Chembur for which, according to Jagdish Kurdia, they paid more than Rs 10 lacs. After dismantling the original construction, MRT built a new community hall and an expenditure of Rs 2 lac was incurred on it which was borne by MRT. The size of the hall is 10 x 80 sq feet. MRT appealed to caste fellows to donate liberally to it and their names were inscribed on the wall of the hall. This hall was meant to hold caste meetings, solemnise marriages and also provide boarding facilities to guests, Sadhus and Sanyasis, etc. It has toilet and bathroom facilities. MRT is a registered body, its Registration No. is E. 15166 Mumbai dated 22.6.1994.

Saint Ravidas Seva Samiti, 1999[28]

Raigars made big organisational efforts in the year 1999, by celebrating Ravidas Jayanti for the first time at Basant Nagar TB Colony, Chembur. Such kind of function provides an opportunity for the organisers to invite VIPs and voice their grievances and demonstrate their organisational strength.

It may be noted that the plot where the Jayanti Samaroh was held, belonged to a society called Pragati Society. In 2000, the Raigars under the local leadership of Durga Shankar Bora, Shanker Khorwal, Jagdish Kurdia and others, as also with the support of Pramod Shivwalkar, a very influential BJP MLA, took the plot under their possession by fencing it with wire. Some of the members, viz., Govind Mogalgavore, Mahendra Daste, Dilip More, Hari Shinde and others of the Pragati Society, filed petition in a court of law in Mumbai on November 29, 2000, against seven Raigars, viz. Jagdish Kurdia, Durga Shanker Bora, Shanker Khorwal, Hari Kharat, Sohan Shersiya, Chhotu Ram Kurdia and Pooran Mal Balotia.

On September 13, 2001, according to Jagdish Kurdia, the lower court passed an interim order in response to petition filed by Members of Pragati Society and directed the opposite party (Saint Ravidas Seva Samiti) to open one side of the encroached space. On October 1, 2001 the Raigars filed an appeal against the order seeking a vacation of its order in Bombay High Court because their interests were adversely affected by lower court verdict. According to Jagdish Kurdia Bombay High Court reversed the order made by the lower court. Thus, High Court protected the interest of the Raigars. In December 2000, Pramod Shivwalkar, BJP MLA wrote two letters to Collector, Mumbai and Mumbai Slum Improvement, Mumbai respectively regarding the issue of NOC for construction of Samaj Kalyan Kendra on open land City Survey No. 122, Basant Nagar, TB Colony, Chembur.

Over a period of time, Collector, Mumbai, issued the directions to the Tehsildar to submit the report. According to Jagdish Kurdia, a favourable report was submitted by the concerning authorities to Collector, Mumbai. Then the Collector obtained NOC from various agencies such as Development Planner, Brihan Mumbai, Traffic and Lighting authorities, Tata Power etc. The Collector worked for the welfare of the Raigars in Chembur and allowed them to build the Samaj Kalyan Kendra.

It is noteworthy that Pramod Shivwalkar was responsible for Saint Ravidas Bhavan scheme. On Saturday, July 19, 2003, Sri Saint Ravidas Seva Samiti organised a foundation laying ceremony. A large contingent of Raigars of Mumbai attended this 'vishal samaroh' and Swami Gopal Ram Maharaj laid the foundation stone. Among others present were: Kirit Somai, MP Mumbai; Ashwani Kumar Daboria and Shiv Karan Daboria.

According to Jagdish Kurdia, Pramod Shivwalkar donated generously Rs 20 lacs from his MLA Development Fund for the scheme, and built Saint Ravidas Bhawan for low untouchable caste – the Raigar. Saint Ravidas Bhawan was completed within a record time of 7 months. On February 6, 2004, it was inaugurated by Pramod Shivwalkar in the presence of a huge gathering. The size of the Bhawan is 33 x 58 sq feet. Four social activities are run by the Bhawan, viz., small Dava Khana for the poor, temple for Raigars, Women Welfare Centre and Balwadi.

The present office-bearers of Saint Ravidas Seva Samiti are: Manga Ram Tungaria, President; Govind Balotia, Secretary and

Deva Ram Chorotia, Treasurer. It was registered in 2000. Its Registration No. is 328/OBBS, 2000. It is necessary to point out that aims and objects of Saint Ravidas Seva Samiti are the same as those of MRT.

Dharmguru Gian Swaroop Vyasan Sudhar Samiti 2001[29]

On April 23, 2001, Raigars established another organisation called Dharmguru Gian Swaroop Vyasan Sudhar Samiti (DGSVSS) in Chembur. The founder members are: Kishna Ram Phoolwadia, Shiv Ram Jajoria, Madan Lal Dholpuria, Shrawan Balotia and Madan Lal Mundotia.

The main programme of the Samiti is to launch a campaign against the social vices with a view to inculcate good habits among the caste-fellows and whenever the Raigars assembled on certain occasions, there is a public exhibition. For instance, Aasha Ram Kurdia, a social activist of Beawar, Rajasthan, prepared a pictorial exhibition which worked for awakening of consciousness among the Raigars to get rid of socialvices. Aasha Ram Kurdia has been playing a leading part in awakening the socio-religious consciousness. Samiti advised Raigars to give up liquor and gambling as they ruined families. Samiti also advised them to educate their children. The DGSVSS also pressed for vegetarianism and teetotaller. The DGSVSS also called for reforms in their caste customs and for socio-religious reformation. It is exclusively reformative in its orientation and supports the policy of socio-religious reforms.

Thakkar Bappa Footwear Materials Merchants Welfare Association, 2002[30]

As has been noted earlier, Raigars of Chembur in spite of being well-established manufacturers of chappals, sandals and other leather goods since 1947, did not form their own trade association as other traders like clothes, steel, iron and other businessmen had formed their own associations.

Purushottam Bora, a businessmen of TB Colony, Chembur first felt the need for an association and took an active interest and founded Thakkar Bappa Leather Merchant Association (TBLMA) in 1998. The main object of TBLMA was to protect and safeguard the business interest of the traders. The traders who benefited from this association were not merely confined to Raigars of Chembur, but were also drawn from other castes.

To organise the general body meeting of the association was a major activity of TBLMA. The first general body meeting was held at Purushottam Bora's shop on August 6, 1998. This enabled the members to discuss issues regarding Sales Tax and Income Tax, to issue the certificate and identity cards to members, to get the Association registered, to appoint the watchman and the security-guard for night, to observe the holiday on *Puranmasi* and *Amavasiya* and close the shop after 9 pm positively.

The name of the association was later changed to Thakkar Bappa Footwear Material's Merchant's Association. Later again a new word – 'Welfare' was added. Thus, Thakkar Bappa Footwear Materials Merchants Welfare Association is registered body with its own constitution. Its registration No. is 1296/8/2002/GBBSD, September 7, 2002.

Membership was increased from 190 in February 2004 to 220 in May 2004, and there are more than 70 Raigar members who took part in various meetings especially the annual meetings. The first office-bearers were: Jeet Narayan Chavan, President; Nazarali Valji Jaria, Vice President; Purushottam Bora, Secretary; Khiya Ram Naval, Treasurer; Tara Chand Dholkeria, Joint Secretary; and six members.

The most significant factor in the process of the formation of the association was the emergence of the Raigars as business elite.

It is necessary to point out that Raigars' associations played a significant role at the time of natural calamities. For instance, during Gujarat earthquake in 2001 the Maharashtra Raigar Samaj and Thakkar Bappa Footwear Materials Merchants Welfare Association[31] took an active part in helping the Gujarat earthquake victims by raising funds and enlisting volunteers for holding relief camps in earthquake affected areas. Thus, under the leadership of Purushottam Bora and other office-bearers, DD No. 438139 dated April 23, 2004 for Rs 75,000.00 and another DD No. 438724 dated May 18, 2004 for Rs 25,000.00 (Total Rs 1,00,000.00) were handed over to the then Chief Minister Vilas Rao Deshmukh, Chief Minister of Maharashtra for Chief Minister's Gujarat Earthquake Relief Fund.

Besides financial help, in February 2001, the organisers with the prior permission of Maharashtra and Gujarat Government, a group of 14 Volunteers under the leadership of Deva Ram Chorotia left

Mumbai for Gujarat and organised several relief camps in different parts of Gujarat in order to distribute tea, rice, dal, sugar, milk powder, sarees, bed sheets, chappals and sandals, water bottles, blankets, medicine, etc. amongst the poor and needy victims. Other members were: Jagdish Kurdia, Purushottam Bora, Vinod Savasia, Sohan Jajoria, Pawan Kurdia, Jiv Raj Banshi Lal etc. Their efforts were appreciated.[32] According to Purushottam Bora, in relief work in Gujarat these organisations had distributed materials worth Rs 6 lacs. For purpose of mentioning the places, where relief camps were held were: Nigard, Chandia, Worli, Chakar, Hazapar, Harudi, Vadva, Lakhod, Kali Talwadi, Bhuj, Machau, Kukma, Gandhidham, Dhrangdhara, Aanjar and Nana Revidi.

The Raigars on the Frontiers of Politics: Local Level

Political Participation in Brihan Mumbai Mahanagar Palika (BMMNP) Election, 1979[33]

It was not until 1978 that Raigars demanded party tickets for Brihan Mumbai Mahanagar Palika (BMMNP) election. However, the Raigars in Chembur, for the first time, realised the value and usefulness of politics and started organising themselves to demand party tickets for BMMNP election, 1979.

In Maharashtra, Raigars had a positive reference group in Mahars and Chamars who had entered into the state politics long back and also had their own political parties. Around 1979, the Raigars in Chembur started organising themselves, thanks to the efforts of Jagdish Kurdia and his colleagues. They organised the first meeting of caste-fellows at Hanuman Mandir. This was attended by 500-600 Raigars from Chembur. Jagdish Kurdia took a leading part in organising the meeting. The meeting addressed itself specifically to two issues, the demand for party ticket for Raigars or to nominate caste-fellows as independent candidate. The leaders of Raigars visited all the leaders of political parties requesting for party ticket to a Raigar candidate for BMMNP election, 1979, to which the parties did not respond favourably. With the result Raigars nominated Bhanwar Lal Savasia as an independent candidate. The BJP leadership was dissatisfied with this move and a bitter rivalry developed between them which resulted in withdrawal of Bhanwar Lal in favour of BJP candidate in 1979.

Political Participation in BMMNP Election, 1985[34]

Again in 1985, Raigars in Chembur organised a meeting under the leadership of Deva Ram Chorotia at Madhu Lal Kurdia's residence, an active Congress worker at TB colony, Chembur. Smt. Parvati Gehlot – a local Congress MLA and her husband also attended it. This meeting was attended by about 100 Raigars. Eminent persons of the Raigar Samaj were: Bhag Chand Phoolwadia, Pudha Ram Kurdia, Kunja Kurdia, Kesha Ram Balotia, Deva Ram Chorotia and Jagdish Kurdia. The main purpose of the meeting centred round one prominent issue, the demand for party ticket. Parvati Gehlot assured them to help in giving party ticket. Jagdish Kurdia said that monopoly of the other castes should end now. Similarly, Raigars also approached BJP for party ticket.

As noted earlier, Chembur is a reserved seat for SC. Although Raigars formed a single largest caste in Chembur. Yet the political parties did not support their demand. Jagdish Kurdia narrated that Ravindra Panwar was given Congress ticket who belonged to Matrang caste and Shadashiv Lokhande – a Chamar by caste was BJP candidate. It may be recalled that the leaders of Raigars were irritated by indifferent attitude of political parties, with regard to the election. The Raigars of Chembur continued to nominate their own candidate as an independent candidate. For instance, this time Durga Shankar Bora was nominated, in spite of factions among the Raigars, marked by the bitter personal rivalries. Ravindra Panwar was elected to BMMNP on Congress party ticket.

Political Participation in BMMNP Election, 1992[35]

It was during 1992 that the Chembur seat was reserved for woman candidate. In the history of Raigar community, 1992 was an important year. Smt. Pushpa Bora had emerged as a strong Shiv Sena candidate. There was a natural urge on part of the Raigars to support her. With this aim in mind the Raigars in Chembur whole-heartedly supported her. Thus, Pushpa Bora was elected to BMMNP in 1992 on Shiv Sena party ticket.

Political Participation in BMMNP Election, 1997[36]

Two things are common to Raigar caste. First, they claim for party ticket. Secondly, some caste candidates had fought the election as independent candidates. This indicates that there was no consensus among them. For instance, in 1997, seven Raigar candidates fought the BMMNP election. The candidates who contested were: Jagdish Kurdia, Vishnu Goswami, Durga Das Phoolwadia, Chakradhari Kurdia, Arjun and Madhu Lal Kurdia – all independent. Madan Lal Dholpuria fought the election on Samajwadi party ticket. Thus, there seems to be no consensus regarding nomination of caste candidate for election.

According to Jagdish Kurdia all were defeated miserably.

Political Participation in BMMNP Election, 2002[37]

As noted earlier, the political parties' indifferent attitude created hindrances in political progress of Raigars. In 2002, none of the political parties gave ticket to Raigars and Jagdish Kurdia and Madan Dholpuria contested the election as independent candidates. Ravindra Panwar switched from Congress party to Nationalist Congress Party (NCP).

There are two main factions among the Raigars of Chembur, one led by Ram Swaroop Goel, Harish Nirwan and Jagdish Kurdia (all BJP) and other by M.P. Kurdia (Congress) and when Jagdish Kurdia was defeated in 2002, he switched to BJP and was nominated as President of Ward No. 180, Sahakar Nagar area, TB Colony, Chembur.

Raigars Launched a Campaign for Inclusion in Scheduled Castes Category

Another problem which attracted the attention of Raigars was the inclusion of Raigars in the list of Scheduled Castes.

Raigars belonged to the broad category of the untouchable caste, but since they are not designated as SC in Maharashtra, they are not entitled to enjoy the benefits of protective discrimination policy. For instance in Rajasthan, Delhi, Haryana, Punjab and Madhya Pradesh, Raigars belonged to Scheduled castes. In Maharashtra, Uttar Pradesh and Gujarat, they do not belong to SC category and therefore, suffered from political and educational privileges and government jobs.

The Raigar caste sought to overcome this problem by not only claiming SC status but also by social agitation. As pointed out Raigars are referred to both SC/non-SC category.

It is necessary to mention here that emergence of awareness among the Raigars was a gradual process. Raigar consciousness among the Raigars of Maharashtra existed long back. However, after 1980 many channels of communications were established and Raigars of Maharashtra came into contact with Raigars of Rajasthan, Delhi and Madhya Pradesh, who have been enjoying the benefits of reservation policy since independence. While MRS was responsible for taking up the issue with the Government of Maharashtra, the inclusion of Raigars in the list of SC, came into focus only when they protested with the state government. However, SC issue developed among the Raigars first at the state level and it was not until the formation of MRS in 1980, that SC issue emerged at the central level.

Now, we shall examine the socio-political agitation of claiming SC status in the following section.

One of the first accounts of their efforts in this direction is reflected in the letter written by Treasurer, MRS[38] on October 6, 1980 to the then Chief Minister, Government of Maharashtra and urged the government to concede to the demand for inclusion of Raigars in the list of SC and said that if done so, all the Raigars residing in Maharashtra would be highly obliged.

The demand for inclusion in the list of SC had some significant effect on the government. In his reply entitled "Request for inclusion of the Raigars Samaj in the list of Scheduled Caste", M.P. Damlo, Assistant Secretary, Social Welfare Department, Government of Maharashtra wrote a letter No. CBC – 1080/80440 (542) D-V dated May 29, 1981 to MRS for an early reply and added that MRS must furnish the following information immediately, if government were to accept their demand. They were: 1. Population, 2. Historical and Social background, 3. Education, 4. Trait and Characteristics, 5. Language, 6. Customs, 7. Religious ceremonies, 8. Deity, and 9. Profession.

The letter also asked to send the above information to: 1. Director, Social Welfare, Maharashtra State, Pune, and 2. Director, Tribal Research and Training Institute, Maharashtra State, Pune.

This became a new basis for inclusion in the list of SC.

The other notable leader who took the lead with Government of Maharashtra, supporting poor Raigars in a formal way, was Guru Das Kamat, Member of Parliament from Mumbai. In December 1994, he wrote to Sharad Pawar, the then Chief Minister, Maharashtra to include Raigars of Maharashtra in the list of SC. In this venture Kamat cooperated with the MRS.

Soon after the assumption of the post of the Minister, Social Welfare, Tourism, Welfare of SC/ST, Government of National Capital Territory of Delhi, Surendra Pal Ratawal wrote a DO letter No. 1639 dated July 22, 1996 and requested Manohar Joshi, the then Chief Minister, Maharashtra for inclusion of Raigars in SC category. It is a important to note that Ratawal himself is a Raigar from Delhi. The next effort came in 1997 when Pramod Shivwalkar, local BJP MLA from Chembur too wrote a letter to Manohar Joshi to include Raigars as SC in the schedule.

Between 1996 and 2001 the following associations wrote letters regarding inclusion of Raigars in the list of SC category: 1. Maharashtra Charmo-Udyog Vikas Mahamandal (November 20, 1996); 2. Maharashtra Raigar Trust, Chembur (January 14, 1998); 3. Rajasthan Ambedkar Mahasangh, Ajmer (December 18, 1999); 4. Sri Kachhi Maheshwari Meghwar Samaj, Mumbai (June 24 and July 18, 2000); 5. Ashok Gehlot, the then Chief Minister, Rajasthan (D.O. letter June 7, 2001); and 6. Dr Baba Saheb Ambedkar Academy, Mumbai (October 5, 2001).

This is significant that most of the Associations which wrote letters and whose main object was to support the Raigars issue, adopted an agitational approach in 1998.

Although Shiv Ram Jajoria, Secretary MRS submitted the required information to the Maharashtra Government with reference to letter No. CBC. 1097/Pra. Ka. 320/Mavak – 5 dated December 18, 1998, yet the government of Maharashtra did not accept the demand and the demand for inclusion of Raigars in SC category is still alive.

The demand for SC status, discussed above had two effects on the Raigar agitation. First, all the social activists and leaders among the Raigars started taking active interest in this matter, as they considered the case worth fighting for. As a result of this, MRS emerged as a strong organisation representing the population of Raigars. Second, although the Government of Maharashtra has not accepted the demand, yet the demand for SC status has boosted the self-image of the Raigars and they have gained the sympathy from other castes. An indirect effect of growing consciousness among the Raigars has been that BJP, Congress, Samajwadi Party and Shiv Sena have supported the Raigars cause – in Maharashtra so that they can enlarge their political base.

In November 1999, Sri Saint Ravidas Seva Samiti, held its meeting in Chembur under the leadership of Jagdish Kurdia, who is the founder member of Samiti and also its Chairman. The meeting passed many resolutions. The main one was that Kurla Signal Flyover Bridge should be named after Saint Ravidas.[39] Besides, Jagdish Kurdia also submitted a memorandum to Vilas Rao Deshmukh, the then Chief Minister of Maharashtra and also to Navab Malik, the then State Minister for Housing (Grah Nirman), Government of Maharashtra, demanding for naming of Kurla Signal Flyover Bridge after Saint Ravidas. Besides Jagdish Kurdia, there were: Sahdev Taratode and Bhou Kamble. The Raigars supported the demand made by Sri Saint Ravidas Seva Samiti because the entire Raigar Samaj was involved.

Notes

1. The most important source for early migration and background of the Raigars in Mumbai is Mana Ram Rasgania, aged 80. Conversation with him, Dadar, May 18, 2004.
2. Ibid.
3. Ibid.
4. Conversation with Shyam Lal Sevania, Corner, U. 35, 3rd Floor, Gokhale Road (North), Dadar, May 18, 2004.
5. Ibid.
6. Ibid.
7. Conversation with Sita Ram Rasgania, Dadar, May 18, 2004.
8. Conversation with Shyam Lal Sevania. Ibid.
9. Ibid.
10. Conversation with Vijay Kumar, Dadar, May 18, 2004.
11. Mana Ram Rasgania, *Sri Guru Maharaj ka Bhav Prasad*, Dadar, 2004.
12. *The Express Estates*, Mumbai, May 23, 2004.
13. Ibid.
14. As narrated by Mana Ram Rasgania, Ibid. May 18, 2004.
15. Conversation with Uda Ram Parbhuji Kurdia, aged 85, Chembur, May 21, 2004. For background and early arrival of Raigars in Chembur, other useful sources are: "Thakkar Bappa Colony – Asuvidhao key Registan mein ek Laghu 'Rajasthan'", *Jansatta*, Mumbai, Thursday, 24 October 1996; "Mumbai mein Raigar Samaj

and Mumbai mein Samaj Kab Sey", *Raigar Sudhar*, November 15-30, 2001.

16. Conversation with Shiv Ram Jajoria, Chembur, May 23, 2004.
17. Conversation with Dr. Vishnu Kumar, Chembur, May 21, 2004.
18. Conversation with Dr Paras Kumar, Chembur, May 22, 2004.
19. Conversation with Hemant Kumar Kurdia, Chembur, May 22, 2004.
20. Conversation with Rajesh Jajoria, Chembur, May 22, 2004.
21. Conversation with Ashok Kurdia, Vashi, Navi Mumbai, May 20-21, 2004.
22. Raj Kumar Phoolwadia, *Rajasthan Raigranan: Pahachan*, published by Chela Ram Phoolwadia, B-101, Sector 3, Vashi, Navi Mumbai, 1994, pp. 47-48.
23. The detailed account of BRCHS, 1967 and some other relevant information of it were provided by Mana Ram Rasgania, Jagdish Kurdia and Harish Kurdia in their conversation with author, May 18 and 20, 2004. See, also Bharatiya Raigar Cooperative Housing Society, *Raigar Sudhar*, November 15-30, 2001
24. Detailed account of MRS and some other relevant information of it, were given by Jagdish Kurdia in his conversation with author, Chembur, May 20, 2004.
25. Kesha Ram Khatnawalia provides detailed account of a meeting of Raigars held in the year 1980 in which Rajasthan Trijan-Mitra Mandal came into existence.
26. Shiv Ram Jajoria gives the detailed account of a meeting of Raigars held in Chembur in the year 1984 in which Shiv Shankar Seva Sansthan came into existence.
27. Jagdish Kurdia gives a detailed documentation of this organisation. A full account is provided in documents submitted to the Registrar's office Mumbai, for its registration in 1994. See, also its constitution.
28. Jagdish Kurdia gives a detailed documentation of this newly formed organisation. A full account is provided in a12-page document submitted to the Registrar's office, Mumbai for its registration in 1999. See also its constitution and *Saint Ravidas Bhawan ka Udghatan*, Raigar Jyoti, Barmer, March 2004.
29. Conversation with Shiv Ram Jajoria, Chembur, May 23,2004. See, also "Gian Swaroop Vyasan Sudhar Samiti ka Gathan", *Raigar Sudhar*, November 15-30, 2001; "Gian Swaroop Vyasan Sudhar Samiti dwara Satsang, Pravachan, Vyasan Mukti Pradarshan", *Raigar Jyoti*, Barmer, March 2004.

30. Purushottam Bora gives a detailed documentation of this organisation. A full account is provided in the documents submitted to the Registrar's office, Mumbai, for its registration in September 2002. See, also its constitution.
31. The most authoritative account of relief camps for distribution of food, clothes, medicines and other rehabilitation work for earthquake victims in Gujarat by Maharashtra Raigar Samaj, Chembur and Thakkar Bappa Footwear Merchants Association, Chembur, is given by Purushottam Bora, Chembur, May 23, 2004. See, Collector, Mumbai, Suburb District letter No. C/Desk-7/Earthquake/Gujarat/2001 dated January 31, 2001 to Maharashtra Raigar Samaj and Thakkar Bappa Footwear Materials Merchants Association. See, also Chairman, Thakkar Bappa Footwear Merchants Association letter dated May 19, 2001 to Vilas Rao Deshmukh, the then Chief Minister of Maharashtra regarding handing over of DD No.438139 of Rs 75,000 and another DD No. 438724 of Rs 25,000 for earthquake victims in Gujarat.
32. Almost all the newspapers appreciated their action. See, *Mahanagar* Mumbai, March 7, 2001; *Do Bajey Dopahar*, Mumbai, March 7, 2001; *Vichar aur Awaj*, Mumbai, March 8, 2001; *Nagar Up-nagar*, Mumbai, March 8, 2001; *Kalbadevi Times*, Mumbai, March 8-14, 2001; *Pratah Kal*, Mumbai, May 21, 2001.
33. For an important discussion of relation of the Raigar caste to National Political Parties of the Region, Jagdish Kurdia provided some detailed information of this basic issue to the author, Chembur, May 20-22, 2004.
34. Ibid.
35. Ibid.
36. Ibid.
37. Ibid.
38. MLA, MP, Minister, Chief Minister of other States and Social organisations, etc., supported in 1980, the Raigar demand for their inclusion in Scheduled Castes list of Maharashtra, however, the Government of Maharashtra did not accept their genuine demand. For details regarding inclusion in SC list, see, specifically, the Treasurer Maharashtra Raigar Samaj letter dated October 6, 1980, addressed to Chief Minister, Maharashtra, Government of Maharashtra, Guru Das Kamat; Member of Parliament, Mumbai's letter dated December 4, to Sharad Panwar, the then Chief Minister, Maharashtra; Adhiyaksha, Ramesh Medhekar, Maharashtra Charmo-udyog Vikas Mahamandal Mardayit, Mumbai, letter dated

May 20, 1996, to Manohar Pant Joshi, Chief Minister Maharashtra; S.P. Ratawal, Minister Social Welfare, Tourism and Welfare of SC/ST, Government National Capital Territory of Delhi's D.O. letter No. 1639, dated July 22, 1996 to Manohar Joshi, the then Chief Minister, Maharashtra; Pramod Shivwalkar, MLA's letter No. Ja-Kra-A-1/1966/97 dated May 31, 1997 to Manohar Joshi, Chief Minister, Maharashtra; Maharashtra Raigar Trust letter dated January 14, 1998 to Welfare Minister, Government of Maharashtra, Mumbai; Deputy Secretary, Social Welfare, Cultural Affairs and Sports Department, Government of Maharashtra letter No. CBC – 1097/Pra-ka-320 dated December 18, 1998 to Deputy Director, Social Welfare, Maharashtra State, Pune and copy endorsed to Shiv Ram Jajoria, Mantri, Maharashtra Raigar Samaj, Chembur; State President, Rajasthan Ambedkar Mahasangh, Ajmer letter No. 330 dated December 18, 1999; Ramji M. Maheshwari Sanjot, Mahamantri, Sri Kachhi Maheshwar Meghwar Society, Thane letter No. 25/2000 dated July 18, 2000 to Deputy Director, Social Welfare, Directorate, Maharashtra State, Pune; Ashok Gehlot, Chief Minister, Rajasthan, letter No. A. Sha. Mum 4/Pa 5 (i) Sak/2001/4842, Jaipur dated June 7, 2001 to Vilas Rao Deshkmukh, the then Chief Minister, Maharashtra and Section Officer, Social Justice, Cultural Affairs and Sports Department, Government of Maharashtra letter No. CBC – 10/2001/Vkak 2799 Pra. Kra. 216/Mavak – 5, dated July 13, 2001 to Director, Social Welfare, Maharashtra State, Pune.

Also all newspaper reporting indicate indifferent attitude of Government of Maharashtra to Raigar's demand. See: "Raigar Samaj ko anusuchit jati ki manyata nahi", *Nagar Up-nagar*, Mumbai, Thursday, March 30, 2000; "Menka Gandhi sey maang, anusuchit jati 'raigar' samaj ko manyata di jaya" *Yug Sagar*, Chembur, July 8-14, 2000; "Raigar samaj ko anusuchit jati mein shamil karney ki mang", *Nav Bharat*, Mumbai, Saturday, July 15, 2000; "Raigar samaj ko anusuchit jati mein shamil kiye janey ki mang", *Satyamev Jayatey*, Mumbai Sandhya, Wednesday, July 18, 2000; "Anusuchit jati ki suchi mein 'raigar' samaj ko manyata diye janey ki mang", *Do Bajey Dopahar*, Mumbai, Thursday, July 20, 2000; "Raigar Samaj ko Manayata di jaye: Sri Kachhi", *Sanjha; Jansatta*, Mumbai, Thursday, July 20, 2000; "Kendriya Kalyan Mantri Menka Gandhi sey Mang, Anusuchit jati ki suchi mein Raigar Samaj ko manyata di jaye", *Azad Chingari, Mumbai*, Thursday, July 20, 2000; "*Raigar Samaj ki mang*" *Nav Bharat Times*, Mumbai, July 21, 2000; "Anusuchit jati ki suchi mein raigar samaj ko manyata diye janey ki mang", *Sanjha Lok Swami*, Mumbai, Monday, July 24, 2000; "*Raigar Samaj ko anusuchit jati mein shamil kiya jaye"*, *Sabject Mańthan*, Mumbai, July 25-31, 2000; "Raigar Samaj ko anusuchit jati mein shamil karney ki mang", *Nirbhaya Pathik*, Mumbai, Thursday, July 29, 2000; "Raigar samudaya ko anusuchit jati ka darja doo", *Nutan Savera*, Mumbai, August 6-12, 2000; "Maharashtra sarkar dwara Raigar samaj par annaya", *Maharashtra Crime (Weekly)*, Mumbai, Friday, October 6-12, 2000 and "Azadi key pachas saloo key bad bhi Maharashtra mein Raigar Samaj anusuchit jati mein samavesh nahi", *Mahanagar*, Mumbai, Thursday, August 23, 2001.

39. "Kurla key nav nirmit pul ka nam sant Ravi Das key nam par karney ki mang, *Nav Bharat Mahanagar*, Mumbai, Monday, November 29, 1991. Also, see: "Kurla signal udan pul ka nam sant Ravi Das pul rakhey janey ki mang", *Kurla Samachar* (Hindi Saptahik).

11

Raigars' Periodicals

During the pre-independence period, Raigars were involved in social reform movement, but their political participation was limited. Being untouchables, most of the Raigars were politically inactive. Only a few persons were active, who participated in the independence movement. The formation and growth of the ABRM during the British Raj cannot be attributed to a single factor. The need for such an organisation was felt differently by different leaders and at different times. With the advent of independence, a large number of Raigar leaders of Mahasabha felt the necessity of publications of a caste periodical for all-round development of Raigar activities as also one of the important mediums of communication between the central body of ABRM, the Regional Mahasabha and castemen. The community journal will provide a platform for reform movement and ABRM would expound its views on socio-political issues. It will also give a living picture of the community. But ABRM could not launch the publication of Community paper on account of certain social and political differences and economic constraints and ABRM dropped the idea for the publication.

However, along with social, economic and political activities, the Raigar saints and social activists could also see the need for a powerful community paper to bring to the notice of the general community and government as also to well-wishers of untouchables, their miserable conditions and to propagate the philosophy of religious saints and to motivate their vast following. Such an attempt helped crystallise the ideology and worked out a programme of action for fighting against the various kinds of social evils, discriminations and deprivation.

As mentioned earlier, Swami Gian Swaroop's attempt to organise an Akhil Bharatiya Raigar Mahasabha to carry on the agitation and in 1948 soon after the independence of the country, he infused enthusiasm among the activists, which made them realise that community paper would be essential for their progress in an educationally backward community, and therefore, decided to launch the paper. Swamiji discussed these issues with Surya Mal Maurya – a freedom fighter and resident of Beawar, Ajmer, the necessity for socio-political regeneration of the masses and impressed upon him for having a strong organisational base all over North India to spread the message.

In the history of Raigar movement, the year 1948 was an important year. RSS had emerged as a pivotal organisation enlisting the cooperation of Raigars from Delhi. There was a natural urge on the part of RSS to publish its own paper. With this aim in mind and also to fulfil the dream of late Atma Ram Lakshya a committee called Jagrati Patra Prakashan Samiti (JPPS) was formed in 1948[1] under the chairmanship of Swami Gian Swaroop Maharaj. Bihari Lal Jagrat became the first General Secretary of JPPS. Thus, the first issue of *Jagrati*, a national monthly newspaper, was published on October 2, 1948 and it was first dedicated to Rashtrapita Mahatma Gandhi. The first editor was Surya Mal Maurya from Delhi. The JPPS had published 30 issues of the Jagrati. After this the committee could not continue its publication as it had to face a financial crisis. Hence, it stopped its publication.

These were the views of the Raigar leaders 56 years ago, at the time of inception of the ABRM. But during the last six decades various welfare and economic institutions had grown up. The traditional occupational structure had undergone considerable change. The percentage of educated persons had gone high. In the 14th Elections to Parliament, people had cast their votes. In short, the conditions of the 1944s had undergone considerable change in the year 2006. Hence, an obvious question arises. Why ABRM has not been able to launch the publication of its own paper even today, viz., 2006. The author raised this question with some of the Raigar leaders. In reply, some showed reservations while others blamed the inactiveness of ABRM. Some leaders expressed their grievances that nobody in the organisation listened to their views.

However, most of the Raigars felt the necessity of a community periodical for giving a living picture of the community and to expound its views on socio-political issues. After 41 years, in December 1981, Kalu Ram Jajoria, and Sita Ram Maurya launched the publication of a monthly "*Raigar Pragatisheel Patrika*", which they edited themselves as chief editor and associate editor respectively. The aim of the paper, as expressed in the early issues was to rouse the consciousness among the community for developing self-consciousness, the social reform and highlight their grievances and problems through this paper and thereby defend the Raigar community. It further expressed that although Raigars are in huge numbers yet they are disunited. In their social, political and educational aspects they are still backward as they were centuries ago. This is the time that we should give them a break to come out of this darkness. It, therefore, requires that they should be organised and re-united. Thus the paper tried to foster in them, the caste consciousness and unity in order to assert political power.

Besides, the publication of the above Patrikas the Raigars are reported to have published the following periodicals:

1. *Raigar Pragatisheel Patrika*[2] (1981) by Kalu Ram Jajoria from Jaipur, Rajasthan,
2. *Phalak*[3] (1992) by Smt G.S. Jatolia from Jaipur, Rajasthan,
3. *Raigar Uthan*[4] (1993) by Smt Kanta Devi Verma (Kankhedia) from Indore, Madhya Pradesh,
4. *Raigar Sudhar*[5] (1999) by Ashwani Kumar from Fatehabad, Haryana,
5. *Raigar Jyoti*[6] (2000) by Govind Jatolia from Barmer, Rajasthan,
6. *Raigar Rakshak*[7] (2001) by Umesh Peepliwal from Jaipur, Rajasthan,
7. *Vikas Kiran*[8] (2001) by Babu Lal Khamokhariya from Tonk, Rajasthan,
8. *Parivarik Jyoti Raigar Samaj*[9] (2001) by Smt Vimla Parsoya from Bhilwara, Rajasthan,
9. *Lakshya-Rakshak*[10] (2001) by Smt Meira Kanwaria from New Delhi, and
10. *Gadegaonlia Times*[11] (2003) by Mukesh Kumar from Jaipur, Rajasthan.

These periodicals are published by different individuals and local organisations from different places and are still being published.

Out of these periodicals, some were published as weekly, fortnightly, quarterly and monthly with 18 to 20 pages. The periodicals generally contained the news on education, social and economic attainment of Raigars, news of Raigar activities at various places, enquiries from the readers, articles, stories and poems on current topics of general interest, problems of community and its other related fields. The editorial describing the activities of Dr Ambedkar, criticising political parties, also appeared in the periodicals. In its news section the atrocities perpetrated by the caste Hindus on scheduled castes, indifferent attitude of the government officials to safeguard the rights of SC/ST, poems depicting socio-economic conditions of the Raigars, scheduled castes and similar other items are reported prominently. Political news – local, national or international often appeared in the periodicals. Occasionally, special number on festivals, conventions or various problems are published. The periodicals propagated the views of influential leaders during the elections. It asked the Raigars and scheduled castes to vote for a particular political party. the party's policy and programmes are also explained. At the same time grievances of the individuals or a section of the Raigars are also expressed. The periodicals are often mailed to the person concerned in order to influence or inform him regarding the community's views and problems.

The columns of these periodicals are open to any type of contribution. These caste periodicals discharge the function of establishing and reinforcing contact between widely depressed castemen and news items published in the periodicals contributed by the scholars, reflect the aspirations and achievements of castemen and their problems. There are some examples of typical articles that have been published in the periodicals. They are on the explanation of the word Raigars, origin of Raigar with reference to the religious texts, the fusion and fission of different castes of Raigar caste cluster, necessity of periodicals etc.

These papers carry diverse materials in its issues devoting its space on matters relating to the caste problems and welfare, elite biographics, work of caste leaders, atrocities on the Raigars in particular and SCs/STs in general. Some of the space is filled up by the editor who may discuss subjects covering religion, politics, social, economic, reservation, etc. Besides, the papers also carry material relating to matrimonials, diseases and their treatments, issues related to public litigation, legal advice, etc. Among caste problems and welfare activities, inter sub-caste commensal rules, child marriage, preparation of directory of castemen, etc., figure prominently. The papers carry 80 per cent material in its issues endorsed by writers from Rajasthan.

The financial condition of the papers is not sound. Most of the issues contain an appeal for enrolling new membership and raising the funds for the papers. The papers have reminded again and again that if castemen do not help the papers financially, they will have to stop their publication. *Raigar Pragatisheel Patrika* had two types of subscriptions in 1981. The annual subscription was Rs 15 and permanent subscription was Rs 100. In spite of low subscription, the members had not remitted their subscription for a long period. Out of the listed subscribers, almost all are from Rajasthan.

Among other caste periodicals, Raigar Jyoti had three types of membership in 2001, according to amount of money donated. They are annual subscription (paying Rs 50), three-year subscription (paying Rs 125) and *Aajeevan* membership (paying Rs 500). During a very short span of time, subscribers have increased by February 2001 with 43 *Aajeevan* members. Likewise, the *Raigar Rakshak* was started by Umesh Peepliwal, an educated social worker in 2001. The first issue was published on August 15, 2001 with message from Governor of Rajasthan, Chief Minister of Rajasthan along with a few other eminent persons. The first issue of this periodical has 8 pages. The periodical has 4 types of membership according to the amount of money donated. They are: Three-years subscription (paying Rs 100), six-year subscription (paying Rs 150), ten-year subscription (paying Rs 250), and *Aajeevan* (paying Rs 1,100). During very short span of time, subscribers have increased by October 2001 with 10 *Aajeewan* members.

Notes

1. Bakolia, Chiranji Lal and Gadegaonlia, Rajendra Prasad, *Raigar Kaun aur Kya?* New Delhi, Asian Printers, Hardhyan Singh Road, Karol Bagh, 1964, p. 134.

2. For details see, Issues of *Raigar Pragatisheel Patrika.*
3. See, issues of *Phalak.*
4. See, issues of *Raigar Utthan*.
5. See, issues of *Raigar Sudhar.*
6. See, issues of *Raigar Jyoti.*
7. See, issues of *Raigar Rakshak.*
8. See, issues of *Vikas Kiran.*
9. See, issues of *Parivarik Jyoti aur Raigar Samaj.*
10. See, issues of *Lakshya Rakshak.*
11. See, issues of *Gadegaonlia Times.*

12

Political Parties and the Raigar Leadership

Perspective/Policy/Strategy

Caste, Party and Political Representation in State Assembly

Since the political elite form the driving force in any social movement, it is necessary to give a brief account of their growth and strength. Although modern Raigar politicians emerged from 1944 onward when they formed All India Raigar Mahasabha (AIRM) and launched a campaign against the socio-economic atrocities, untouchability and socio-religious disabilities in Rajasthan, Madhya Pradesh, Uttar Pradesh and Delhi, a steady growth of professional politicians occurred only after 1952 general elections.

Since 1952 the Congress party established nearly complete hegemony over SC/ST politics. Within Congress, supremacy has increasingly been shown towards Chamars, Bhambis, Meghwals, Bairwas, Khateeks and Raigars. The sentiments within caste/community, however, were shifting slowly.

A point worth consideration in this respect is the fact that in the state assembly election held in 1952 in the state of Rajasthan which was the first of its kind, the Congress party in all the constituencies, reserved for scheduled castes, fielded large number of candidates from all major castes/communities, such as Chamars, Meghwals, Bhambis, Raigars, Khateeks, etc. The fact that related to the elections of 1952 to the state assembly revealed that Jai Chand Mohil contesting from Badi Sadri, Kapasan, Chittorgarh, Kewar Lal Jelia from Ladpura and Prabhu Dayal from Churu won the election. All the three candidates were of Raigar community and were sponsored by Congress.[1]

The 1957 general elections marked a further increase in the representation of Raigar community in the state politics. In this election (1957), Smt. Anandi Devi Jelia from Bara, Kota district, Hajari Mal Bakolia from Kekri, Ajmer; Jai Chand Mohil from Kapasan, Chittorgarh and Kanhaiya Lal from Shahpura, Bhilwara, were elected to the state assembly and all the four were nominated by the Congress party. The total number of Raigar candidates had increased from 3 in 1952 to 4 in 1957.[2]

For the first time, in the history of Rajasthan, in the third general elections of the legislative assembly held in the year 1962, a move was made by some leaders of the Raigar community that they should associate themselves with some other political parties to fight elections to defeat Congress party. For this purpose, Jai Narain Shalodia and Bhanu Prashad contested elections on the Swatantra Party ticket from Niwai, Tonk district and Chomu, Jaipur district respectively and were declared elected.[3] Thus, the neglect of Raigars interest by the Congress party, created a crisis in the Raigar organisation, which led to vertical split in this organisation. Some members of this community owed allegiance to Congress and others to other political parties. In this process, of course, Niwai and Chomu Raigars moved closer to the Congress. Virda Ram Phoolwaria contested from Jalore and Kana Bhai Naval from Shahpura on Congress tickets and were declared elected.[4] Although as per the results declared officially, Congress won only two seats, actually it lost three seats. This was an indication of political alienation of the Raigar elite from the Congress as it was a change in political alignments.

On the eve of the fourth general election in 1967 for the State Legislative Assembly, again a change took place in the attitudes of Raigars towards the Congress. However, most of the Raigars, as in the previous elections, remained associated with the Congress. It would be noted that during the 1962 general elections, the number of representatives of Raigar caste in the assembly was four only; two each from the Swatantra and Congress parties. During 1967 elections, the number of candidates who were declared elected increased from four to five. These newly elected candidates were from Swatantra party. Thus Chuni Lal Jelia from Khandar, Sawai Madhopur district, Jai Narain Shalodia from Niwai, Tonk district and Paras Ram from Parbatsar, Nagaur district. All these Raigar Swatantra candidates were declared elected.[5] It will be worthwhile to note here that like in 1962; again in 1967 the Congress bagged only two seats of Raigar candidates in the state assembly. They were Virda Ram Phoolwadia from Jalore district and Ganesh Ram Palia from Gangrar, Chittorgarh district.[6] Thus, the Raigar leaders emphasised the need for multi-political ideologies for the community.

The 1972 general elections marked a sudden decline in the number of candidates of this caste in the State politics. In this election (in 1972), both Congress candidates Virda Ram Phoolwadia from Jalore and Bhuralal from Shahpura, Bhilwara districts were successful,[7] but the total number of Raigar candidates had decreased from 5 in 1967 to 2 in 1972.

The most significant feature of the sixth general elections of 1977 in the country and in the various states, of general or reserved constituencies, was of a general feeling of disappointment in the minds of the people towards the Congress – the ruling party because of the emergency imposed in the country in 1975. Decades of the rule by the Congress party had not delivered the expected goods, but casteism, groupism, nepotism and attendant rapacious corruption was the order of the day. The people were also bound to be frustrated by the police atrocities and compulsory retirement of government servants.

All these had made the Congress rule unpopular and this determined the trend of the canvassing done by various political parties who were in opposition, so much so that they amalgamated themselves into a United front. Thus, in May 1977, the Congress (O), the Bharatiya Lokdal, Bharatiya Jansagh, the Socialist Party, the Congress for Democracy and a few independents belonging to the Congress merged in a single party to form the Janta Party. It was because of these reasons that several young canvassers in different areas were found to be working on behalf of Jansangh, Socialist, Congress (O) parties, etc. Their main object was to defeat the Congress in any possible manner.

The number of candidates, as per the figures of sixth general elections of 1977, indicate that all the three Raigar candidates Chuni Lal Jelia from Khandar, Sawai Madhopur district, Jai Narain Shalodia from Niwai, Tonk district and Mangi Lal from Gangrar, Chittorgarh district had exclusively won election as the Janta party candidates.[8] Thus, crushing defeat of the Congress was a spectacular feature of the sixth general election in the state as a whole.

As stated earlier, it was the Janta Party which won the election in 1977, but in the mid-term election of 1980s, caused due to the failure of Janta Party, the picture radically changed. Thus, in the mid-term election Congress party improved its position. Thus three Raigar candidates namely Chhoga Ram Bakolia from Revdar, Sirohi, Chhoga Lal Kanwaria from Dudu, Jaipur and Dhara Ram Phoolwadia from Siwana, Barmer district were declared successful.[9] All were Congress candidates. However, it may be added here that BJP succeeded in sending one Raigar candidate from Khandar. It was Chuni Lal Jelia.[10]

The most significant feature of the general elections of 1985 in the country was the general sympathy in the minds of the people toward Congress party because of the assassination of Mrs Indira Gandhi, the then Prime Minister of India, who remained in power for nearly 18 years. The overwhelming victory of the Congress was a spectacular feature of the eighth general election in the country as a whole. The number of candidates in the whole state assembly was only three candidates from the Raigar community. Congress being at the top who bagged two, i.e., Chhoga Ram Bakolia from Revadar, Sirohi district and Bhudar Mal Verma from Dausa.[11] It will, thus be seen here that BJP which had returned the candidates in 1980 could not muster any seat this time. It will be worth mentioning here that the Lok Dal candidate Mohan Lal Chauhan[12] who won the election from Parbatsar reserved constituency of Nagaur district belonged to the Raigar community.

The elections of 1990 showed a sudden increase in the number of BJP candidates of this caste in the state politics. The two BJP candidates Tikam Chand Kant from Revdar, Sirohi district and Mangi Lal from Gangrar were successful. Thus, the number of BJP Raigar candidates had increased from zero in 1985 to two in 1990.[13] Two Raigar candidates namely Chunni Lal Indora from Nokha, Nagaur district and Mohan Lal Chauhan from Parbatsar were declared successful. They were Janta Dal candidates.[14] Congress bagged one candidate only from Kesharsinghpur. He was Heera Lal Indora.[15] Thus, again the crushing defeat of Congress was spectacular feature of 1990 elections.

The elections of 1993 were significant because of sudden decrease in the number of professional politicians. Rajasthan had 2

MLAs against 5 in 1990. Of these two were one each from the BJP and Congress. Tikam Chand Kant was from Siwana, Barmer district[16] and Heera Lal Indora from Kesharsinghpur.[17] They were BJP and Congress candidates respectively.

The elections of 1998 were all the more significant because BJP could not send even a single Raigar MLA as against 1 in 1993 and there were in all, four MLAs. Chhoga Ram Bakolia from Revdar, Babu Lal Singharia from Kekri, Ajmer district, Mohan Lal Chauhan from Parbatsar and Heera Lal Indora from Kesharsinghpur. All the four were Congress candidates.[18]

As stated earlier it was the Congress Party which won the election in 1998 with two-thirds majority (153 seats) but in the 12th legislative assembly election of December 1, 2003, the picture radically changed. Thus, the overwhelming victory of BJP with 120 seats (out of 200) and crushing defeat of Congress is spectacular feature of 12th general election in the state. The number of reserved-seats in the whole state assembly is only 57. Similarly Congress being at the top who bagged 29 SC and 20 ST seats out of 57 in the whole state assembly in 1998, could not muster even 10 seats this time (2003). The number of BJP SC/ST candidates in the whole of state assembly was 4 (SC – 3, ST – 1). Janta Dal bagged 3, while there was one independent SC. The number of Congress SC/ST candidates in the whole state assembly is 9 only (5 SC and 4 ST). This is a indication of political alienation of the weaker section of the society in general and SC and ST in particular from Congress. The most significant feature of state assembly election of 2003 was of a general feeling of disappointment in the mind of SC and ST people towards Congress – the ruling party – because of indifferent attitude of Chief Minister Ashok Gehlot. The SC and ST people were also bound to be frustrated for failure in protecting their genuine interest by the Congress government.

The elections of 2003 are all the more significant because Congress could not send even a single Raigar MLA as against 4 Congress MLAs in 1998. Thus, all the three Congress candidates – Babu Lal Singharia from Kekri, Ajmer district; Chhoga Ram Bakolia from Revdar, Sirohi district and Mohan Lal from Parbatsar, Nagaur district were defeated. This is an indication of alienation of Raigar elites from Congress as it was a change in the political alignment.

As per the result declared officially, out of 2 BJP candidates, one Raigar candidate Hira Lal from Niwai, Tonk district was successful, the number of BJP Raigar candidates has increased from zero in 1998 to 1 in 2003.

Table 12.1

Rajasthan Vidhan Sabha Elections and Raigar Caste Representation from All-over Rajasthan in State Assembly since 1952-2003

Year	*Number of Assembly Seats*				*Name of Scheduled Caste/Community (by party affiliation)*		
	General	*Scheduled Castes*	*Scheduled Tribes*	*Total*	*Raigar Caste*	*Other Scheduled Castes/ Communities*	*Total*
1952-57	139	16	5	160	3 Congress	13	16
1957-62	128	28	20	176	4 Congress	24	28
1962-67	128	28	20	176	2 Swatantra Party 2 Congress	24	28
1967-72	132	31	21	184	3 Swatantra Party 2 Congress	26	31
1972-77	132	31	21	184	2 Congress-I	29	31
1977-80	143	33	24	200	3 Janta party	29	32
1980-85	143	33	24	200	3 Janta Party 1 Bharatiya Janta Party	28	32
1985-90	143	33	24	200	2 Congress-I 1 Lok Dal	29	32
1990-92	143	33	24	200	2 Bharatiya Janta Party 2 Janta Dal 1 Congress-I	27	32
1993-98	143	33	24	200	1 Bharatiya Janta Party 1 Congress-I	30	32
1998-2003	143	33	24	200	4 Congress-I	28	32
2003-2008	143	33	24	200	1 Bharatiya Janta Party	31	32

Source: 1. *Trimasik* Patrika, *Vidhan Bodhani,* Vol. 4, No. 4, October 1997, Rajasthan Vidhan Sabha Sachivalaya, Jaipur.
2. *Doorbhash Nirdeshika,* 2000, Rajasthan Vidhansabha Sachivalaya, Jaipur.

It is important to note that Raigar politicians belong to diverse political parties. For instance in 1980, 4 MLAs out of 200 in Rajasthan were: 3 Congress and 1 BJP. Similarly, in 1990, 5 MLAs out of 200 in Rajasthan were 2 BJP, 2 JD and 1 Congress – 2 Raigar MLAs in 1993, one each from BJP and Congress.

Thus, the Raigars had been successful in their endeavour to gain caste representation like Meghwals, Chamars, Bairwas, etc., in the state assembly since 1952. Since 1981 at least one member of state level Raigar group in the state assembly had been a member in the ministry. The Table 12.1, shows the position of parties since 1952-2003.

Raigar Caste Representation in Madhya Pradesh State Assembly and Delhi Metropolitan/Government of NCT of Delhi Since 1952-2003

Since we have already discussed about the Raigar MLAs from the Rajasthan State, we will now consider in this section the feedback of the growth of the political elites among the Raigars of Madhya Pradesh and Delhi.

As the social and political consciousness increased over a period of years, the scheduled castes including Raigars joined other political parties especially after the imposition of emergency. During these years the participation of scheduled castes in different political parties also increased and this was the period when they achieved success in sending their members from other parties also. Thus the fact, related to the election of 1962 to the state assembly, revealed that Champa Lal Arya contesting from Suwasara reserved constituency, won the election.[19] The candidate was from the Raigar community and was sponsored by Bharatiya Jan Sangh. Thus, he was the first Raigar MLA in the history of Madhya Pradesh. Not only elected for the first time to the state assembly, but also won the election in 1967 as the Bharatiya Jan Sangh candidate.[20]

The 1977 general election marked a further increase in the representation of Raigar community in the state politics. In this election (1977), Champa Lal Arya from Suwasara constituency[21] and Satya Narain Jatia from Shojapur constituency were elected to the state assembly and both were sponsored by the Janta Party.[22]

The election of 1980 showed a sudden decrease in the number of Raigar community in the state politics. The lone BJP candidate Champa Lal Arya from Suwasara constituency was successful.[23]

Thus the number of Raigar candidates had decreased from two in 1977 to one in 1980.

Similarly, the fact that related to the election of 1952 to the then Metropolitan Council, Delhi, revealed that Daya Ram Jalutharia contested from the reserved constituency in Delhi, on Congress ticket, was declared elected. Thus, he was the first Raigar member in the history of the Delhi Metropolitan Council.[24]

On the eve of the general elections held in 1967 for Delhi Metropolitan Council a change took place in the attitudes of Raigars towards the Congress. It would be noted that during 1967 election the number of candidates who were declared elected however remained the same, i.e., one. But the newly elected candidate was Shiv Narain Sarsunia and was sponsored by Bharatiya Jan Sangh.[25]

The 1972 general elections marked again a change in the representation of Raigar community in the state politics. In this election Moti Lal Bakolia was elected to the state assembly and was nominated by the Congress party. In 1972 Bakolia was not only elected to state assembly but also won the election three times in 1977, 1980 and 1985, respectively. Thus, he was elected MLA four times.[26]

The 1977 general election marked increase in the representation of Raigar community in the state politics. In this election (1977), Moti Lal Bakolia, Bhore Lal Shastri and Smt. Sundar Devi Naval Prabhakar were elected to the State Assembly and all the three were nominated by Congress party.[27]

On the eve of the general election of 1993 for the state legislative assembly again a change took place in the attitude of the Raigars towards the Congress. It would be noted that during 1977 general election the number of representatives of Raigar castes in assembly was three and all were from Congress Party. During the 1993 election the number of candidates who were declared elected decreased from 3 in 1977 to 1 in 1993. The newly elected candidate was Surendra Pal Ratawal and was sponsored by BJP.[28]

In the 1998 general election one Congress candidate Moti Lal Bakolia[29] was successful but the total number of the Raigar candidates had remained one. Table 12.2 shows the position of the parties from 1952 to 2003.

Table 12.2

Madhya Pradesh Vidhan Sabha and Delhi Metropolitan/NCT Elections and Raigar Caste Representation in the State Assembly since 1952-2003

State/Metropolitan Government of NCT of Delhi	*Year*	*Raigar Caste (by party affiliation)*
Madhya Pradesh	1962	1 Bharatiya Jan Sangh
	1967	1 Bharatiya Jan Sangh
	1997	2 Janta Party
	1980	1 Bharatiya Janta Party
Delhi	1952	1 Congress
	1967	1 Bharatiya Jan Sangh
	1972	1 Congress-I
	1977	3 Congress-I
	1993	1 Bharatiya Janta Party
	1998	1 Congress-I
	2003	1 Bharatiya Janta Party

Source: Chandanmal Naval, *Raigar Jati-ka-Itihas*, Jodhpur, Shyam Printing Press, 1986, pp. 80-83.
Also gleaned from S.P. Ratawal, former Minister, Government of NCT of Delhi, on phone on 26/27 February 2002.

On the eve of general election of December 1, 2003 for Delhi legislative assembly both Surendra Pal Ratawal and Mrs Durgesh Mohanpuria were nominated by BJP and Congress respectively from Karol Bagh reserved constituency, Delhi. Thus, both Raigar candidates were fighting against each other. The fact that related to the election of 2003 to Delhi assembly revealed that Surendra Pal Ratawal a BJP candidate was declared elected. Thus, the number of Raigar candidates has remained one.

In addition to MPs and MLAs, the other Raigar elites who had been the Chairmen and members of Delhi Nagar Palika/Nagar Nigam were: Gotam Chakrawal, Congress (1954-57), Daya Ram Jalutharia, Congress (1958-62), Khoob Ram, Congress (1962-67), Gopal Krishan Ratawal, Jansangh (1967-75), Laxman Singh Atal, Jan Sangh (1975-80), Kushal Chand Mohanpuria, Congress-I (1977-85), Hem Chandra Mohanpuria, Congress-I (1985-90), Dharam Pal Atal, BJP (1997-2002) and Smt. Meira Kanwaria, Chairman BJP (1997-2000), Tulsi Ram Sablania, Congress-I (2002-2007), Yogendra Chandolia, BJP (2002-2007).[30]

Some of the famous professional politicians can be listed for the sake of illustration: Shiv Narain Sarsunia was an active RSS worker and he was also a member of Bharatiya Jana Sangh Committee constituted to remove untouchability in Delhi. He took an active part in Kashmir agitation and was arrested and sent to jail. He was one of the nominees of Bharatiya Jan Sangh in Delhi's interim Nagar Parishad which was formed in 1966 and became an executive councillor (Revenue) of Delhi Nagar Parishad in the year 1967 and was also MLA (BJP) in 1967.[31]

S.P. Ratawal was also an active BJP worker. In 1993 when BJP formed a Ministry at NCT of Delhi, Ratawal was also MLA and later became the first Raigar Cabinet Minister in 1993 and was allotted the portfolio of Labour, Tourism and the Scheduled Castes and Scheduled Tribes.[32]

Smt Meira Kanwaria was a BJP worker and became the first woman Raigar Chairman of Delhi Nagar Nigam in 1997.[33]

Caste and Representation in Parliament

Apart from all this, a few Raigars became members of the Parliament. For instance in 1952 Naval Prabhakar, was not only elected for the first time to Parliament from Karol Bagh, Delhi, but he also won the elections twice in 1957 and 1962. Thus, he was elected MP thrice and stayed for a long time (15 years).[34] Dharm Das Shastri (1967) and Smt. Sundar Devi Naval Prabhakar (1972) were elected as MPs from Karol Bagh Delhi respectively.[35] The first three MPs from Raigar community were the Congress candidates, the fourth candidate being Shiv Narain Sarsunia (1977) was from BJP.[36] In witnessing this change over to BJP, we can interpret this as an example of anti-Congress attitude. In 1980 Virda Ram Phoolwadia from Jalore Parliamentary reserved constituency, Rajasthan was elected as Congress (I) candidate. He was from Raigar community.[37]

Since we have already mentioned about the Raigar MPs from Delhi and Rajasthan states, we will now mention about Dr Satya Narain Jatia, one of the prominent Raigar MPs from Madhya Pradesh, who was not only elected for the first time in 1980 to Parliament from Ujjain constituency but also subsequently won the elections five times in 1989, 1991, 1996, 1999 and 2004 respectively.[38] Thus, he was elected MP six times (continued for a long period). The first member of Parliament from Raigar Community was a BJP candidate.

For the first time, in the history of Rajasthan, in the 14th general elections of the parliament held in the year 2004, a move was made by some leaders of the Raigar community that they should associate themselves with other political parties to fight election to defeat both Congress and BJP. For this purpose Ram Babu Raigar (a resident of Tonk district) and Smt Shakuntla Kansotia wife of Dr Padam Singh Kansotia (a resident of Delhi) who contested election on BSP ticket from reserved Parliamentary Constituency Tonk and Bayana (both in Rajasthan) respectively, lost. Thus, the neglect of Raigar interest by Congress and BJP created a crisis in the Raigar caste.

Table 12.3, shows the position of the parties since 1952-2004 in various states.

Table 12.3

Parliamentary Elections and Raigar Caste Representation from Delhi, Rajasthan, Madhya Pradesh in Lok Sabha since 1952-2004

State/Union Territory	*Year*	*Raigar Caste (by party affiliation)*
Delhi	1952	1 Congress
	1957	1 Congress
	1962	1 Congress
	1977	1 Janta Party
	1980	1 Congress-I
	1984	1 Congress-I
Rajasthan	1980	1 Congress-I
Madhya Pradesh	1980	1 Bharatiya Janta Party
	1989	1 Bharatiya Janta Party
	1991	1 Bharatiya Janta Party
	1996	1 Bharatiya Janta Party
	1998	1 Bharatiya Janta Party
	1999	1 Bharatiya Janta Party
	2004	1 Bharatiya Janta Party

Source: 1. Chandanmal Naval, *Raigar Jati-ka-Itihas*, Jodhpur, Shyam Printing Press, 1986.

2. *Trimasik Patrika, Vidhan Bodhani*, Vol. 4, No. 4, October 1997. Rajasthan Vidhan Sabha Sachivalaya, Jaipur.
3. *Doorbhash Nirdeshika, 2000. Rajasthan Vidhan Sabha Sachivalaya*, Jaipur.
4. Pamphlet published and circulated by Ministry of Labour, Government of India, New Delhi. See also, Pamphlet published and circulated by Ministry of Information and Broadcasting, Government of India, November 10, 1999.

In addition to MPs, MLAs, the other Raigar elites who had been the chairmen and members of the Nagar Palikas in the State were: Kaju Lal Jajoria, Chairman, Nagar Palika, Jobner;[39] Members: Bansi Lal Arya and Mishri Lal Malviya (both from Jodhpur), Bhika Ram Phoolwadia, Chhagan Lal Jatolia and Basti Ram Bakolia (all from Barmer), Mishri Mal Chauhan and Mishri Lal Khatnawalia (both from Peepar), Bheem Raj Naval (Pali), Magha Ram (Churu) and Keshri Mal Jatolia (Balotra).[40]

Since the introduction of the Panchayati Raj in Rajasthan the number of Raigar Panch and Sarpanch had increased considerably. Their names were: Ramesh Chandra Dholkhedia (Bikaner), Sita Ram Maurya (Bhanda Rang), Girdhari Lal Maurya (Kharkada), Jagnath Moralia (Devli) and Prabhu Dayal Sabal (Kotdi).[41]

Thus, there is a significant political elite among the Raigars of Rajasthan.

Caste and Representation in Congress Ministries

Raigars were also represented in the Congress ministries since 1981 and had held different portfolios. Since 1981 at least one member of Raigar community had been a member in the Ministry. For instance in 1952 Chhoga Lal Kanwaria, was selected as RAS officer and served the State in various capacities.[42] After serving nearly 25 years, in 1977 he took voluntary retirement from the state service and joined the Congress.[43] In 1980 he was elected as a Congress candidate from Dudu reserved constituency.[44] When Shiv Charan Mathur was heading the State, Kanwaria was inducted for the first time in Mathur's Ministry as a Cabinet Minister with the portfolio of Medical and Health.[45] He remained Minister from July 19,1981 to October 16, 1982.[46]

Another notable leader, who was associated with the activities of Congress during his early days in the border district of Barmer in western Rajasthan, was Chhoga Ram Bakolia. Born on January 1, 1944, in a poor Raigar family of Jai Ram Bakolia, Chhoga Ram obtained his Diploma in Mechanical Engineering from Jodhpur Polytechnic and joined RSEB as Junior Engineer.[47] He was promoted to the post of Assistant Engineer in the year 1976. He was not interested in the service and in 1980, he took voluntary retirement from the service and joined the Congress Party.[48] In the elections held in the year 1980, he was nominated as the Congress candidate from

Revdar reserved constituency, in Sirohi district and won the election.[49]

In 1981 he became the President of Rajasthan Handloom Project; Member of State Town Planning, Secretary of State Unit of Akhil Bharatiya Anusuchit Jati Parishad; Member, Board of Directors of Rajasthan State Transport Corporation and Board of Directors of Rajasthan Anusuchit Vikas Mandal. Later on he was promoted to the post of Vice-President of District Congress, Sirohi.[50] He was also member of the delegation of Government of India sent under Food and Agriculture Programme in the year 1982 and visited South Korea, Japan, Hong Kong, Thailand and Singapore.[51] Similarly, he was the Member of Scheduled Castes Welfare Committee and was also Member of the Parliamentary Advisory Committee for Irrigation, Public Health Department, Revenue, Land Reforms, Energy, Food and Famines.[52] He was also President of Raigar Mahasabha Rajasthan. From October 16, 1982 to 1985 he was Deputy Minister for Energy, Social Welfare and Underground Water Works.[53] In 1985, he again contested the election from the same constituency and won.[54] In March 1985, he became the Minister of State and in October 1985, he was elevated to the rank of a Cabinet Minister of Food and Supplies.[55] In 1998, he again contested the election and won the election as Congress candidate. He had been a Cabinet Minister in Ashok Gehlot Ministry (2002).[56]

Notes

1. Chandanmal Naval, *Raigar Jati ka Itihas*, Jodhpur, Shyam Printing Press, 1986, p. 81.
2. Ibid.
3. Ibid.
4. Ibid.
5. Ibid.
6. Ibid.
7. Ibid.
8. Ibid., p. 82.
9. Ibid.
10. Ibid.
11. Ibid.

12. Ibid.
13. *Trimasik Patrika, Vidhan Bodhani,* October 1997, *Swaran Jayanti Visheshank,* Rajasthan Vidhan Sabha Sachivalaya, Jaipur, pp. 205-210.
14. Ibid.
15. Ibid.
16. Ibid., pp. 211-216.
17. Ibid.
18. *Doorbhas Nirdeshika 2000,* Rajasthan Vidhan Sabha Sachivalaya, Jaipur.
19. Chandanmal Naval, *Raigar Jati ka Itihas,* Jodhpur, Shyam Printing Press, 1986, p. 82.
20. Ibid.
21. Ibid.
22. For detailed information, please see, Pamphlet issued by the Ministry of Labour, Government of India, New Delhi, 10 November, 1999.
23. Chandanmal Naval, op. cit., p. 82.
24. Telephonic conversation with S.P. Ratawal, Delhi on 26-27 February 2002.
25. Ibid.
26. Ibid.
27. Ibid.
28. Ibid.
29. Ibid.
30. Ibid. Also, "Delhi Nagar Nigam key Chunab mein Raigar Samaj key Char Pratiashi Chunav Maidan mein, Tulsi Ram Sablania and Yogendra Chandolia, Delhi Nagar Nigam, *Chunav Geetey*", *Raigar Sudhar,* dated 1-15 March 2002 and 16-31 March 2002, respectively. Also see, Chandanmal Naval, 1986, p. 83.
31. Ibid.
32. Ibid.
33. Ibid. Also see, Roop Chand Jalutharia, *Raigar-Jati-ka Itihas,* Jaipur, Capital Printers, 2001, pp. 80-81.
34. Chandanmal Naval, 1986, op. cit., p. 80.
35. Ibid.
36. Ibid.
37. Ibid.

38. For detailed information, please see, Pamphlet issued by the Ministry of Labour, Government of India, 10 November, 1999.
39. Chandanmal Naval, 1986, op. cit., p. 83.
40. Ibid.
41. Ibid.
42. Ibid., p. 78.
43. Ibid.
44. Ibid.
45. Ibid., p. 79.
46. Ibid.
47. Ibid.
48. Ibid.
49. Ibid.
50. Ibid.
51. Ibid.
52. Ibid.
53. Ibid.
54. Ibid., p. 80.
55. Ibid.
56. *Rajasthan Sujas*, October 5-January 1999.

13

Mahasabha and Transformation

Three consequences of ABRM movement can be identified. First, the movement has a bearing on the upward social mobility of the Raigars and this is reflected in the growth of different kinds of elite and ritual, educational and economic gains that they have achieved and quantum of power they have enjoyed. Second, as a result of upward mobility, by protest and increase of political power there is a shift in traditional balance of power in Rajasthan society. Third, the movement has an impact on the nature of traditional caste system. All these changes were transformative in character offering the basic organisation of the Indian society and culture. We may begin with the consideration of growth of an elite and upward social mobility through protest.

Social Mobility through Protest

The Raigars have been able to lift themselves up from the position of untouchables. They have achieved equality of opportunity in several spheres of social life starting from a position of all-round severe deprivation. They have attained a higher status in the ritual hierarchy compared to other untouchable castes/communities by a series of positive measures. They have also achieved equality of opportunities with regard to modern education, government employment, representation in legislatures, parliament and right of entry into caste Hindu temples, through a series of agitations. They have also shed their civic disabilities in the matters pertaining to dress, ornaments, houses and general lifestyles.

While these are general indicators to show the trend of upward social mobility of caste as a whole, there are also specific indicators which pertain to the individuals. Individual mobility which is considered to be characteristic feature of the class systems, is interrelated with group mobility, which is considered to be the feature of the caste system. The importance of the individual mobility is that it leads to the development of an elite within the castes, who occupy a higher status through the process of exclusion within their distinct social status and they maintain a distance between themselves and the masses or the non-elite. However, many of them feel that they have responsibility of contributing their shares to the upliftment of the masses of their community. In so far as they do so, individual social mobility comes to have a bearing on group mobility.

Growth of Elite

The social and cultural process underlying the emergence of the modern elite will be demonstrated in the following pages. The point at this juncture is how to treat the growth of different kinds of elite as an indicator of the upward social mobility of individuals and to see the reaction it has on the movement as a whole.

The growth of a differentiated modern elite reveals the diversity of individual talent and level of achievement, which has to be seen in relation to the level of deprivation, in the traditional structure on the one hand and the general performance of the so-called progressive castes, which were also relevant as opposition – reference groups on the other hand.

The notion of an elite is a relative one. In a community which has been denied opportunities of various kinds, the individuals with a certain level of achievements are considered to be in an elite position. By this standard, the first generation graduate school and college teachers, lawyers, doctors, engineers, industrialists and administrators belong to the elite category. Raigars were denied the modern educational opportunities which they acquired after a series of intense agitations. Thus, when a Raigar graduate was employed by the state as a teacher, it was a big event for the community. Similarly, when Raigars started the liquor factory or constructed a cinema house, then they were considered to be big ones whereas their parents were mostly leather workers only. Like all the other untouchables, Raigars were also denied all kinds of socio-political and religious participation. After 1947, when the country achieved independence they were elected to legislature and thus the first generation of politicians emerged. The Raigars were also kept out of Brahminical Hinduism and when Swami Laxmandas Maharaj came under the influence of Arya Samajists, he was trained and learned Vedas, Vedanta, and ritual to fill in religious office in temples, a religious elite, parallel to those among the Brahmins came into existence. This is the rationale for treating those employed as priests, doctors, lawyers, engineers, government officers, businessmen, industrialists and professional politicians as a part of the elite.

Madan Lal Chandolia, advocate and the Deputy Maha Prabandhak (Karmick), Power Finances Corporation (Government of India Undertaking), New Delhi, published a '*Raigar Samaj Directory*' (in Hindi) in February 1996, in memory of his father late Nonda Ram Chandolia 'Kuntli Wale' which contains information about 'Who is Who' among the Raigars in different states. The information available about the occupation for all persons, can be made use of in classifying different types of elite. The data suffer from two limitations. First, they do not include the members or supporters of the ABRM but consist mainly of the influential members of the Raigar community. Second, they do not provide data of all states or regions but consist mainly of Delhi, Rajasthan and a few other states. However, the data is indicative of the growth of different types of elite in selected states. Table 13.1 gives the distribution of individuals who have achieved an elite status in different categories.

The basis for a discussion on the growth of an elite, particularly in Rajasthan, is based on the information collected from various government offices regarding Raigars who are employed in the state government. Thus, all the data collected may be classified in 13 categories depending on each individual occupation: (1) Teachers as the school teachers and principals, (2) Teachers including college and university lecturers, readers, professors. These two categories represent the intellectual elite while professional elite are: (3) Vaidyas and modern doctors including those who practicised Ayurvedas, Homeopathy and Allopathy; (4) Vakils and lawyers; (5) Engineers. The remaining types of elite are: (6) IAS, IPS and allied service personnels; (7) IRS, IFS; (8) Judicial officers such as Munsif Magistrate, District and Session Judge and Additional District and Session Judge; (9) State Administrative Officers which include –

Table 13.1

Distribution of Raigar Elite in the Different States (as on 2001)

Types of elite	*Number of Elite in Different States*												
	Delhi	*Madhya Pradesh*	*Mahara-shtra*	*Gujarat*	*Punjab*	*Uttar Pradesh*	*West Bengal*	*Goa*	*Tamil Nadu*	*Bihar*	*Andhra Pradesh*	*Karnataka*	*Chattish-garh*
School teachers and Principals	6	103	-	2	1	-	-	-	-	-	-	-	-
College and University teachers	1	1	-	-	-	-	-	-	1	-	-	-	-
Doctors/Vaidya	7	4	-	2	-	1	-	-	-	-	-	-	-
Vakil and Lawyers	5	1	-	-	-	-	-	-	-	-	-	-	-
Engineers	2	6	1	-	-	-	-	1	1	-	1	1	-
IAS/IPS	3	6	-	2	-	-	-	-	-	-	-	-	-
Administrative Officers*	16	1	-	-	1	-	-	-	-	1	-	-	-
JRS,IFS, IES**	9	4	3	4	1	-	1	-	-	-	-	-	1
Management and Personnel***	12	-	-	1	-	-	-	-	-	-	-	-	-

Contd...

Contd...

Government Officers	42	-	-	-	1	2	-	-	-	-	-	-	-
Bank Officers	22	-	-	1	1	-	-	-	-	-	-	-	-
Inspectors	12	9	-	3	-	-	-	-	-	-	-	-	-
Politicians and Social Workers	57	15	5	1	-	-	-	-	-	-	-	-	-
TOTAL	194	150	9	16	5	3	1	1	2	1	1	1	1

Source: Figures for Raigar Caste doctors, engineers, college and university teachers, IAS, IPS, IFS and other officers, serving in various Government Departments, etc., have been derived from the following sources:

1. Chandanmal Naval, *Raigar-Jati-ka-Itihas*, Jodhpur. Shyam Printing Press, 1986,pp. 55-60.
2. Madan Lal Chandolia, *Raigar Samaj Directory*, Delhi, Karol Bagh, 1996, pp. 1-50.
3. Aasu Lal Umaji Kurdia (Editor) Raigar Samaj Shiksha Samiti, Ahmedabad, *Smarika* 1999, Ahmedabad, p. 11.

* Includes: Law Secretary, Joint Secretary, Over Secretary, Deputy Director, Regional Director.

** Includes: Income Tax Commissioner, Deputy Commissioner, Assistant Commissioner, Income Tax Officer, District Forest Officer, Indian Revenue Service, Indian Forest Service, Indian Education Service, Director/Joint Commissioner, Customs and Central Excise, Divisional Controller, Transport, Manager Videsh Sanchar Nigam, Deputy Collector, Deputy Superintendent of Police, Passport Officer.

*** Includes: Senior Prabandhak, Manager and Deputy Manager Indian Air Lines, Chief General Manager, Sahayak Prabandhak

Government Officer includes House Tax Officer, Social Welfare Officer, Section Officer, Hindi Officer, Chief Propaganda Inspector, Principal Berak Stores, Udyog Prasar Adhikari, Administrator, Supervisor, Superintendent, Foreman, Zila Bachat Adhikari, Marketing Manager, Field Officer, Computor Officer, Transport Officer, Officer Incharge, Administrative Officer.

Bank Officer includes Bank Manager, Assistant Manager, Finance Officer, Branch Manager, Deputy Manager, Accounts Officer, Currency Inspection Inspector.

Inspector includes Income Tax, Sales Tax, Police Inspector, Inspector IB, Inspector CID, Telephone Revenue Inspector, Station Incharge, Inspector in Defence Ministry, Commercial Taxation, Inspector, Cooperative Inspector, Sub-Inspector, Assistant Commercial Taxation Officer, Custom Inspector, Revenue Taxation Officer, Senior Drug Inspector (IB), Assistant Sub-Inspector etc.

RAS and RPS; (10) Government officers which include Assistant Administrative Secretary, House Tax Officer, Social Welfare Officer; (11) Bank officers which include Bank Manager, Account Officer (12) Inspectors include Income Tax Inspector, Inspector, Assistant Sale Tax Inspector, Police Inspector, CID Inspector, IB. Inspector, Custom Inspector, etc. and, finally (13) The politicians and social workers, political party workers, members of Nagar Palikas, Nagar Nigam, Panchas, Sarpanchas, MLAs and Ministers.

In order to get an idea of the growth of the elite over a period of time – 232 persons were divided into 13 categories. Thus, the growth of elite class covered more than 38 years from 1960 to 1998.

Table 13.2 gives the distribution of different types of elite category-wise. It will be seen that all the intellectual elites put together account for 33.62 per cent while all the professional elites comes to 26.32 per cent, followed by the government and bank officers with 17.67 per cent, politician and social workers with 9.48 per cent, administrators (IAS, IPS, IRS, RAS and RPS) with 8.62 per cent, judicial officers with 1.72 per cent and others with 2.15 per cent.

We may now consider the growth of different types of elite among the Raigars, over a period of four decades.

Prior to independence, there were no Raigars who were literate like other untouchables as they were not admitted in the schools. The modern intellectual elite developed after the independence, when untouchables including Raigars started acquiring modern education. They are employed as school teachers, college lecturers and university professors. 23 college lecturers are serving in the government colleges of the state and 1 university Associate Professor is Kishori Lal Raigar. Kishori Lal is in Hindi Department in Jai Narain Vyas University, Jodhpur. One outstanding intellectual is Lekh Raj. Lekh Raj is serving as Professor in Delhi University.[1]

Besides teachers, there are journalists and writers who have made a name for themselves. Some of the known journalists are Umesh Peepliwal (Jaipur), Govind Jatolia (Barmer), Ashwani Kumar (Haryana) and Babu Lal Khamo Khariya (Kota).

Some of the famous writers may be listed for the sake of illustration. Dr Kishori Lal Raigar is a known Hindi writer of National repute, who obtained his Master's degree in Hindi from University of Rajasthan, Jaipur in 1987 and later on M. Phil in 1988. In 1991 under the able supervision of Associate Professor Dr (Mrs) Kalawati Prakash, D. Litt., Department of Hindi, University of Rajasthan,

Table 13.2

Distribution of Raigar Elite in Rajasthan (as on 2001)

Types of Elite	*Number of Persons*
School teachers and Principals	54
College and University teachers	24
Doctors and Vaidyas	27
Vakils and Lawyers	29
Engineers	6
IAS and IPS	4
IRS, IFS*	5
Judicial Officers	4
State Administrators (RAS and RPS)	11
Government Officers**	29
Bank Officers***	12
Inspectors	5
Politicians and Social Workers	22
Total	232

Sources: Figures for all scheduled castes, doctors, engineers, college and university teachers, IAS, IPS officers, RAS and RPS officers, serving in various state government departments were collected as on 1989 and 1999 and presented category-wise in a Register. The register is with Dr Puran Mal Bairwa. The data for Raigars of Rajasthan have been derived from this register. Besides, figures have been gleaned from following sources also.
Chandanmal Naval, *Raigar Jati-ka-Itihas*, Jodhpur, Shyam Printing Press, 1986, pp. 55-60.
Madan Lal Chandolia, *Raigar Samaj Directory*, Delhi, Karol Bagh, 1996, pp. 1-50.
Vimla Parsoi, Parivarik Jyoti Raigar Samaj, Pratham Aank. Bhilwara, Housing Board Shastri Nagar, 2001 (page number not mentioned).
*includes Custom Collector, DFO, IRS, IFS, Income Tax Officer.
**includes House Tax Officer, Social Welfare Officer, Reception Officer, Superintendent, Registrar Cooperative, Section Officer, Supply Officer, DET, Deputy DET, BDO, Joint/Assistant Registrar, PO, ACTO, RTS, Joint Director and Deputy Director.
***includes Bank Manager, Probation Officer and Accountant.
Inspector includes CTI, Cooperative Inspector, Sub-Inspector Police, Income Tax Inspector.

Kishori Lal was awarded Ph.D. degree by University of Rajasthan. The topic was *Dr Rangay Raghav ke katha sahitya mein gramya jiwan*. In order to become eligible for college lecturership he passed NET examination conducted by UGC, New Delhi and later on UGC granted him JRF and SRF in order to promote the research work in Hindi. K.L. Raigar, after completion of his M.A. started his career as a school teacher and later joined as lecturer in Hindi at Kendriya Hindi Shikshan Sansthan, Kolkata (Raj Bhasha). After a few years, he joined his new assignment as Investigator at Rajasthan Prachiya Vidhya Pratisthan, Jaipur. Again in 1992, he was selected as lecturer in Hindi in Jai Narain Vyas University, Jodhpur. In 1997, during his service period he was selected as Associate Professor in the same University. He has also published a few books.[2]

Chandanmal Naval is another writer of national repute, who obtained his master's degree in Political Science from the then Jodhpur University (now JNV University, Jodhpur) after obtaining his degree of M.A. in 1967, he joined as a lecturer and was posted in different government colleges of Rajasthan, namely Sardar Shahar, Kota, Neem-ka-Thana, Kotputli, Jaisalmer and Barmer. For three years he also served in Government College, Kharton, Madhya Pradesh as lecturer in Political Science. In 1977, during his service period, he was selected by the Rajasthan Public Service Commission, Ajmer, as Deputy Superintendent of Police and was posted at Bheem (Udaipur) and subsequently, Jalore, Makrana, etc. Several times he delivered Radio talks on SCs/STs issues from All India Radio, Jodhpur and Jaipur stations. He is a regular writer in the regional daily newspapers as well as in the community papers. He is well known for his writing, oratory in Hindi, honesty and sincerity of purpose. In 1986, ABRM, New Delhi, honoured him. In 1991 and 1992 Bharatiya Dalit Sahitya Academy, New Delhi, honoured him with 'Pandit Rahul Sanskrityanan' award and Dr Ambedkar Vishist Award respectively. Similarly in 1992, Mahatma Jyoti Rao Phoole Satya Shodhak Sansthan Jodhpur honoured him with Dr Ambedkar award. In order to portray the good image of the police in public he did a lot of work in his department and published a book *Bharatiya Police* in Hindi, for which he was honoured with Pandit Govind Vallabh Pant Award 1992-1993 by Bureau of Police Research and Development, Ministry of Home Affairs, Government of India, New Delhi. He has written several books on the Raigar community. Some of the important books are: *Raigar Jati-ka-Itihas* (1986), *Marwar-ka-Amar Sahid: Raja Ram* (1994) and *Bharatiya Police*. Now he has retired as Additional Superintendent of Police, Jodhpur.[3]

Another notable writer, who has written several books on crime, terrorism, vigilance management, women, Ambedkar, etc., is P.N. Rachhoya, Inspector General of Police, Rajasthan. His father was a man with progressive ideas, who always encouraged the members of his family to learn English. P.N. Rachhoya did his M.A. (Hindi) in 1967 and LL.B in 1972 from University of Delhi and after completion of his studies, he served various government departments in different capacities. He was not interested in practising law and therefore in 1972, he appeared in civil service examination and was selected in the Indian Police Service. He worked as Superintendent of Police at Jaisalmer, Jhalawar, Tonk, Sikar, Pali and also in Anti-corruption Department, CID (Crime) Branch Rajasthan. In 1989, he was promoted as Deputy Inspector General of Police, Bharatpur Range and also of Jaipur Range. In 1996, he was again promoted as IGP Crime and also as IGP (Vigilance). Now, he has retired as Director, Rajasthan Police Academy.

As stated above, he also took the lead in writing of books and is also a poet having an imaginative power and uncommon aptitude for passion and sentiments. His important books are: Laws Relating to Terrorism and Disturbance; Bombs and Explosives; Investigation and Security Guide; Vigilance Management: Practice and Procedure; Law of Explosives and Bombs and Honour and Display of National Flag. Besides all this, his books in Hindi are *Apradh Anvekshan: Vidhi avam Prakriya; Khoj Kala aur Apradh Anveshan*; *Bhishma Pitamah*; *Nari Bhari Peer*; *Dard key Deep* and *Pankhudi Gulab Ki*.

In 1997, Arun Shourie, the former Chief Editor, *The Indian Express* had published a book entitled 'Worshipping False Gods'. Rachhoya's concern and anguish about Arun Shourie cannot be described better than in his own words. He says:

> "...with prejudiced mind and pre-fixed ideas by intentionally distorting facts with a view to maligning not only Dr Ambedkar but also the followers of social change and equal justice in the society. The nation expects the expression of rightful facts and does not respect the authority of yellow journalism that strengthen ignorance and oppression that authority which destroyed Babylon and shook the foundation of Jerusalem and left Rome in ruins... Progeny of writers has ugly selfishness which is the course of blind superiority which believes to discord and subjugation".

Therefore, Rachhoya has answered almost all the questions raised by the author of 'Worshipping False Gods" in his recently published book *Dr Ambedkar: Rediscovered* (2000) with supporting evidences and documents. Rachhoya not only has criticised bitterly Arun Shourie but also challenged him about it. He stated:

> '... I have rediscovered the real and truthful facts about Dr Ambedkar which have been erased with malafide intention by the above said author and found in Ambedkar the incense of love for humanity and fragrance of beauty for human society and natural law of justice... the challenge to "worshipping False Gods" is a challenge to the orthodox society, social evils, prejudiced mind, oppressors of human values and; ultimately to the "Worshipping of Gods of Falsehood". Readers may please read, judge and decide about the "False Gods".

In 1999, he was awarded the Police Medal for Meritorious Services as well as for distinguished service by the President of India.[4] Recently, he published a book entitled *Rajasthan Police ka Itihas* for which he was honoured by Bureau of Police Research and Development, Ministry of Home Affairs, Government of India in 2003. Also he was presented a memento and citation along with Rs 15,000 in cash.

Pooran Mal Jalutharia is now Additional District and Session Judge Malpura, District Tonk. He is a regular writer in the community paper *Raigar Sudhar* (Haryana) as well as in *Raigar Jyoti*, Barmer.[5]

Besides, some of the known writers and the poets are: Madhav Shokaria, Jaspat Rai Girdhar and Chandan Mal Maurya 'Chand', Bhagat Bhagirath, Kanwar Sen Maurya, Ghisu Lal, Jeevan Ram Gusaiwal, Roop Chand Jalutharia, Khem Chand Phoolwadia – editor of *Mazdoor Kalyan Times* (Weekly), New Delhi.

Another line in the intellectual elite is the emergence of a religious literate elite which is an entirely new category created by various religious sects. Traditionally, the Raigars were not permitted to study the religious texts and were not allowed to worship the high caste Hindu deities. The various sects like Kabir, Arya Samaj, Nath sect, etc., had trained a number of Sadhus, who possessed the knowledge of their religions. As noted earlier, several temples, 'ashrams', 'dharmshalas', etc. were established by the founding fathers and are managed by these Sanyasis. Some of the outstanding personalities are: Gusai Baba Saint Pitambar Maharaj, Laxmandas Maharaj, Gian Swaroopanand Maharaj, Swami Jiwan Ram Maharaj, Swami Atma Ram Maharaj, Swami Ramanand Maharaj, Gopal Ram Maharaj, Swami Brahma Nand Maharaj, Swami Moji Ram Maharaj and Saint Ananta Nand Maharaj, Swami Atma Ram Maharaj were the moving spirit behind Raigar movement and launched the socio-religious movement amongst the downtrodden in general and Raigars in particular.

A few Raigars have strong traditions of medical practice. They are well versed in Ayurveda, the indigenous system of medicine, which required deep knowledge of Sanskrit text. One of the famous Vaidyas was Swami Rama Nand Maharaj.[6] Besides Ayurveda the Raigars have also taken to the practice of Homeopathy.

Modern Allopathic doctors made their debut with Dr Khoob Chand Jajoria in the year 1937-1938.[7] Just before independence of the country in 1946-1947 he was nominated as one of the members by the British government in the then Chief Commissioner's Advisory Committee. For this important Committee, membership was an award legitimising their high status and 'good conduct'. Since then there have been many doctors of high repute. Dr Kewal Goswami was working as Professor, All India Institute of Medical Sciences, New Delhi.[8] Dr Padam Singh was the Director, ICMR, New Delhi.[9] Another notable man was Dr Sandeep Kumar son of Yad Ram, who was doctor in Irvin Hospital, New Delhi.[10] Dr Balkishan son of Chiranji Lal of Pachimpuri, New Delhi, was medical officer in the Airport Authority of India, Allahabad,[11] Dr (Mrs) Sumitra wife of Om Prakash of Raigarpura was doctor at Dr Girdhari Lal Hospital, Ajmeri Gate, Delhi,[12] while Dr Lakhpat Rai son of Nathu Ram and Dr Kishan Lal son of Bhura Lal were eye specialists. After getting their degrees from Delhi they established their own clinics at Bidanpura, Karol Bagh and Sunder Vihar, New Delhi, respectively. Similarly Dr (Mrs) Indira wife of Subhash Chandra after getting her degree from the Rajasthan University established her clinic at Bassi in Jaipur district.[13] Dr Rajendra Kumar was educated in Rajasthan and was working as Medical Officer at SMS Hospital, Jaipur.[14] Dr Hari Prasad Gusaiwal, MS was gynaecologist at Hari Maternity and Nursing Home, Bharuch, Gujarat.[15]

A lot of modern medical talent seems to have been accumulated in Raigars which indicates a transformation of the Raigar talent into medical talents. The point of interest here is that the Raigars were able to achieve a breakthrough in this medical profession which involved touching caste Hindu patients who still believed in touch pollution. It will be noted that the present strength of modern Raigar doctors constitutes one-tenth of the total strength.

Another profession in which Raigars achieved a level of excellence is law. The modern legal profession came into existence with the establishment of the courts. But untouchable castes/communities including Raigars were denied education for centuries and, therefore, joined this profession after independence. The first lawyer of this caste in Rajasthan is Naval Kishore Nidar. Since independence there had been a significant growth of lawyers. Thus according to Pooran Mal Jalutharia, out of a total of 29 lawyers, there are 4 lawyers in Ajmer, 8 in Jaipur, 3 in Dausa, 4 in Jodhpur, 3 in Udaipur, 2 in Bikaner, 3 in Sikar, 2 in Alwar and 1 in Tonk (all in Rajasthan). Besides Rajasthan it may be noted that there are quite a large number of advocates and lawyers in Delhi – 12, in Ujjain – 8 and in Indore – 9, who have made a name for themselves. Some of the advocates were educated in countries like UK and Netherlands and one of the outstanding advocates is Madan Lal Chandolia son of Nonda Ram. Madan Lal did his DPM from Delhi. After DPM, he did his SPM from UK and APM from Netherlands. In addition to his professional activities he is also Managing Director, Power Finances Corporation Limited, New Delhi.[16]

Some of the Raigar lawyers were selected and appointed in the Law Ministry, Government of India and these two outstanding officials are Kundan Lal son of Ganeshi Lal[17] and Panna Lal son of Jyoti Prasad, both residents of New Delhi.[18] The former is an eminent official, who studied in Delhi and later on joined the Law Ministry and subsequently became Secretary (Law), Ministry of Law and Justice and Company Affairs, Government of India and the other was a good lawyer. Panna Lal resident of Kidwai Nagar, New Delhi, got his degree from Delhi and practised in Delhi and was working as Joint Secretary, in the Ministry of Law and Justice and Company Affairs.

While there are some lawyers among the Raigars, there are only a few judges. The category of the judges includes mostly Munsif Magistrates, Additional District and Session Judges and District and Session Judges. This represent judicial elites. Some of the notables were: Dev Bax, District and Session Judge, Bhilwara; Mangi Lal Nogia, Additional Session Judge (Retd); Prayag Chand Verma, Additional Session Judge, Khetri and Pooran Mal Jalutharia, Chief Judicial and Civil Judge, Dausa.

A notable lawyer who was associated with the activities of social reform movement during its early days in Jaipur, was Pooran

Mal Jalutharia. His father Ram Dev was a man with progressive ideas. He encouraged the members of his family to go to schools and colleges. His father was an ordinary man. After passing his matriculation examination in 1968, Pooran Mal Jalutharia joined Telecommunication Department as a telegraphist in 1971. In 1975, he got his BA degree from the University of Rajasthan and did his LLB in 1978 from the same university. In 1980 he appeared in the examination for Rajasthan Judicial Services and was selected by the Rajasthan Public Service Commission, Ajmer and was posted as Judicial and Munsif Magistrate, Ajmer city. After more than one decade or so he was promoted as Additional Chief Judicial Magistrate, Gangapur, District Bhilwara. Again in 2001, he was promoted to the post of Chief Judicial Magistrate, Dausa.[19]

While there are some doctors and lawyers among the Raigars, there are only a few engineers, many of whom are employed under the centre and state governments. Rudradev Sakkarwal was the first engineer graduate from Delhi University in 1959 and later on he studied and had his training in USSR, from 17 May 1963 to November 1964 at LMZ. On his return he was posted as Design Engineer at BHEL, Haridwar, Uttar Pradesh.[20] Some of the other notable ones are Banshidhar Maurya, Divisional Engineer, Telephones, Ahmedabad, Manoj Kumar Maharam Lal, Software Engineer, Gandhinagar, Ahmedabad.

Most of the employees/officers come under the category of government servants. This represents the administrative officers, including IAS, IPS, IRS, IFS and Indian Forest Service and RAS. Some of the notable ones are: modern bureaucrats and top ranking administrators made their debut with Vinod Jagoria,[21] the first IAS (1965 batch) son of Dr Khoob Chand Jagoria and was the Managing Director, Finance Corporation, Madhya Pradesh Backward Class, Bhopal. Yad Ram Dhuria[22] son of Balu Ram Dhuria, resident of Narain Vihar, New Delhi, was selected for the first time (1965 batch) as IPS who was holding the post of Director General of Police, Home Guard and Civil Defence, New Delhi. Similarly Chiranji Lal Bakolia son of Panna Lal of Prasad Nagar, New Delhi was educated in Delhi and got success in IRS[23] (1967 batch) and was posted as Income Tax Commissioner, Kolkata. Since then there have been many IAS, IPS and IRS officers of high repute, who have achieved an even higher level of elite status by their dedication, sincerity and honesty. Umrao

Shalodia son of Narotam Lal resident of Niwai, Tonk did his B.Sc. from Rajasthan University. After getting his degree from Rajasthan University he did his further studies in UK and received his MA degree from UK and was selected into IAS in 1978.[24] He served as Divisional Commissioner, Ajmer and was Divisional Commissioner, Jaipur. T.R. Verma, did his BA Hons in 1967 from Rajasthan University. After getting his degree, he did his further studies in the same university, received his MA degree in English literature in 1969. He was selected as an IAS officer in 1975.[25] Jai Narain Kansotia son of Anna Lal of Kuchaman city, District Nagaur, Rajasthan, did his B.Sc and MA from Rajasthan and was successful in IAS examination in 1989. He was Collector at District Raigarh, Madhya Pradesh,[26] while G.R. Aaloria is the Commissioner, Municipal Corporation, Baroda.[27] G.L. Verma received his M.Com degree from Rajasthan University in 1970 and was selected as RAS officer in 1972. Later on he was promoted in the senior scale of RAS in 1978 and subsequently became IAS in 1994-1995. He was working as Deputy Secretary, Medical and Health Department, Government of Rajasthan, Jaipur. Some other notable ones are Narendra Malparia, IAS, Mukesh Chand Gadegaonlia, IPS.

Besides IAS, there are quite a few IPS and IRS officers who speak for themselves. Some of the well-known IPS officers are: Banwari Lal Atal, Inspector General of Police, Madhya Pradesh,[28] S.K. Dass and Balwant Ray Nirmal, both are Additional Director Generals of Police, Bhopal, Madhya Pradesh and IGP (Retd) Bhopal respectively.[29] Another notable IPS is Gyan Chand, Additional Director General of Police, Ahmedabad.[30] Other notable IPS officers include Parma Nand Rachhoya and Banwari Lal.[31] Banwari Lal who was selected in the year 1974 and after getting his training at Dehradoon, was posted as Superintendent of Police and later on in 2002 became Additional Director general of Police (Railway).[32]

Besides IAS and IPS officers, there are quite a few IRS officers. Some of the well-known personalities are: C.M. Chandolia, Joint Commissioner, Customs and Central Excise, Kandla Port, Gujarat,[33] and Bhawani Shanker, Income Tax Officer, Income Tax Department, Ahmedabad.[34] Gulab Chand Udenia is Income Tax Officer, Ajmer.[35]

While there are good number of IAS, IPS and IRS officers amongst the Raigar community, there are more RAS, RPS and Allied

Service Administrative Officers also. Some of the notable personalities are: Ram Swaroop Verma[36] (Retd), Udai Ram Kurdia (Retd), Nathu Lal Verma, Deputy Secretary, Agriculture (Group–I), Department, Government Secretariat, Jaipur.[37] Madho Lal Bhatt was posted as Registrar, Jai Narain Vyas University, Jodhpur, and Bhanwar Lal Naval, Special Assistant to Transport Minister, Government of Rajasthan and Ratan Lal, Tehsildar at Revdar, District, Sirohi (all RAS). Chandanmal Naval, was Company Commander of RAC, Jodhpur, and later on became Additional Superintendent of Police, Jalore. He was Additional S.P Crime Branch, Jaipur, Nathulal Maurya, Additional Superintendent of Police, Nagaur; Lokesh Sonwal, Jai Narain Sher, Prem Chand Kurdia, Ramesh Maurya, Ramji Lal Chandel, Smt. Anukriti Ujawal, Shiv Nath Kurdia, and Nathu Lal Verma all Deputy Superintendent of Police and posted indifferent districts; Mahendra Hingonia, Deputy Superintendent of Police, Jaipur and G.L. Verma, Additional Superintendent of Police (Retired)(all RPS).

Besides male police officers, there is one lady police officer, who had made a name for herself. One such officer is Smt Sita Kansotia. While serving in the Cooperative Societies in Rajasthan Government she appeared for RAS and Allied Services examinations in 1999 and was subsequently selected as Deputy Superintendent of Police in Rajasthan. Thus, she became the first police officer in the community. She hails from Kuchaman city in Nagaur district.

It would not be out of place to mention here that earlier to this, she had appeared in the competitive examination conducted by the Rajasthan Public Service Commission, Ajmer, for selecting the candidates for RAS and Allied Services, in which she was selected for Cooperative Services. She did her MA in History. She had an academic interest. She appeared in an eligibility test conducted by RPSC and UGC for selection of the candidates for college and university lecturership, in which she passed SLAT and NET examinations. However, she could not get a teaching job. Her brother Jai Narain Kansotia is an IAS officer in the Madhya Pradesh government.

Besides teachers, doctors, engineers and administrators, etc., there are a few who are officers in defence services and who have made a name for themselves. One well known navy officer is Ved

Prakash Chokdayat as Navigator in the Shipping Corporation of India Limited.[38] Another army officer is Major Durga Lal, son of Bhori Lal (Kekri, Ajmer); Major Durga Lal was in 17th Rajputana Rifles.[39] Some other notables are Lt. Colonel Jai Ram Kanwa (Retd) and Captain Prem Chand Dangalia (Retd) – Lt. Colonel Kanwa took part in 1971 Bangladesh war.[40]

The growth of professional and administrative officers largely account for the bulk of educated middle class. This significant growth is an indicator of the upward social mobility of any community, for it means increasing access to and control of scarce resources of education and employment where there is a keen competition and its achievement is difficult.

It is obvious that growth of the professional elite with internal variations is closely related to the educational mobility.

The growth of business elite calls for a different kind of talent, namely entrepreneurial ability with regard to mobilisation of capital and organisation of other resources. The main occupation of Raigars before independence was traditional one. After 1947 and thereafter, the number of those with non-traditional occupations and those with entrepreneurial ability with regard to mobilisation of capital and organisation of other resources steadily increased. There are some contractors such as Sita Ram Rasgania,[41] building contractor and interior decorator, Dadar, Mumbai, who is doing the job of construction of buildings and roads. Similarly, Mana Ram Rasgania of Mumbai is also a contractor who has received recognition as 'A' Class Contractor from Maharashtra government. Besides Sita Ram Rasgania and Mana Ram Rasgania in Maharashtra, there are some other contractors constructing road and buildings for government and one of the other well-known contractor is Bhagwan Das of Surat, Gujarat who was awarded recognition as 'A' Class contractor from Gujarat government. Besides Bhagwan Das, Babu Lal Mistri, is another government contractor from Surat, who also has received recognition as 'A' Class contractor from the Gujarat government. Similarly, Asha Ram is also Class-I, Government contractor for air conditioners at Surat, Gujarat. In this way, there are numerous private contractors also.

Later on, commercial and industrial entrepreneurs came into existence. They opened provision stores, sewing machine works, leather stores, chappals manufacturers, manufacturers and distributors of *mangal sutras,* manufacturers of plastic extrusion system and its ancillaries. Automobiles, flower factories, sales corporations are the other business concerns, where they have their own contribution.[42] Mangi Lal Khorwal opened Harish Enterprises where 0.25 HP to 3 HP one-phase electric motor, 0.5 HP to 20 HP three-phase electrical motor and submersible pumps are manufactured. Naragam D. Devatwal opened Navin Trading Company for rejected PCB, laminate sheet scrap, solder copper liquid, plastic paper, waste merchant, in Ahmedabad. Similarly, Jagdish Bhai Jai Ramdass Khorwal started Saibaba Enterprise dealing in all kinds of chappals and shoes materials such as rubber sheets, wooden heels, rexines, rubber solution and all kinds of leather goods at Ahmedabad. Besides all this, there are also a large number of footwear stores and leather stores at Ahmedabad. Jute bags is another big business for Raigars also. Narain Das Thawar Dass Gusaiwal is a big businessman of the gunny bags at Kabutar Khana, Chokha Bazar, Kalupur, Ahmedabad.[43]

They have mills of different types. Jagdish Bugradia was the first Raigar to open a mill at Mohanpura, Bassi, Jaipur (1990), while Mangi Lal Dulara owns a rag mill. Raigars are also prominent in trade of welding. Daya Chand Puran Mal Dulara opened the Baba Ram Dev Welding Workshop at Mohanpura, Bassi, Jaipur. Similarly, his relative Radhey Shyam Dulara also opened welding workshop at Mohanpura, Jaipur.

Besides all this, they also opened a leather goods manufacturing factory, tent house, etc. Keshri Chand Poonam Chand Dholkheria, resident of Bikaner, Rajasthan, opened a leather goods manufacturing factory namely Madras Leather Store at Kolkata, whereas his relative Bhagirath Dholkheria opened Vijay Leather Store at Hardiyan Singh Road, New Delhi. Similarly Madan Lal Maurya, another Raigar industrialist opened Maurya Leather Store at Bappa Nagar, New Delhi. Photography is also another business for Raigars – Muniraj Kansotia is a film distributor at New Delhi.

Tent house, government agencies, petrol pumps, taxi, transport, etc., are big business for the Raigars and Nand Lal Jajoria is owner of Chand Tent House at Ramrajpura, Rakdi, Jaipur. Similarly, Prahlad Mandawaria is the owner of Mandawaria Tent House at Jaisinghpura Khor at Jaipur and Jhotwara Tent House, Jhotwara, Jaipur, respectively. Transport is another big business for Raigars and Girdhari Lal Bakolia, P.K. Sethi and Devi Lal Kansotia of Bakolia Tour and Travellers Company, Sethi Transport and Kansotia Transport, Jaipur, are owners of a fleet of trucks and buses, etc. Raigars also have hotels and restaurants. Kishan Lal Kurdia is owner of hotel/restaurant at Karol Bagh, New Delhi. Besides all this, there is also one petrol pump of Bhagirath Nogia at Jobner, Jaipur. Damodar Salodia and Gomasagar Jatolia are owners of Bharat Gas Agency, Niwai, Tonk, and Sagar Gas Agency at Khandela, District Sikar, respectively.[44]

There is keen interest among the Raigars with regard to the opening of schools. It was realised by the Raigars that those who control the educational resources also control economic opportunities. Education itself offers jobs to several men and women. With this in mind the Raigars are attempting to open schools and coaching centres in different parts of Rajasthan. Baldev Prasad Hingania is the first Raigar who took the lead in opening modern education and opened Vikramaditya Senior Secondary School at Ambedkar Nagar, Jaipur. In his endeavour, apart from schools started in 1980, he also opened Kids Paradise in 2002 at Ambedkar Nagar, Jaipur. Similarly, B.L. Chomia, Joint Registrar Cooperative Society, Jaipur, started Meira Public Secondary School at Kalyan Nagar, Jaipur in the year 1990. Murli Manohar Chomia, a relative of B.L. Chomia, opened a Primary School, namely Appu Ghar at Kalyan Nagar, Jaipur in 2002. Jagdish Kuldeep also opened Vikas Public Secondary School, Mansarovar, Jaipur, in 1989. Besides all this, there are others also like Jagdish Khorwal, Satpal Chandolia, Jagdish Narain Naval and Rajesh Singh Hingonia, who opened Navin Public Middle School (1996) at Raigaro-ki-Kothi, Ghat Gate, Jaipur, Vishakha Public School (1997) at Rampura Road, Sanganer, Deepshikha Public School (1997) at Pratap Nagar, Sanganer, Jaipur and Raj Public School (1999) at Dharash Ajmer Road, Jaipur (all middle schools). In 1998 Satya Narain Uchenia also opened a primary school namely Gayatri Public School at Saini Colony, Kartarpura, Jaipur.[45]

Political elite including politicians began to appear only around the fourth decade of the twentieth century, with the growth of the national movement and later under the Gandhi-Ambedkar Poona Agreement for reforms amongst the downtrodden. After independence and introduction of adult franchise and the representative institutions at different levels, the number of the professional politicians increased. They now hold positions in the new structure of power at various levels, i.e., at the parliament, the state assembly, the municipality, the three tiers of the Panchayati Raj. They are also office bearers of different political parties and active workers.

Some of the famous politicians may be listed for the sake of illustration. Jai Chand Mohil was an active Congress worker and he was a member of Mewar Praja Mandal and took an active part in Bharat Chhodo Aandolan and aroused socio-political awakening amongst the untouchable communities. In the first general election held in the year 1952, he was elected as an MLA from the constituency comprising Choti Sadri, Kapasan, Chittorgarh as a Congress nominee. Similarly, in the second general election held in the year 1957, he was again elected as a Congress candidate from a reserved constituency of Kapasan, Chittorgarh. Jai Narain Salodia and Bhanu Prasad both Swatantra party leaders were MLAs of Rajasthan Assembly in 1962. Chuni Lal Jelia, Jai Narain Salodia and Mangilal, the Janta party leaders were MLAs in 1977. In 1980 Chhoga Lal Kanwaria was elected as a Congress candidate. When Shiv Charan Mathur was heading the state, Kanwaria became the first Raigar minister in 1981. Chhoga Lal Bakolia was also the leader of Congress party and became another Raigar deputy minister in 1980 and the Minister of State in 1985. He was a Cabinet Minister in Ashok Gehlot's ministry. In 1980 Virda Ram Phoolwaria was also the leader of the Congress party and became the first Raigar MP from Jalore, Rajasthan.

Raigar politicians are members of one or the other political parties of different regions. For instance, in the year 1952, Naval Prabhakar, was not only elected for the first time to the parliament from Karol Bagh, New Delhi, but subsequently also won the elections twice in the years 1957 and 1962 respectively. Thus, he was elected as MP thrice (15 years). Dharm Das Shastri was also the leader of Congress party and an MP from Karol Bagh, New Delhi, in 1967. Mrs Sundar Devi Naval Prabhakar was also an MP in 1972. Naval Prabhakar became the first Raigar MP in whole of the country. He remained in close contact with Congress party. He was one of the chief patrons of All India Raigar Maha Sabha. These three MPs from Raigar community were Congress candidates. Shiv Narain Sarsunia, a BJP leader was MP in 1977 from Karol Bagh, New Delhi.

Besides MPs, there are a few MLAs from Delhi. Daya Ram Jalutharia was the MLA of Delhi Assembly. In addition to MPs and

MLAs, there are a few Raigar elites who became the members of Delhi Mahanagar Parishad (DMP). These were: Dharmdas Shastri, Shiv Narain Sarsunia, Smt. Sunder Devi Naval Prabhakar, Moti Lal Bakolia, Naval Prabhakar, Laxman Singh Atal, Bhori Lal Shastri, Khushal Chand Mohanpuria and Hemendra Kumar Mohanpuria.

Champa Lal Arya (Hindunia clan) was an active Jan Sangh worker and he was a member of the committee to remove untouchability in Madhya Pradesh. In 1962, he was elected to Madhya Pradesh legislative assembly from Suwashra constituency, district Mandsore (MP) on Bharatiya Jan Sangh party ticket. He became the first Raigar MLA. He was also elected as an MLA of Janta party ticket in 1977 and again as an MLA on BJP ticket in 1980. Thus, Champa Lal Arya had been the key leader of BJP and was elected to Madhya Pradesh Legislative assembly for four consecutive terms. Here, it will suffice to note that during the emergency period, Champa Lal Arya was arrested and sent to jail.

Elite and the Mass

The foregoing account of the emergence of different types of elite shows the diversified patterns of individual achievement in the professional, administrative business and industrial and political fields. The level of achievement, in a competitive and democratic society, depends on an increasing degree of excellence. The Raigars have achieved to some extent a level of excellence in professional and political field, comparable to other untouchable communities in Rajasthan. These intellectuals have reputation at state and national level – they are either doctors who are serving in AIIMS and other national reputed hospitals, or a few lawyers and bureaucrats who are trained abroad, or judges at state level, secretaries and under-secretaries at the state and centre level and ministers at the state and centre level and MPs. There are also a few who have excellence in police service, medical service and administrative service. All these impressive achievements of individuals represent instances of upward social mobility of the community as a whole, because the Raigars are proud of themselves and community gains a lot of prestige in the eyes of other progressive castes/communities. Those untouchable castes which are behind in the race of mobility look up to the Raigars, Bairwas, Chamars and Meghwals as reference groups, as they have demonstrated the upward movement.

Within the caste, however, gaps exist between elite and the masses. A few of those who had achieved an elite status feel that they had, therefore, risen by their own merit and hard work and that they do not owe to their poor fellow caste-men any obligation. On the other hand their caste-men look upon those persons holding the elite position for help in securing seats in the educational institutions, jobs, moral and financial support and preferential treatment. The increasing expectations of the masses with regard to those occupying higher positions have often remained unfulfilled and they complain that the elite are not only indifferent to their poor fellow caste-men but also treat them in the same way, as the upper caste persons had treated the untouchables in the earlier days. As this frustration increases the poor masses tend to move towards socialists/Congress parties whereas the affluent elites tend to align themselves with the BJP.

Transformation of Caste into an Ethnic Block

The ABRM movement was responsible for the emergence of a large ethnic block. During the princely rule, there were several isolated local endogamous groups and named caste groups of Raigars among whom there was little communication. However, with the growth of the movement, all these small groups came on a single platform, establishing their identity on the basis of common ideology, lifestyle, and programme of action. As a result of politicisation, a large ethnic block of Raigar has emerged.

The organisation of this ethnic block is of the federal type. There is a ABRM at the centre with regional associations at the state level and branches at the district level. This type of federal organisation provides internal autonomy to the local and regional associations and yet at the same time are subject, in varying degrees to the external control of the central organisation.

Ethnicity is a new form of caste organised on a new set of elements, such as common ideology, identity of interests (ritual, educational, economic and political) a federal organisation characterised by the democratic political process and volunteers covering a wider geographical area and a higher degree of politicisation characterised by opposition to and confrontation with other ethnic groups and parties. The emergence of wider ethnic identity is a common phenomenon to be found among many castes which are subjected to a politicisation. For instance, Shyam Lal (2000) shows how the sub-caste identity is merged in the wider 'bhangi' identity, through the pivotal organisation of All India Safai Mazdoor Congress.

Notes

1. Chandolia, Madan Lal, *Raigar Samaj Directory*,1996, p. 43.
2. Lal, Kishori, *Dr Rangay Raghav ke katha sahitya mein gramya jiwan*, Jaipur, Rachna Prakashan, 1997.
3. Naval, Chandanmal; *Raigar Jati ka Itihas*, 1986. Also see, *Marwar Ka Amar Shahid: Raja Ram, 1994*. Conversation with Naval, Jodhpur 22 May, 2003.
4. See, P.N. Rachhoya's book, *Dr Ambedkar – Rediscovered*, Jaipur, Kirti Publications, 2000. Also talk with Rachhoya at Jaipur, January 2003.
5. Conversation with Pooranmal Jalutharia, Jaipur, 3 August 2003.
6. *Smarika: Sri Dharmguru Swami Gianswaroop Janam Shatabdi avam Akhil Bharatiya Raigar Mahasabha Jayanti Samaroh*, dated 6-7 October, 1955.
7. Conversation with Rajendra Nath Chandolia, New Delhi, 10 June 2003. Also see: Chiranji Lal Bakolia and Rajendra Prasad Gadegaonlia, *Raigar Kaun aur Kya?*, New Delhi, Asian Printers, Hardhiyan Singh Road, Karol Bagh, 1964, p. 54.
8. Chandolia, Madan Lal, op. cit., p. 14.
9. Ibid., p. 7.
10. Ibid., p.25.
11. Ibid., p.32.
12. Ibid., p.12.
13. Ibid.
14. Ibid., p.6.
15. Kurdia, Aasu Ram Umaji (Ed.), *Raigar Samaj Shiksha Samiti*, Ahmedabad, *Smarika* 1999, p. 11.
16. Chandolia Madan Lal, op. cit., p.15.
17. Ibid., p.37.
18. Ibid., p.46.
19. Conversation with Pooranmal Jalutharia, Jaipur, 3 August 2003.
20. Letter from Rudra Dev Sakkarwal, Delhi to author, received on 25 June 2003. Also conversation on phone on 17 July 2003, New Delhi.
21. *Raigar Sudhar*, dated 1-15 February 2001.
22. Ibid.

23. Ibid.
24. *Smarika: Shi Dharmguru Swami Gianswaroop Janam Shatabdi avam Akhil Bharatiya Raigar Mahasabha Jayanti Samaroh,* dated 6-7 October, 1955. (page number not mentioned).
25. Conversation with T.R. Verma on phone, Jaipur, February 2003.
26. Conversation with Jai Narain Kansotiya, Ramgarh, Madhya Pradesh February 2002. Chandolia Madan, op. cit., p. 8.
27. Kurdia, Aasu Ram Umaji (Ed.), *Raigar Samaj Shiksha Samiti,* Ahmedabad, *Smarika* 1999, op. cit., p. 11.
28. Chandolia Madan Lal, op. cit., p. 1 and 27.
29. Ibid., p. 36.
30. Kurdia, Aasu Ram Umaji (Ed.), *Smarika* 1999, op. cit., p. 11.
31. Conversation with P.N. Rachhoya, Jaipur, January 2003.
32. Chandolia, Madan Lal, op. cit., p. 1.
33. Kurdia, Aasu Ram Umaji (Ed.), *Smarika* 1999, op. cit., p. 11.
34. Ibid.
35. *Smarika: Sri Dharmguru Swami Gianswaroop Janam Shatabdi,* op. cit., 1995.
36. Conversation with Ram Swaroop Verma, Jaipur, 19 August 2003.
37. Kamal, K.L. (Ed.), Raigar Vikas Sansthan, Rajasthan, Jaipur, 18 June 2003, p. 40.
38. Kamal, K.L (Ed.), *Raigar Samaj Samuhik Vivah Ayojan Samiti, Dutiya Samuhik Vivah Samorah,* 14 February 1999, p. 33.
39. Kamal, K.L. (Ed.), Raigar Vikas Sansthan, Rajasthan, Jaipur, 2000, Ibid., p. 41. Also, *see,* particularly '*Major Raigar: Raigar Samaj ka ek ojamaya vyaktitya*', Lakshya Rakshak, September 10, 2001, pp. 3-5.
40. Conversation with K.L. Kamal, Jaipur, 23 July 2003.
41. Ibid.
42. Recent published *Smarika,* Raigar Samaj Shiksha Samiti, Ahmedabad, 1999. Also see, *Ahmedabad mein Raigar Samaj,* 1998.
43. Ibid.
44. Conversation with Bal Dev Prasad Hingonia, Jaipur, 23 February 2003.
45. Ibid.

Bibliography

Primary Sources

The major sources of information for this study are derived from Raigar movement. The historical data was collected from Rajasthan, Delhi, Uttar Pradesh, Madhya Pradesh, Gujarat, Haryana, Punjab, and Maharashtra. A major part of the bibliographic material, however, is contemporary, consisting of publications of Raigar socio-economic and political movements. This material has not been systematically collected or organised in any public or private library either in Rajasthan or in the neighbouring states. The Raigar organisations and individuals made valiant efforts to maintain collection of contemporary (and historical) publications. Lack of caste consciousness, money and lack of literacy among the caste fellows, however, render this is a Herculean task. I was fortunate in being given access to some private collections, notably those of K.L. Kamal in Jaipur, Chandanmal Naval in Jodhpur, Aashu Ram Kurdia in Gujarat, Arjun Singh Mohanpuria in Uttar Pradesh, Rajendra Nath Chandolia, Shiv Narain Sarsunia and Kisan Lal Kurdia all in New Delhi. In addition, I was given various pamphlets, magazines, newspapers and booklets that were put out by contemporary Raigar political and cultural organisations, which are now part of my private library. Many of these publications appear at no fixed interval, having a shifting leadership and locus. They also lack an established distribution network. A few Raigar Smarikas are published at periodic intervals – for example, Smarikas of Raigar Vikas Sansthan, particularly in Rajasthan. Due to the kindness of Ashwani Kumar, editor of *Raigar Sudhar*, Fatehabad, Haryana, he supplied me issues of this periodical. The other major Raigar periodicals that I consulted extensively are *Raigar Pragatisheel Patrika, Jaipur Phalak*, Jaipur; *Raigar Joyti*, Barmer; *Raigar Rakshak*, Jaipur; *Vikas Kiran*, Tonk; *Parivarik Jyoti Aur Raigar Samaj*, Bhilwara; *Gadegaonlia Times*, Jaipur; all from Rajasthan and *Raigar Utthan*, Indore, Madhya Pradesh; which are continuously published periodical of Raigar activities. Finally, I am also grateful to Jagdish Kurdia, Purushottam Vora and Shiv Ram Jajoria, Chembur, Mumbai, for making available to me some material from their collections.

The sources used in this study are exclusively in Hindi language. Much of this work is inaccessible to any researchers due to non-availability of literature. A special effort has been made to collect the work of Raigar writers who have written most of the part in Hindi. The reasons for utilising as thoroughly as possible the work of Raigar writers pertain to a major goal of this study, which is to provide a view from within the Raigar movement. The phenomenon of Raigar writers writing on the history, sociology, politics and culture of their own community is a development which in itself testifies to the change which have overtaken the Raigars in free India.

Finally, interviews have also been conducted in Rajasthan, Delhi, Uttar Pradesh, Haryana, Punjab, Gujarat and Maharashtra. Structured questionnaire have not been used. I had conversations during which I took notes. I tried to talk to as many ordinary people as possible.

The Raigar Movement: History, Politics, Literature

Raigar Jati ka Mahatva, 1941.

Jati Bijak Mool Prakash: Raigar Samaj (year not mentioned).

Gar Kshatriya Updesh Gian, 1942.

Sri Raigar Navyuwak Sabha, Karachi, 1944.

Unnati Path Pradershan Athva Dhan Ka Durupayog, 1947.

Bharatiya Janganana Vibhag, Rajasthan, Ajmer-Rajya Ki Bulletin No. 12, Parishist No. 2, Ke Prashano ki Pariganit Raigar Samaj ka Uttar, 1950.

Asamarth Sahayata Samiti, 1957.

Asamarth Sahayata Samiti Ki Pratham Varshik Sankshipta Vivran Patrika, 1957.

Vidhan Asamarth Sahayata Samiti, 1958.

Akhil Bharatiya Raigar Mahasabha: Vidhan 1965.

Sri Sanatan Dharm Satsang Sabha Raigarpura Avam Bhagwan Sri Vishnu Mandir Ka Sankshipt Vivran Patrika.

Smarika, Kalyan Sangh, 1971.

Rajasthan Prantiya Raigar Mahasabha, Jaipur, Smarika, 1972.

Dilli Prantiya Raigar Mandir Prabandhak Committee ka Aaya-Vyaya Prativedan, 1972-1979.

Prachin Raigar Itihas, 1973.

Dilli Prantiya Raigar Panchayat: Aaya-Vyaya Vivran Avam Varshik Prativedan, 1979-1980.

Raigar Itihas ki Khoj Tatha Jat path Sambandhi Vichar, 1980.

Akhil Bharatiya Raigar Mahasabha Karya Karini Samiti Avam Karyakarta Sammelan, 8 Avam 9 November, 1981.

Akhil Bharatiya Raigar Panchayat, Pushkar Mandir, Vyavyasthan Committee, Pushkar, Rajasthan, Aaya Vyaya Vivran (1982-83), (year not mentioned).

Raigar Dharmshala Birla Road, Haridwar-Aaya-Vyaya Vivran (1982-83) (year not mentioned).

Dandata Namavali Avam Aaya-Vyaya Vivran, 1982-83.

Raigar Samaj, Atma Ram 'Lakshya', 1986.

Pancham Akhil Bharatiya Raigar Mahasabha, Raigar Gaurav Smarika, 1986.

Dilli Prantiya Raigar Swayam Sewak Mandal, Dev Nagar, New Delhi, Swaran Jayanti, 1938-1987, 1987.

Swaran Jayanti 1938-1987, Smarika, 30 May, 1987.

Smarika: Dashak Samaroh, 3-31 May, 1993, 1993.

Smarika, Sri Dharmguru Swami Gian Swaroop (Janam Satabdi Avam Akhil Bharatiya Raigar Mahasabha, Swaran Jayanti Samaroh, 1995.

Sri Gian Bhajan Prabhakar, 1998.

Prachin Raigar Itihas, 1998.

Akhil Rajasthan Raigar Yuva Mahasabha Pratham Maha Sammelan, Smarika, 1998.

Raigar Samaj Samuhik Vivaha Ayojan Samiti, Jaipur, Madhur Smiriti, Smarika, 1998.

Raigar Samaj Shiksha Samiti, Ahmedabad, 1999.

Raigar Shikshit Samaj, Smarika (year not mentioned).

Raigar Samaj Samuhik Vivaha Ayojan Samiti, Jaipur: Dwitiya Samuhik Vivaha Samaroh Madhur Smiriti, Smarika, 1999.

Raigar Vikas Sansthan Rajasthan, Jaipur, Tritiya Samuhik Vivaha Samaroh Sammelan Madhur Smiriti Smarika, 2000.

Raigar Vikas Sansthan, Rajasthan, 2000.

Surya Sagar Ganga Smarika, Tritiya Raigar Samaj, Samuhik Vivaha Sammelan, Pushkar, 2001.

Kavya Piyush, 2001.

Raigar, 2002.

Arya Kanya Pathshalla: Platinum Jayanti Smarika, 2003.

Raigar Vikas Sansthan, Rajasthan, 2003.

Letters

Letters from Rudra Dev, son of late Chaudhary Padam Singh Sakkarwal to the author dated June, 2003.

Letter circulated by Yashpal Singh Khorwal, Mahamantri ABRM, New Delhi, dated April 16, 2001.

Miscellaneous

Bakolia, Chiranji Lal Aur Gadegaonlia, R.P., *Raigar Kaun Aur Kya*? New Delhi, Asian Printers, Hardhiyan Singh Road, Karol Bagh, 1964.

Bhagat, Bhagirath, *Jati Bijak Mool Prakash: Raigar Samaj*, Nasirabad (Ajmer), Jain Printers (Year not mentioned).

Chandolia, Madan Lal, *Raigar Samaj Directory*, New Delhi, 1996.

Naval, Chandanmal, *Raigar Jati Ka Itihas*, Jodhpur, Shyam Printing Press, 1986.

Naval, Chandanmal, *Marwar Ka Amar Shahid: Raja Ram*, Jodhpur, Rajasthani Granthagaar, 1994.

Naval, Madan Lal, *Anusuchit Jatia Avam Janjatia: Rajasthan ke Pariprekshaya Mein*, New Delhi, Brilliant Publishers, 1989.

Jalutharia, Roop Chand, *Raigar Jati ka Itihas*, Jaipur, Capital Printers, 2001.

Documents and Government Publications

Marwar Census Report 1891, Jodhpur, 1896 (Reprinted in 1997).

Census of India, 1971, Serial – I, Paper 1 of 1975, Scheduled Castes and Scheduled Tribes, 1975.

Census of India, 1991, Caste-wise Break-up 1981 and 1991.

Census of India, 1991, Distribution of Scheduled Castes Population by Sex, Population 1991, Sheet – 1, Serial No. 17.

Ethnographic Atlas of Rajasthan, with reference to Scheduled Castes and Scheduled Tribes, 1969.

Dr Baba Saheb Ambedkar: Writings and Speeches. Vol. 5, Mumbai, Government of Maharashtra, 1989.

Newspapers and Periodicals

Community Papers

Raigar Pragatisheel Patrika, Jaipur, Rajasthan, 1982 onwards.

Phalak, Jaipur, Rajasthan, 1992 onwards.

Raigar Utthan , Indore, Madhya Pradesh, 1993 onwards.

Raigar Sudhar, Fatehabad, Haryana, 1999 onwards.

Raigar Jyoti, Barmer, Rajasthan, 2000 onwards.

Raigar Rakshak, Jaipur, Rajasthan, 2001 onwards.

Vikas Kiran, Tonk, Rajasthan, 2001 onwards.

Parivarik Jyoti Aur Raigar Samaj, Bhilwara, Rajasthan, 2001 onwards.

Lakshya Rakshak, New Delhi, 2001 onwards.

Gadegaonlia Times, Jaipur, Rajasthan, 2003 onwards.

News Papers

Koli Rajput, Ajmer, 1950 onwards.

Rajasthan Patrika, Jaipur, 1990 onwards.

Dainik Navjyoti, Jaipur, 1990 onwards.

Dainik Bhaskar, Jaipur, 1999 onwards.

Nav Bharat, Mumbai, February 5, 1999.

Kurla Samachar (Hindi Weekly), November, 1999.

Maharashtra Crimes (Weekly), Chembur, Mumbai, October 6-12, 2000.

The Times of India, New Delhi, 2001 onwards.

Hindustan Times, New Delhi, 2001 onwards.

Secondary Sources

Bailey, F.S., *Caste and Economic Frontier: A Village High Land in Orissa*, Manchester, the Manchester University Press, 1957.

Blunt, E.A.H., *The Caste System of Northern India*, New Delhi, S. Chand and Company, First Indian Reprint, 1969.

Cohn, Bernard S., "The Changing Status of a Depressed Caste" in Mackim Marriott (ed.), *Village India*, Chicago, University of Chicago Press, 1960.

Chaudhary, P.S., *Rajasthan Between The Two World Wars (1919-1939)*, Agra, Sri Ram Mehra and Company, 1968.

Divekar, V.D. (ed.), *Social Reform Movements in India: A Historical Perspective*, Mumbai, Popular Prakashan, 1991.

Fuchs, Stephen, *At the Bottom of Indian Society: The Harijan and Other Low Castes*, New Delhi, Munshi Ram Manohar Lal Publishers, 1981.

Gunarthi, Ram Chandra, *Rajasthani Jatio-ki-Khoj*, Ajmer, Vedic Yantralaya, 1950.

Gokhale, Jayashree., *From Concession to Confrontation: The Politics of an Indian Untouchable Community*, Mumbai, Popular Prakashan, 1993.

Gokuldas, Swami, *Meghvans Itihas*, Ajmer, Arya Brothers Book Seller, 1993.

Gopinathan, G., "The Process of Re-humanisation Initiated by Sri Narayan Guru and Its Impact on the Kinship and other Social Relationships in Kerala" in Asko Parpola and Sirpa Tenhunen (ed.) *Changing Pattern of Family and Kinship in South Asia*, Helsinki, 1998.

Jatav, D.R., *A Silent Soldier: An Autobiography*, Jaipur, Samata Sahitya Sadan, 2000.

Kuber, W. N., "Dalit Movements in India" in V.D. Divekar (ed.), *Social Reform Movements in India*, Mumbai, Popular Prakashan, 1991.

Keer, Dhananjay, *Dr Ambedkar: Life and Mission*, Mumbai, Popular Prakashan, 1995.

Lohia, Bajrang Lal, *Rajasthan-ki-Jatia*, Kolkata, Vishal Bharat Book Depot, 1954.

Lynch, Omen M., *The Politics of Untouchability, Social Mobility and Social Change in a City of India*, Delhi, National Publishing House, 1974.

Omvedt, Gail, *Dalit and Democratic Revolution: Dr Ambedkar and the Dalit Movement in Colonial India*, New Delhi, Sage Publications, 1994.

Patwardhan, S., *Change Among India's Harijan*, New Delhi, Orient Longman, 1973.

Puran Mal, *Asprashyata Avam Dalit Chetna*, Jaipur, Pointer Publishers, 1999.

Rao, M.S.A., *Social Movements and Social Transformation: A Study of two Backward Classes Movement in India*, Chennai, Macmillan and Company of India, 1979.

Rachhoya, P.N., *Dr Ambedkar Re-discovered*, Jaipur, Kirti Publications, 2000.

Sachchidanand, *The Harijan Elite: A Study of Their Status, Network, Mobility and Role in Social Transformation*, Faridabad, Thomson Press, 1977.

Shyam Lal, *Caste and Political Mobilisation: The Bhangis*, Jaipur, Panch Sheel Prakasthan, 1981.

—, *From Higher Caste to Lower Caste: Process of the Asprashyeekaran and Myth of Sanskritisation*, Jaipur, Rawat Publications, 1997.

—, *The Changing Bhangis of India: A Study of Caste Association*, Jaipur, Sublime Publications, 1999.

—, *Untouchable Movement in India*, Jaipur, Sublime Publications, 2002.

Singh, K.S., (ed.), *People of India, Rajasthan, Part Two*, Bombay, Popular Prakashan, 1998.

Sato, Mananori, "The Chamars of South Eastern Rajasthan, A.D. 1650-1800" in H. Kotani (ed.), *Caste System, Untouchability, Depressed*, New Delhi, Manohar Publications, 1997.

Shah, Ghanshyam, "Untouchability in Rural Gujarat", Revisited in Ghanshyam Shah (ed.), *Dalits and the State*, New Delhi, Concept Publishing Company, 2002.

Vidhyarthi, L.P. and Mishra, N., *Harijan Today*, New Delhi, Prentice Hall of India, 1977.

Index